MW00803940

PATERNOSTER THEOLOGICAL MONOGRAPHS

Paradox in Christian Theology

An Analysis of Its Presence, Character,
and Epistemic Status

PATERNOSTER THEOLOGICAL MONOGRAPHS

PATERNOSTER THEOLOGICAL MONOGRAPHS

Paradox in Christian Theology

An Analysis of Its Presence, Character, and Epistemic Status

James Anderson

WIPF & STOCK · Eugene, Oregon

Wipf and Stock Publishers
199 W 8th Ave, Suite 3
Eugene, OR 97401

Paradox in Christian Theology
An Analysis of Its Presence, Character, and Epistemic Status
By Anderson, James and Fergusson, David
Copyright©2007 Paternoster
ISBN 13: 978-1-55635-271-3
Publication date 2/8/2007
Previously published by NP, 2007

"This Edition Published by Wipf and Stock Publishers
by arrangement with Paternoster"

Series Preface

In the West the churches may be declining, but theology—serious, academic (mostly doctoral level) and mainstream orthodox in evaluative commitment—shows no sign of withering on the vine. This series of *Paternoster Theological Monographs* extends the expertise of the Press especially to first-time authors whose work stands broadly within the parameters created by fidelity to Scripture and has satisfied the critical scrutiny of respected assessors in the academy. Such theology may come in several distinct intellectual disciplines—historical, dogmatic, pastoral, apologetic, missional, aesthetic and no doubt others also. The series will be particularly hospitable to promising constructive theology within an evangelical frame, for it is of this that the church's need seems to be greatest. Quality writing will be published across the confessions— Anabaptist, Episcopalian, Reformed, Arminian and Orthodox— across the ages—patristic, medieval, reformation, modern and counter-modern—and across the continents. The aim of the series is theology written in the twofold conviction that the church needs theology and theology needs the church—which in reality means theology done for the glory of God.

To Catriona

Contents

Acknowledgements

The author wishes to thank Cambridge University Press for permission to reproduce and expand on parts of his previously published article, 'In Defence of Mystery: A Reply to Dale Tuggy', *Religious Studies* 41.2 (2005).

Abbreviations

ANF   Alexander Roberts and James Donaldson (eds), *The Ante-Nicene Fathers* (10 vols; Edinburgh, 1867)

CD   Karl Barth, *Church Dogmatics* (14 vols; eds Thomas F. Torrance and G. W. Bromiley; Edinburgh: T. & T. Clark, 1936-1977)

HCC   Philip Schaff, *History of the Christian Church* (8 vols; New York: Charles Scribner, 1910)

NPNF1   Philip Schaff (ed.), *The Nicene and Post-Nicene Fathers: Series I* (14 vols; New York, 1886)

NPNF2   Philip Schaff and Henry Wace (eds), *The Nicene and Post-Nicene Fathers: Series II* (14 vols; New York, 1890)

ST   Thomas Aquinas, *The Summa Theologica of St. Thomas Aquinas* (trans. Fathers of the Dominican Province; 22 vols; London: R. & T. Washbourne, 2nd edn, 1911-1920)

CHAPTER 1

Introduction: The Problem of Paradox

One should not think slightingly of the paradoxical; for the paradox is the source of the thinker's passion, and the thinker without a paradox is like a lover without feeling: a paltry mediocrity.[1]

1.1 Paradox in Christian Theology

Credo quia absurdum—as Tertullian probably never said. Still, the sentiment behind the misquotation is a provocative one: that the Christian faith is absurd, because it asserts the impossible event of a divine death, yet this very assertion functions as a reason *for* belief rather than *against*. Few have been so bold as to champion such a counterintuitive stance, but a somewhat weaker contention has proven far more popular, namely, that certain tenets of the Christian faith are paradoxical yet may be reasonably believed *in spite* of this feature (if not *because* of it). It is this view that forms the subject of the present book.

The notion that traditional Christian conceptions of God and his relation to the world suffer from internal logical difficulties has a long history, having enjoyed currency among thinkers at every point on the scale of theological belief and unbelief. These alleged logical conflicts have been denoted in various ways, from the negatively connotative 'incoherence', 'self-contradiction', and 'absurdity', to the more forgiving labels of 'paradox', 'antinomy', and 'mystery'. Terminological differences aside, the significance of these difficulties lies in the potential implications for the epistemic status of Christian beliefs. On the one hand, atheists and agnostics have marshalled such considerations in support of their stance of non-belief or outright disbelief. This strategy is typified by Michael Martin, who argues that incoherences in the very idea of God, given the standard

---

1   Søren Kierkegaard, *Philosophical Fragments* (Princeton: Princeton University Press, 2nd edn, 1962), 46.

divine attributes of *omniscience, omnipotence,* and *freedom,* warrants
the conclusion that no such being exists.[2] Richard Gale highlights
further problems: the notion that God is *immutable* seems to be
inconsistent with the claims that God is omniscient and God created
the world, while the notion that God is *timeless* conflicts with the
claim that God is personal and interacts with his creatures.[3]

Beyond these conceptual difficulties with generic theism,
distinctively *Christian* claims have also come under fire. Alleged
internal contradictions in the doctrines of the Trinity and the
Incarnation are regularly cited as grounds for believing that
Christianity, in its traditional forms, cannot be true.[4] Remarking on
the profusion of paradoxes generated by the typical claims of
Christian theologians, Ronald Hepburn contends that such 'grave
logical difficulties' provide an insuperable obstacle for the
'religiously minded person' who would like to embrace the
'religious orientation of life' associated with Christian orthodoxy.[5]
Hepburn chides those theologians of paradox who refuse to take
seriously the complaints of analytical philosophers, arguing that
such scholars are obligated to provide excellent justification for their
religious beliefs and claims, given their paradoxicality.

Within the Christian camp, on the other hand, attitudes toward
theological paradox have ranged from abomination to near
adoration. The conservative Calvinist philosopher Gordon Clark
warns that 'dependence on ... paradox ... destroys both revelation

---

2   Michael Martin, *Atheism: A Philosophical Justification* (Philadelphia, PA:
    Temple University Press, 1990), 286-316. Further examples of this line of
    argument can be found in Michael Martin and Ricki Monnier (eds), *The
    Impossibility of God* (Amherst, NY: Prometheus Books, 2003).
3   Richard Gale, *On the Nature and Existence of God* (Cambridge: Cambridge
    University Press, 1991), 37-39, 52-55, 57ff.
4   Unitarians have made much hay out of apparent inconsistencies in the
    doctrine of the Trinity. For recent examples, see Anthony F. Buzzard and
    Charles F. Hunting, *The Doctrine of the Trinity: Christianity's Self-Inflicted
    Wound* (Lanham, MD: International Scholars Publications, 1998); Donald R.
    Snedeker, *Our Heavenly Father Has No Equals* (Lanham, MD: Rowman &
    Littlefield, 1998). On conceptual problems with the doctrine of the
    Incarnation, see Michael Goulder, *Incarnation and Myth: The Debate
    Continued* (London: SCM Press Ltd., 1979); Michael Martin, *The Case Against
    Christianity* (Philadelphia, PA: Temple University Press, 1991); John H.
    Hick, *The Metaphor of God Incarnate* (London: SCM Press, 1993).
5   Ronald W. Hepburn, *Christianity and Paradox: Critical Studies in Twentieth-
    Century Theology* (London: Watts, 1966), 2, 22.

and theology and leaves us in complete ignorance.'[6] Similarly, the
open theist David Basinger (illustrating that antipathy toward
paradox is represented at diverse points on the theological
spectrum) takes much the same view as Clark: there is no good
reason to affirm paradoxical doctrines in Scripture; indeed, the
notion is a 'confusion that ought to be avoided.'[7] Still other writers,
operating on the assumption that the intellectual propriety of the
Christian faith requires the elimination of any apparent logical
inconsistencies, have laboured to set forth non-paradoxical
interpretations of its central theological claims.[8]

More remarkable, however, is the number of Christian thinkers
who have conceded the presence of paradox in Christian theology,
some going so far as to deem it an essential feature of the faith.
Kierkegaard is well known for his conviction that the Incarnation
constitutes the 'absolute paradox' of Christianity.[9] Donald Bloesch
asserts that 'the truth of faith cannot be translated into a finalized,
coherent system which denies the mystery and paradox in faith.'[10]

---

6   Ronald Nash (ed.), *The Philosophy of Gordon H. Clark* (Phillipsburg, NJ:
     Presbyterian & Reformed, 1968), 78. Clark memorably dismissed paradox as
     'a charley-horse between the ears that can be eliminated by rational
     massage.' In keeping with this spirit, he attempted to articulate
     demonstrably consistent formulations of the doctrines of the Trinity and the
     Incarnation: Gordon H. Clark, *The Trinity* (Maryland: The Trinity
     Foundation, 1985); Gordon H. Clark, *The Incarnation* (Maryland: The Trinity
     Foundation, 1988).
7   David Basinger, 'Biblical Paradox: Does Revelation Challenge Logic?',
     Journal of the Evangelical Theological Society 30.2 (1987), 213.
8   For representative examples, see Richard Swinburne, *The Coherence of
     Theism* (Oxford: Clarendon Press, 1977); David W. Brown, *The Divine Trinity*
     (London: Gerald Duckworth & Co. Ltd., 1985); Thomas V. Morris, *The Logic
     of God Incarnate* (Ithaca, NY: Cornell University Press, 1986); Cornelius
     Plantinga, Jr., 'The Threeness/Oneness Problem of the Trinity', *Calvin
     Theological Journal* 23.1 (1988), 37-53; Ronald J. Feenstra, 'Reconsidering
     Kenotic Christology', in Ronald J. Feenstra and Cornelius Plantinga, Jr.
     (eds), *Trinity, Incarnation, and Atonement: Philosophical and Theological Essays*
     (Notre Dame, IN: University of Notre Dame Press, 1989), 128-52; Richard
     Sturch, *The Word and the Christ: An Essay in Analytic Christology* (Oxford:
     Clarendon Press, 1991); Richard Swinburne, *The Christian God* (Oxford:
     Clarendon Press, 1994).
9   Kierkegaard, *Philosophical Fragments*; C. Stephen Evans, 'Is Kierkegaard an
     Irrationalist? Reason, Paradox, and Faith', *Religious Studies* 25.3 (1989), 347-
     62.
10   Donald G. Bloesch, *Essentials of Evangelical Theology*, Vol. 1 (San Francisco,
     CA: Harper & Row, 1978), 18. He later adds, 'the mysteries of the faith defy

Donald Baillie contends that 'the element of paradox comes into all religious thought and statement', identifying the Christian doctrines of creation, providence, salvation by grace, the Incarnation, and the Trinity as cases in point.[11] J. I. Packer, addressing the perceived tension between divine sovereignty and human responsibility, speaks of biblical 'antinomies': apparently conflicting revelational truths that are surely reconciled 'in the mind and counsel of God' yet present us with 'a mystery which we cannot expect to solve in this world.'[12] Still more strident is the view of Cornelius Van Til:

> Since God is not fully comprehensible to us we are bound to come into what seems to be contradiction in all our knowledge. Our knowledge is analogical and therefore must be paradoxical.[13]

For this reason, he remarks, 'while we shun as poison the idea of the really contradictory we embrace with passion the idea of the *apparently* contradictory.'[14]

Other 'theologians of paradox' could be cited to reinforce the point.[15] Yet presumably each of these writers takes it that affirming

---

rational comprehension and can be expressed only in symbolic and paradoxical language.' Bloesch identifies the doctrine of the Incarnation and the doctrine of salvation by grace as particular cases of theological paradox. Bloesch, *Essentials of Evangelical Theology*, 86, 126-27, 201.

11　Donald M. Baillie, *God Was In Christ: An Essay on Incarnation and Atonement* (London: Faber and Faber, 2nd edn, 1961), 108, 111-14, 144.

12　J. I. Packer, *Evangelism and the Sovereignty of God* (Downers Grove, IL: InterVarsity Press, 1961), 23. Cf. Anthony A. Hoekema, *Saved by Grace* (Grand Rapids, MI: Eerdmans, 1989), 5-7.

13　Cornelius Van Til, *The Defense of the Faith* (Phillipsburg, NJ: Presbyterian & Reformed, 3rd edn, 1967), 44.

14　Cornelius Van Til, *Common Grace and the Gospel* (Phillipsburg, NJ: Presbyterian & Reformed, 1972), 9, emphasis original. Van Til finds paradox in the doctrines of the Trinity and the Incarnation, the necessity and freedom of God's will, the interplay between divine sovereignty and human responsibility, the tension between God's goodness and his foreordination of evil, and the notion that God is self-sufficient yet chose to create the world. For a survey of Van Til's claims about theological paradox, see John M. Frame, 'The Problem of Theological Paradox', in Gary North (ed.), *Foundations of Christian Scholarship: Essays in the Van Til Perspective* (Vallecito, CA: Ross House Books, 1979), 295-330.

15　For further examples, see Roger Hazelton, 'The Nature of Christian Paradox', *Theology Today* 6 (1949), 324-35; Vernon C. Grounds, 'The Postulate of Paradox', *Bulletin of the Evangelical Theological Society* 7 (1964), 13-14; John V. Dahms, 'How Reliable is Logic?', *Journal of the Evangelical Theological Society* 21.4 (1978), 369-80; Denis R. Janz, 'Syllogism or Paradox: Aquinas and Luther on Theological Method', *Theological Studies* 59.1 (1998), certain paradoxical doctrines is acceptable, even *reasonable* in some sense. As such, the various positions with respect to theological paradox mentioned thus far may be broadly divided as follows:

(P1) It is *always* irrational to affirm a paradoxical doctrine; and *some* central Christian doctrines are unavoidably paradoxical; therefore, adherence to the Christian faith is *always* irrational (on account of paradox).

(P2) It is *always* irrational to affirm a paradoxical doctrine; but *no* central Christian doctrines are unavoidably paradoxical; therefore, adherence to the Christian faith is *not always* irrational (on account of paradox).

(P3) It is *not always* irrational to affirm a paradoxical doctrine; and *some* central Christian doctrines are unavoidably paradoxical; therefore, adherence to the Christian faith is *not always* irrational (on account of paradox).

Each position has its problems, however. (P1) is intolerable for Christians who believe they have good epistemic grounds for their religious convictions; (P2) faces the difficulty of countering the widespread contention (among both believers and non-believers) that there *are* unresolved paradoxes in traditional Christian theology; and (P3) is problematic inasmuch as it fails to offer a satisfactory account of the circumstances under which a paradoxical doctrine might be rationally believed (and whether such circumstances ever obtain). While some advocates of (P3) have offered sketchy defences of the intellectual propriety of paradox, none of these treatments addresses in any depth the prior question of what *constitutes* rationality: what is required for belief to be judged 'rational' and whether adherence to paradoxical doctrines can ever meet the relevant epistemic requirements.

1.2 Paradox Defined

I trust that the particular concept of 'paradox' with which this book is concerned will be evident from the discussion above, but since the term has historically carried a number of distinct meanings, it would be remiss not to provide an explicit definition at the outset. As I will be using the term, it is synonymous with *apparent contradiction*. A 'paradox' thus amounts to *a set of claims which taken in conjunction*

3-21; Augustine Holmes, 'The Paradox of God: Thoughts on Christian Theism', *Faith Magazine* (May-June 2002); also the authors discussed in §2.3.4 and §3.3.3.

appear to be logically inconsistent.[16] Note that according to this definition, paradoxicality does not entail logical inconsistency *per se*, but merely the *appearance* of logical inconsistency. Of course, what appears to be the case very often *is* the case—but this definition is deliberately adopted so as not to beg any crucial questions about the logical status of Christian doctrines.[17]

1.3 Outline of the Book

The three positions identified above suggest that there are two key questions concerning paradox in Christian theology:

(1) Are any essential Christian doctrines genuinely paradoxical?

(2) Can a person rationally believe a paradoxical doctrine?

Answers to these questions will determine which of the positions (P1), (P2), and (P3) is closest to the mark.

Part I of the book considers the *first* key question and concludes in the affirmative. In Chapter 2, I argue that the Christian doctrine of the Trinity is paradoxical. This conclusion is reached by way of (i) a survey of the early trinitarian controversies leading up to the formulation of two definitive statements of orthodoxy, the Niceno-Constantinopolitan Creed and the Athanasian Creed, and (ii) a critical examination of contemporary interpretations of the doctrine, especially those developed with an eye to avoiding paradox while

---

16 For similar definitions in a theological context, see William H. Austin, 'Complementarity and Theological Paradox', *Zygon* 2.4 (1967), 366-67; Van Til, *The Defense of the Faith*, 45; Dahms, 'How Reliable is Logic?', 375; Michael Goulder, 'Paradox and Mystification', in Michael Goulder (ed.), *Incarnation and Myth: The Debate Continued* (London: SCM Press Ltd., 1979), 51-54; Jeffrey Astley, 'Paradox and Christology', *King's Theological Review* 7.1 (1984), 9; Basinger, 'Biblical Paradox', 205; Evans, 'Is Kierkegaard an Irrationalist?', 353; Sturch, *The Word and the Christ*, 17; David M. Ciocchi, 'Reconciling Divine Sovereignty and Human Freedom', *Journal of the Evangelical Theological Society* 37.3 (1994), 397; Janz, 'Syllogism or Paradox', 6. According to Nicholas Rescher, 'a paradox arises when a set of individually plausible propositions is collectively inconsistent', and furthermore, 'the inconsistency at issue here must be real rather than merely seeming.' Nicholas Rescher, *Paradoxes: Their Roots, Range, and Resolution* (Chicago and La Salle, IL: Open Court, 2001), 6. Thus what I and others call a 'paradox', Rescher would label an 'apparent paradox'—the disagreement here being merely semantic.

17 This presupposes that a meaningful distinction can be made between *apparent* contradiction and *real* contradiction, a distinction that I take up and defend in due course (see §6.2.1 and §7.4.1).

preserving orthodoxy. In Chapter 3, I argue that the Christian doctrine of the Incarnation is also paradoxical using a similar two-stage argument, considering both the early christological controversies and contemporary interpretations of the doctrine. I have chosen to focus on these two doctrines, first, because they have often been regarded as 'paradoxical', and second, because of their ecumenical appeal and early credal status.[18] (For those readers not persuaded by the conclusions reached in these early chapters, I would ask that final judgement be withheld until the end of the book, since my later analysis of the epistemic status of paradoxical doctrines may render these conclusions somewhat more palatable.) Chapter 4 considers a range of responses to the paradoxicality of Christian doctrines: coping strategies for dealing with the epistemic anxieties induced by the appearance of contradiction. Each of these strategies is inadequate on philosophical or theological grounds, so I contend, and thus the path is cleared for the presentation of (what I take to be) a more satisfactory approach in Part II.

Part II considers the *second* key question and also concludes in the affirmative. Chapter 5 lays the epistemological groundwork by providing an account of how the affirmation of Christian doctrines *in general* can be rational. This chapter introduces a number of important notions, such as epistemic warrant, proper function rationality, and epistemic defeaters, which play central roles in the later argument. Chapter 6 then sets forth a model for construing theological paradox according to which believers, with varying degrees of intellectual sophistication, can be perfectly rational in holding to paradoxical interpretations of Christian doctrines. In Chapter 7, I defend this model against a range of potential objections. Finally, in Chapter 8, I briefly highlight what I take to be the main implications of the conclusions reached and suggest some avenues for further study.

---

18 Thus the argument presented here will be of interest, I trust, to readers from all Christian traditions. I believe a case can be made for the paradoxicality of several doctrines distinctive to the Reformed tradition, as I indicate in later chapters, but to focus on these would inevitably diminish the relevance of this work to the wider Christian community.

PART I

The Presence of Paradox

The question 'How are you coping with your drink problem?' is hardly appropriate for one who imbibes only in moderation. Likewise, the question 'How can Christians be rational in holding to paradoxical doctrines?' is rather beside the point if no Christian doctrines (at any rate, no *essential* doctrines) suffer from paradox. Hence the question of the *presence* of paradox must precede the question of its *propriety*. In the first part of this book, I argue that at least two major articles of the Christian faith—the doctrine of the Trinity and the doctrine of the Incarnation—are indeed paradoxical. If this is the case, the rationality of traditional Christian beliefs is cast into some doubt. Still, a range of options are open to the Christian theologian in response to this state of affairs, each of which purports either to eliminate or to excuse the paradoxicality of the doctrines in question. In the closing chapter of Part I, I consider the main contenders in the arena, arguing that each one fails to provide a philosophically defensible and theologically satisfying solution to the problem; thus the conclusions of Part I will pave the way for Part II, in which I develop a model for understanding paradoxical Christian doctrines according to which belief in such doctrines can be entirely rational, their deep logical perplexities notwithstanding.

CHAPTER 2

The Paradox of the Trinity

2.1 Introduction

The doctrine of the Trinity is one of the most debated doctrines of the Christian faith; but if both its defenders and its detractors can agree on anything, it is that the doctrine is a mysterious one. In its briefest formulation, the doctrine asserts that there is only one God who exists in three distinct persons. Although much more needs to be said in order to fully specify the boundaries of orthodox trinitarian belief, as dictated by the Christian scriptures and creeds, already this minimal statement raises questions about the logical status of this defining doctrine. Is not God (at least in the Judeo-Christian tradition) a *personal* being? Does this not suggest that if there is only one God, there is only one divine person? How then can this one divine person also be *three* divine persons? Put another way: if there are three numerically distinct persons, each fully divine, does this not imply that there are *three* Gods, rather than *one*?[1]

It is answers to questions such as these (or perhaps a lack of answers) that have driven many thinkers, both inside and outside the church, to argue that the doctrine of the Trinity is not merely mysterious: it is *paradoxical*, if not outright self-contradictory. In this chapter, I propose to show that this conclusion is well justified.[2] Still,

---

1 'Here one instinctively feels the point of the seventeenth-century antitrinitarian complaint that trinitarians simply do not know how to *count*.' Plantinga, 'The Threeness/Oneness Problem', 41.

2 It is worth reiterating that as I have defined the term, 'paradox' entails only *apparent* contradiction and not *real* contradiction. In other words, a paradoxical set of statements is one that strikes us as inconsistent, but may or may not turn out to be genuinely inconsistent. Given this usage, my conclusions in this chapter and the next should not be taken as entailing that the doctrines of the Trinity and the Incarnation are (or must be interpreted as) logically inconsistent. The relevance of the distinction between apparent contradiction and real contradiction is developed and defended in Chapters 6 and 7.

any such claims about trinitarian theology must recognise that while there may be only one God, there is surely more than one doctrine of the Trinity; at any rate, there is more than one *interpretation* of that distinctive Christian teaching expressed in the ancient creeds and confessions of the church.

Consequently, sophisticated theses about the logical status of this doctrine usually incorporate statements about the boundaries of orthodoxy regarding its interpretation. Few scholars would deny that interpretations of the Trinity have been offered which, under the closest scrutiny, appear to be free of any *logical* difficulty. However, many more would question whether such interpretations are free of any *theological* difficulty; that is, whether they pay sufficient heed to the religious concerns of those who originally forged the early statements of trinitarian orthodoxy. As such, criticisms of the doctrine of the Trinity based on its logical status are often presented in the form of a *dilemma*: it is alleged that the trinitarian who wishes to remain orthodox will inevitably face paradox, while the trinitarian who aims to banish paradox will end up heterodox.

Given this framing of the problem, I propose to assess the validity of this purported dilemma in two stages. In the first, I will chart the original development of the doctrine of the Trinity from the decades of debate culminating in the Council of Nicea in 325, through the decades of reflection following the Council of Constantinople in 381, and closing with the formulation of the Athanasian Creed some centuries later. The focus here will be not merely on the *wording* of the trinitarian statements arising from this period, but also on the *concepts* associated with that vocabulary and the *theological concerns* which conditioned the development of orthodox doctrine. Although this historical survey will be somewhat distilled, my aim is to secure an adequate understanding not only of the formal specification of the doctrine of the Trinity, but also of the constraints placed on its legitimate interpretation. In so doing, not only will we see how the contours of the doctrine naturally give rise to paradox, but some indication will be gained as to what extent the pioneers of trinitarian doctrine were prepared to tolerate paradox within their theology.

If an orthodox interpretation of the trinitarian creeds *does* raise acute logical difficulties, the next question to ask is whether these difficulties have been resolved in the centuries following their formulation. In the second stage of my analysis, therefore, I will review various representative contemporary explications of the doctrine, with a particular focus on those which purport to avoid, in part or in full, the charge of paradox or self-contradiction.[3] Each treatment will be assessed according to two criteria: (i) its fidelity to orthodoxy, in light of the conclusions reached in the first stage, and (ii) its success in avoiding paradoxical formulations of the Trinity. In addition, a selection of Christian writers who *concede* that the doctrine is unavoidably paradoxical will be examined, before drawing some final conclusions about the present-day status of the trinitarian dilemma.[4]

2.2 Early Trinitarianism

2.2.1 The Road to Nicea

As most historians have acknowledged, the seeds of trinitarian theology were present in Christian thought from the earliest times. Leaving to one side the question of the New Testament witness to the triune nature of God, the established practice of the church—for example, baptism in the threefold name of God (following Matthew 28:19) and worship directed toward Jesus as 'God'—strongly suggests that at the heart of newborn Christian faith lay the conviction that Jesus Christ was, in some real sense, *divine*.[5] Even so,

---

3   Of the writing of books on the Trinity, there is no end. The reader should therefore note that my selection is guided by the relatively narrow remit of this work.

4   Due to space constraints, the discussion in this chapter will not incorporate either exegesis of key biblical texts or analysis of significant contributions to the interpretation of trinitarian doctrine between the fifth and twentieth centuries. I hope that reference to the former will be implicit in my treatment of the debate among the Fathers, while the latter will be taken into account (again, implicitly) by my examination of contemporary contributions (most of which are sensitive to, and seek to advance the achievements of, their historical predecessors). The direct biblical support for a paradoxical doctrine of the Trinity is discussed in Chapter 7.

5   Jaroslav Pelikan cites various evidences for this, concluding that 'clearly it was the message of what the church believed and taught that "God" was an appropriate name for Jesus Christ.' He notes that the strength of this conviction is further underlined by the existence of early docetic heresies. Jaroslav Pelikan, *The Christian Tradition, Vol. 1: The Emergence of the Catholic Tradition (100-600)* (Chicago, IL: University of Chicago Press, 1971), 173-74. For an exhaustive treatment of early Christian devotion to Jesus, and its foundational contribution to later doctrinal developments, see Larry W. Hurtado, *Lord Jesus Christ: Devotion to Jesus in Earliest Christianity* (Grand Rapids, MI: Eerdmans, 2003).

a precise theological formulation of this conviction was lacking and would not be brought to maturity for several centuries to come.

The first steps towards a definitive trinitarian theology came in response to various Monarchian teachings arising in the third century. The driving axiom of Monarchian theology was the numerical unity and absolute sovereignty of God as required by a robust monotheism. From this axiom it appears to follow with seamless logic that no substantial distinction can be made between the Father and the Son; for if Christ is deemed to be God in any *literal* sense, then he cannot be any other God than the Father (whom all parties agreed was to be identified with the 'Yahweh' of the Old Testament). Thus Praxeas of Rome and Noetus of Smyrna declared at the turn of the third century that the Father and the Son were the same person,[6] while Sabellius would later appeal to texts such as Isaiah 44:6 to support the same basic thesis, albeit with the greater sophistication of allowing for a threefold distinction between the *names* and *activities* of God.[7]

The response of the church to these teachings is instructive insofar as it indicates the theological constraints within which trinitarian doctrine would be forced to develop. Although it may seem obvious, it is important to note that apologists such as Tertullian and Hippolytus at no point challenged the basic monotheistic axiom of Monarchian thought; after all, it enjoyed such impeccable support from Scripture and tradition. Instead, they took a threefold approach to countering Monarchianism. In the first place, they sought to rebut the ultimate conclusions of their opponents by appealing to *other* biblical texts. Pelikan identifies four categories of scriptural passages which played key roles in the debates over the relation between Christ and God: passages of *adoption* (suggesting that divinity was conferred on Jesus by the Father at some point in time); passages of *identity* (positing a simple identification of Christ with God); passages of *distinction* (supporting a real distinction between the Father and the Son); and passages of *derivation* (suggesting that Christ derived his divinity from the Father, perhaps with some subordinationist overtones).[8] The tactic of the Fathers in refuting the modalism of the Monarchians was to try to meet the force of the monotheistic texts and the passages of identity with the force of the

---

6   Bernard Lonergan, *The Way to Nicea: The Dialectical Development of Trinitarian Theology* (trans. Conn O'Donovan; London: Darton, Longman & Todd, 1976), 38, 43.

7   Lonergan, *The Way to Nicea*, 39; Pelikan, *The Christian Tradition*, 179.

8   Pelikan, *The Christian Tradition*, 175.

passages of distinction and of derivation.[9] In short, these theologians challenged the validity of the modalist inferences, not by questioning their monotheistic premises or by correcting their understanding of logic but by appealing to the authority of Scripture—an authority acknowledged at least formally by their opponents.

Secondly, borrowing heavily from Hellenist philosophy, the anti-Monarchians offered accounts of the ontological relationship between the Father and the Son that sought to make clear the distinction between them whilst striving to avoid the charge of 'dividing the monarchy' and thus abandoning biblical monotheism. Tertullian, whose approach was typical of the ante-Nicene writers,[10] spoke of the Son being a distinct substance 'emitted' from the substance of the Father, but maintained that the motivating concerns of the Monarchians could be satisfied by emphasising the intimate union and non-separation of the Father and the Son.[11] Origen likewise posited the distinct substantiality of the Son, designating him the 'invisible image of the invisible God' and related to the Father by something akin to Platonic participation, such that the Son shares the divine nature of the Father. On this account, thought Origen, the unity of God is preserved.[12] Although the proffering of such ontological models proved effective to a degree, they invariably suffered from ambiguity and dubious coherence, leading their proponents to fall on occasion into either self-contradiction or subordinationism. These weaknesses would later return to haunt the church, most notably in the championing of Origen by the Arians.

Thirdly, the Fathers drew attention to the unpalatable (since patently unbiblical) *implications* of the Monarchian position. Thus Tertullian famously charged that 'in Rome, Praxeas accomplished two things for the devil: he expelled prophecy and brought in heresy, drove out the Paraclete and crucified the Father.'[13] The line

---

9   It is commonly acknowledged that overemphasis of the latter led ante-Nicene authors such as Tertullian and Origen perilously close to ontological subordination, although a charitable assessment need conclude no more than that further elucidation and precision was required of trinitarian thinking. Cf. Lonergan, *The Way to Nicea*, 40-42.

10   Lonergan, *The Way to Nicea*, 50.

11   'This conception of the trinity … is in no way opposed to the monarchy, and it preserves the order of the divine economy.' Tertullian, *Against Praxeas*, 7-8; in *ANE*, Vol. 3.

12   Origen, *De Principiis*, I, 2.6; in *ANE*, Vol. 4. See also Origen, *In Joan.*, II, 2, quoted in Lonergan, *The Way to Nicea*, 61.

13   Tertullian, *Against Praxeas*, 1.

of reasoning illustrated here is instructive once again: although the Monarchians began with theologically impeccable premises, their conclusions were heretical; therefore, argued the Fathers, their inferences—however *seemingly* logical—could not be valid.

It thus appears that even in the earliest stages of trinitarian development, defenders of orthodoxy were struggling with limited success to hold fidelity to Scripture and tradition together with the demands of logic. And although this first wave of defence against the Sabellian heresy and its stable-mates was successful up to a point, the problems raised by inferences from the defining axiom of Monarchianism would before long arise in a new form, that of Arianism, forcing the church to an even more sophisticated and nuanced defence of orthodox trinitarianism.

2.2.2 The Nicene Settlement

The debate over the deity of Christ that eventually culminated in the formulation of the Nicene Creed was sparked off by the rise of Arianism at the beginning of the fourth century.[14] Arius, a presbyter of the church in Alexandria, had garnered attention by his controversial teaching that only the Father was truly God, and that the Son was an ontologically inferior being created by the Father. The details of Arius's theology and the later arguments of his followers are well documented,[15] but the important point to note here is this: Arius, along the same lines as the Monarchians, grounded his theology on a perfectly orthodox premise; namely, 'the affirmation of the absolute uniqueness and transcendence of God, the unoriginate source (ἀγέννητος ἀρχή) of all reality.'[16] From this premise Arius reasoned that God (the one whom Jesus called 'Father') could not possibly fully communicate his divine essence to another being and thus Christ must be less than fully divine: hence the Logos was demoted to the status of a created being (albeit more than a mere human) having a beginning in time.

The parallels between the argument of the Arians and the argument of the Monarchians should not be missed. Both parties

---

14 J. N. D. Kelly, *Early Christian Doctrines* (London: A. & C. Black, 5th edn, 1977), 223; Christopher Stead, *Divine Substance* (Oxford: Clarendon Press, 1977), 223-24.

15 Lonergan, *The Way to Nicea*, 68-87; Pelikan, *The Christian Tradition*, 191-200; Kelly, *Early Christian Doctrines*, 226-31.

16 Kelly, *Early Christian Doctrines*, 227.

began with the orthodox conviction of absolute monotheism.[17] Both parties conjoined this premise with another uncontroversial theological tenet: for the Monarchians, the affirmation that Christ is God; for the Arians, the affirmation (previously defended by the *anti*-Monarchians) that the Son is distinct from the Father. Both came to conclusions which, despite their logical appeal, were ultimately deemed to be biblically and theologically unacceptable. The very emergence of these two trinitarian heresies, not to mention the degree to which their proponents persuaded others of the irresistible logic of their position, serves as strong evidence that the emerging orthodox doctrine of the Trinity was faced with the spectre of paradox from the outset. The three basic premises involved in these formative debates appear to be such that one cannot consistently affirm two without denying the third.[18]

Seven years after Arius's influential teaching had first come to light, the Council of Nicea condemned his view of Christ as heretical, based on the firm conviction that both Scripture and tradition testified to the full divinity and immutability of the Logos.[19] The rebuttal of Arius consisted of both positive and

---

17 Moltmann rightly observes that both Sabellianism and Arianism were driven by a commitment to monotheism, although their strategies for safeguarding this axiom led to different conclusions. The remarkable conclusion he draws from this is that trinitarians should distance themselves from monotheism altogether—an approach which involves, so it would seem, rejecting the *homoousios* of the Nicene Creed and the *unus Deus* of the Athanasian Creed. Jürgen Moltmann, *The Trinity and the Kingdom of God* (trans. Margaret Köhl; London: SCM Press, 1981), 132-37, 149-50, 189-90. This radical recommendation smacks of Wittgenstein's ladder, kicked away once it has been climbed. An uncompromising commitment to monotheism was one of the central components in the religious matrix of the early Christians, out of which developed the doctrine of the Trinity. See Hurtado, *Lord Jesus Christ*, 29-53.

18 Using formal logical notation, A. P. Martinich sets out with admirable clarity the acute logical difficulties faced by orthodox trinitarianism in its opposition to both Sabellianism and Arianism. A. P. Martinich, 'Identity and Trinity', *The Journal of Religion* 58.2 (1978), 169-81. As I argue below, however, Martinich's proposed solution to the problem is unsatisfactory. For a similarly clear formulation of the logical problems faced by trinitarians, see Dale Tuggy, 'The Unfinished Business of Trinitarian Theorizing', *Religious Studies* 39.2 (2003), 165-83.

19 Kelly, *Early Christian Doctrines*, 232-33. By this time, the terms 'Logos' and 'Son of God' had become standard designators for the divine person in Christ as distinct from the Father, and as such were employed with great

negative arguments: the former appealing to scriptural passages supporting the 'consubstantiality' of the Son with the Father, and the latter refuting Arius's appeal to passages suggesting that the Son was *created* by the Father. As I noted earlier concerning the response of the Fathers to Monarchianism, it is worth remarking here that at no point did the Nicene authors challenge the basic premises of the Arian theological argument. Both sides in the debate adhered to a conception of deity as absolute, unique, and indivisible; both sides held that, in some real sense, the Son was distinct from the Father. What the Council challenged, on the basis of what they took to be unacceptable conclusions, was *the legitimacy of Arius's inferences from those premises*. In short, the overriding concern of the Fathers was not so much to develop a scrupulously coherent theology (that was arguably the principle motivation of their *opponents*)[20] but to be faithful to Scripture and tradition. As a result, the Council resolved to maintain a classical monotheist view of God in conjunction with an uncompromisingly high christology despite the apparent logical tension between the two.

Further insight into the logical status of Nicene theology can be obtained by considering more closely its famous declaration that the Son is 'of the same substance' (*homoousion*) with the Father. There has been extensive debate over the exact meaning of this term, both as employed at the time of the Council and as interpreted by subsequent defenders of Nicene orthodoxy. A particular concern is whether it expresses merely a *generic* identity (such that the divinity of the Son is the same as the divinity of the Father, just as the humanity of Peter is the same as the humanity of Paul) or something akin to *numerical* identity (such that the Son is one and the same divine being as the Father). The latter view has tradition heavily in its favour, but has been challenged more recently on the basis of the common usage of *homoousios* prior to Nicea (which most frequently reflected the *generic* sense) and its technical usage within post-

---

effect to interpret and synthesise the four types of biblical passages mentioned previously. Cf. Pelikan, *The Christian Tradition*, 191.

20 Thus Kelly describes Arius and his ilk as 'rationalists at heart', while Philip Schaff remarks of Arianism and Athanasian orthodoxy, respectively, that 'the one made reasonableness, the other agreement with Scripture, the criterion of truth.' Kelly, *Early Christian Doctrines*, 243; *HCC*, Vol. 3, Ch. 9, §123. Cf. Lonergan, *The Way to Nicea*, 134-35; William J. Hill, *The Three-Personed God: The Trinity as a Mystery of Salvation* (Washington, DC: Catholic University of America Press, 1982), 42.

Nicene Christian theological writings (which made use of both senses).[21]

There is legitimate doubt, therefore, as to whether the Nicene Fathers consciously and unanimously intended for the term to bear the connotation of numerical identity.[22] Nevertheless, it is clear that its employment at Nicea was at the very least designed to outlaw Arianism and to uphold the full divinity of the Son and his co-eternality with the Father.[23] Moreover, a strong case can be made that in light of the *other* theological commitments of the Fathers (namely, their strict adherence to monotheism, divine simplicity, and divine indivisibility) the Nicene *homoousion* ought to be taken to imply something akin to identity of substance between the Father and the Son if orthodoxy is to be upheld.[24] On such grounds as these, Schaff concludes that

---

21   See the discussion in Kelly, *Early Christian Doctrines*, 234. Kelly expresses some reservations about the traditional view, but remarks that *homoousios* 'in the last resort requires' the stronger numerical sense. Pelikan and Schaff both suggest that the original Nicene usage was ambiguous, although Schaff concurs with Kelly that on theological grounds that it *should* be (and later was) taken in a sense connoting numerical identity. Lonergan contends that while the latter sense is not explicit in the Nicene statement, it follows implicitly from the theology expressed therein. Gerald O'Collins expresses little doubt: 'It is clear from the whole tenor of the Nicene Creed that the former meaning [i.e., numerical identity rather than generic identity] was intended.' Gerald O'Collins, *The Tripersonal God: Understanding and Interpreting the Trinity* (London: Geoffrey Chapman, 1999), 117. Basil Studer remarks that the term *homoousios* 'had not been closely defined' at Nicea and suggests that it was originally intended only to express *equality* of essence (and thus to uphold Christ's true divinity against the Arians) rather than *unity* of essence. This deficiency, however, was remedied by the post-Nicene theologians with the introduction of the *'mia ousia, treis hypostaseis'* formula. Basil Studer, *Trinity and Incarnation: The Faith of the Early Church* (Edinburgh: T. & T. Clark, 1993), 106, 109-10, 140ff.

22   On the basis of a detailed historical investigation, Christopher Stead concludes that the word does not signify the triumph of Western theology (which tended toward a stronger view of the unity of the divine *hypostases*) over Eastern theology; rather, its original ambiguity made it suitable as a formula of compromise that could be defended by bishops of either persuasion. Nevertheless, he agrees that the 'ultimate effect' of the Nicene settlement was to assert 'not merely the equality, but also the essential unity, of the three Persons.' Stead, *Divine Substance*, 251. One might say, then, that the Nicene Fathers spoke better than they knew.

23   A point reaffirmed by the Council of Constantinople in 381.

24   Further evidence is provided by the fact that the term *homoousios* suffered more from suspicion of *Sabellian* connotations than from suspicion of

the homoousion ... must be understood as identity or *numerical* unity of substance, in distinction from mere generic unity. Otherwise it leads manifestly into dualism or tritheism.[25]

Lonergan likewise asserts, on the basis of Athanasius's commentary on the Nicene declaration, that

the affirmation of a single substance is *logically contained* in the Nicene decree. ... Athanasius thus testifies to the fact that the Nicene decree is intended to go beyond the affirmation of a mere similarity between the Father and the Son, to an affirmation of identity.[26]

Now if this understanding of consubstantiality is correct, being demanded by Christian orthodoxy, then it has direct implications for the paradoxicality (or otherwise) of the doctrine of the Trinity. For it has long been recognised that the numerical identity view of the *homoousion* relation between the Father and the Son leads to logical perplexities that do not trouble the generic identity view. Given the predominantly neo-Platonist philosophical atmosphere in which these early doctrinal debates were played out, to say merely that the Father and the Son share the same divine 'form' or 'genus' would invite no charge of incoherence. Indeed, had it been considered consistent with biblical monotheism, this solution would have sufficed to remove the sharpest teeth from the Arian argument (hence the fact that it was *not* unambiguously advocated by the Nicene theologians is instructive). In contrast, the claim that both the Father and the Son are *numerically identical* with the divine essence, while yet distinct individuals, is considerably more difficult for a rationalistic mindset to digest. Nonetheless, the insistence of the Fathers on the indivisibility of God, and their frequent charge of 'polytheism' levelled against the Arians,[27] naturally inclined them toward a stronger understanding of consubstantiality, logical difficulties notwithstanding.[28]

---

tritheistic or subordinationist connotations, both at the time of the council and subsequently. Pelikan, *The Christian Tradition*, 207-10, 220; G. L. Prestige, *God in Patristic Thought* (London: S.P.C.K., 2nd edn, 1952), 222-23; O'Collins, *The Tripersonal God*, 117. Eusebius of Caesarea, in particular, was apparently hesitant to accept the term on account of its potentially modalistic implications.

25 *HCC*, Vol. 3, Ch. 9, §127.
26 Lonergan, *The Way to Nicea*, 95, emphasis added.
27 Pelikan, *The Christian Tradition*, 199-200.
28 I have not addressed here the post-Nicene debate over *homoiousion* as an alternative to *homoousion*—a debate that, while important in some respects,

The road to Nicea marked a real progression in the church's understanding of the triune God as revealed in the biblical witness to Jesus Christ, not least in its identification of the boundaries of orthodoxy. Still, this increase in conceptual clarity came at a price, namely, the advocacy of a paradoxical doctrine. As Lonergan observes,

> [The emergence of the Nicene dogma] marks a transition from the mystery of God as hidden in symbols, hinted at by a multiplicity of titles, apprehended only in a vague and confused manner in the dramatico-practical pattern of experience, to the mystery of God as circumscribed and manifested in clear, distinct and *apparently contradictory* affirmations.[29]

2.2.3 The Post-Nicene Fathers

A distinct tendency toward a stronger, paradoxical understanding of the relationships within the Trinity can be clearly seen in the most prominent of the post-Nicene writers, beginning with the influential writings of Athanasius. Kelly remarks:

> [Athanasius's] theology represents the classic exposition of the Nicene standpoint. As a Christian thinker he stood in complete contrast to Arius and even to Eusebius of Caesarea. Rationalists at heart, they started from *a priori* ideas of divine transcendence and creation. The Word, they held, could not be divine because His being originated from the Father; since the divine nature was incommunicable, He must be a creature, and any special status He enjoyed must be due to His role as the Father's agent in creation. In Athanasius's approach philosophical and cosmological considerations played a very minor part, and his guiding thought was the conviction of redemption.[30]

Athanasius's primary concern, then, was not to avoid any apparent logical difficulties in his theology but to be faithful to the theological constraints placed upon him by preceding Christian orthodoxy regarding the nature of God and Christ's redemptive work. While his opponents rested heavily on 'philosophical and cosmological considerations', coupled with seemingly impeccable inferences, Athanasius's greater commitment was to 'the conviction of

---

arguably bears only tangentially on my concerns here. See Pelikan, *The Christian Tradition*, 210; Studer, *Trinity and Incarnation*, 140-41.

29   Lonergan, *The Way to Nicea*, 137, emphasis added.
30   Kelly, *Early Christian Doctrines*, 243.

redemption' and thus to the strongest affirmations of Christ's divinity and unity with the Father.

As a consequence of this theological outlook, Athanasius was compelled in his opposition to the Arian heresy to emphasise that the Son is of the very same substance and nature as the Father. I have already noted Athanasius's understanding of the Nicene *homoousion*, insisting that the identity between the Father and the Son is stronger than mere generic identity and is tantamount to identity of substance.[31] Even so, Athanasius could by no means compromise his equally strong commitment to a genuine distinction between the Father and the Son, resulting in a considerable tension within his thought. On the one hand, he insisted that 'the Monad of the Godhead is indivisible'[32] and that 'the Godhead of the Son is the Father's' such that there is 'identity of Godhead'[33]—as clear an indication of numerical unity of substance as one might hope to find.[34] On the other hand, he was also resolutely opposed to the Sabellian heresy of denying the distinctions between the Father and the Son.[35] With two such seemingly incompatible commitments in

---

31 Prestige, *God in Patristic Thought*, 213-18; Kelly, *Early Christian Doctrines*, 245; Hill, *The Three-Personed God*, 46. It should be noted that Athanasius's conception of consubstantiality apparently involves *more* than an identity claim, not least because he viewed the relation as asymmetric (the Son is *homoousios* with the Father, but not vice versa). Still, given how he characterizes the relation, it certainly seems to *imply* identity of substance.

32 Athanasius, *Four Discourses Against the Arians*, Discourse 4, 1-2; in *NPNF2*, Vol. 4.

33 Athanasius, *Four Discourses*, Discourse 3, 4.

34 It would be misguided to object that Athanasius could be speaking here only of a generic unity, since this would suggest that the Godhead is a *third* entity, an abstract nature distinct from the Father and the Son in which both participate.

35 See, e.g., Athanasius, *Four Discourses*, Discourse 4, 2. Stead offers correctives to both a 'rationalistic' misreading of Athanasius, which interprets him in line with the 'generic unity' view discussed previously, and a 'romantic' misreading, 'which represents him as leading an advance towards an unrestricted view of the unity of the Persons, and as upholding their "numerical identity of substance"…' Stead, *Divine Substance*, 265-66. Certainly Athanasius's view of the triune unity was not *unrestricted*, given his stalwart opposition to modalism. Nevertheless, his characterisation of *homoousion* is hard to square with anything weaker than numerical identity. Stead's analysis thus supports my view that there was a considerable logical tension within Athanasius's trinitarian theology. If Athanasius did indeed hold to a paradoxical doctrine of the Trinity, then it would not be at all surprising to find such diametrically opposed misreadings of him.

his theology, it comes as little surprise to find Lonergan concluding that although Athanasius derived his understanding of the consubstantiality relation from various creaturely images employed in Scripture, when reflecting on the divine *homoousion* as it truly is, he conceded that 'there is nothing imaginable in which it can be grasped or understood.'[36]

The debate culminating in the declarations of Nicea had been focused on the divinity of Christ. It was not until afterwards that much thought was concentrated on the divinity of the Holy Spirit and thus on formulating a full-orbed trinitarian theology. Athanasius had started the ball rolling with his argument that the Holy Spirit is also *homoousion* with the Father.[37] His lead was followed and further developed by the Cappadocian Fathers, to whom I now turn.

It is often remarked in contemporary discussions of the Trinity that the Cappadocians were the intellectual forebears of modern 'social trinitarians', who favour the weaker, generic understanding of the unity of the Persons within the Godhead.[38] Such suggestions often rely in great measure on (i) the 'three men' analogy employed by Gregory of Nyssa, by which he compares the sharing of one divine essence by Father, Son, and Spirit with the sharing of one human nature by Peter, James, and John;[39] and (ii) a mistranslation of the word *koinonia*, used frequently by the Cappadocians to describe the unity of the Godhead, as 'community' rather than the more accurate 'communion'.[40]

---

36 Lonergan, *The Way to Nicea*, 103.

37 Kelly, *Early Christian Doctrines*, 255-58.

38 See, e.g., Brown, *The Divine Trinity*, 243; Morris, *The Logic of God Incarnate*, 212; Cornelius Plantinga, Jr., 'Social Trinity & Tritheism', in Ronald J. Feenstra and Cornelius Plantinga, Jr. (eds), *Trinity, Incarnation, and Atonement: Philosophical and Theological Essays* (Notre Dame, IN: University of Notre Dame Press, 1989), 31-32.

39 Gregory of Nyssa, *Ad Ablabium* (also known by the title 'Not Three Gods'); in *NPNF2*, Vol. 5.

40 Sarah Coakley provides ten textual evidences against the idea that the Cappadocians can be fairly claimed for the 'social trinitarian' camp. She concludes that Gregory's trinitarianism, at least, is more in line with the Western, Augustinian tradition with its stronger expression of identity between the each *hypostasis* and the one *ousia*. Sarah Coakley, '"Persons" in the "Social" Doctrine of the Trinity: A Critique of Current Analytic Discussion', in Stephen T. Davis, Daniel Kendall, and Gerald O'Collins (eds), *The Trinity: An Interdisciplinary Symposium on the Trinity* (Oxford: Oxford University Press, 1999), 123-44.

A closer examination of the writings of the Cappadocians in their historical and philosophical context leads to a different conclusion. In the first place, as Gregory indicates in the opening paragraphs of *Ad Ablabium*, the 'three men' analogy originated not with him but with his opponent, who demands to know how trinitarians like Gregory can avoid falling into tritheism. Secondly, in discussing the analogy Gregory takes a rather idiosyncratic view of the commonality of nature between three *human* persons, leading him to argue that strictly speaking Peter, James, and John are 'one man' and therefore talk of 'many men' is 'a customary abuse of language.' His understanding of unity-in-plurality is thus not straightforward even in the creaturely case, let alone the divine case.

Thirdly, the Cappadocians were frank in admitting that their illustrations of the relationship between the Persons and the Godhead were only *approximations* to the truth and did not fully capture the reality of the intratrinitarian relations. Basil of Caesarea, for example, writes as follows:

> Yet receive what I say as at best a token and reflection of the truth; not as the actual truth itself. For it is not possible that there should be complete correspondence between what is seen in the tokens and the objects in reference to which the use of tokens is adopted.[41]

Significantly, Basil notes that such illustrations, while imprecise, are nonetheless easier on the mind than more abstract statements of doctrine whose literal meaning is beyond human understanding:

> My argument thus teaches us, even by the aid of the visible creation, not to feel distressed at points of doctrine whenever we meet with questions difficult of solution, and when at the thought of accepting what is proposed to us, our brains begin to reel. In regard to visible objects experience appears better than theories of causation, and so in matters transcending all knowledge, the apprehension of argument is inferior to the faith which teaches us at once the distinction in hypostasis and the conjunction in essence.[42]

In a similar vein, Basil denies that ordinary arithmetic applies to the persons of the Trinity such that they can be 'added up' in the way that (say) Peter, James, and John can be counted as numerically three

---

41 Basil of Caesarea, *Letter 38*; in *NPNF2*, Vol. 8. Some scholars now attribute this letter to Gregory of Nyssa; its authorship remains a matter for debate.
42 Basil, *Letter 38*.

individuals.[43] This is evidently not the case for contemporary 'social' conceptions of the Trinity.

Finally, like all orthodox (and indeed unorthodox) theologians of their day, the Cappadocians were firmly committed to the *indivisibility* and *simplicity* of God, a stance requiring a considerably stronger ontological union than that offered by mere commonality of nature (even when strengthened by emphasising unity of purpose and activity).[44] Thus the trinitarian theology of these Fathers ought to be located nearer to the paradoxical views of Athanasius before them, and Augustine after them, than many modern scholars would wish to grant.[45] The logical tensions within the expositions of the Cappadocians, despite their pioneering appropriation of the terms *ousia* and *hypostasis* to explicate the relationship between the One and the Three, is frankly admitted by Pelikan:

> Formulas such as homoousios, three hypostases in one ousia, and mode of origin were metaphysically tantalizing; but the adjudication of their meaning was in many ways a defiance *not only of logical consistency, but of metaphysical coherence.* How, for example, could the Father be the source of Son and Spirit within the Trinity and yet fatherhood be a property not only of his hypostasis, but of the divine ousia as such? Or, to put it in liturgical terms, was the Lord's Prayer addressed only to the hypostasis of the Father as 'our Father' and the Father of the Son, or to the entire ousia of the

---

43 Basil of Caesarea, *On the Spirit*, 18.4; in *NPNF2*, Vol. 8.

44 Prestige, *God in Patristic Thought*, 229, 242-44; Kelly, *Early Christian Doctrines*, 268-69. According to David Coffey, the Cappadocians 'had reached the point of realizing that the divine persons were each identical with the single concrete essence of God'—a conception of divine unity far stronger than that posited by modern social trinitarians. David M. Coffey, *Deus Trinitas: The Doctrine of the Triune God* (New York: Oxford University Press, 1999), 68.

45 One notable exception is T. A. Noble, who documents Gregory Nazianzen's 'deliberate embracing of paradox' and argues that this should be seen as 'an expression of his apophaticism'. Gregory states, for example, that 'Monad is worshipped in Triad, and Triad in Monad—a paradox both in division and union' (*Oration* 25.17) and elsewhere prays that 'one illumination may come upon us from the one Godhead, unitedly divided and dividedly united, which is a paradox' (*Oration* 28.1). In fact, Gregory sees *two* paradoxes in the doctrine of the Trinity: first, that the Three are One; and second, that the Father as ἀρχή (Origin) and αἴτιος (Author) of the Son and the Spirit is the *greater* of the three Persons, yet they are nonetheless *equal* in essence, deity, glory, power, and dignity. T. A. Noble, 'Paradox in Gregory Nazianzen's Doctrine of the Trinity', *Studia Patristica* 27 (1993), 94-99. Cf. Studer, *Trinity and Incarnation*, 145.

Godhead? Basil's answer to this and to any such difficulty was to declare that what was common to the Three and what was distinctive among them lay beyond speech and comprehension *and therefore beyond either analysis or conceptualization.*[46]

Athanasius and his Cappadocian successors were representative of doctrinal development in the East, but among the Western theologians, the tendency toward paradox in expositions of the Trinity is clearer still. The treatise *On the Trinity* by Hilary of Poitiers provides a prime example, in which we find its author striving to maintain the distinct individuality of the Father, Son, and Spirit, while nonetheless insisting in the strongest terms on their absolute unity and ontological interpenetration (*perichoresis*).[47] Hilary's exposition of trinitarian doctrine is not particularly novel, aligning for the most part with those of Athanasius and Augustine. Of greater interest are his candid comments on the antagonism between the orthodoxy he defends and 'human logic', which arguably reflect a certain self-consciousness regarding the paradoxical character of his theology:

> The words of the Lord, *I in the Father, and the Father in Me,* confuse many minds, and not unnaturally, for the powers of human reason cannot provide them with any intelligible meaning. It seems impossible that one object should be both within and without another, or that ... these Beings can reciprocally contain One Another, so that One should permanently envelope, and also be permanently enveloped by, the Other, whom yet He envelopes. This is a problem which the wit of man will never solve, nor will human research ever find an analogy for this condition of Divine existence.[48]

> To human logic it may seem ridiculous and irrational to say that it can be impious to assert, and impious to deny, the same doctrine, since what it is godly to maintain it must be godless to dispute; if it serve a good purpose to demolish a statement, it may seem folly to dream that good can come from supporting it. But human logic is fallacy in the presence of the counsels of God, and folly when it would cope with the wisdom of heaven; its thoughts are fettered

---

46   Pelikan, *The Christian Tradition*, 223-24, emphasis added.
47   The notion of *perichoresis* or *circumincession*—the deep mutual indwelling of the Persons of the Trinity—is also to be found in the Cappadocians, although Hilary's treatment is more developed and exegetical.
48   Hilary of Poitiers, *On the Trinity*, 3.1; in *NPNF2*, Vol. 9.

by its limitations, its philosophy confined by the feebleness of natural reason.[49]

The last post-Nicene theologian to be reviewed here is Augustine of Hippo, in whose writings, according to one commentator, the predominant Western understanding of trinitarian theology found 'its mature and final expression'.[50] One of the first points to acknowledge regarding Augustine's treatment of the Trinity is that he follows prior Christian tradition in affirming the absolute indivisibility and simplicity of God; indeed, he is perhaps more explicit and self-conscious in this regard than any previous writer.[51] As such, he was bound to reject a 'generic unity' view of the relation between the Persons of the Trinity,[52] even though he doubtless appreciated its appeal in alleviating the logical problems inherent in orthodox doctrine. The majority of contemporary scholars are therefore comfortable endorsing the traditional view that Augustine posited numerical identity between each divine person and the divine essence: a view usually deemed to be paradoxical if not outright incoherent.[53]

Nevertheless, like Athanasius before him, Augustine refused to allow his unwavering commitment both to the unity and indivisibility of the Godhead, and to the identity of substance between the Persons, to undermine his equal commitment to the real distinctness of the Persons, as demanded by Scripture and the church:

All those Catholic expounders of the divine Scriptures, both Old and New, whom I have been able to read, who have written before

---

49 Hilary, *On the Trinity*, 5.1.

50 Kelly, *Early Christian Doctrines*, 271.

51 See, e.g., Augustine, *On the Trinity*, Bk. 1, 4.7; Bk. 7, 1.2; in *NPNF1*, Vol. 3. Augustine's reliance on neo-Platonic thought at this point, rather than catholic tradition grounded in Scripture as he professes here, is often overstated. For a re-evaluation of this common reading of Augustine's trinitarian theology, see Michel René Barnes, 'Rereading Augustine's Theology of the Trinity', in Stephen T. Davis, Daniel Kendall, and Gerald O'Collins (eds), *The Trinity: An Interdisciplinary Symposium on the Trinity* (Oxford: Oxford University Press, 1999), 145-76.

52 Augustine, *On the Trinity*, Bk. 7, 6.11.

53 Kelly, *Early Christian Doctrines*, 272; Coffey, *Deus Trinitas*, 68-69; Plantinga, 'The Threeness/Oneness Problem', 45-46. David Brown favours a weaker interpretation of Augustine, primarily on the ground that the numerical identity view suffers from 'complete incoherence'. Even on this more charitable reading, however, he concludes that Augustine's theology 'bristles with difficulties'. Brown, *The Divine Trinity*, 243, 301.

me concerning the Trinity, Who is God, have purposed to teach, according to the Scriptures, this doctrine, that the Father, and the Son, and the Holy Spirit intimate *a divine unity of one and the same substance in an indivisible equality*; and therefore that *they are not three Gods, but one God*: although the Father hath begotten the Son, and so He who is the Father is not the Son; and the Son is begotten by the Father, and *so He who is the Son is not the Father; and the Holy Spirit is neither the Father nor the Son*, but only the Spirit of the Father and of the Son, Himself also co-equal with the Father and the Son, and pertaining to the unity of the Trinity. ... This is also my faith, since it is the Catholic faith.[54]

While Augustine infamously expressed a lack of enthusiasm for the word 'person' as applied to the *hypostases*,[55] and has been charged with modalism for his alleged overemphasis on the divine unity,[56] he is nonetheless forthright in his condemnation of Sabellianism and in his defence of the distinctness of the Persons, both by appealing to Scripture and by offering analogies for the diversity-in-unity of the Trinity.

One final aspect of Augustine's treatment to observe is that the driving motivation behind his dogged adherence to such a logically awkward set of beliefs is simply fidelity to Scripture and to received orthodoxy. Much has been made of the influence of neo-Platonic thought in Augustine's theology, but the fact remains that the earlier books of *De Trinitate*, not to mention his earlier writings on the Trinity, are replete with appeals to biblical texts and to the 'Catholic' faith inherited from Nicea.[57]

In my survey of the development of trinitarian orthodoxy, it remains only to examine the last major classical statement of trinitarian doctrine, the Athanasian Creed.[58] The creed dates to the

---

54 Augustine, *On the Trinity*, Bk. 1, 4.7, emphasis added.

55 Augustine, *On the Trinity*, Bk. 7, 6.11.

56 Adolf von Harnack, *History of Dogma*, Vol. 4 (trans. E. B. Speirs and James Millar; 7 vols; London: Williams & Norgate, 1898), 130; Karl Rahner, *The Trinity* (trans. Joseph Donceel; London: Burns & Oates, 1970), 17-18.

57 Barnes, 'Rereading Augustine's Theology of the Trinity'; Hill, *The Three-Personed God*, 61. Hill defends Augustine from the charge of modalism and from being held hostage to neo-Platonism, but still finds his theology to be underdeveloped in such a way as to render it susceptible to modalist tendencies.

58 The creed is held as an authoritative statement of orthodoxy by Roman Catholics, Anglicans, and most conservative Protestant denominations. The Eastern Orthodox do not regard the Athanasian Creed as infallible, since not only was it not decreed by an ecumenical council but also it

early fifth century, if not before, and represents the catholic consensus in the West concerning trinitarian and christological belief. Despite the name, the theology of the creed is more Augustinian than Athanasian; indeed, some of its statements are taken almost verbatim from Augustine's *De Trinitate*.[59] Its statements regarding orthodox trinitarianism are a model of simplicity and completeness. But as might be expected given the discussion thus far, many subsequent readers have found them to be the quintessential expression of a paradoxical doctrine of the Trinity. Its offending statements in this regard read as follows:

3. And the catholic faith is this: That we worship one God in Trinity, and Trinity in Unity;

4. Neither confounding the persons nor dividing the substance.

5. For there is one person of the Father, another of the Son, and another of the Holy Spirit.

15. So the Father is God, the Son is God, and the Holy Spirit is God;

16. And yet they are not three Gods, but one God.

Statement 3 reflects a commitment to classic monotheism: there is only one deity, although that one deity exists as a triunity. The fourth statement expresses both a rejection of Sabellianism and an affirmation of something close to the 'numerical identity' conception of consubstantiality (consistent with Augustinian thought), while the fifth statement reinforces the anti-modalist stance. Statement 15 establishes the full and equal deity of Father, Son, and Spirit.[60] Statement 16 denies what would otherwise be a natural inference from its predecessor taken in isolation, namely, that there are three deities.[61] Thus, the creed carefully rules out three anti-trinitarian heresies: modalism, subordinationism, and tritheism.

The difficulty of conceiving an ontology in terms of which these statements may be logically reconciled, while preserving the

---

unmistakeably bears the stamp of Western, Augustinian theology. Nevertheless, the Orthodox hold it in high regard. Timothy Ware, *The Orthodox Church* (London: Penguin Books, rev. edn, 1997), 202.

59 Kelly, *Early Christian Doctrines*, 273; Pelikan, *The Christian Tradition*, 351-52.

60 Compare statements 8, 9, 10, and 13, which ascribe uncreatedness, incomprehensibleness, eternality, and omnipotence to each of the Persons.

61 Compare statements 11, 12, and 14, which deny that there are three 'uncreateds', three 'incomprehensibles', three 'eternals', or three 'omnipotents'.

theological intentions of its authors, should be apparent.[62] Yet this creed is the culmination of a trinitarian orthodoxy refined through centuries of debate by the premier theologians of the church and bequeathed to subsequent generations of Christians. In the Athanasian Creed, one finds the clearest and boldest expression of the trinitarian paradox.

With this focused historical survey complete, it will be appropriate to summarise the main points established regarding the constraints of trinitarian orthodoxy and their implications:

(T1) An orthodox doctrine of the Trinity must uphold biblical monotheism: there can be only one absolute, transcendent, indivisible, sovereign God. (Hence, all forms of polytheism should be excluded.)

(T2) An orthodox doctrine of the Trinity must maintain the full and equal divinity of each of the three persons: the Father is fully God, the Son is fully God, and the Spirit is fully God. (Hence, all forms of ontological subordinationism should be excluded.)

(T3) An orthodox doctrine of the Trinity must posit genuine distinctions between the three persons: the Father is not the same as the Son or the Spirit, and the Son is not the same as the Spirit. (Hence, all forms of modalism should be excluded.)

(T4) On the one hand, the conjunction of (T1) and (T2) seems to require that the consubstantiality relation between the divine persons be construed in terms of *numerical* identity rather than *generic* identity: the Father is identical with, not distinct from, the one divine *ousia* (essence, substance, Godhead); likewise for the Son and the Spirit. This understanding is implicit in the Nicene Creed and became increasingly explicit in the writings of those who subsequently defended and expounded Nicene orthodoxy.

---

62 In his detailed analysis of the Athanasian Creed, Kelly explicitly concedes the paradoxicality of its trinitarian theology. 'The fundamental idea is that, as understood by Catholic Christians, the Godhead is at once a Trinity in unity and a unity in Trinity. More precisely, the Godhead, while one indivisible substance, is simultaneously three persons. The paradox is that the threeness of the persons does not violate the oneness of the substance, while the oneness of the substance in no way impairs the real distinction of the persons.' Thus its opening statements set down 'two apparently contradictory truths which are to be held in tension'. J. N. D. Kelly, *The Athanasian Creed* (London: A. & C. Black, 1964), 73-74.

(T5) On the other hand, (T3) seems to require that each divine person is numerically distinct from (i.e., not numerically identical to) each of the other two persons.

(T6) Consequently, any interpretation of the doctrine of the Trinity that seeks to fulfil requirements (T1), (T2), and (T3) will be paradoxical, given our natural intuitions about the concepts employed.

If these conclusions are correct, then trinitarians face an awkward dilemma: an apparent choice between orthodoxy and clear logical consistency. Still, a number of contemporary writers have maintained that interpretations of the doctrine of the Trinity are now available which uphold orthodoxy whilst minimising, even eliminating, any hint of incoherence. In the remainder of this chapter, with the concerns and presuppositions of those who defined orthodoxy in mind, I propose to assess these claims.

2.3 Recent Trinitarianism

The last fifty years or so have seen a formidable number of theologians and philosophers offering defences, explications, and novel interpretations of the ancient doctrine of the Trinity. Many of these treatments are proffered on the basis that previous accounts have been lacking in one or more respects, often with regard to their logical coherence. The implicit or sometimes explicit assumption is that paradoxical formulations of trinitarian doctrine are inherently unsatisfactory and therefore in need of conceptual clarification or alteration. In what follows I will examine some representative and influential contributions to this field, with a view to determining whether interpretations of the doctrine of the Trinity are now available which fully uphold the concerns of Christian orthodoxy whilst avoiding any charge of apparent contradiction; that is, whether the problems faced by the Fathers are now behind us.

My survey is divided under four headings so as to bring out the common themes in the interpretations reviewed. (1) *Modalistic* interpretations of the doctrine of the Trinity are those that emphasise the ontological unity of the Godhead to the extent that (so critics argue) they tend unacceptably toward modalism. (2) *Social trinitarian* interpretations are those schemes that for the sake of logical consistency eschew the 'numerical identity' understanding of consubstantiality in favour of the weaker 'generic identity' understanding, resulting in a conception of the Trinity as something like a 'society' or 'community' of divine individuals (albeit one with a greater degree of unity among its members than any creaturely community). Whereas modalistic interpretations run the danger of lapsing into full-blown modalism, social trinitarianism is often thought to insufficiently distinguish itself from tritheism. (3) *Relative identity* interpretations are those that attempt to secure both orthodoxy and logical consistency by offering an account of the intratrinitarian identity relations that avoids positing an 'absolute' or 'numerical' identity between each divine person and the Godhead by appealing to the notion of 'relative' identity. (4) Finally, I conclude by reviewing a selection of contemporary authors who admit to holding a *paradoxical* interpretation of the doctrine.

2.3.1 Modalistic Interpretations

Credited by many as the most influential theologian of the last century, Karl Barth has also been criticised for propounding a modalistic doctrine of the Trinity.[63] It will therefore be appropriate to examine his trinitarian theology to determine (i) whether the charge of modalism is a fair one, and (ii) if Barth avoids falling into heterodoxy, whether he also avoids paradox.

In my judgement, it should be acknowledged from the outset that Barth is no modalist in the original, Sabellian sense.[64] Barth explicitly rejects modalism as 'heresy', remarking that it 'entails a denial of God' insofar as it denies the existence of the true God who has revealed himself to us.[65] Moreover, this disavowal of modalism is no empty protest, for Barth clearly affirms that the threefoldness of God is 'an unimpaired differentiation within Himself' which is 'irremovable and ... ineffaceable'[66]—an affirmation no third-century Sabellian would be prepared to echo. His rationale for insisting on the immanent reality of this threefold distinction follows from his belief that the triunity of God is bound up in his self-revelation. For Barth, if God's unity is to be upheld then he must be *identified* not only with his *act* of revelation but also with the *effect* of that act: the

---

63 The most notable criticism comes from Moltmann, *The Trinity and the Kingdom of God*, 139-44.

64 Geoffrey Bromiley deems 'absurd' the idea that Barth advocates modalism. Geoffrey W. Bromiley, *An Introduction to the Theology of Karl Barth* (Grand Rapids, MI: Eerdmans, 1979), 16. For a recent analysis of the charge, and a qualified defence of Barth, see Dennis W. Jowers, 'The Reproach of Modalism: A Difficulty for Karl Barth's Doctrine of the Trinity', *Scottish Journal of Theology* 56.2 (2003), 231-46.

65 *CD*, I/1, 368, 382.

66 *CD*, I/1, 299, 361.

one God is thus at once 'Revealer', 'Revelation', and 'Revealedness'.[67] Yet it is just this identification that secures the reality of his inner differentiation, Barth maintains, for such distinctions are no less real than the distinction between the subject, object, and predicate involved in the very concept of 'revelation'.[68]

Why then should Barth have attracted the label of 'modalist' (or the slightly less damning 'modalistic')? The main reason for the charge comes from Barth's dissatisfaction with the term 'person' applied to the divine *hypostases*. He maintains that personality, in the modern sense of the term, 'belongs to the one unique essence of God' and therefore to ascribe personality to each *hypostasis* would imply 'the worst and most extreme expression of tritheism'.[69] For Barth, then, God is strictly speaking *one person* and it is therefore theologically safer to speak of God as existing in three 'modes (or ways) of being'.[70]

This denial of three personalities, subjectivities, or consciousnesses in God has prompted some writers to complain that Barth's doctrine of the Trinity contradicts the testimony of the New Testament and undermines the economy of salvation that Barth himself affirms. Even if these criticisms have weight, however, it is not altogether clear that the orthodox creeds *require* that personality (in the modern sense) be ascribed to each of the divine persons. For this reason, it cannot be said with confidence that Barth is less than credally orthodox.[71]

Given that Barth's explication of the unity and the plurality of the Godhead falls within the limits of orthodoxy, the question remains as to whether it also avoids any apparent inconsistency. Insisting as he does on the simplicity of God and the identity of substance between Father, Son, and Spirit,[72] but also their real differentiation, Barth would seem hard-pressed to escape the charge of paradox in his trinitarian theology. Indeed, he appears to admit as much:

---

67 *CD*, I/1, 296, 299.
68 *CD*, I/1, 353-55; Alan Torrance, 'The Trinity', in John Webster (ed.), *The Cambridge Companion to Karl Barth* (Cambridge: Cambridge University Press, 2000), 81.
69 *CD*, I/1, 350-51.
70 *CD*, I/1, 355.
71 Alan Torrance goes further in his defence of Barth, drawing attention to affirmations of interpersonality in his trinitarian theology, such as his discussion of 'mutual knowing' within the Godhead and his exposition of the 'perichoretic "fellowship"'. Torrance, 'The Trinity', 82.
72 *CD*, I/1, 350.

The great central difficulties which have always beset the doctrine of the Trinity at this point apply to us too. ... We, too, are unable to say how in this case 3 can really be 1 and 1 can really be 3. ... None of the terms used, whether it be essence or mode of being or relation of origin, whether it be the numeral 1 or the numeral 3, can adequately say what we ought to say and are trying to say in using it. If we pay attention only to what the terms as such can say in their immanent possibility of meaning; if we are unwilling or unable to accept the indication they are supposed to give, we shall only cause ourselves endless vexation.[73]

Barth thus concedes that while the opposing heresies of tritheism and modalism must be avoided at all cost, steering a 'middle course' means that the '*mysterium trinitatis* remains a mystery.' Against those who might be tempted to rationalise this mystery, Barth warns that there can be 'no question' of doing so, for 'rationalisation is neither theologically nor philosophically possible here.'[74] Barth's treatment of the doctrine of the Trinity provides further support for the notion that on this issue, one must choose between heterodoxy and paradox.

The second most influential contemporary trinitarian theology to be labelled 'modalistic' is that of Karl Rahner. Rahner criticises Barth for suggesting that we abandon altogether the word 'person' in our formulations of trinitarian orthodoxy, but he nevertheless concurs with Barth's warning that its modern connotations, if carried over into the doctrine of the Trinity, would lead to tritheism.[75] He therefore recommends the expressions 'relative concrete ways of existing' and 'distinct manners of subsisting' as more theologically precise and less prone to misleading inferences.[76] It is this uneasiness with speaking of 'one God in three persons', and his denial of 'three centres of consciousness and activity' in the Godhead, that have led critics to categorise Rahner's view as modalist or neo-modalist.[77]

In Rahner's case, however, the charge of outright modalism appears to be even less warranted than when laid at Barth's door. Rahner quite clearly wishes to emphasise the reality of the threefold distinction within God and thus to distance himself from

---

73   *CD*, I/1, 367.
74   *CD*, I/1, 368.
75   Rahner, *The Trinity*, 42-44, 56-57.
76   Rahner, *The Trinity*, 74, 109.
77   Moltmann, *The Trinity and the Kingdom of God*, 144-48; Hill, *The Three-Personed God*, 145; Plantinga, 'The Threeness/Oneness Problem', 39.

Sabellianism.[78] On this count, then, one would be hard-pressed to maintain that Rahner falls beyond the boundaries set by the Nicene and Athanasian Creeds. He is careful to avoid modalism and meticulous in his eschewal of tritheism. The question, however, is whether his middle course directs him into the path of paradox.

Like Barth, Rahner acknowledges that if tritheism is to be excluded then the consubstantiality relation must be construed as something far stronger than mere generic identity, lest the 'absolute unity' of the Godhead be compromised. As we have seen, however, this presents him with an acute logical problem insofar as he wishes to maintain the real distinctness of the *hypostases*—a problem Rahner openly acknowledges. He therefore presents a 'negative defence' of this 'basic logical difficulty' following from the Thomistic approach of construing the divine persons as *relations*: specifically, as the 'opposed relations' by virtue of which the threefold differentiation arises.[79] From this vantage point, Rahner argues that the divine persons should be treated as 'relative realities' rather than 'absolute realities'. The crucial difference between these two species of reality is just this: while identifying each of two *absolute* realities with a third would entail the identity of the first two, it is possible for two *relative* realities (such as the Father and the Son) to be identical with an *absolute* reality (such as the Godhead) without being 'really identical' with each other. By making this crucial distinction, Rahner believes, the charge of formal contradiction can be deflected.[80]

Does Rahner's strategy relieve him from having to admit to a paradoxical doctrine of the Trinity? While his distinction enables him to avoid *formal* contradiction—as indeed *any* formal contradiction may be dissolved by positing a distinction on those terms that give rise to the inconsistency—it is far from clear that Rahner renders the identity relations within the Godhead logically unproblematic. The problem, in a nutshell, is that the distinction introduced here is no less formal than the contradiction it serves to remove. As Stephen Davis has noted, it is far from clear how Rahner's 'relative reality' differs from an 'absolute reality' (i.e., our standard notion of an individuated entity).[81] Neither is it clear how the identity relation obtaining between a relative reality and an absolute reality differs from our basic concept of numerical identity—except, of course, that it conveniently exhibits the lack of

---

78 Rahner, *The Trinity*, 38.
79 Rahner, *The Trinity*, 68-69.
80 Rahner, *The Trinity*, 72.
81 Stephen T. Davis, *Logic and the Nature of God* (London: Macmillan, 1983), 139-40.

transitivity required to avoid a contradictory doctrine of the Trinity! Rahner's defence smacks of special pleading, amounting as it does to little more than the question-begging insistence that the laws of logic which we apply to everything else in our experience should not be applied to the persons of the Trinity. As such, this proposal does not carry us very far along the path of paradox elimination—a fact that Rahner seems to concede, as this later caution about the relational view of the *hypostases* indicates:

> This relationality should not be considered first of all as a means for solving apparent logical contradictions in the doctrine of the Trinity. As such a means, its usefulness is quite restricted.[82]

I conclude that Rahner's trinitarian theology no more avoids the problem of paradox than that of Barth. Although both treatments of the doctrine of the Trinity scrupulously avoid the heresies excluded by the creeds, in favouring the stronger interpretation of the *homoousion* relation—correctly, if my earlier conclusions hold—both face logical difficulties that their advocates cannot fully resolve. In the next section, I turn to consider several authors who prefer a weaker construal of *homoousion* in order to allow a more obviously consistent interpretation of the doctrine of the Trinity.

2.3.2 Social Trinitarian Interpretations

The motivation to find an interpretation of divine triunity that avoids any hint of paradox is far more evident with so-called 'social views' of the Trinity than with the modalistic views just examined (a fact evidenced not least by the willingness of Barth and Rahner to concede a residue of apparent contradiction). A typical example comes from an article by Cornelius Plantinga, Jr.[83] Plantinga begins by correctly noting that 'many of the church's central doctrinal

---

82 Rahner, *The Trinity*, 103.
83 Plantinga, 'The Threeness/Oneness Problem'. Other than the three social trinitarian interpretations examined here, variations on this theme can be found in William Hasker, 'Tri-Unity', *Journal of Religion* 50 (1970), 1-32; Timothy W. Bartel, 'Could There Be More Than One Almighty?', *Religious Studies* 29 (1993), 465-95; Timothy W. Bartel, 'Could There Be More Than One Lord?', *Faith and Philosophy* 11 (1994), 357-78; C. Stephen Layman, 'Tritheism and the Trinity', *Faith and Philosophy* 5.3 (1988), 291-98; Thomas D. Senor, 'The Incarnation and the Trinity', in Michael J. Murray (ed.), *Reason for the Hope Within* (Grand Rapids, MI: Eerdmans, 1999), 238-60; J. P. Moreland and William Lane Craig, *Philosophical Foundations for a Christian Worldview* (Downers Grove, IL: InterVarsity Press, 2003), 575-96; Edward Wierenga, 'Trinity and Polytheism', *Faith and Philosophy* 21.3 (2004), 281-94.

claims have traditionally been stated in ways that look paradoxical or else mysterious in some other way', the doctrine of the Trinity being a pre-eminent example. For this reason, he suggests, 'the attempt to work out a relatively *coherent* account of major doctrinal claims ... ranks high on the agenda of traditional systematic theology.'[84]

Plantinga locates as the object of his analysis the formulation of the doctrine expressed in statements 15 and 16 of the Athanasian Creed:

15. So the Father is God, the Son is God, and the Holy Spirit is God;

16. And yet they are not three Gods, but one God.

This formulation, he remarks, 'is a statement of daunting ambiguity and paradox.'[85] He then proceeds to distinguish three options for interpreting these statements: (1) the 'standard Western Latin' option, which he attributes to Augustine; (2) the 'modalist' option; and (3) the 'social view' option. He rightly defends Augustine against the charge of modalism, recognising that Augustine clearly acknowledged the scriptural affirmations of real plurality within the Godhead and in so doing carried on 'the Johannine tradition of referring to Father, Son, and Spirit as wholly divine entities yet distinct.'[86] However, Plantinga considers it unfortunate that Augustine complicated this biblical view of the Trinity with the doctrine of simplicity, such that Augustine is forced to say in consequence that each divine person is identical with the divine essence.[87] These two trinitarian tenets, Plantinga argues, are logically incompatible:

The proper conclusion on the first option, I believe, is that it is impossible to hold. The threeness part of it is biblical and plausible; the oneness part of it is both implausible and unbiblical, and is, in any case, inconsistent with the threeness part. ... To say [that each divine person is identical with the divine essence] is to say

---

84 Plantinga, 'The Threeness/Oneness Problem', 37, emphasis original.
85 Plantinga, 'The Threeness/Oneness Problem', 41.
86 Plantinga, 'The Threeness/Oneness Problem', 44.
87 That the doctrine of simplicity was the primary motivation for Augustine's conclusions is debatable; but nevertheless, Plantinga's characterisation of Augustine's conclusions is uncontroversial. More significantly, Plantinga overlooks the fact that Augustine's commitment to divine indivisibility was hardly exceptional among the early trinitarian theologians.

something both unbiblical and—because self-contradictory—
necessarily false.[88]

Plantinga thus takes the view that Augustine's doctrine of the
Trinity is paradoxical and, moreover, that it is mistaken for just that
reason.

Dealing relatively briefly with the second option, Plantinga rightly
notes that modalist theories, which 'reduce three divine persons to
modes or roles of one person', are incompatible with both orthodox
dogma and the New Testament witness regarding the interrelation
between Father, Son, and Spirit.[89]

Having rejected the first option as inconsistent and the second as
heterodox, Plantinga turns to the third option in the hope that this
will prove immune to both ailments. Recognising that this view
requires a weaker, generic understanding of the *homoousion* relation,
such that the divine essence is taken to be a set of attributes fully
possessed by each divine person rather than a substance with which
each person is identical, Plantinga also admits that such a view has
been historically susceptible to the charge of tritheism. He therefore
proposes various ways of bolstering the social model of the unity
between the persons, specifically by highlighting the *familial*
relationships between the members of this divine community and
the notion that the *personal* essences (i.e., those three distinct natures
which individuate the divine persons) unify just as much as the
generic essence by ensuring that the three 'relate each to the other
two in unbroken, unbreakable love and loyalty.'[90]

Even with these qualifications in place, the question still arises as
to why Plantinga's scheme should not be thought tritheistic, since it
remains that the social view he espouses posits three numerically
distinct divinities. Plantinga therefore considers how the Athanasian
Creed's denial of 'three Gods' should be understood according to
advocates of the social view:

> We could mean any or all of three things: (1) If *God* is used as the
> peculiar name of the Father, as much of the New Testament uses it,
> then Father, Son, and Spirit are all divine persons, but there is only
> one *fount* of divinity, only one Father, only one God in *that* sense of
> *God*. (2) Or suppose *God* is the name of the divine essence, as it is in

---

88 Plantinga, 'The Threeness/Oneness Problem', 47.
89 Plantinga, 'The Threeness/Oneness Problem', 49. He charges each of Karl
     Barth, Otto Weber, Eberhard Jüngel, Hendrikus Berkhof, Robert Jenson,
     Karl Rahner, Dorothy Sayers, and E. Y. Postma with holding to a variant of
     modalism (whether they admit it or not).
90 Plantinga, 'The Threeness/Oneness Problem', 52.

much Latin Christianity; then there are three divine persons but only one generic divinity, one *divinitas* or *deitas*, one Godhead, or Godhood, or Godness—only one God in *that* sense of *God*. Or (3), following Augustine's usage, we could say that *God* is the designation of the whole Trinity. Without falling for Augustine's simplicity program, we could then mean by the Athanasian formula that the Father is a divine person, the Son is a divine person, and the Holy Spirit is a divine person; yet there are not three ultimate monarchies, but only one, the holy Trinity.[91]

We should first observe that what Plantinga (or any other social trinitarian for that matter) means by the phrase 'not three Gods' is beside the point in the present context, unless one is prepared to embrace a postmodernist free-for-all on credal interpretation. The question at hand is whether the creed *as intended and understood by the Fathers* is compatible with Plantinga's social view of the Trinity.

Let us therefore consider each of Plantinga's suggested readings in turn, asking whether it can plausibly be attributed to the original authors. While the monotheism of the creed's formulators no doubt involved the belief that there is but one 'fount of divinity', Plantinga's reading (1) requires a conspicuous equivocation between statements 15 and 16 of the creed, for neither the Son nor the Spirit are to be identified with the 'fount of divinity'. Reading (2) raises an immediate question: why would anyone want to *deny* that there is one divine essence, one *generic* divinity? Surely countering such a bizarre idea was not an immediate concern of those wishing to delineate trinitarian orthodoxy. A similar question arises for reading (3). Was an affirmation of multiple Godheads—multiple *Trinities*—a troublesome heresy in Christian circles during the fourth and fifth centuries? If so, it has gone unrecorded.

The fundamental inadequacy of Plantinga's readings of the Athanasian Creed may be brought out in two ways. The first is to recall the Augustinian origins of the creed. Its authors were almost certainly thinking in terms of what Plantinga dubs the 'standard Western option' and thus would have rejected outright these weaker readings of statements 15 and 16 along with the degree of ontological distinctness between the divine persons that such readings aim to accommodate.

Secondly, Plantinga's approach simply fails to do justice to the two small words 'and yet' with which the sixteenth statement

---

91 Plantinga, 'The Threeness/Oneness Problem', 52.

begins.[92] This phrase reflects a strong logical connection between this statement and the previous one, the thought being that statement 16 serves as an important *qualification* to statement 15. Read in isolation, the first of the two statements might naturally lead one to think that the creed speaks of *three ontologically distinct beings, each of which is divine*; the second statement, however, is intended to immediately scotch such an inference as heterodox. This crucial grammatical and conceptual connection between the two statements renders inadmissible the degree of equivocation in the term 'God' that Plantinga needs to introduce, and thus, when read carefully and in its historical context, it is hard to avoid concluding that the Athanasian Creed effectively outlaws the version of social trinitarianism championed by Plantinga.

A second example of social trinitarianism in contemporary philosophical theology is provided by Richard Swinburne.[93] By far the greater proportion of Swinburne's works are devoted to the rational defence of Christian theism. Part of that project, as Swinburne understands it, is to rebut charges of incoherence against the Christian conception of God by explicating it in ways that are (as best one can tell) logically and metaphysically harmonious. In keeping with this general programme, Swinburne unashamedly opts for a view of the Trinity as a unique group of divine individuals: three distinct persons each possessing the full set of attributes required for divinity. He spends many pages explaining just how it can be that multiple divine beings could still enjoy such traditional attributes as necessity and omnipotence, not to mention spelling out the metaphysics of *generation* (of the Son by the Father) and *procession* (of the Holy Spirit by the Father and the Son), even going so far as to develop an argument for why there should be specifically *three* divine individuals.

As far as I can tell, Swinburne's trinitarian model is indeed logically consistent. However, my concern is not whether his interpretation of the doctrine of the Trinity succeeds in avoiding paradox, but whether that interpretation is faithful to the demands of orthodoxy. In the course of his exposition, Swinburne directly addresses this question, first by considering how the credal statement 'there is only one God' ought to be understood:

> If 'there is only one God' meant 'there is only one divine individual', then the doctrine of the Trinity would be manifestly

---

92 Latin, *et tamen*: otherwise translatable as 'even so', 'however', or 'nevertheless'.
93 Swinburne, *The Christian God*.

self-contradictory. So clearly Church councils in affirming both must have understood 'there is only one God' in a somewhat subtler sense—since no person and no Council affirming something which they intend to be taken with utter seriousness can be read as affirming an *evident* contradiction. What in denying tritheism, the view that there are three Gods, were Councils ruling out? I suggest that they were denying that there were three *independent* divine beings, any of which could exist without the other; or which could act independently of each other.[94]

Unfortunately, Swinburne provides no historical evidence for what he takes to be 'clearly' the case, namely, that the Fathers shared the same rationalistic mindset as certain twentieth-century philosophers of religion. As my earlier survey indicated, the situation is not nearly so straightforward as Swinburne's effortless deduction suggests. Even if the Fathers took 'there is only one God' to mean 'there is only one divine individual', it is rather doubtful that they would have found themselves guilty of flagrant self-contradiction, since their unwavering concern to uphold a robust biblical monotheism would have inclined them even less to speak of *three* 'divine beings' or 'divine individuals' in the sense that Swinburne recommends.[95] While the original formulators of trinitarian orthodoxy were careful to avoid explicit contradiction (i.e., stating that something both is and is not the case), they held to a far stronger notion of God's unity and indivisibility than Swinburne is inclined to grant them—so much so that the most prominent post-Nicene theologians naturally inclined toward saying that each divine *hypostasis* is numerically identical with the divine *ousia*. In contrast to their Arian and Sabellian opponents, the orthodox were less concerned with avoiding charges of implicit contradiction or irrationality than with defending the theological boundaries prescribed by Scripture and tradition.

Swinburne also attempts to reconcile his social model with the credal identification of each divine person with 'God', suggesting that it should be understood 'simply as the claim that each is divine—omnipotent, perfectly good, etc.'[96] He argues that the Greek and Latin words for 'God' (θεός and *deus*) are ambiguous in a way not evident from the English translation, such that the one word can

---

94 Swinburne, *The Christian God*, 180.

95 One thinks, for example, of the Cappadocians' denial that the divine persons can be literally numbered off.

96 Swinburne, *The Christian God*, 181.

be used in either a predicative sense (i.e., 'divine') or a referring sense (i.e., 'God'). 'Given this ambiguity,' Swinburne writes,

> it is not implausible to read the creeds as asserting that three divine individuals (in my sense) together constitute one God (in my sense). The creeds are less paradoxical in Greek or Latin than their English translation makes them.[97]

Swinburne's proposal certainly removes the paradox. But even granting this ambiguity at the individual word level, it by no means follows that Christians are therefore at liberty to choose whichever sense suits their own theological agendas. The meanings of the credal statements are not as flexible and indeterminate as Swinburne seems to suggest: the immediate literary, historical, and theological contexts of those statements also bear crucially on their proper interpretation—and we have seen that those contexts support a meaning quite at odds with Swinburne's preference.

Moreover, it is evident throughout Swinburne's discussion that his guiding hermeneutical criterion is the notion that the authors of the creeds *could not* have meant to affirm anything that would appear logically problematic. As he writes in the conclusion of his discussion:

> I derived the traditional formulas by reading the *deus* (θεός), which the Father, Son, and Spirit are each said to be, differently from the *deus* (θεός) which is used when it is said that there are not three *dei* but one *deus*. Unless we do this, it seems to me that the traditional formulas are self-contradictory.[98]

The idea that self-evident logical consistency trumps all other considerations when interpreting the theology of the creeds is dubious, to say the least. I have already noted not only that the writings of the Nicene and post-Nicene Fathers favour an interpretation of *homoousios* which leads to the trinitarian paradoxes that Swinburne is so keen to avoid, but also that the Fathers themselves simply did not manifest the kind of rationalistic concerns that would warrant a hermeneutic such as this.

The upshot is that Swinburne's weaker interpretation of the credal denial of tritheism faces the same objections as Plantinga's: although necessary to accommodate his own agenda, it fails to square with the theological outlook of those who formulated the creeds (and thus with the original intention of their affirmations and denials). No doubt various interpretations can be attached to the key terms of the

---

97 Swinburne, *The Christian God*, 182.
98 Swinburne, *The Christian God*, 186.

Nicene and Athanasian Creeds so as to permit a theology that posits three numerically distinct divinities, none of which is numerically identical to 'God'. But unless that interpretation aligns with the authorial intentions of the Fathers (insofar as we can reconstruct them from surviving documentary evidence) the notion of credal orthodoxy becomes altogether worthless.[99]

The third social trinitarian interpretation I propose to consider is that of David Brown.[100] Brown devotes a chapter of his work *The Divine Trinity* to a defence of the coherence of the doctrine of the Trinity, focusing on what he takes to be, historically speaking, the two most reputable interpretations of the doctrine. The first he labels the 'Unity Model' (UM), which he ascribes to Augustine and Thomas Aquinas; the second he dubs the 'Plurality Model' (PM), for which he takes the Cappadocians, especially Gregory of Nyssa, to be representative. Brown summarises the basic difference in outlook of the two models thus:

> UM may be characterised as the belief that what is ultimately a unity, the Godhead, is also fundamentally a trinitarian plurality; PM as the belief that what is fundamentally a trinitarian plurality is also ultimately a unity in the Godhead.[101]

It is not entirely clear how Brown means to distinguish between the two qualifiers 'ultimately' and 'fundamentally', but the idea seems to be that the approach of the Unity Model is to begin with a conception of the Trinity as a metaphysical *unity* and then to consider how this unity may be further understood as a *plurality*, while the approach of the Plurality Model is to start with a conception of the Trinity as a metaphysical *plurality* before turning

---

99 One might argue that since the Athanasian Creed is so problematic, and does not command the level of ecumenical assent enjoyed by the earlier creeds, it should simply be jettisoned (or at least revised). Cf. Dale Tuggy, 'Tradition and Believability: Edward Wierenga's Social Trinitarianism', *Philosophia Christi* 5.2 (2003), 454. If my earlier conclusions are correct, however, then the line of paradox was crossed well before this venerable creed was composed. In any case, the triple of errors excluded by the Athanasian Creed—modalism, subordinationism, tritheism—must still be avoided by any trinitarian theology worth its salt.

100 Brown, *The Divine Trinity*. See also David W. Brown, 'Trinitarian Personhood and Individuality', in Ronald J. Feenstra and Cornelius Plantinga, Jr. (eds), *Trinity, Incarnation, and Atonement: Philosophical and Theological Essays* (Notre Dame, IN: University of Notre Dame Press, 1989), 48-78.

101 Brown, *The Divine Trinity*, 243.

to explain how this plurality may be also thought of as a significant *unity*.[102]

In his assessment of the Unity Model, Brown focuses on Augustine's theology, noting that Augustine explicitly rejects the notion that the relation between the divine essence and each divine person should be construed in terms of 'genus' or 'species'. Even so, he suggests that Augustine himself did not write consistently on whether he took this relation to be one of numerical identity or the weaker notion of *constitution*.[103] Believing as he does that the former view is altogether incoherent, Brown charitably takes Augustine to be committed only to the weaker construal of consubstantiality.[104] Nevertheless, his final assessment is that UM 'bristles' with conceptual problems to the degree that a defence of its coherence is all but impossible.[105]

Brown's defence of the coherence of the Plurality Model, on which he grounds his hopes for a rationally tenable doctrine of the Trinity, follows the same basic approach as Plantinga. On this view, the persons of the Godhead are 'essentially and permanently distinct' individuals.[106] Indeed, the term 'person' is to be understood in something like the modern psychological sense: the Father, Son, and Holy Spirit should be thought of as 'three distinct centres of

---

102 There is some ambiguity here as to whether these two models differ merely in terms of *epistemological* priority or also in terms of a corresponding *metaphysical* priority. It certainly seems that our thinking about the Trinity must at any one time proceed either from the unity to the plurality or *vice versa*, but it does not follow that one must thereby affirm a corresponding *metaphysical* priority in the Trinity. It is possible for one to hold that neither the unity nor the plurality of the Godhead is 'more ultimate' than the other. Cf. Coffey, *Deus Trinitas*, 25. If this is the correct position to take, then the paradoxicality of the doctrine of the Trinity is all too apparent.

103 Brown, *The Divine Trinity*, 291. Put crudely, this latter relation reflects something like the idea that the Father, Son, and Holy Spirit are constituted by the same 'divine stuff'. A contemporary defence of the coherence of the Trinity mounted along similar lines will be considered shortly.

104 Brown, *The Divine Trinity*, 243, 291. As my earlier historical survey suggests, I would take issue with Brown's analysis on three points: (i) the understanding of *homoousios* required to uphold the concerns of orthodoxy; (ii) the claim that the Cappadocians were the forefathers of the social model; and (iii) the alleged ambiguity in Augustine's view of the consubstantiality relation. Brown seems inclined to employ the same hermeneutic as Swinburne in interpreting early expressions of trinitarian theology.

105 Brown, *The Divine Trinity*, 301.

106 Brown, *The Divine Trinity*, 280.

consciousness, each with its own distinctive mental content.'[107] Brown recognises that while PM avoids the *logical* problems that plague its rival, its greatest challenge is to turn aside the *theological* charge that it amounts to tritheism. Thus, like Plantinga, he accepts the burden of showing that a unity between the divine persons can be identified which allows us to speak of 'one God' in an intelligible and religiously adequate way.

One cannot help but admire Brown's candidness in his treatment of this difficulty. He concedes that, if the Plurality Model is correct, then strictly speaking it would be accurate to speak of the Trinity as being 'three gods'—although such frank expressions should be avoided when dealing the 'ordinary layman'![108] His case for harmonising PM with Christian monotheism involves arguing that the superlative degree of intimate relation and mutual comprehension between the divine persons is sufficient to sanction talk of 'a single reality, the Godhead'.[109] Furthermore, evidence from anthropology and sociology supports the coherence of a notion of 'group consciousness' which, in cases of communities enjoying a high degree of intimacy and union, can assume primacy over the individual consciousnesses of members.[110]

Although space forbids a full critique of Brown's trinitarian theology, this brief exposition should be sufficient to show that while evading the charge of incoherence, his conception of divine unity no better staves off the spectre of tritheism than Plantinga or Swinburne. As Brown's admissions suggest, his trinitarian theology diverges significantly from the theological sentiments and concerns of those whose thinking shaped the Nicene and Athanasian Creeds.

Indeed, I suggest that the expositions of these three contemporary writers illustrate the essential inadequacy of *all* social trinitarian

---

107 Brown, *The Divine Trinity*, 244, 289.

108 Brown leans heavily on his interpretation of the Cappadocians in defending the orthodoxy of the Plurality Model, an interpretation that I have challenged. Even so, Brown acknowledges that none of these Fathers would countenance talk of 'three gods'—a fact that sheds further doubt on whether, given the 'degree of logical rigour' in their discussions, they truly represent the PM position. Brown, *The Divine Trinity*, 276, 293.

109 Brown, *The Divine Trinity*, 293.

110 Brown elaborates this line of defence in his essay 'Trinitarian Personhood and Individuality', where he concludes that while consciousness is still to be attributed to the individual persons of the Trinity, *self*-consciousness is better thought of as residing in the Godhead as a whole. The fact that Brown feels obliged to speak of the Godhead 'as a whole' further distances him from the mindset of the Fathers.

interpretations, that is, all trinitarian models in which the divine persons are numerically distinct from the divine substance (however the latter is construed). Such interpretations weaken the ontological unity within the Godhead to the point where a collapse into tritheism is unavoidable. After a rigorous examination of the various strategies available to advocates of social trinitarianism, Brian Leftow concludes that the prospects for defending such a view against heterodoxy are bleak:

> [O]ne basic problem for ST [i.e., social trinitarianism] is showing that it is a form of monotheism, and I have examined three broad ways ST's friends have tried to show this. 'Trinity' and 'group mind' monotheist moves try to treat the sum of the Persons as the 'one God' of the Creed. I have argued that these moves denigrate the Persons or are unorthodox even on ST's reading of the Creed. ST's third strategy is functional monotheism. I have raised a variety of problems for this; my overall claim has been that merely functional monotheism is not enough for Christian purposes. So if my arguments are sound, it is not clear that ST can be orthodox or truly monotheist.[111]

I concur with Leftow's assessment. The besetting problem of social trinitarianism interpretations is that their advocates cannot adequately accommodate a commitment to historical Christian monotheism. All will argue that in *some* sense they can affirm that 'there is only one God'. But as Daniel Howard-Snyder notes, 'academic trinitarians cannot mean whatever they like when they insist that they are monotheists.'[112] The proper interpretation of the

---

111 Brian Leftow, 'Anti Social Trinitarianism', in Stephen T. Davis, Daniel Kendall, and Gerald O'Collins (eds), *The Trinity: An Interdisciplinary Symposium on the Trinity* (Oxford: Oxford University Press, 1999), 249. Dale Tuggy raises a separate, but closely related, problem. On any normal understanding of the terms, being a deity or divinity entails *being a person*; yet according to Plantinga, Swinburne, and Brown, God is not a person but a *community* of persons. It thus follows that God is not a deity or divinity—a conclusion both counterintuitive and hard to reconcile with Scripture. Tuggy, 'Trinitarian Theorizing', 168. Elsewhere, Tuggy mounts two 'biblical-moral' arguments against social trinitarian interpretations, to the effect that if social trinitarianism is true then God was deliberately deceptive in his (or rather *their*) self-revelation in the Old and New Testaments. Dale Tuggy, 'Divine Deception, Identity, and Social Trinitarianism', *Religious Studies* 40.3 (2004), 269-87. I highlight some of the biblical obstacles for social trinitarians in §7.2.1.

112 Daniel Howard-Snyder, 'Trinity Monotheism', *Philosophia Christi* 5.2 (2003), 402.

creeds is constrained both by grammar and by historical context; and as such, they demand a commitment to monotheism that social trinitarian interpretations, however sophisticated, simply cannot satisfy.[113]

2.3.3 Relative Identity Interpretations

It should be evident from the foregoing discussion that the logical difficulties faced by the doctrine of the Trinity boil down to a question of *identity*; specifically, how to interpret the identity claims in statements such as 'the Father is God' and 'the Son is God'. If one interprets such statements in terms of *numerical* identity, with a concern to uphold monotheistic convictions, then it is hard to avoid either modalism or paradox; and if one interprets them in terms of mere *generic* identity, with a view to preserving the ontological equality but genuine distinctness of the divine persons, then the spectre of tritheism looms large. What is needed here, so it would seem, is a *via media*: some other kind of identity relation that could be used to express the doctrine of the Trinity in a formally consistent way yet without falling into either modalism or tritheism. In this section, I consider two approaches that purport to dissolve the paradox of the Trinity by appealing to the notion of 'relative' identity.

The first, and more straightforward, of these approaches has been presented with admirable clarity by A. P. Martinich. Martinich begins by framing the problem presented by the Christian doctrine of the Trinity and quickly dismisses metaphysical solutions such as those offered by modalistic and social trinitarian interpretations:

> All theologians understand that the central problem involving the mystery of the Trinity is to explain the possibility that there is one God but three persons in God without falling into contradiction. Many, if not most, contemporary theologians who write about the Trinity believe that the key to the solution of this problem lies in adequately analyzing one or more of the concepts of a person, a nature, a substance, or God, or in constructing some new concept,

---

113 Howard-Snyder puts the historical point particularly well. 'After all, when the early Christians were accused by their Jewish contemporaries of being polytheists, they responded by insisting that, *like their accusers*, they too affirmed that there exists exactly one God. They *agreed* with them. What they agreed to was what the Jews themselves believed, that there exists a certain number of Gods, and that that number is *one*.' Howard-Snyder, 'Trinity Monotheism', 402. Cf. Leftow, 'Anti Social Trinitarianism', 236-37.

say, that of "persons in community" or "a society of persons." ... Worse, such discussions mislocate the source of the problem, which is that the Father, Son, and Holy Spirit are somehow identical and yet not identical. As the notion of identity is generally construed, this is incoherent no matter how "person," "nature," or what-have-you is analyzed.[114]

Statements typically taken to express the core claims of the doctrine, such as those of the Athanasian Creed, 'seem to form an inconsistent set' and as such are 'paradoxical' when interpreted according to standard first-order logic.[115] According to Martinich, this explains how heresies such as Arian and Sabellianism gain rational support, for 'if faced with the alternatives of being a heretic and asserting a contradiction, the rational person will always choose heresy and trust himself to the mercy of God.'[116] If self-contradiction is to be avoided, it seems one or more of the statements of orthodoxy must be denied: thus Arianism rejects the claims that 'the Son is God' and 'the Spirit is God', while Sabellianism rejects the claims that 'the Father is not the Son or the Spirit' and 'the Son is not the Spirit'.[117]

Martinich's proposed solution to this trinitarian dilemma, with its apparent choice between rationality and orthodoxy, is to interpret the credal identity statements in terms of *relative* identity as opposed to *absolute* identity. In general, a relative identity claim always takes the qualified form '*A* is (or is not) the same Φ as *B*', where Φ is a sortal term—that is, a term designating a particular *kind* of thing. Examples of such claims would include 'Cicero is the same *man* as Tully' and 'Mars is not the same *planet* as Venus'. Moreover, Martinich wishes to go further by insisting that there really is no such thing as absolute identity, since the meaning of an identity claim of the form '*A* is the same as *B*' is *indeterminate* until the particular respect in which *A* and *B* are said to be identical is specified. As such, 'there is no bare self-identity' and thus 'numerical identity is a fiction'.[118]

Once this position is taken, a solution to the trinitarian problem immediately presents itself, for the 'indeterminate' identity claims of the creeds can be expanded, as explicit statements of *relative* identity, without any formal contradiction: the Father is the same *God* as the

---

114 Martinich, 'Identity and Trinity', 169.

115 Martinich, 'Identity and Trinity', 170.

116 Martinich, 'Identity and Trinity', 172.

117 The 'irrational' solution of denying that the laws of logic apply to God, or to our doctrine of God, Martinich dismisses as inexcusable.

118 Martinich, 'Identity and Trinity', 175.

Son, but the Father is not the same *person* as the Son, and so forth. Thus, argues Martinich, abandoning the misguided notion of absolute identity (along with a few dispensable logical principles which go hand in hand with it) enables the orthodox trinitarian to deflect with ease the arguments of the Arian and the Sabellian.

Martinich's proposal for avoiding paradox is elegant and appealingly simple, but must ultimately be judged untenable, both on philosophical and historical grounds. In the first place, his rejection of absolute (i.e., numerical) identity is highly controversial, less than adequately supported, and philosophically problematic. Martinich's cavalier dismissal notwithstanding, the reality of absolute identity—roughly, the notion that the world is constructed of distinct things such that each thing is the same thing as itself and no other thing—has considerable intuitive support, such that a defence of the rationality of orthodox trinitarianism built upon its denial will hardly attract widespread acceptance.

Moreover, Martinich does little more than *assert* that non-relative statements of identity are always semantically underdetermined; in comparison, persuasive arguments have been proffered in defence of absolute identity. David Wiggins argues that the relativity of identity is inconsistent with Leibniz's Law, which in turn undergirds the principle of substitutivity, according to which natural inferences such as the following are valid: 'Cicero denounced Catiline; Cicero is identical to Tully; therefore, Tully denounced Catiline.'[119] Martinich openly admits that his scheme requires one to abandon these logical principles, but the counterexamples he raises against them can be satisfactorily explained without recourse to relativizing the identity relation.[120] Frederick Doepke contends that our concept of absolute identity is a necessary precondition of our capacity to individuate objects in the world.[121] Michael Rea, meanwhile, has recently argued that a denial of absolute identity goes hand in hand with an anti-realist metaphysic, according to which the distinctness of objects in the world is not independent of our thoughts about them but depends on the way in which we 'carve up' the world by our theorizing about it (such that alternate theories will lead to different

---

119 David Wiggins, *Sameness and Substance Renewed* (Cambridge: Cambridge University Press, 2001), 24-28.

120 See the treatment in Wiggins, *Sameness and Substance Renewed*, 34-50.

121 Frederick C. Doepke, *The Kinds of Things: A Theory of Personal Identity Based on Transcendental Argument* (Chicago: Open Court, Carus Publishing Company, 1996), 191-92. Richard Swinburne argues similarly in his assessment of Peter van Inwagen's relative-identity interpretation of the doctrine of the Trinity. Swinburne, *The Christian God*, 13-16, 187-88.

ontological inventories).[122] Metaphysical anti-realism is not every philosopher's cup of tea, but for an orthodox Christian its implications are simply intolerable: it would follow that the very existence of the Trinity depends on our *theorizing* about the Trinity, thus turning the Creator-creature dependence relation on its head.

In my judgement, Martinich's solution faces insurmountable philosophical objections. Yet even if it were philosophically defensible, his proposed interpretation of the orthodox creeds is quite untenable. The modern distinction between absolute and relative identity was certainly not familiar to the Christian theologians of the fourth and fifth centuries; if it had been readily available to them, it is reasonable to suppose they would have evidenced that by disambiguating any identity statements of the creeds which they viewed in a relative, and not absolute, sense. As my earlier historical survey indicated, however, the authors of the creeds appear to have understood those identity claims in precisely the paradoxical fashion that Martinich finds so unpalatable.

Relative identity interpretations such as Martinich's are clearly too radical a means of circumventing paradox, but perhaps a more plausible appeal to relative identity can be found nearby. Michael Rea has helpfully distinguished between 'pure' and 'impure' strategies for defending the doctrine of the Trinity via relative identity.[123] Both strategies propose that the crucial identity and distinctness claims required by the doctrine of the Trinity be interpreted as *relativized* identity and distinctness claims (e.g., 'the Father is the same *God* as the Son' yet 'the Father is not the same *person* as the Son') rather than as absolute ones. However, while the pure strategy involves an outright denial of absolute identity, the impure strategy does not. The weighty objections to solutions that employ the pure strategy (such as Martinich's) have already been rehearsed. The weakness of the impure strategy, on the other hand, is that taken alone it offers an *incomplete* solution to the problem; for by remaining neutral on the question of whether absolute identity exists, it does not adequately rule out polytheism. After all, the doctrine of the Trinity involves a clear affirmation of monotheism: that there is *numerically* exactly one God. It seems that the trinitarian must therefore deny that the Father, the Son and the Holy Spirit are numerically distinct, which is to say, he must affirm that they are absolutely (numerically) identical—and thus that there really is such

---

122 Michael C. Rea, 'Relative Identity and the Doctrine of the Trinity', *Philosophia Christi* 5.2 (2003), 431-45.

123 Rea, 'Relative Identity and the Doctrine of the Trinity', 437-38.

a thing as absolute identity.[124] All this is to say that advocates of the impure strategy for dissolving paradox cannot simply dodge the question of whether absolute identity exists and, if it does, whether it holds between the divine persons. Whichever way they choose to jump, they need to provide some plausible metaphysical account of the identity relations within the Trinity according to which one can meaningfully say 'there is only one divine being' (contra polytheism) but also 'the Father is distinct from the Son' (contra modalism).[125]

It so happens that Rea, in collaboration with Jeffrey Brower, believes that there is just such an account.[126] The context for their proposal is the infamous philosophical problem of material constitution. Consider a statue made of bronze; let the statue and the lump of bronze be labelled 'Athena' and 'Lump', respectively. Intuitively, we would want to say that there is only *one* object here, for Athena is just the same thing as Lump. Thus, if one wanted to purchase the statue, one would not expect to have to pay *twice*: once for the statue and again for the lump of bronze. According to Leibniz's Law, however, if *A* is identical to *B* then whatever is true of *A* must also be true of *B*; in which case, if Athena could be destroyed by melting then Lump could *also* be destroyed by melting. Yet common sense also tells us that after melting, it would be correct to say Athena no longer exists but that Lump remains. Is Athena identical to Lump or not? Depending on which intuitions we privilege, different answers follow.

There is no consensus among philosophers as to how this vexing metaphysical conundrum ought to be resolved. Brower and Rea recommend an Aristotelian solution according to which there exists a unique and irreducible relation, distinct from absolute identity, which they call 'accidental sameness without identity'. On this view, Athena is not *absolutely identical* to Lump (and thus violations of Leibniz's Law are avoided) but stands in the relation of *accidental sameness* to Lump. In general, this relation holds between a 'hylomorphic compound' (i.e., a form-matter complex, such as a statue or a horse) and the material or 'stuff' of which it is

---

124 It is for this reason that Peter van Inwagen's proposal must be judged inadequate, given its agnosticism on the question of whether absolute identity exists. Peter van Inwagen, 'And Yet They Are Not Three Gods But One God', in Thomas V. Morris (ed.), *Philosophy and the Christian Faith* (Notre Dame, IN: University of Notre Dame Press, 1988), 241-78; Rea, 'Relative Identity and the Doctrine of the Trinity', 438-41.

125 Rea, 'Relative Identity and the Doctrine of the Trinity', 441-42.

126 Jeffrey E. Brower and Michael C. Rea, 'Material Constitution and the Trinity', *Faith and Philosophy* 22.1 (2005), 57-76.

constituted. It is a relation of 'sameness' because one may properly say that the statue is 'the same as' the lump of bronze; and it is 'accidental' because the latter *might* have existed without the former existing (and could continue to exist after the former has been destroyed).[127] The 'form' of a hylomorphic compound is only *contingently* instantiated by its 'matter'.

On this scheme, one must be careful how one goes about counting things. Counting is normally taken to proceed in terms of absolute identity: *A* and *B* count as one object just in case *A* is absolutely identical to *B*. If there is such a relation as accidental sameness, however, then our enumerative method will depend on *what it is* we take ourselves to be counting (i.e., what sortal we are employing). Specifically, when counting 'material objects' we should proceed in terms of accidental sameness and not absolute identity: *A* and *B* count as one material object just in case *A* is accidentally the same as *B*. Thus while Athena and Lump are distinct, they only count as one material object (which seems intuitively correct).

How does this bear on the coherence of the doctrine of the Trinity? Brower and Rea suggest that some metaphysical relation akin to accidental sameness holds between the divine persons and the divine essence:

> [L]ike the familiar particulars of experience, the Persons of the Trinity can also be conceived of in terms of hylomorphic compounds. Thus, we can think of the divine essence as playing the role of matter; and we can regard the properties *being a Father*, *being a Son*, and *being a Spirit* as distinct forms instantiated by the divine essence, each giving rise to a distinct Person. As in the case of matter, moreover, we can regard the divine essence not as an individual thing in its own right but rather as that which, together with the requisite 'form', constitutes a Person. Each Person will then be a compound structure whose matter is the divine essence and whose form is one of the three distinctive Trinitarian properties. On this way of thinking, the Persons of the Trinity are directly analogous to particulars that stand in the familiar relation of material constitution.[128]

Clearly the relation in question cannot be accidental sameness *itself*, for it would follow that each divine person exists only contingently; rather, it should be thought of as something like 'essential sameness without identity'. In this way, both relations can be considered species of a more general relation of 'numerical sameness without

---

127 Brower and Rea, 'Material Constitution and the Trinity', 60-61.
128 Brower and Rea, 'Material Constitution and the Trinity', 68.

identity'—a relation such that if it holds between *A* and *B* then *A* and *B* are distinct and yet can be treated as numerically one. So according to the authors' proposal, the Father, Son, and Holy Spirit are distinct (i.e., not absolutely identical) and yet they are all the same *God*; hence, there is numerically one God (since the sortal 'God' functions like 'material object') and monotheism is saved.

Brower and Rea claim that their solution 'seems to us to be the most philosophically promising and theologically satisfying solution currently on offer.'[129] It is certainly ingenious and I am inclined to agree with their bold claim. Explicating the *homoousios* relation in terms of 'numerical sameness without identity' offers an attractive middle path between generic identity (which invites tritheism) and absolute identity (which invites modalism).

Nevertheless, it still faces some serious, perhaps even fatal problems. In the first place, the Aristotelian solution to the problem of material constitution, to which their trinitarian model appeals, is controversial in its own right. The authors admit that the notion of numerical sameness without identity is initially 'hard to swallow', but counter that *every* solution to the problem is counterintuitive. This may be true; however, it remains that defending the coherence of the Trinity by positing a *sui generis* metaphysical relation on analogy with another counterintuitive metaphysical relation smacks of explaining a mystery with a mystery. Moreover, one wonders how much *disanalogy* can be admitted before the argument is weakened beyond all plausibility. Is it really appropriate to think of each divine person as consisting of some kind of 'immaterial stuff'?[130] And doesn't the very idea of a constituting substance that can take on multiple 'forms' suggest at least the *potential* for alternative instantiations? Such would be at odds with the *essentiality* of God's triunity (which Brower and Rea are careful to affirm); yet if this supposed 'divine stuff' is not susceptible to counterfactual instantiations, the analogy with matter is rather questionable.[131]

---

129 Brower and Rea, 'Material Constitution and the Trinity', 70.

130 Brower and Rea, 'Material Constitution and the Trinity', 68. It is worth noting that a number of key figures in the development of trinitarian doctrine—namely, Origen, Eusebius of Caesarea, Athanasius, Hilary, and Basil—maintained that the divine *ousia*, and thus the *homoousios* relation, should not be understood on analogy with material constitution, as if it were some kind of 'divine stuff'. Lonergan, *The Way to Nicea*, 60, 89-91; O'Collins, *The Tripersonal God*, 119.

131 After all, the logical independence of matter *as such* from its potential forms is arguably one of its most distinctive properties.

A further difficulty arises with respect to the *multi*-personality of the Godhead. Even if one is prepared to grant that a statue can be distinct from a lump of clay while also being the same material object, it seems obvious that *three* statues cannot be distinct from a lump of clay *and* distinct from one another whilst all being one and the same material object.[132] Yet according to the Brower-Rea model, 'person' functions analogously to 'statue' and 'God' functions analogously to 'material object'. If three distinct statues cannot be one and the same material object, the appeal to analogy would suggest that three distinct persons cannot be one and the same God.

Finally, it is difficult to know just what the proper name 'God' or 'Yahweh' is supposed to identify on this proposal. In the Athena-Lump scenario, according to the authors, a definite description such as 'the material object' is ambiguous and indeterminate as it stands; it must be disambiguated as either referring to Athena or to Lump.[133] Yet when Christians make general statements about 'God' (e.g., 'God exists' or 'God is good') the term is not normally intended to refer to one of the divine persons and not the other two. On the other hand, if 'God' is taken to refer to the divine essence, it is hard to make sense of claims that a non-personal 'immaterial stuff' can be omnipotent, omniscient, all-good, all-merciful, and so forth. Instinctively one would like 'God' to mean something like 'the Deity' or 'the uniquely divine being'; but on this view, there is no such thing in any determinate sense.

Given these difficulties, I must conclude that the scheme presented by Brower and Rea does not offer an adequate resolution to the logical problem of the Trinity.[134] The fact that it comes closer than any alternative solution, yet still falls short, perhaps tells us something about the intractability of trinitarian paradox.

2.3.4 Concessions to Paradox

In this final section, I draw attention to a number of contemporary writers whose treatments of the doctrine of the Trinity appear to concede its inherent paradoxicality. For brevity's sake, I do not

---

132 Cf. David Wiggins, 'On Being in the Same Place at the Same Time', *The Philosophical Review* 77.1 (1968), 90-95; David S. Oderberg, 'Coincidence Under a Sortal', *The Philosophical Review* 105.2 (1996), 145-71.

133 Brower and Rea, 'Material Constitution and the Trinity', 66.

134 Cf. William Lane Craig, 'Does the Problem of Material Constitution Illuminate the Doctrine of the Trinity?', *Faith and Philosophy* 22.1 (2005), 77-86. The criticisms of the Brower-Rea model expressed in this section were developed prior to the publication of Craig's article.

propose to discuss in detail the trinitarian theology of each writer; in keeping with the narrow focus of the chapter, my purpose here is simply to draw attention to their concessions to paradox and their rationales for so doing.

Stephen Davis's *Logic and the Nature of God* provides a particularly telling example of such a stance. As an analytic philosopher standing in the Protestant tradition, Davis offers his monograph as a defence of the coherence of the Christian conception of God. Like Swinburne, Davis is not reluctant to adopt less traditional and more controversial interpretations of Christian doctrines where such interpretations best suit his aim of avoiding logically problematic descriptions of God. On this basis he rejects the traditional doctrines of divine immutability and necessary goodness, for example, and advocates a kenotic model of the Incarnation. Even so, when he finally comes to examine the doctrine of the Trinity, Davis not only notes its 'inherently paradoxical character' but also resists the temptation of advocating either a modalistic or a social trinitarian interpretation.[135] He expresses dissatisfaction with the proposals of Rahner and Martinich, considered above, before concluding that the doctrine is a 'mystery'—to be carefully distinguished from a real contradiction, but nonetheless deemed 'an apparent contradiction which there is good reason to believe'.[136] In short, Davis is forced to concede that the orthodox doctrine of the Trinity is a paradox, though he maintains that it can be rationally believed nonetheless.[137]

A second example comes from David Coffey, who has provided a book-length treatment of the doctrine of the Trinity in which he aims to do justice both to the New Testament expressions of the triune nature of God and also to the orthodox creeds. His own contribution to the vast literature on this subject is particularly notable for seeking to combine insights from the Western and Eastern traditions in order to provide an ecumenical resolution to the debate over the *filioque* clause. In dealing with the Threeness-Oneness problem, Coffey endorses the standard Augustinian-Thomist approach of understanding the persons of the Trinity as 'subsistent relations'. On this view, while the Father, Son, and Holy Spirit are each identical with the divine substance, they are distinguished at root by their opposing relations toward one another. In order to uphold the simplicity and essentiality of the divine nature, furthermore, these

---

135 Davis, *Logic and the Nature of God*, 132.
136 Davis, *Logic and the Nature of God*, 141.
137 As it turns out, Davis's defence of paradox, though far less developed, is similar in direction to the strategy I propose in later chapters.

relations must be thought of as *identical* with the persons and thus with the divine substance itself.[138]

Coffey's starting point for addressing the problem is thus that 'in God there are one absolute and three relative subsistences.'[139] From this he reasons that, if we understand 'personhood' as something communicated (like the other divine attributes) from the Father to the Son and to the Spirit, we should think of God as being 'one absolute and three relative persons'—a result he considers sufficient to reconcile 'the one person of God of the Old Testament with the three persons of the New.'[140] Even so, it is another question whether this explication of the Trinity is free from paradox. As with Rahner, Coffey avoids *formal* contradiction by appeal to an 'absolute/relative' distinction, but he concedes nevertheless that

> there is no known philosophical principle that can be used to integrate absolute personhood and relative personhood in God in a single vision. All we can do is to proceed on the basis of the negative principle that they are not contradictory.[141]

In other words, although we can state *that* our conception of the Trinity is not contradictory, we are at a loss to specify or explain just *how* it is not contradictory.

Coffey later confirms the merely formal adequacy of his Thomistic distinction by admitting that it fails to 'bestow positive intelligibility on the situation under consideration.'[142] The point is clear: while we are able to introduce distinctions in order to avoid *literal* contradiction, we must admit that we have effectively no grasp of how these distinctions cash out in metaphysical terms. Hence any attempt to conceive a concrete state of affairs in which all the orthodox statements regarding the Trinity are true is bound to lapse into paradox.

William Hill, who takes a similarly conservative stance to Coffey in his concern to uphold Catholic orthodoxy and tradition, is even more forthright about the presence of paradox within his historical and theological exposition of the doctrine of the Trinity.[143] In his account of the historical development of credal trinitarianism, he reaches similar conclusions to those I presented earlier: the Arian heresy was 'rationalistic in doing away with apparent

---

138 Coffey, *Deus Trinitas*, 68-69.
139 Coffey, *Deus Trinitas*, 70.
140 Coffey, *Deus Trinitas*, 72.
141 Coffey, *Deus Trinitas*, 76.
142 Coffey, *Deus Trinitas*, 104.
143 Hill, *The Three-Personed God*.

contradictions'; Athanasius came to see that the Godhead must be 'numerically one in concrete being or essence (*homoousios*)'; and the Cappadocians conceived of the divine oneness not merely in terms of three substances sharing an abstract nature but as 'a matter of ontological identity on the level of *ousia*.'[144]

Hill's own interpretation of the Trinity, set out in the final chapters of his book, aims to be faithful both to this tradition and to the developments that followed in Augustine and Aquinas. Accordingly, he chides social trinitarians for downgrading the unity between the divine persons to the level of generic identity, rather than numerical identity.[145] Hill's straightforward admission that such a stance inevitably results in paradox is evident from the following passages:

> The Scylla and Charybdis of trinitarianism are modalism on one side and subordinationism on the other. ... There is, after all, no dead center here; no theology entirely succeeds in holding the two horizons in focus at once, and the most that seems possible is a dialectical move of the mind shuttling between the two, maintaining a certain tension without capitulating to either extreme.[146]

> [T]he Christian theologian is aware at the very outset ... that the reality of God is at once One and Three. Thus, any critical dealing with this paradox (which has no parallel in the phenomenal order) calls for the mind to distinguish what faith confesses as in reality beyond all such distinction.[147]

> [The notion of 'appropriation'] is a language device of believers that seeks in a paradoxical way to suggest the personal identity of the members of the Trinity, but one that has always functioned in tradition. [Such a device] violates to a degree the logic of ordinary discourse...[148]

In a now familiar fashion, Hill maintains that *formal* contradiction can be avoided by means of introducing distinctions, but nonetheless all attempts to flesh out the *content* of those distinctions by drawing from our immanent experience lead to seeming violations of logic.

---

144 Hill, *The Three-Personed God*, 43, 46, 48-49.
145 Hill, *The Three-Personed God*, 218.
146 Hill, *The Three-Personed God*, 235.
147 Hill, *The Three-Personed God*, 256.
148 Hill, *The Three-Personed God*, 269.

The three contemporary trinitarians considered above are not the only writers to concede that their desire to stay unambiguously within the bounds of orthodoxy leads them into paradoxical discourse regarding God's triune character. I have already noted the admissions from Barth and Rahner regarding the logic of trinitarian theology. Similar concessions, both explicit and implicit, can be adduced from the writings of other conservative Christian thinkers.[149] For those who do not consider the Christian theologian to be bound by a yoke of philosophical rationalism, obliged to formulate every cardinal doctrine with perspicuous logical consistency, there is little doubt about the paradoxicality of the orthodox doctrine of the Trinity.

2.4 Conclusion

In this chapter I have sought to examine the question of whether the Christian doctrine of the Trinity, interpreted in an orthodox fashion, is paradoxical in the sense that its metaphysical affirmations appear to be logically contradictory. I proceeded in two stages. In the first, I surveyed the historical development of the orthodox doctrine of the Trinity, as expressed particularly in the Nicene and Athanasian Creeds, reaching the conclusion that these definitive statements of orthodoxy appear to be logically inconsistent when interpreted in a way faithful to the theological intentions of those who originally formulated those statements.

This result was further confirmed by the conclusions of the second stage of my investigation, in which I examined a selection of contemporary interpretations of the Trinity from writers for whom alignment with orthodoxy is a significant concern. In fact, I suggest that if the doctrine of the Trinity were to be placed in the dock and charged with the crime of apparent contradiction, nearly all of the writers I have considered might profitably be called as witnesses for the prosecution (regardless of their own views on the guilt of the

---

149 Baillie, *God Was In Christ*, 142-44; Cornelius Van Til, *An Introduction to Systematic Theology* (Phillipsburg, NJ: Presbyterian & Reformed, 1974), 229-31; Lonergan, *The Way to Nicea*, 92-93; Harold O. J. Brown, *Heresies: Heresy and Orthodoxy in the History of the Church* (Peabody, MA: Hendrickson Publishers, 1988), 62, 127-28, 150; Thomas F. Torrance, *Trinitarian Perspectives: Toward Doctrinal Agreement* (Edinburgh: T. & T. Clark, 1994), 87, 121-22, 142; Thomas F. Torrance, *The Christian Doctrine of God, One Being Three Persons* (Edinburgh: T. & T. Clark, 1996), 172-73; David S. Cunningham, *These Three are One: The Practice of Trinitarian Theology* (Oxford: Blackwell, 1998), 7-8.

defendant). By tacitly dividing the witnesses into two groups—those whose trinitarianism properly observes the boundaries of credal orthodoxy and those whose trinitarianism does not—an astute counsel for the prosecution could effectively play off the testimonies of the former against the testimonies of the latter in order to secure a conviction. For what one invariably finds is that the first group is accused of paradox or self-contradiction by the second (and, as I have noted, the first group is often prepared to concede the point), while the second group (for whom the avoidance of paradox is paramount) is accused by the first of deviating from orthodoxy.

As the debate stands today, no writer from the first century to the twenty-first century has offered an explication of the doctrine of the Trinity that is both clearly orthodox and free from apparent contradiction. It seems that the careful theologian inevitably faces a dilemma: that of embracing either paradox or heterodoxy. In the next chapter, I argue that the doctrine of the Incarnation presents the very same dilemma.

CHAPTER 3

The Paradox of the Incarnation

3.1 Introduction

In the previous chapter, I examined the claim that the traditional Christian doctrine of the Trinity is paradoxical; the conclusion reached was that its metaphysical affirmations indeed appear to be logically inconsistent. Adherents of the doctrine are thus presented with a dilemma: either the doctrine must be abandoned in favour of some revised (but unorthodox) interpretation, or else its paradoxicality must be accepted and the awkward questions that follow regarding the rationality of believing it must be squarely faced.

The doctrine of the Trinity is by no means the only article of Christian faith to have been charged with being paradoxical or outright incoherent. The doctrine of the Incarnation, no less central to the church's witness, has been likewise summoned into the dock to defend its logical credentials. The very idea that God—an eternal, infinite, immortal, transcendent spirit—could become a human being—a temporal, finite, mortal, material creature—is one that seems *prima facie* impossible, if not altogether absurd. Secularists and theological liberals have made much hay from the apparent conceptual problems inherent in the traditional doctrine,[1] while a good number of conservative believers have conceded that such difficulties defy rational explanation, some going so far as to suggest that this should be reckoned a virtue rather than a vice. Kierkegaard famously held that the Incarnation was the 'absolute paradox' of the biblical religion.[2] In similarly superlative terms, Donald Baillie considered the doctrine to be the 'supreme' and 'central' paradox of the Christian faith.[3] Philip Schaff conceded that the biblical teaching on the person and nature of Jesus Christ 'cannot be exhaustively set

---

1 See, e.g., Martin, *The Case Against Christianity*, 125-46; John H. Hick (ed.), *The Myth of God Incarnate* (London: SCM Press, 1977).
2 Kierkegaard, *Philosophical Fragments*, 46-67.
3 Baillie, *God Was In Christ*, 106, 110.

forth by any formulas of human logic.'[4] Evidently the idea that this central Christian doctrine defies rational penetration enjoys some considerable sympathy and thus merits close examination.

In this chapter, I therefore ask the same questions of the traditional Christian doctrine of the Incarnation as I asked previously of the doctrine of the Trinity. What are the boundaries of orthodoxy for interpreting the defining claims of the doctrine? Is it possible to affirm an orthodox doctrine of the Incarnation whilst avoiding any apparent contradiction in one's affirmations? In short, is the Christian faced here with a similar dilemma to that presented by the doctrine of the Trinity, that is, a choice between paradox and heterodoxy?

As before, my investigation will proceed in two stages. In the first, I chart the development of the doctrine of the Incarnation in the early church, beginning with the definitive affirmations of the Councils of Nicea and Constantinople regarding the divinity of Christ, following through the christological debates which culminated in the Council of Chalcedon, and concluding with a review of the Athanasian Creed. As before, my historical survey will be concerned not merely with the *wording* of the doctrinal statements arising from these decades of debate but also with the key *theological concerns* which motivated those statements and provide the context for their proper interpretation. Having thus identified the boundaries of orthodoxy, I will review a selection of contemporary treatments of the doctrine of the Incarnation, with a particular focus on those expositions developed as responses to the charge of incoherence. Each one will be assessed with respect to (i) its theological acceptability in light of the conclusions reached in the first stage, and (ii) its success in avoiding paradoxical formulations of the Incarnation.[5]

---

4   *HCC*, Vol. 3, Ch. 9, §142.

5   As in the previous chapter, my treatment will not incorporate either exegesis of key biblical texts or discussion of significant contributions to the interpretation of christological doctrine between the fifth and twentieth centuries. I trust the reader will accept that such factors are acknowledged at least implicitly in my treatment of the christological debates within the early church and in my critique of contemporary interpretations of the Incarnation (the most influential of which have been self-consciously formulated as defences, refinements, or replacements of their historical predecessors). The direct biblical support for a paradoxical doctrine of the Incarnation, and its relationship to the creeds, is discussed in Chapter 7.

3.2 Early Christology

3.2.1 *The Road to Chalcedon*

With the formation of the Niceno-Constantinopolitan Creed, a line had been drawn in the sand regarding the divinity of Jesus Christ, the Son of God. The Son was declared to be *homoousion* or 'consubstantial' with the Father; that is to say, the divine essence, by virtue of which the Father is God, is also fully possessed by the Son. Consequently, whatever may be truly said of the Father *qua* God may likewise be truly said of the Son. This historic statement of Christian orthodoxy would inevitably serve as the baseline for the subsequent debates within the church regarding the nature of the Incarnation.[6] However, although the Nicene decree had settled the issue of the divinity of the Son of God, the question of the precise relationship between the human and the divine in Jesus Christ remained open. Since the first issue is logically prior to the second, and was the more pressing given the various aberrant views being propounded at the time, this is understandable. Nevertheless, it was inevitable that once the absolute divinity of Christ had been established as a non-negotiable article of faith, it would only be a matter of time before the implications for his humanity would have to be considered and clarified.

The aphorism that orthodoxy owes a debt to heresy is no less apt for the doctrine of the Incarnation than for the doctrine of the Trinity. Just as the controversy culminating in the Council of Nicea was sparked off by the controversial teaching of Arius, so the heated debate prior to the Council of Chalcedon was precipitated in the first instance by the teaching of Apollinarius.[7] To be fair, Apollinarius had not brought something entirely novel to the theological table; rather, he was merely working through the logical implications (as he saw it) of a certain framework for understanding the Incarnation, one already incipient in the christological writings of several bastions of orthodoxy.

Kelly dubs this christological framework the 'Word-flesh' view and identifies Athanasius, that champion of Nicene trinitarianism, as

---

6   That this proved to be so is evidenced by a common complaint made by each of the parties in the subsequent christological debates, namely, that their opponents were deviating from Nicene orthodoxy. Pelikan, *The Christian Tradition*, 227-28.

7   Kelly, *Early Christian Doctrines*, 280.

its classic representative.[8] This view, associated with the Alexandrian school, tended toward seeing Jesus Christ as the divine Logos inhabiting a human body. Accordingly, we find Athanasius writing that the Word of God 'fashioned His body for Himself from a Virgin'; the Logos 'takes unto Himself a body, and that of no different sort from ours' and 'prepares the body in the Virgin as a temple unto Himself, and makes it His very own as an instrument, in it manifested, and in it dwelling.'[9] Consistent with this tradition, in which the Logos is typically treated as the sole centre of consciousness, Athanasius could comfortably speak of one and the same Word as performing miracles, suffering on the cross, and expressing ignorance of the date of the Parousia. Nonetheless, he was careful to qualify those statements attributing human weakness and mortality to the Word as applying to him only 'in the flesh' and not in his divine nature.[10] Convinced that the divine Logos could not *truly* lack knowledge of any matter, Athanasius argued that Christ's professions of ignorance were effectively feigned; he was speaking *as a man*, that is, as any normal human in his position *would* speak.[11]

It should be clear from this summary of Athanasius's christology that it is open to an obvious line of criticism. While scrupulous in avoiding any denigration of Christ's *divinity* (as evidenced by his insistence that the Word remained omnipresent and continued to uphold the universe *during* his incarnation), Athanasius is rather more liberal in his willingness to play down his *humanity*. This problematic imbalance of the Word-flesh framework was never worked through to its logical conclusions by Athanasius, perhaps due to the restraining influence of his commitment to the biblical data. However, the same degree of moderation cannot be attributed to his friend Apollinarius of Laodicea.

Apollinarius arguably took the Alexandrian perspective to its logical endpoint in his declaration that the 'man' Jesus of Nazareth was merely a human body animated by the divine Logos. On this

---

8   Kelly, *Early Christian Doctrines*, 284. Kelly's analysis is based on the influential work by Aloys Grillmeier, *Christ in Christian Tradition: From the Apostolic Age to Chalcedon (451)* (trans. J. S. Bowden; London: A. R. Mowbray, 1965).

9   Athanasius, *On the Incarnation of the Word*, 18.5, 8.2, 8.3; in *NPNF2*, Vol. 4.

10 'But these affections were not proper to the nature of the Word, as far as He was Word; but in the flesh which was thus affected was the Word...' Athanasius, *Four Discourses Against the Arians*, Discourse 3, 55; in *NPNF2*, Vol. 4.

11 Athanasius, *Four Discourses*, Discourse 3, 42ff.

model, the Word effectively substituted for an absent human soul.[12] For Apollinarius, this position was the only one consistent with three theological convictions: (i) the full divinity of Christ as demanded by Nicene orthodoxy; (ii) the unity of Christ's person; and (iii) the *a priori* impossibility of the fullness of deity and the fullness of humanity residing in one person.[13] (The last of these axioms, as we shall see, arose again in connection with other christological heresies.) Apollinarius and his followers were careful to posit the closest possible connection between Christ's divinity and his human flesh, such that they were keen to affirm along with other Alexandrian thinkers the *communicatio idiomatum*: the principle that the names and attributes of divinity may be properly applied to Christ's flesh and *vice versa*.[14] Nevertheless, his unambiguous teaching concerning the extent to which Christ may be considered 'human' caused a furore and invoked a host of criticisms. The chief objections to Apollinarius's christology concerned its denial of a rational soul in Christ (an essential component, so it was argued, of genuine humanity) and its failure to properly uphold the human psychology of Christ as presented in the Gospels.

It is fair to say that the driving force behind such criticisms was fundamentally a soteriological concern: if Jesus Christ were less than truly human, as Apollinarianism seemed to imply, then how could he serve as the redeemer of humanity?[15] As Gregory of Nazianzus famously put it, 'What has not been assumed cannot be restored; it is what is united with God that is saved.'[16] The immediate question, however, was an *anthropological* one—what is it to be human?— albeit one whose answer carried the gravest soteriological implications.

Apollinarianism served to bring the 'christological problem' into sharp relief. The Cappadocians recognised early on the theological errors invited by this extreme variety of Alexandrian thought and sought to counter it with a precursor of the Chalcedonian 'two natures' formula, so as to emphasise that whilst Jesus Christ was fully divine, he was also fully human. Gregory of Nazianzus

---

12 Kelly, *Early Christian Doctrines*, 292; Pelikan, *The Christian Tradition*, 248.

13 Kelly, *Early Christian Doctrines*, 290, 296; HCC, Vol. 3, Ch. 9, §136.

14 R. V. Sellers, *The Council of Chalcedon: A Historical and Doctrinal Study* (London: SPCK, 1953), 142.

15 Sellers, *The Council of Chalcedon*, 166-67. It is only fair to note, however, that Apollinarius's position was also driven in part by soteriological concerns; see Studer, *Trinity and Incarnation*, 194.

16 Gregory of Nazianzus, *First Letter to Cledonius*; quoted in Kelly, *Early Christian Doctrines*, 297.

declared that the incarnate Word possessed 'two natures (δύο ψύχεις) concurring in unity'; at the same time, he was careful to insist that Jesus Christ was not thereby two *persons*, but one.[17] Still, despite availing himself of this useful distinction Gregory exhibited a tendency to speak of these two natures being 'fused' or 'mixed' within one individual (a turn of phrase that would later be considered misleading if not altogether heterodox). Moreover, like Athanasius before him, Gregory was evidently uncomfortable with directly attributing human experiences to the Logos, preferring instead to explain away such phenomena as Jesus' childhood learning. Although these problems would have been more naturally dealt with by ascribing a human mind or soul to Christ (distinct from his divine mind or soul), at no point did Gregory of Nazianzus resort to such a solution.

In the writings of Gregory of Nyssa, however, rather more credit is given to the New Testament statements about Christ's humanity. While likewise distinguishing between a divine nature and a human nature, Gregory resisted the tendency of his namesake both to combine and confuse the two natures and to play down the reality of Christ's human experiences.[18] By keeping Christ's two natures separate, Gregory thought it legitimate to ascribe those experiences only to his humanity and thus to avoid the theologically unacceptable conclusion that the immutable, impassible God had suffered on the cross. On the same basis, he held that one should identify both a divine will and a human will in Jesus. Moreover, unlike others in the Alexandrian tradition, Gregory was even prepared to speak of a *human soul* in addition to the divine Word. As such, he could go so far as to describe the Incarnation in terms of God entering into a *man* (not merely a human body). At one point, for example, he refers to Jesus as 'the Man in whom [the Only-begotten God] tabernacled, taking to Himself humanity in completeness.'[19]

Gregory's christology marks the furthest point of reaction in the Alexandrian school away from the extreme of Apollinarianism. The predominant christological matrix in this period was that of the Word-flesh framework, with its resistance to positing a human soul in Christ and a concomitant reluctance to take at face value the biblical statements regarding Christ's human psychology and limitations. It was thus left to theologians of the opposing

---

17   Kelly, *Early Christian Doctrines*, 297.
18   Kelly, *Early Christian Doctrines*, 298-300.
19   Gregory of Nyssa, *Against Eunomius*, 5.4; in *NPNF2*, Vol. 5.

Antiochene school, notably Diodore of Tarsus and Theodore of Mopsuestia, to redress the balance by promoting a 'Word-man' christology over against the Word-flesh approach of the Alexandrians.[20] This contrasting view unashamedly affirmed Christ's possession of a human soul, which functioned alongside the divine 'soul' of the Logos. The basic argument for such a view was straightforward, arising as it did from dissatisfaction with the reductionist tendencies of the Alexandrians: the New Testament speaks of Jesus as having distinctly human experiences (of suffering, ignorance, temptation, etc.); a divine mind or soul could not, by its very nature, be the subject of such experiences; ergo, Jesus must have also possessed a human soul to serve as the bearer of those experiences. Given this Word-man scheme, in which the Logos is conjoined with the fullness of humanity, body and soul, it is hardly surprising to observe the popularity of the metaphor of *indwelling* among the Antiochene theologians. Thus, according to Theodore, God the Son 'assumed' and 'indwelt' the man Jesus of Nazareth, uniting himself with that one man and accomplishing his redemptive purposes through him.[21]

By its very design, the Word-man framework was far better equipped to accommodate the reality and comprehensiveness of Christ's humanity. But the price to pay was the awkward question of whether it adequately preserved the unity of his person; and the Alexandrians were all too eager to point to the grammar of a christology of 'indwelling' in order to dismiss it as heterodox.[22] Theodore was evidently aware of this difficulty, straining as he did to point out that Scripture itself emphasises the unity of the two natures by often attributing to Christ 'as a whole' what properly belongs only to his divinity or his humanity. He further insisted that Christ, despite possessing two distinct natures, was 'one *prosopon*', that is, one subject who can be addressed both as God and as man.[23]

Needless to say, this defence of Word-man christology did not persuade the Word-flesh theologians to concede the debate—a fact

---

20 I should mention that I do not take the 'Alexandrian school' and the 'Antiochene school' to be *clearly defined* schools of christology (and the argument of this chapter does not require it). However, I do maintain that these designations are historically defensible and useful in identifying two discernible (and divergent) trends of christological thinking.

21 Kelly, *Early Christian Doctrines*, 305.

22 Sellers, *The Council of Chalcedon*, 169. No doubt the awkward pronouns of the final sentence of the preceding paragraph illustrate the conceptual problems raised by Antiochene christology.

23 Kelly, *Early Christian Doctrines*, 306-7.

due in no small part to the intellectually gifted but somewhat pig-headed patriarch Cyril of Alexandria, who by the early decades of the fifth century had inherited the mantle of Athanasius as the champion of the Alexandrian cause. Despite his protestations to the contrary, Theodore was charged by Cyril with the heresy that would later be associated with the name of Nestorius: that of overemphasising the humanity of Christ to the point of dividing him into two persons, one human and one divine.

From our detached perspective, it is not difficult to see that this attack on Theodore's theology was uncharitable and unfair. The worst that can be said of Theodore is that his exposition of Christ's humanity *logically implied* a duality of persons, which in turn conflicted with his insistence on the unity of Christ's person; in other words, Theodore may have been logically inconsistent, but he was no heretic. As Kelly remarks, 'Theodore was no Nestorian, and the doctrine of the "two Sons" repelled him.'[24] Nevertheless, the tremors from Cyril's assault would resurface over a century later in Theodore's condemnation by the Fifth General Council of Constantinople in 553.

Theodore had rightly resisted the undeniable tendency within his theology toward a two-person view of Jesus Christ, just as Athanasius had resisted the tendency within his own theology toward denying Christ's full humanity. Yet just as the Alexandrian camp had to accommodate an Apollinarius as well as an Athanasius, so the Antiochenes were to find in their ranks an outspoken bishop who could not resist carrying the arguments of Theodore to a seemingly more consistent endpoint.

3.2.2 *The Chalcedonian Settlement*

If Apollinarianism was the spark that ignited the fire of christological debate, it was the ascendance of Nestorianism that fanned it into the furnace that would prove to be a make-or-break period in the Christian church. Nestorius, patriarch of Constantinople, came to prominence in the debate over the person of Christ through his vehement opposition to the liturgical use of the title *Theotokos* (lit. 'God-bearer'), which was commonly ascribed in Alexandrian circles to Mary the mother of Jesus. The term had already become something of a shibboleth for Alexandrians, emphasising as it did the unity of the person of Jesus Christ. As *Theotokos*, Mary was deemed not merely to have borne Christ with

---

24 Kelly, *Early Christian Doctrines*, 308.

respect to his 'flesh', but to have given birth to the *incarnate Logos*, God the Son. For an Antiochene like Nestorius, however, to claim that God had a mother was intolerable if not altogether blasphemous; after all, one of the chief motivations for favouring a Word-man christology had been the desire to *avoid* having to attribute such creaturely characteristics to God. Although his opponents no doubt shared this theological concern, Nestorius was not prepared to compromise (as he saw it) the biblical testimony regarding Christ's genuinely human life of growth, temptation, and suffering.

If the rejection of *Theotokos* represented the negative dimension of Nestorius's christology, the positive dimension was expressed in his teaching on Christ's two natures. Whereas Theodore had insisted that Jesus Christ was but one *prosopon*, Nestorius took his distinctively Antiochene convictions further and found himself unable to affirm a moderate position such as that of his predecessor. In conscious opposition to Cyril's doctrine of the 'hypostatic union' of Christ's divine and human natures, he emphasised not only that the two natures retained their individuality and independence in the Incarnation but furthermore that each should be thought of *concretely* rather than as a set of abstract qualities.

> As he explained, he could not think of two natures except as each having its *prosopon* (i.e. its external aspect, or form, as an individual) and its *hypostasis* (i.e. concrete subsistence). By this he meant to convey, not that each nature was an actually subsistent entity, but that it was objectively real.[25]

Although it is now widely acknowledged that Nestorius never went so far as to claim that Christ was two *persons* or *individuals*, and thus strictly speaking was not guilty of 'Nestorianism' as commonly defined,[26] his talk of multiple *prosopa* and *hypostases* was hardly liable to endear him to his Alexandrian adversaries. Nestorius's error was not so much that he divided the person of Christ, but that he neglected to guard against the implicit inference to this conclusion by stating in unambiguous terms just how Christ's single personhood was to be affirmed and expounded. If not a heretic himself, Nestorius had at least prepared a bed for heresy.

Cyril's response to Nestorius was two-pronged, both theological and political. In the face of what he perceived to be Nestorius's dangerous separation of Christ's two natures, he vigorously promoted a 'one nature' christology in which Christ's divinity and

---

25 Kelly, *Early Christian Doctrines*, 313.
26 Kelly, *Early Christian Doctrines*, 311-12, 316; Baillie, *God Was In Christ*, 91.

humanity were united in his person, in a manner analogous to the union of body and soul in an ordinary human person. In addition, he secured the support of Pope Celestine and subsequently engineered the anathematisation and deposition of Nestorius (*in absentia*) via a general council convened at Ephesus in 431. Cyril's polemics not only ensured the downfall of Nestorius, but also raised the hackles of more moderate Antiochenes who found his 'one nature' formula to be an unacceptably extreme expression of Alexandrian christology.

In the two decades following Nestorius's condemnation at Ephesus, the debate veered back and forth with vehement recriminations on both sides and little sign of progress toward a compromising position (or even of a desire to attain one). Just as Nestorius had become the scapegoat for the extremes of two-nature christology, so the archimandrite Eutyches became the whipping-boy for extremist Antiochenes reacting against the one-nature view. Nevertheless, despite the hindrances of human pride and obstinacy, an agreement was eventually reached amidst this controversy between the two Eastern parties—although in the end it required the mediating assistance of the West.

Before turning to the definitive statement of orthodoxy forged at the Council of Chalcedon in 451, it will be worthwhile to pause and recall the context of this historical survey—the question of the paradoxicality of the doctrine of the Incarnation—and, in light of it, to reflect on the acute challenge faced by those who sought to combine the equally valid insights of both the Word-flesh and the Word-man perspectives into one biblically and theologically faithful doctrine.

In the first place, it should be emphasized that all parties in the debate (just as in the disagreements that had precipitated the formulation of trinitarian doctrine) were firmly committed to the highest view of divine transcendence and perfection. As Pelikan comments,

> the early Christian picture of God was controlled by the same self-evident axiom, accepted by all, of the absoluteness and the impassibility of the divine nature. Nowhere in all of Christian doctrine was that axiom more influential than in christology, with the result that the content of the divine as revealed in Christ was itself regulated by the axiomatically given definition of the deity of God. No one wanted to be understood as setting forth a view of

Christ in which this definition was in any way compromised or jeopardized.[27]

The central metaphysical problem faced by the disputants, given this non-negotiable axiom and the Nicene *homoousios* confession, was simply that of explaining how creaturely limitations and experiences—temporality, ignorance, suffering, and so forth—could be attributed to the Logos. The solutions variously proposed, however, diverged in accordance with whatever *additional* theological or biblical restraints were considered by their advocates to be of comparable importance.

For the Alexandrian school, from Athanasius and Apollinarius through to Cyril and Eutyches, the prominent concern was to preserve *the unity of Christ's personhood*. If this meant that the Gospel record of Christ's human experiences had to be played down or explained away, then that was the price to be paid for protecting the undiminished deity of the Son.[28] Likewise, whilst formally acknowledging Christ's full participation in two natures, godhood and manhood, the unity of his person seemed to require the union of those natures into one.

For the Antiochene school, meanwhile, a greater premium was placed on securing *the genuineness and distinctness of Christ's humanity*. Conjoined with an axiomatic commitment to the impassibility and immutability of God, it followed that Christ must possess a human mind or soul, as well as a human body, to serve as

---

27 Pelikan, *The Christian Tradition*, 229.

28 There are indications that the more moderate Alexandrians were less than satisfied with this rationalistic policy. As Pelikan comments, '[T]he question was: "In what sense does not [the impassible Logos] himself suffer?" Cyril replied that it was "by suffering in his own flesh, but not in the nature of his deity," *in a manner that transcended all reason and all language.*' Pelikan, *The Christian Tradition*, 231, emphasis added. Cyril was thus prepared to assert that 'the Word suffered impassibly', a claim which could hardly be more paradoxical and which earned him sustained criticism from Nestorius. The methodological difference between Nestorius and Cyril is informative. Paul Gavrilyuk remarks that while the former 'dissolved the paradox of the incarnation', the latter 'carefully preserved it, by keeping the tension between Christ's undiminished divinity and his suffering in the flesh at the center of his theology.' Paul Gavrilyuk, '*Theopatheia*: Nestorius's Main Charge Against Cyril of Alexandria', *Scottish Journal of Theology* 56.2 (2003), 207. Cf. John J. O'Keefe, 'Impassible Suffering? Divine Passion and Fifth-Century Christology', *Theological Studies* 58.1 (1997), 39-60.

the seat of those human experiences incompatible with divinity.[29] Jesus Christ was no mere man, but neither was he *less* than a man. And if this stance required one to concede that in Christ there are two *prosopa* or *hypostases*, with the risk of encouraging the inference of dual personhood, then so be it.

As I noted earlier, soteriological and liturgical concerns were also prominent in the arguments on both sides. In order for God to raise man to himself, contended the Alexandrians, the redeemer and mediator must be none other than the incarnate Son, whose divinity is in no way compromised by his human condition. Yet in order for Christ to fulfil that redemptive, mediating role, retorted the Antiochenes, he must be fully human and genuinely suffer on our behalf—and that requires a distinct human psyche in addition to the divine psyche.

Both perspectives represented entirely valid concerns, being based on impeccable theological and biblical considerations, yet each faced the danger of serving as a seed-bed for heretics bent on forcing their various christological distinctives to seemingly more consistent conclusions. I suggest that this christological dilemma provides a strikingly parallel to the trinitarian dilemma faced at the turn of the fourth century. In the earlier case, all of the pre-Nicene parties were firmly committed to the monotheistic tradition inherited from Judaism. Yet the Sabellians, rightly emphasising the deity of Christ, illegitimately inferred that the Son must be essentially the same divine person as the Father, while the Arians, rightly emphasising the distinctness of the Son, illegitimately inferred that Christ must be less than fully divine.[30] Similarly, in the debates leading up to the Council of Chalcedon, all parties were equally committed to the same monotheistic tradition with its doctrines of absoluteness and immutability. Yet the Apollinarians and Eutychians, rightly emphasising the unity of Christ's person, illegitimately inferred that his human nature and experiences were less than distinct and comprehensive, while the Nestorians, rightly emphasising the full humanity of Jesus, leaned toward (if not actually embracing) a two-

---

29 Sellers, *The Council of Chalcedon*, 172. As R. P. C. Hanson comments, 'The chief reason why any of the ancients wanted to acknowledge a human mind in Christ was that it could sluice off the human passions which can only with danger (they thought) be ascribed to the Godhead.' Quoted in A. T. Hanson, 'Two Consciousnesses: The Modern Version of Chalcedon', *Scottish Journal of Theology* 37.4 (1984), 476.

30 As I noted previously, Jürgen Moltmann makes much of this point in his critique of 'Christian monotheism'. Moltmann, *The Trinity and the Kingdom of God*, 129-37.

person christology in which the divine Word 'indwelt' a complete human person. Just as the heresies on either side of trinitarian orthodoxy may be seen as evidence of its inherent paradoxicality, so the heresies on either side of christological orthodoxy can be taken as confirmation of its own paradoxical character.[31]

Nevertheless, to the extent that the church required a definitive doctrinal statement serving to exclude decisively the anti-trinitarian heresies, so it also needed such a statement designed to exclude heterodoxy regarding the nature of the Incarnation. A way forward to such an achievement, without simply favouring one party over the other, was provided by the theology of the Westerns. Adopting a formula found in embryonic form in the writings of Tertullian,[32] Hilary of Poitiers had spoken of '*one Person*, God and man ... being in *two natures* united'.[33] On the one hand, Hilary was concerned (in Antiochene fashion) to uphold the comprehensiveness of Christ's humanity, writing of the 'full reality of each nature' and arguing that Jesus had not only a human body but also a human soul.[34] In keeping with this concern, he insisted that in his human life Christ 'passed through all the circumstances of our nature' while yet retaining all his divine attributes.[35] Nevertheless, at the same time, Hilary was equally careful (in Alexandrian fashion) to stress the unity of the personhood of Christ:

> Yet it was not another and a different Person Who emptied Himself and Who took the form of a servant. ... The emptying of the form does not then imply the abolition of the nature: He

---

31 Sellers analyses the early christological debates in terms of two fundamental principles: 'the principle of Christological confession' (which amounts to the identity claim that Jesus Christ *is* the Son of God) and 'the principle of Christological enquiry' (which amounts to the predicate claim that Christ is *genuinely and fully human*, as well as genuinely and fully divine). His thesis is that all three schools—Alexandrian, Antiochene, Western—were ultimately committed to these principles, but differed from one another in their emphases and preferred expressions; thus, the Definition of Chalcedon (which balances and cements these two principles) fairly represents an underlying, if rarely acknowledged, theological consensus. Sellers, *The Council of Chalcedon*, xiii-xvi, 203, 211. Of course, the fact that the disputants were not so far apart as they perceived, and that Chalcedon sought to do equal justice to these two axiomatic principles, does not remove any of the logical perplexities from the resultant christological confession.

32 Tertullian, *Against Praxeas*, 27; in *ANF*, Vol. 3.

33 Hilary, *On the Trinity*, 9.3; in *NPNF2*, Vol. 9.

34 Hilary, *On the Trinity*, 9.3, 10.22.

35 Hilary, *On the Trinity*, 9.7.

emptied Himself, but did not lose His self: He took a new form, but remained what He was. Again, whether emptying or taking, He was the same Person...[36]

For Hilary, the fullness and distinctiveness of the Christ's natures could not be allowed to divide his person, 'for the whole Son of Man is the whole Son of God'.[37] Rather than allowing one christological truth to annul the other, Hilary was content to rest with their dual affirmation, a position he described repeatedly as a 'mystery'. Acknowledging that this approach gives rise to paradoxes which defy rational penetration, he nonetheless believed this to be the only theologically acceptable path to take.[38]

In Augustine's writings, practically the same formula can be found: 'the one person, Jesus Christ, [is] the Son of God and the Son of man ... one personality as consisting of two substances, the divine and the human'.[39] On the one hand, Augustine affirmed that Christ's humanity is comprehensive: against the Apollinarians, 'there was also in Christ a human soul, a whole soul; not merely the irrational part of the soul, but also the rational, which is called mind.'[40] On the other hand, he insisted that this assumption of the fullness of conscious human life by the divine Word does not result in a duality of personhood:

He Himself unites both natures in His own identity, and both natures constitute one Christ ... not two Sons of God, God and man, but one Son of God: God without beginning; man with a beginning, our Lord Jesus Christ.[41]

Like Hilary, Augustine was scrupulous in avoiding both the errors of an unrestrained Word-flesh christology and those of an unrestrained Word-man christology.

This Western strain of theology made its decisive contribution to the Definition of Chalcedon by way of its expression in the *Tome to Flavian*, a letter from the pen of Pope Leo. This short treatise on the

---

36 Hilary, *On the Trinity*, 9.14.

37 Hilary, *On the Trinity*, 10.22.

38 Of particular interest are Hilary's discussions of Christ's suffering ('He willed to suffer what He could not suffer') and the seeming incompatibility of his pre-existence and his birth. According to Hilary, the latter paradox 'transcends thought'; it 'cannot be determined under the conditions of our thought' and 'ever eludes the grasp of our thought.' Hilary, *On the Trinity*, 9.7, 12.31-32.

39 Augustine, *Tractates on the Gospel of John*, 99.1; in *NPNF1*, Vol. 7.

40 Augustine, *Tractates*, 23.6.

41 Augustine, *Enchiridion*, 35; in *NPNF1*, Vol. 3.

Incarnation contained little original material, but was rather a polemical yet perspicuous restatement of the christology developed by earlier Latin theologians.[42] Although it vehemently opposed the one-nature doctrine of Cyril in favour of the 'one person in two natures' formula, it was by no means a defence of Antiochene christology over against its Alexandrian rival. As Pelikan remarks,

> when its polemically conditioned overtones have been subtracted from it, this theology is seen to have manifested a concern for the oneness of Jesus Christ in his person and saving acts that sets it apart from the [Antiochene] theology of the indwelling Logos no less than its stress upon the distinctness of the natures sets it apart from the [Alexandrian] theology of the hypostatic union.[43]

As such, Leo's *Tome* opened the door to a compromise position that sought to do justice to the legitimate concerns of both Eastern parties. In due course, an ecumenical council was called at Chalcedon in 451, by the authority of the Eastern and Western emperors, with the remit of settling the controversy over christological orthodoxy once and for all. After several weeks of heated discussion, and not a little pressure applied to those factious parties less inclined to come to agreement, the following definitive statement of christology was formulated and ratified:

> In agreement, therefore, with the holy fathers, we all unanimously teach that we should confess that our Lord Jesus Christ is one and the same Son, the same perfect in Godhead and the same perfect in manhood, truly God and truly man, the same of a rational soul and body, consubstantial with the Father in Godhead, and the same consubstantial with us in manhood, like us in all things except sin; begotten from the Father before the ages as regards His Godhead, and in the last days, because of us and because of our salvation begotten from the Virgin Mary, the *Theotokos*, as regards His manhood; one and the same Christ, Son, Lord, only-begotten, made known in two natures without confusion, without change, without division, without separation, the difference of the natures being by no means removed because of the union, but the property of each nature being preserved and coalescing in one *prosopon* and one *hupostasis*—not parted or divided into two *prosopa*, but one and the same Son, only-begotten, divine Word, the Lord Jesus Christ,

---

42 Kelly, *Early Christian Doctrines*, 337; Pelikan, *The Christian Tradition*, 256.
43 Pelikan, *The Christian Tradition*, 259.

as the prophets of old and Jesus Christ Himself have taught us about Him and the creed of our fathers has handed down.[44]

This classic formulation of Christian orthodoxy was for the most part a synthesis of excerpts from Leo's *Tome*, two influential letters by Cyril, and the Symbol of Union (the last being a statement drawn up in 433 as an attempted compromise which affirmed a union of two natures in one person). It clearly reflects the Western 'one person in two natures' formula, whilst aiming to satisfy both the concerns of the Antiochene school (by declaring that the two natures are united 'without confusion, without change', preserving their distinctive characteristics) and those of the Alexandrian school ('without division, without separation', avoiding any duality of personhood). Nestorianism was ruled out decisively by the use of *Theotokos* and the insistence on 'not ... two *prosopa*, but one and the same Son', just as Eutychianism was excluded by the endorsement of 'two natures' whose difference is 'by no means removed because of the union'. The Definition of Chalcedon remains to this day the standard of orthodox doctrine for all conservative Christian denominations: Protestant, Roman Catholic, and Eastern Orthodox.

Despite its achievements, the settlement has been criticized for failing to solve (or worse, ignoring altogether) the knotty metaphysical problems faced by a harmonization of the two warring schools of christological thought.[45] But then it was never intended to accomplish such. It is best understood not as an attempt to set forth a detailed exposition of incarnational metaphysics, but as a reaffirmation of Nicene orthodoxy with the additional prescription of two further essential christological principles: (i) the unity of Christ's personhood and (ii) the genuineness and fullness of his humanity. Negatively, it was designed to exclude all relevant heterodoxy whilst refraining from taking a particular line on just *how* the content of orthodoxy might be systematically elucidated. In short, it laid down the ground rules for future christological theorizing. This restricted goal was, naturally, a far easier one to achieve; even though it would thereafter leave the church open to the charge of committing herself to a statement of doctrine which, by attempting to synthesis the essential tenets of two fundamentally incompatible theologies, cannot be rationally explicated.[46]

---

44   The translation used here is taken from Kelly, *Early Christian Doctrines*, 339-40.

45   Pelikan, *The Christian Tradition*, 266; cf. 256.

46   Cf. Hick, *The Metaphor of God Incarnate*, 45.

3.2.3 Post-Chalcedonian Developments

It would be a historical gloss to suggest that the Council of Chalcedon put an end to the controversy. Although the bulk of the church was prepared subsequently to stand by its conclusions, pockets of dissent remained for many years to follow (and continue even today in the form of the Coptic Church). Monophysite groups in the East continued in their opposition to the 'two natures' formula, believing that Leo's *Tome* sailed too close to the shores of Nestorianism. Likewise, Nestorian sects lived on beyond Chalcedon and extend to the present day. Notwithstanding these exceptions, the mainstream Christian church has acknowledged that the essential parameters of a theology that properly upholds Christ's untarnished deity, unrestricted humanity, and unity of personhood, are all reflected in and secured by the Chalcedonian statement.

It remains to review briefly several significant refinements and reaffirmations of this christological orthodoxy in the centuries following Chalcedon. The Second Council of Constantinople in 553 provided both reaffirmation and refinement: it formally endorsed Chalcedon as a 'holy synod' but further added, in an attempt to appease certain Monophysite bishops still opposed to its doctrine, a condemnation of anyone who denied that God the Son had suffered on the cross. This arguably added nothing of substance to the theology of Chalcedon, which had already settled the issue of Christ's unity of person; moreover, the council failed in its immediate goal of bringing the dissenters into the fold (although, over time, the two parties would steadily converge in their interpretation of the Incarnation).[47]

A second refinement resulted from the Monothelite controversy during the seventh century. In short, a dispute arose as to whether or not Christ possessed two wills (one associated with each nature) or only one (associated with his singular person). The issue was settled—formally, at least—by a general council at Constantinople in 680, which ruled that Christ's full humanity necessitated that he have a human will distinct from his divine will. While this may strike some as a rather abstract and trivial point of doctrine, unworthy of such ecclesiastical posturing, it nevertheless serves to underline the commitment of orthodoxy to two suppositions: (i) that Jesus Christ was human in every essential respect, psychological as well as physical; and (ii) that his divinity must not be confused with, or compromised by, his humanity.

---

47 Pelikan, *The Christian Tradition*, 274-77. Cf. Sellers, *The Council of Chalcedon*, 269-70; Sturch, *The Word and the Christ*, 7, n. 3.

Finally, I turn to consider the contribution of the Athanasian Creed. Its endorsement of Chalcedonian christology is as unmistakable as its reaffirmation of Augustinian-Nicene trinitarianism:

> Furthermore it is necessary to everlasting salvation that he also believe rightly the incarnation of our Lord Jesus Christ. For the right faith is that we believe and confess that our Lord Jesus Christ, the Son of God, is *God and man*. God of the substance of the Father, begotten before the worlds; and man of substance of His mother, born in the world. *Perfect God and perfect man*, of a *reasonable soul and human flesh* subsisting. Equal to the Father as touching His Godhead, and inferior to the Father as touching His manhood. Who, although He is God and man, yet He is *not two, but one Christ*. One, not by conversion of the Godhead into flesh, but by taking of that manhood into God. One altogether, *not by confusion of substance, but by unity of person*. For as the reasonable soul and flesh is one man, so God and man is one Christ...[48]

All the essential components of Chalcedonian orthodoxy are present here: (i) Christ participates perfectly in two natures, divine and human; (ii) he possesses the fullness of human life in all its physical, mental, and spiritual components; (iii) his two natures are not combined into a third kind of nature; but (iv) they are nonetheless united in one person.[49]

One further detail of both the Definition of Chalcedon and the Athanasian Creed should be noted: the use of the present tense throughout. This seemingly minor grammatical point reflects a significant theological point, for it was the conviction of the theologians who drafted those statements that Jesus Christ not only *had been* fully human during his earthly life, but *continued to be* fully human following his ascent to the Father, remaining so eternally.[50] This easily overlooked element of credal orthodoxy will prove relevant in my assessment of contemporary models of the Incarnation.

Arriving at the end of this survey of the development of the doctrine of the Incarnation, the constraints of christological orthodoxy (as indicated by a historically and theologically

---

48 *HCC*, Vol. 3, Ch. 9, §132, emphasis added.
49 Kelly observes that Apollinarianism is ruled out by statement 32 of the creed, which affirms that Christ is a 'perfect (i.e., complete) man' possessing a 'human rational mind', while Nestorianism is ruled out by statements 31, 35, and 36. Kelly, *The Athanasian Creed*, 91-108.
50 Baillie, *God Was In Christ*, 151-52.

contextualized reading of the Definition of Chalcedon and the Athanasian Creed) and their implications may be summarised as follows:

(I1) An orthodox doctrine of the Incarnation must protect the *personal unity* of Jesus Christ: the redeemer of mankind is none other than the Son of God.

(I2) An orthodox doctrine of the Incarnation must uphold the *full divinity* of Christ, where divinity is construed in terms of undiminished transcendence and perfection.

(I3) An orthodox doctrine of the Incarnation must maintain the *full humanity* of Christ, in all its essential physical and psychological respects, along with the concomitant experiences and limitations.

(I4) An orthodox doctrine of the Incarnation must affirm that even now Christ remains fully human as well as fully divine.

(I5) On the one hand, (I1) and (I2) imply that Christ was omniscient, omnipotent, omnipresent, immutable, impassible, etc.

(I6) On the other hand, (I1) and (I3) imply that Christ was limited in knowledge and power, was spatially constrained, underwent change, suffered pain, etc.

(I7) Consequently, any interpretation of the doctrine of the Incarnation that seeks to fulfil requirements (I1), (I2), (I3), and (I4) will be paradoxical, given our natural intuitions about the concepts employed.

It is hardly surprising then that the doctrine of the Incarnation has been considered by many to be irremediably paradoxical, given the central theological concerns that directed its formulation and constrain its interpretation. For it apparently requires believers to affirm that one individual, one *person*, is the bearer of two sets of attributes, many of which appear to be directly incompatible.

Without wanting to kick a doctrine when it is down, a further logical problem may be noted in passing. If the doctrine of the Trinity is inherently paradoxical, as I argued earlier, then the doctrine of the Incarnation necessarily inherits that paradoxicality. Here is the argument: if the Son assumed a human nature, and the Son is God, then God assumed a human nature; but if the Father did not assume a human nature, and the Father is God, then God did *not* assume a human nature; therefore, God both did and did not assume a human nature.[51]

To sum up: the Christian doctrine of the Incarnation is expressed definitively in the Definition of Chalcedon and the Athanasian Creed, but any interpretation of these statements faithful to the historical and theological context in which they were formulated appears to lead to irreconcilable metaphysical claims. Still, it would be premature to conclude at this point that an orthodox view of the Incarnation inevitably involves paradox, since numerous attempts have been made in the last two centuries to set forth interpretations of the traditional doctrine that avoid any appearance of incoherence. In the remainder of the chapter, I evaluate the most promising of these attempts.

3.3 Recent Christology

In Chapter 2, I noted that the twentieth century has enjoyed a plethora of defences, explications and original interpretations of the doctrine of the Trinity. The doctrine of the Incarnation has garnered no less attention. A good proportion of these works on the Incarnation are presented either as improvements on previous expositions considered to be lacking in clarity or coherence, or as responses to the charge that the doctrine suffers from unavoidable confusion and contradiction. As with works on the Trinity, the operative assumption often seems to be that paradoxical formulations of the doctrine of Christ's two natures are inherently unsatisfactory and therefore in need of either life-saving theological surgery or (less radically) a thorough conceptual makeover. In the second part of this chapter, I will assess a selection of representative and influential contributions to this field with a view to determining whether interpretations of the doctrine of the Incarnation are now available which maintain conformance to orthodoxy whilst adequately dissolving any alleged logical difficulties.

I have divided my survey of contemporary treatments of the doctrine of the Incarnation into three sections, corresponding to three basic approaches to the christological problem. (1) *Kenotic*

---

51 It might be objected that this presupposes an Augustinian model of the Trinity, whereas alternative models (e.g., social trinitarianism) would render the argument obviously invalid. Cf. Brown, *The Divine Trinity*, 251. This observation is correct. However, it was earlier argued that Augustinian trinitarianism comports best with (i) the most natural interpretation of the creeds and (ii) the theological concerns which motivated their authors. In any case, my conclusions in this chapter do not stand or fall on this point.

interpretations, in which the drive for clear logical consistency is arguably most conspicuous, hold in common that God the Son had to divest himself of certain divine characteristics, such as omniscience and omnipotence, in order to become incarnate. (2) *Dual-psychology* interpretations are offered by writers who, dissatisfied with the kenotic solution, suggest instead that the incarnate Christ possessed two distinct minds or consciousnesses: one serving as the subject of his divine attributes and experiences, the other serving as the subject of his human attributes and experiences. (3) Finally, I review a selection of contemporary theologians who have effectively acceded to a *paradoxical* interpretation of the doctrine of the Incarnation.

3.3.1 Kenotic Interpretations

Kenotic theories of Christ's nature derive their label from the Greek word *kenosis* ('emptying') and their chief biblical support from Philippians 2:7 in which a variant of the word features.[52] The common theme of such theories is that God the Son, in order that he might appropriate a full human nature and thus accomplish mankind's redemption, was required to divest or 'empty' himself of various divine attributes thought to be metaphysically incompatible with being genuinely human. The motivation for this relatively novel approach to christology lies not only in a desire to avoid the charge of incoherence but also in a concern to uphold the genuine humanity and personal integrity of Jesus. Kenoticism is associated historically with certain German and British theologians writing between the mid-nineteenth and the early-twentieth century, such as Gottfried Thomasius, Charles Gore, and P.T. Forsyth. However, my focus here will not be on these early proponents but on the expositions of three recent defenders of kenotic theory: David Brown, Ronald Feenstra, and Stephen Davis. These writers are of particular relevance to my present concerns, not only because they have sought to defend and refine earlier kenoticism in the face of subsequent criticisms, but also because they have offered their treatments in the explicit context of developing *logically consistent* interpretations of the doctrine of the Incarnation.

In his 1985 work *The Divine Trinity*, David Brown devotes three chapters to defending the logical coherence of the traditional

---

52 For a brief overview of the history and theological character of kenoticism, see B. E. Foster, 'Kenoticism', in Sinclair B. Ferguson and David F. Wright (eds), *New Dictionary of Theology* (Leicester: InterVarsity Press, 1988), 364.

doctrines of the Trinity and the Incarnation. Concerning the latter, Brown reviews six historically significant models for explicating the incarnation of the Son of God.[53] These are: (1) the two-nature christology endorsed at Chalcedon (TNC); (2) Apollinarianism (emphasising Christ's unity of personhood but at the expense of his human nature); (3) Nestorianism (emphasising Christ's complete humanity but at the expense of his personal unity); (4) the kenotic model (KM); (5) the model of grace (attributed to Donald Baillie and John Robinson);[54] and (6) the mythological model (advocated by John Hick and similarly minded revisionists).

Brown's first question concerns the orthodoxy of each of these models. He argues, somewhat controversially, that the ultimate criterion for the orthodoxy of any incarnational model is its conformance to the Definition of Chalcedon rather than to the Bible.[55] Whether or not Brown is correct in his prioritizing of ecclesiastical authorities, it can be agreed that conformance to Chalcedon is (either directly or derivatively) a necessary condition of orthodoxy. On this basis, Brown states that any orthodox christology must involve the following two propositions:

> (a) the identity claim that Christ was a single person, and (b) the constitutive claim that he possessed both a fully human and a fully divine nature.[56]

Despite the impression given by his labelling of TNC as 'Chalcedonian', Brown does not believe that this characterisation of orthodoxy eliminates all but the first of the six proffered models. The reason, he suggests, is that TNC involves a *third* proposition, one that distinguishes it from KM:

> (c) that the two natures were simultaneously present in the one person.[57]

Brown's contention is that the Chalcedonian definition does not explicitly require this third proposition to be an ingredient of any orthodox view of the incarnate Christ. Whilst conceding that the Fathers would have given no consideration to any alternative to (c), Brown counters that their soteriological motivation for holding it is

---

53 Brown, *The Divine Trinity*, 224-39. The abbreviations TNC and KM are Brown's.

54 Baillie, *God Was In Christ*; J. A. T. Robinson, *The Human Face of God* (London: SCM Press, 1973).

55 Brown, *The Divine Trinity*, 226.

56 Brown, *The Divine Trinity*, 228.

57 Brown, *The Divine Trinity*, 228.

in fact adequately secured by (a) and (b) without recourse to (c). This third proposition, he further remarks, was 'simply the most natural reading of the Scriptures at the time.'

Brown's defence of the Chalcedonian credentials of kenoticism is inventive and charitable, but nonetheless cannot reasonably be sustained. In the first place, the question arises as to what extent the theological convictions of those who author a doctrinal statement should be brought to bear on its legitimate interpretation. Brown admits that the Chalcedonian theologians would not have given any thought to the negation of proposition (c), but surely he understates the matter here, for there is little doubt that they would have defended it in the strongest terms. Thomas Morris rightly complains that a kenotic perspective is hard to reconcile with Leo's *Tome*, to which the Definition of Chalcedon is indebted, and with Athanasius's view that the incarnate Christ was limited in neither power nor knowledge.[58] It is no secret that a strong doctrine of divine immutability was common to both the Alexandrian theologians and their Antiochene opponents; both parties were concerned not to compromise this conviction in their christological writings.[59] It would have been inconceivable in such a theological environment for the notion that the Logos shed several of his divine attributes to have been given serious consideration.

Be that as it may, however, it does not immediately follow that Chalcedonian orthodoxy requires modern theologians to share that conviction. Adherence to a particular creed does not commit one to endorsing every identifiable theological presupposition of its authors. Nevertheless, where such presuppositions *bear directly on the connotation of key phrases and formulations* (such as 'one person in two natures') then surely adherents to the creed are not free to simply dismiss their contribution to the meaning of the document. Neither of these two extremes reflects a reasonable view of authorial intention in hermeneutical practice. One must ask, then, just what did the authors of the Definition have in mind when they wrote of Christ being 'made known in two natures'? Is it most likely that they thought of him existing in two natures *at one time*—or, as some kenoticists would prefer, that they wished only to say that he existed with a divine nature at one time, a human nature at another, and may or may not have possessed both simultaneously?

---

58 Thomas V. Morris, 'The Metaphysics of God Incarnate', in Ronald J. Feenstra and Cornelius Plantinga, Jr. (eds), *Trinity, Incarnation, and Atonement: Philosophical and Theological Essays* (Notre Dame, IN: University of Notre Dame Press, 1989), 119-21.

59 Pelikan, *The Christian Tradition*, 229, 270-71.

It might be said that we in the twenty-first century are hardly in a position to read the minds of numerous fifth-century theologians as they penned the Chalcedon statement. Even if this were granted — and that in the face of ample documentary evidence of their theological presuppositions — there is no need to rely on inferences based on external data, since the convictions of the authors on this point are perfectly explicit in the text of the Definition itself. A careful reading of the statement is enough to confirm that Brown's claim is untenable. According to the text, Christ *is* (present tense) 'the same perfect in Godhead and perfect in manhood'; he is 'made known in two natures ... without *change* [and] without *separation*'; the differences between the natures are '*by no means removed* because of the union', the properties of each nature being '*preserved* and *coalescing*' in his singular person; and so forth. It is difficult, to put it mildly, for such expressions to accommodate the idea that Christ possessed his two natures successively rather than simultaneously.

As if this were not enough, a further problem arises for the kenotic model (as Brown constructs it) with respect to Christ's post-ascension state. Brown acknowledges this difficulty in his response to Donald Baillie's criticisms of kenoticism: if the kenotic model grants that the fullness of divinity is incompatible with Jesus' humanity during his earthly ministry, then it cannot allow that humanity to continue once his full divinity is recovered in his glorification and return to the Father (John 17:4-5; Phil. 2:9-11).[60] Brown's solution to this dilemma is to suggest that Christ could have retained his humanity, not as the possession of a metaphysical nature, but as 'a remembered experience of the second person of the Trinity'.[61] This compromise would hardly have appealed to the Fathers, probably ranking on a par with the suggestion that the immutable Logos abandoned various divine attributes in the act of incarnation.

Nevertheless, the decisive difficulty of Brown's kenotic model is its contradiction of the most straightforward reading of the Definition. The grammar of the christological statement clearly reflects the indisputable conviction of its authors that Jesus Christ *continues* to possess the same human nature that he appropriated at the first advent. Thus the three points I have identified — the

---

60 Sturch also identifies this as a serious difficulty faced by kenoticism. 'We seem to be driven to conclude either that our Lord ceased to be human after the Ascension or that His divinity has remained limited from that day to this, and will remain so for all eternity. Neither alternative is very attractive...' Sturch, *The Word and the Christ*, 255; cf. 27.

61 Brown, *The Divine Trinity*, 234.

theological context of the Definition of Chalcedon, its expressions regarding the post-incarnation divinity of Christ, and its assumptions regarding his post-ascension humanity—combine to undermine Brown's case for the orthodoxy of a kenotic interpretation of the Incarnation.

Ronald Feenstra has also offered a contemporary defence of kenotic christology.[62] Feenstra, like Brown, professes the twin constraints of orthodoxy and logical consistency. As to the first, he concurs that the standard of christological orthodoxy is to be found in the Definition of Chalcedon. Concerning the logical conundrum, he argues that a kenotic theory need not be committed to denying that the incarnate Son of God lacked *omnipotence* or *omnipresence*; the really thorny problem, he maintains, is whether or not Christ lacked *omniscience* (and in what sense).

The foil for Feenstra's defence is provided by the anti-kenotic arguments of Thomas Morris.[63] Approaching from the standpoint of Anselmian perfect-being theology, with its strong modal claims about the divine attributes, Morris concludes that the kenoticist is committed to saying that God is (by virtue of his divinity) *omniscient-unless-freely-and-temporarily-choosing-otherwise* rather than *omniscient simpliciter*. The problem with this revision of classical theism, Morris suggests, is that it 'fails to be true that any divine person is logically or metaphysically immune to states of extensive ignorance concerning important truths about the world.'[64]

Feenstra's response to this objection is that no such problem arises once we say that (i) *omniscience-unless-kenotically-incarnate* is the relevant divine attribute; (ii) a divine person can only become kenotically incarnate for the purpose of redemption; and (iii) once one divine person has become kenotically incarnate, it is impossible for any other of the three to do so.[65] Leaving aside the suspiciously artificial and *ad hoc* complexity of this metaphysical construction, flying as it does in the face of Anselmian intuitions about divine knowledge, one might ask at this point how well Feenstra's kenoticism accords with his acknowledged standard of orthodoxy. Is it plausible that the Chalcedonian theologians would have accepted as compatible with their conciliar confession a conception of deity that can accommodate divine ignorance, however cautiously qualified? As I have noted, it would be unreasonable to suppose that

---

62 Feenstra, 'Reconsidering Kenotic Christology'.
63 These arguments appear in Morris, *The Logic of God Incarnate*, 88-101.
64 Feenstra, 'Reconsidering Kenotic Christology', 140.
65 Feenstra, 'Reconsidering Kenotic Christology', 142.

adherence to the Definition of Chalcedon requires one to embrace the particular understanding of divinity held by all (or most) of its authors, but the possession of omniscience *simpliciter* by the incarnate Logos nonetheless played a determinative role in the christological debates leading up to Chalcedon and as such must be given all due weight when interpreting the Definition. The Alexandrian commitment to the omniscience of the Word inclined them to explain away Jesus' professions of ignorance. Yet the Antiochenes, in their concern to do better justice to Christ's humanity, were in no way tempted to permit a trade off against their conception of his divinity; instead, they resorted to positing a human soul, distinct from the divine soul, to accommodate Jesus' human ignorance. Not one of the participants in the debate—Alexandrian, Antiochene, or Latin—went anywhere near the kenotic escape hatch.[66] Moreover, the fact that both the Definition of Chalcedon and the Athanasian Creed take care to state that God the Son assumed a human *soul*, as well as a body, is further evidence that no attenuation of his divine psyche was to be tolerated.

Feenstra attempts to address a further major problem for the kenotic view, namely, the *continued* humanity of the exalted Christ. As Morris and other critics have pointed out, kenoticists face a dilemma: if they deny the post-ascension humanity of Christ, they face the charge of heterodoxy; but if they affirm the doctrine, they

---

66 Of all the parties, a kenotic solution would have been most useful to the Alexandrians, given their emphasis on the unity of Christ's person and resistence toward the notion of a distinct human soul that could accommodate Jesus' noetic limitations. Nevertheless, their chief advocate, Cyril, explicitly eschewed such a position: '[W]e confess that the Only begotten Word of God, begotten of the same substance of the Father, True God from True God, Light from Light, through Whom all things were made, the things in heaven and the things in the earth, coming down for our salvation, making himself of no reputation, was incarnate and made man; that is, taking flesh of the holy Virgin, and having made it his own from the womb, he subjected himself to birth for us, and came forth man from a woman, *without casting off that which he was*; but although he assumed flesh and blood, *he remained what he was*, God in essence and in truth. Neither do we say that his flesh was changed into the nature of divinity, *nor that the ineffable nature of the Word of God has laid aside for the nature of flesh; for he is unchanged and absolutely unchangeable, being the same always*, according to the Scriptures. For although visible and a child in swaddling clothes, and even in the bosom of his Virgin Mother, he filled all creation as God, and was a fellow-ruler with him who begat him, for the Godhead is without quantity and dimension, *and cannot have limits*.' Cyril, *Third Epistle to Nestorius*, emphasis added; in *NPNF2*, Vol. 14.

must concede that being omniscient is *not* incompatible with being human and thus disavow one of the chief motivations for adopting a kenotic view in the first place. Feenstra volunteers three potential responses: (i) it is possible to question whether orthodoxy *requires* one to hold that the exalted Christ remains human; (ii) it could be argued that only *becoming* human, and not *being* human, is incompatible with omniscience; and (iii) it may prove fruitful to distinguish the Incarnation from the kenosis of Christ. Feenstra rightly expresses dissatisfaction with the first option, and does not develop the second beyond deeming it 'at least worthy of consideration'.[67] He thereby implies that he considers the third to be the most promising.

The thought behind Feenstra's third option is that the Incarnation and the kenosis are conceptually distinct. Incarnation does not necessarily involve humiliation, but redemption *requires* it; while the act of incarnation does not entail the divesting of attributes such as omniscience, the act of kenosis does. The only relevant point to be made here is that in advancing such a view, Feenstra has effectively abandoned all resistance to the notion that a full human nature and a full divine nature (as traditionally conceived, i.e., without diminution) may be possessed simultaneously by one person. The irony is that kenoticism construed along such lines treats as irrelevant the very feature that might be thought to offset its questionable orthodoxy, namely, its avoidance of the perceived incoherence of a traditional two-natures christology. Feenstra's strategy in defence of kenotic christology thus leads him into an awkward corner: the more modifications and qualifications are introduced to kenoticism in order to bring it into line with orthodoxy, the less it distinguishes itself as a logically superior alternative to the traditional view.

The third and final defence of kenoticism I propose to consider here is that of Stephen Davis in his monograph *Logic and the Nature of God*. As the title of his book suggests, Davis's immediate concern is with the *logical coherence* of Christian theism, and in his treatment

---

67 Feenstra, 'Reconsidering Kenotic Christology', 148. It is hard to see how this distinction could pay the necessary dividends. What could it possibly be about *changing from not being human to being human* that would preclude a person from being omniscient, once it is granted that *being human simpliciter* does not so preclude it? Cf. C. Stephen Evans, 'The Self-Emptying of Love: Some Thoughts on Kenotic Christology', in Stephen T. Davis, Daniel Kendall, and Gerald O'Collins (eds), *The Incarnation: An Interdisciplinary Symposium on the Incarnation of the Son of God* (Oxford: Oxford University Press, 2002), 264-65.

of the doctrine of the Incarnation he identifies two routes open to the
defender of Chalcedonian orthodoxy: the 'classical' route (in which
the full gamut of divine attributes are ascribed to the incarnate
Christ) and the 'kenotic' route. In Davis's view, the first option is
unavoidably paradoxical; he therefore resolves to spell out the
kenotic option and to defend it against charges of incoherence and
heterodoxy.[68]

Following typically kenotic convictions, Davis claims that Jesus as
incarnate must have lacked four divine attributes: omniscience,
omnipotence, necessity, and 'being the creator of the world'. This
requires him to conclude that, contrary to classical theism, these
attributes are *accidental* and not *essential* for a divine being.[69]
Deeming this to be a theologically tolerable price to pay, he
concludes that

> the sentence 'Jesus is truly God and truly man' is coherent. I can
> detect no contradiction or other sort of incoherence here, at any
> rate. The basic idea is this: *Jesus Christ failed to have some divine
> properties but was still God and had some divine properties but was still a
> human being, and he failed to have some human properties but was still a
> human being and had some human properties but was still God.*[70]

Without reiterating the criticisms made of the kenotic interpretations
defended by Brown and Feenstra, it should be clear that Davis's
view is sufficiently similar as to suffer the same objections regarding
its Chalcedonian credentials. Davis evidently holds that there are
some 'divine properties' that are not integral to divine *nature* and
some 'human properties' that are not integral to human *nature*. He
does not specify by virtue of *what* these accidental properties are
distinctively divine or human, given that they are essential to neither
nature, but the upshot is that his conception of divinity deviates
significantly from that implicit in the Definition of Chalcedon.

Davis suggests in his defence that the Chalcedonian authors were
offering a *guideline* rather than an *explanation* of the Incarnation; that

---

68 In light of this strategy, Davis's readers may be surprised to find him
    advocating what he admits to be a paradoxical view of the Trinity in the
    same volume. One cannot help but ask: if, as he later argues, some
    paradoxes are rationally permissible, why is the 'classical' route in
    christology unworthy of further consideration?

69 I merely note in passing the philosophical difficulties involving in claiming
    (i) that *necessary* existence can be a *contingent* attribute and (ii) that Jesus
    was not the creator of the world, yet (as orthodoxy demands) Jesus is
    personally identical to the Logos.

70 Davis, *Logic and the Nature of God*, 129, emphasis original.

is, they were setting out boundaries for orthodoxy rather than setting forth a particular metaphysical explication of that orthodoxy. The kenotic solution, in his judgement, 'affirms the divinity, the humanity and the unity of the person of Christ ... and so falls within the boundaries of Chalcedonic orthodoxy.'[71] While Davis may be right about the intentions of the Fathers, he surely overestimates the latitude of the boundaries that they established. The Definition of Chalcedon does not merely affirm the divinity, the humanity, and the unity of the person of Christ. It also reflects particular conceptions of divine nature, human nature, the manner in which these natures are united, and the chronology of their co-exemplification in the person of Christ—conceptions quite at odds with Davis's kenotic view. Indeed, his interaction with the Definition of Chalcedon seems to be typical of recent defences of kenoticism, which tend to deal with loose summaries and selective excerpts rather than a close examination of the full statement, considered in its original context.

I should mention one further problem of orthodoxy for kenotic interpretations before moving on to consider alternatives. In his discussion of the kenotic model of the Incarnation, David Brown points out that the model is 'heavily dependent' on a social trinitarian view of the doctrine of the Trinity since it cannot be accommodated by an Augustinian interpretation (in which each divine *hypostasis* is thought of as numerically identical with the divine *ousia*).[72] If Brown is correct on this point, then so much the worse for kenoticism; for as I argued in the previous chapter, social trinitarianism is difficult, if not impossible, to reconcile with the theology of the Nicene and Athanasian Creeds.

I therefore conclude that kenotic interpretations face serious objections concerning their faithfulness to credal orthodoxy. The reader will note that I have made no assessment of the *coherence* of such interpretations. For my purposes, the success of kenotic theories on this front may be granted. Few theologians or philosophers have insisted that no logically consistent kenotic christology is possible.[73] Nevertheless, kenotic interpretations still

71 Davis, *Logic and the Nature of God*, 130.
72 Brown, *The Divine Trinity*, 251.
73 One exception is John Hick, who seems inclined toward finding debilitating incoherence in *any* relatively high christology. For a response to Hick's criticisms of kenoticism, see Stephen T. Davis, 'John Hick on Incarnation and Trinity', in Stephen T. Davis, Daniel Kendall, and Gerald O'Collins (eds), *The Trinity: An Interdisciplinary Symposium on the Trinity* (Oxford: Oxford University Press, 1999), 251-72. In my view, Davis adequately

fail one of the two requirements of a non-paradoxical Christian doctrine of the Incarnation and thus offer no escape from a choice between paradox and heterodoxy.

3.3.2 Dual-Psychology Interpretations

In the pre-Chalcedonian debates over the nature and person of Christ, one conviction was held constant among both the orthodox and the unorthodox, namely, Christ's *full divinity*. Moreover, the reigning conception of deity was that of absolute monotheism. With this theological anchor in place, attempts to rationalise the mystery of the Incarnation gave rise to two tendencies in christology: either toward a reduction of the humanity of Christ or toward a division of his person. In contemporary theology, however, the anchor has been relocated: the non-negotiable component in modern christological debate is now the *full humanity* of Jesus.[74] With this shift in the parameters of the discussion, endeavours to formulate a doctrine of the Incarnation free from any apparent contradictions have exhibited a tendency either to reinterpret the *divinity* of the incarnate Son (as in kenotic theories and de-mythologizing christologies) or, once again, to split Christ into two persons. In this section, I propose to examine some prominent examples of christologies that have invited the latter charge by favouring *dual-psychology* interpretations of the Incarnation, according to which Jesus Christ possessed two minds or consciousnesses: one divine, one human.[75]

Thomas V. Morris, in his book *The Logic of God Incarnate*, has offered one of the most thorough and philosophically sophisticated defences of the coherence of Chalcedonian christology in recent

---

defends the coherence of kenotic theory, but the concerns about its theological adequacy remain.

74 Baillie, *God Was In Christ*, 11-20.

75 I use the label 'dual-psychology' because the models in question cover a wide range of mental ascriptions: beliefs, experiences, desires, intentions, etc. Alternative descriptions, such as 'two-minds model' or 'dual-consciousness model', tend to direct attention toward specific features of a person's mental life. Defences of the coherence of the Incarnation by appeal to a dual-psychology model can be found in Morris, *The Logic of God Incarnate*; Morris, 'The Metaphysics of God Incarnate'; Sturch, *The Word and the Christ*; Brown, *The Divine Trinity*; Swinburne, *The Christian God*; Senor, 'The Incarnation and the Trinity'; Jay Wesley Richards, 'Is the Doctrine of the Incarnation Coherent?', in William A. Dembski and Jay Wesley Richards (eds), *Unapologetic Apologetics: Meeting the Challenges of Theological Studies* (Downers Grove, IL: InterVarsity Press, 2001), 131-43.

years. By drawing what he takes to be three plausible metaphysical distinctions—between *individual-essences* and *kind-essences*; between *essential* properties and *common* properties; and between being *merely human* and being *fully human*—Morris suggests it is possible to show that one individual, Jesus Christ, could possess (simultaneously) both a divine nature and a human nature.[76] Furthermore, the concept of divinity with which Morris wishes to work is far from being the pared-down, modally-flexible notion favoured by kenoticists; rather, it is that exalted conception suggested by Anselmian perfect-being theology.[77] I will not embark on a full critique of Morris's strategy for defending the coherence of Chalcedon here.[78] Instead, I wish to focus on his advocacy of a dual-psychology model of the Incarnation in order to resolve particular problems arising from the co-instantiation of Christ's divine and human attributes.

Morris acknowledges that his basic strategy for reconciling Christ's divinity and humanity runs the risk of ending up with a denuded concept of humanity that simply fails to satisfy the soteriological axiom that Jesus fully shared our 'human condition'.[79] The problem is particularly acute with respect to omniscience, which Morris takes to be essential to any divine being conceived along Anselmian lines. How could Jesus grow in knowledge and exhibit ignorance on some subjects (as the biblical record testifies) whilst also being omniscient? After rejecting the kenotic solution as 'a real departure from what most theists, Christian as well as non-Christian, have wanted to say about the nature of God',[80] Morris offers an alternative view in terms of which Christ's simultaneously unlimited and limited knowledge 'is in no way at all *even a paradox* for faith' and thus provides us with 'an important ingredient in a solution to *the single most difficult logical challenge* to the doctrine of the Incarnation'.[81] This is the 'two minds' view, according to which Jesus Christ possessed 'something like two distinct ranges of consciousness':

---

76 For an overview of his strategy in *The Logic of God Incarnate*, see Morris, 'The Metaphysics of God Incarnate', 113-17.

77 Morris, *The Logic of God Incarnate*, 74-88.

78 For some notable criticisms of Morris's christology, see David W. Brown, 'The Logic of God Incarnate', *Modern Theology* 6 (1989), 112-13; John H. Hick, 'The Logic of God Incarnate', *Religious Studies* 25 (1989), 409-23; Keith E. Yandell, 'Some Problems for Tomistic Incarnationists', *International Journal for Philosophy of Religion* 30 (1991), 169-82.

79 Morris, *The Logic of God Incarnate*, 70.

80 Morris, *The Logic of God Incarnate*, 100.

81 Morris, *The Logic of God Incarnate*, 74, 107, emphasis added.

We can view the two ranges of consciousness (and, analogously, the two noetic structures encompassing them) as follows: The divine mind of God the Son contained, but was not contained by, his earthly mind, or range of consciousness. That is to say, there was what can be called an asymmetric accessing relation between the two minds.[82]

In order to explicate this approach, Morris appeals in the first instance to the analogy of 'two computer programs or informational systems, one containing but not contained by the other.'[83] Further analogies aimed at illustrating the basic coherence of this approach are drawn from contemporary psychology: Morris appeals both to the modern notion that there are various strata to the human mind as well as to cases of brain dysfunction or artificial manipulation in which 'we are confronted by what seems to be in some significant sense a single human being, one person, but one person with apparently two or more distinct streams or ranges of consciousness, distinct domains of experience.'[84]

In a follow-up article, 'The Metaphysics of God Incarnate', Morris bolsters his case with more detailed appeals to analogies in artificial intelligence and human psychology, although he rightly admits that such analogies are far from decisive in establishing the coherence of a union of a *divine* mind with a human one. He also addresses two particularly difficult problems introduced by his dual-psychology model: first, the question of how we should speak of Christ's *beliefs* on particular matters; and second, the question of what on this view constitutes the *unity* of Christ's person (since arguably God's mind stands in an 'asymmetric accessing relation' to *every* human mind). In response to the first, Morris suggests that we are forced to divide the question: we can only strictly speak of Jesus' beliefs *with respect to either his divine mind or his human mind*. Thus, Jesus believed *with his divine mind* that he would return on a particular date, but did not so believe *with his human mind*. However, the situation is a

---

82 Morris, *The Logic of God Incarnate*, 102-3.
83 Morris, *The Logic of God Incarnate*, 103.
84 Morris, *The Logic of God Incarnate*, 105. Morris addresses the concern that comparisons with cases of psychological dysfunction hardly befit a man deemed by Christians to be the one historical example of a perfect human life. He points out that the comparisons are merely analogical and, moreover, a state that would be undesirable for a *normal* human person need not be undesirable for the special case of the incarnate Son of God, given the goals he wished to attain. For my purposes here, I will grant the adequacy of his response.

hierarchical one and therefore we should 'represent God the Son's *ultimate doxastic state* as captured in his divine omniscience.'[85]

Morris's answer to the second question, briefly paraphrased, is that while *my* human mental system was intended by God to define a person (distinct from *other* persons), the human mental system of Jesus was not intended *alone* to define a person. Consequently, if *my* mental system were subsumed and overridden by another, my freedom would be abrogated; but since Christ's personhood was never intended to be defined purely by a human mental system, no person's freedom is abrogated through the Incarnation. In this way, Morris suggests, we can preserve the genuineness of Jesus' human knowledge, will, and experiences without falling into the heresy of dividing his person.

With this summary of Morris's christology in hand, we must ask two crucial questions to determine whether Morris's christology succeeds in its claims to uphold orthodoxy whilst avoiding paradox. First of all, is this dual-psychology interpretation harmonious with the credal orthodoxy of Chalcedon? Secondly, does it offer a coherent explication of Christ's divinity and humanity whilst maintaining the unity of his person?

As to the first, the Definition of Chalcedon does not explicitly endorse a 'two minds' or 'two consciousnesses' view of Christ, but neither does it explicitly rule out such a view. No doubt something approximating Morris's view, albeit less clearly articulated, was favoured by the Antiochene school of christology. Indeed, a dual-psychology perspective is intimated by the Definition itself through its claim (echoed by the Athanasian Creed) that Christ's humanity entailed the possession of a 'rational soul'. Still, we should recall that certain phrases of the Definition were meant to proscribe the *extreme* forms of this Antiochene way of thinking: Christ's two natures are said to be united 'without division' and 'without separation'. The question here is not so much whether such phrases were deliberately intended to exclude (among other things) modern dual-psychology interpretations—that would be absurdly anachronistic—but whether whatever degree of division and separation those phrases *were* intended to exclude would *also* serve to render Morris's solution unacceptable. It cannot be denied that Morris 'divides' the two natures in *some* sense, partitioning as he does the consciousness, experiences, and beliefs of Christ with respect to each nature. However, one would be hard-pressed to argue that Morris's view falls outside the boundaries of orthodoxy laid down by Chalcedon,

---

85   Morris, 'The Metaphysics of God Incarnate', 125, emphasis added.

given the difficulty of determining with sufficient precision how the strictures of the Definition are to be understood. In contrast to the kenotic view, then, I conclude that Morris's 'two minds' model is not clearly in violation of conciliar orthodoxy.

Focus therefore turns to the question of coherence—and it is at this point that difficulties are rather more apparent. My critique on this point will include both a negative argument and a positive one: the former will conclude that Morris's defensive strategy is unsuccessful inasmuch as it is mired in ambiguity at crucial points, while the latter will contend that such defences are destined to failure *in principle*.

As I earlier noted, Morris accepts that while his various analogies are helpful in gaining an understanding of the 'two minds' model, they cannot serve as proofs of coherence in the christological case. Analogies employed in this way possess only illustrative and not argumentative force. Moreover, Morris's analogies appear to differ from the incarnational case at just those points at which the charge of incoherence is strongest: artificial intelligence systems, while exhibiting something *analogous* to beliefs, do not possess consciousness or personhood in the way that humans do, and cases of divided human psychologies do not (so far as we can tell) involve the *simultaneous* possession of *contradictory* intentional propositional states (e.g., belief in X and absence of belief in X; awareness of X and lack of awareness of X).[86]

Furthermore, Morris's ascription of two 'ranges of consciousness' to Christ, one 'contained within' the other, is sufficiently vague as to

---

86 Hick makes similar points in criticising what he perceives to be a 'one-dimensional' view of mentality suggested by Morris's computing analogies and 'belief-system' terminology. Hick, 'The Logic of God Incarnate', 417. In a discussion of 'the paradox of Christ's omniscience', Timothy Bartel offers a thought experiment, involving a 'split-brain' patient, which he believes provides a 'clear counterexample to the claim that no-one can simultaneously believe and disbelieve the same proposition.' In fact, his hypothetical scenario shows at most that one can simultaneously hold *logically incompatible* beliefs, which is hardly a controversial conclusion. It would only follow that one can simultaneously believe and disbelieve the same proposition if believing p necessitated believing every proposition deducible from p (in conjunction with one's other beliefs). But then it would also follow that one can believe compound propositions of the form 'p and not p'—which Bartel explicitly denies. In any case, Bartel goes on to argue that solutions to this christological paradox face other formidable difficulties, for which there are no obvious answers. Timothy W. Bartel, 'Why the Philosophical Problems of Chalcedonian Christology Have Not Gone Away', *Heythrop Journal* 36.2 (1995), 153-72.

obscure whether the problem of coherence has really been resolved rather than merely concealed. The most plausible interpretation of this claim is that Jesus' human mind was only aware of a *subset* of those things of which his divine mind was aware; thus, for example, Jesus' human range of consciousness only included awareness of events occurring nearby and not (as his divine range of consciousness encompassed) those events occurring beyond the range of normal human senses. If this is so, the question arises as to whether those items of awareness that *coincide* are also *identical*. To take a concrete example: was the awareness in Jesus' human consciousness that (say) the wine had run out at the wedding in Cana *one and the same* awareness as that present in Jesus' divine consciousness? If they were *not* numerically identical, then it is hard to see why they should be thought of as belonging to the consciousnesses of *one person*; for even if you and I are aware of the same thing (and in the same manner) *my* awareness of it is not identical to *your* awareness of it. And what this suggests is that instances of awareness are individuated by way of the individuality of the *persons* exhibiting those instances of awareness.[87] Given this intuition, coinciding but non-identical instances of awareness would naturally suggest a plurality of persons.

Alternatively, if Jesus' human awareness of the wine shortage *was* numerically identical to his divine awareness, and likewise for all other points of coincidence, it is difficult to see why we should think of him as possessing two distinct consciousnesses (or 'ranges of consciousness') rather than *one* consciousness and a *portion* or *region* of that same consciousness.[88] The problem then returns as to how one might credibly maintain that Jesus *lacked* awareness of certain things in a genuine (rather than Pickwickian) sense.

---

87 Alvin Plantinga reflects this intuition while raising criticisms of the doctrine of divine impassibility: 'Can we say that Christ qua human being (according to his human nature) suffered while Christ qua divine (according to his divine nature) did not? … I'm inclined to think this suggestion incoherent. There is this person, the second person of the divine trinity who became incarnate. It is this person who suffers; if there really were *two* centers of consciousness here, one suffering and the other not, there would be two persons here (one human and one divine) rather than the one person who is both human and divine.' Alvin Plantinga, *Warranted Christian Belief* (Oxford: Oxford University Press, 2000), 319.

88 Tim Bayne raises a similar point in his critique of the Morris-Swinburne strategy. Tim Bayne, 'The Inclusion Model of the Incarnation: Problems and Prospects', *Religious Studies* 37.2 (2001), 130.

However misleading the ambiguity of Morris's claims, this weakness is overshadowed by a more serious conceptual problem concerning the logical relationship between *persons, minds,* and *experiences.* In order to state this problem, however, I must first review an intriguing line of argument presented in one of the most important twentieth-century contributions to analytical philosophy.

In his influential monograph *Individuals,* British philosopher P. F. Strawson developed a transcendental argument for the indispensability and logical primitiveness of our concept of a *person,* where 'person' is taken to denote that type of entity to which both *mental* states (e.g., 'being in pain') and *physical* states (e.g., 'lying down') may be simultaneously and unequivocally ascribed.[89] Against the Cartesian view that a human person is a composite of a material body and an immaterial soul, and the anti-realist view that the metaphysical notion of a real 'ego' or 'self' (distinct from the body) is a mere linguistic illusion, Strawson contended not only that the concept of a person is unavoidable and must be treated as referring to a real entity, but also that it is a *primitive* concept—which is to say, our notions of *body* and *mind* must be logically explicated in terms of our notion of *person* rather than the reverse. Compressing his lengthy discussion, the argument may be paraphrased as follows:

(1) The possibility of ascribing experiences to oneself presupposes the possibility of ascribing experiences to others (of the same type as oneself).

(2) The possibility of ascribing experiences to others presupposes the possibility of distinguishing (individuating) different subjects of experience.

(3) The possibility of distinguishing different subjects of experiences presupposes that those subjects are of a certain

---

89 P. F. Strawson, *Individuals: An Essay in Descriptive Metaphysics* (London: Routledge, 1959), 87-116. A transcendental argument is one that seeks to demonstrate the preconditions of meaningful thought or experience: those necessary concepts that make possible our judgements regarding some domain of experience. Strawson's argument is that the concept of a person, defined in a particular way, is one such concept; that is, we must think of others and ourselves fundamentally as 'persons' (rather than merely 'souls' or 'bodies') if our commonplace ascriptions of mental and physical states (e.g., 'I hope to play tennis this afternoon', 'John is planning to go to London') are to be meaningful. A genuinely transcendental concept is an inescapable feature of our human conceptual schemes.

(logically primitive) type, such that both mental and physical states may be ascribed to individuals of that type.

(4) Therefore, the possibility of ascribing experiences to oneself presupposes that one is just that certain (logically primitive) type of entity: a 'person'.[90]

According to this argument, then, the logical subject or 'owner' of experiences is fundamentally a *person*. States of consciousness are properly ascribed to a mind only indirectly, by way of the person whose mind it is, and not vice versa. Furthermore, in the preamble to his argument, Strawson pointed out that if our statements about particular experiences are to be meaningful, they cannot be logically isolated from the *subjects* of those experiences:

For if we think, once more, of the requirements of identifying reference in speech to *particular* states of consciousness, or private experiences, we see that such particulars cannot be thus identifyingly referred to except as the states or experiences *of* some identified *person*. States, or experiences, one might say, *owe* their identity as particulars to the identity of the person whose states or experiences they are.[91]

It should not be difficult to see that Strawson's argument presents grave difficulties for a dual-psychology model such as Morris's. If claims about Jesus possessing two distinct ranges of consciousness, two distinct sets of experiences, beliefs, etc., are to be coherent then it must be possible to refer to those mental features *without* those features being necessarily owned by any particular person. Yet this is precisely what our concept of a person rules out.[92] If experiences are necessarily individuated with respect to persons, then at the most fundamental logical level it makes no sense to speak of *one* person with *two* distinct consciousnesses (in the sense that each

---

90 Cf. Strawson, *Individuals*, 104.

91 Strawson, *Individuals*, 97, emphasis original.

92 It might be objected here that I am assuming without argument that Strawson's concept of 'person' is the same as Chalcedon's (or Morris's) concept of 'person'. In fact, I reject this assumption. However, it should be obvious enough that Jesus *was* a 'person' in the Strawsonian sense. So if one wishes to ascribe incompatible experiences, beliefs, etc. to Jesus (as Chalcedon seemingly requires) then the problems I discuss here arise nonetheless. Moreover, it seems clear that while Chalcedonian personhood implies rather *more* than Strawsonian personhood, it surely implies no *less*.

consciousness might in principle be ascribed to a different person than the other).[93]

On the same basis, Morris's answer to the question of how we should think of Jesus' beliefs on any particular matter (namely, that we must 'divide the question' and speak of his belief with respect to one or other of his minds) suffers from a similar incoherence. If *persons* and not *minds* are the logically primary subjects of experiences and other mental states then it makes no more sense to say *Christ believed that water is H_2O with respect to his divine mind but did not believe that water is H_2O with respect to his human mind* than it does to say *Christ broke bread with respect to his hands but did not break bread with respect to his feet*. A person either breaks bread or he does not; likewise, a person either believes that water is H_2O or he does not. To try to isolate two distinct minds or consciousnesses within one person, as Morris seeks to do, is to kick against the goads of the very concepts needed to formulate the christological problem in the first place.[94]

If this criticism of Morris's dual-psychology interpretation of the Incarnation is on target then it sounds a death knell for *all* such interpretations, regardless of the details and defensive strategies of each case. Nevertheless, I will briefly consider one other prominent exposition of a dual-psychology model to see whether it fares any better.

Richard Swinburne offers his own defence of the coherence of the Incarnation in his masterful apologetic work, *The Christian God*. In keeping with the modern mindset in christology, Swinburne is concerned to avoid compromising the genuine humanity of Christ. Moreover, like Morris he wishes to uphold the standard of orthodoxy represented by Chalcedon and he judges kenotic interpretations to be unsatisfactory on this count. He suggests that 'with the aid of a modern idea, the divided mind' we can interpret

---

93 This application of Strawson's argument is confirmed by his later remarks on the concept of a 'group mind', i.e., a collection of individual consciousnesses so united as to function as 'one person'. If we go so far as to speak *literally* of a group in this manner, he explains, we remove any basis for distinguishing individual consciousnesses, or subjects of experience, within that 'person'. Strawson, *Individuals*, 112-15.

94 The transcendental character of Strawson's argument means that his conclusions trump any appeals to human psychology in order to defend the cogency of a 'two minds' model. The latter amount to fallible empirical claims about human consciousness, while the former identifies what must be so if *any* meaningful claim about human consciousness can be made *at all*.

the Chalcedonian two-natures christology in such a way as to do justice both to a traditional view of deity and to the biblical expressions of Jesus' humanity (e.g., Luke 2:52 and Mark 13:32).[95] His proposed solution to the logical problem is therefore to attribute two distinct 'belief-systems' or 'belief-acquisition systems' to Christ.[96] On this view, some of Christ's actions are performed on the basis of his divine belief-system, others on the basis of his human belief-system. The overall picture is of 'a divine consciousness and a human consciousness of God Incarnate, the former including the latter, but not conversely.'[97]

Swinburne does not develop and defend his dual-psychology model with the same degree of detail and thoroughness as Morris, but his treatment evidently has much in common with the latter's— including, it must be said, the same basic problem of incoherence. Swinburne wishes to distinguish between a divine consciousness and a human consciousness within one person; but as I have argued, such a distinction cannot be cogently drawn, given the logical primitiveness of our concept of a person.

The same criticism applies to any attempt to attribute conflicting belief-states to a single person. To his credit, Swinburne appears to recognise this latter point, advising that it would be more accurate to speak of 'beliefs' only with respect to Christ's *divine* perspective and mere 'belief-inclinations' with respect to his *human* perspective: insofar as his beliefs determined his actions, 'it would be those inclinations belonging to the human perspective which guided Christ's honest public statements (honest, because guided by those beliefs of which he is conscious in his human acting).'[98] However, such qualifications simply cannot do the work that Swinburne requires of them. Either Christ possessed genuine human beliefs (not mere *inclinations* to belief) or he did not. If he *did*, then those beliefs cannot have conflicted at any time with his divine beliefs (because beliefs are fundamentally ascribable to *persons,* and a person cannot exhibit contradictory belief-states). If he did *not*, then it is hard to see why Christ should be thought of as sharing our human condition in every relevant respect.

Likewise, Swinburne's defence of the honesty of Christ's public statements cannot be sustained, because for Jesus to be conscious only of *some* of his beliefs, he would have to be a logically distinct

---

95 Swinburne, *The Christian God*, 199-201.
96 Swinburne, *The Christian God*, 201-2.
97 Swinburne, *The Christian God*, 202.
98 Swinburne, *The Christian God*, 202-3.

person from the Son of God (who is presumably ever-conscious of all of his beliefs). The veracity of the Gospels would also be called into question on this revised understanding of Jesus' beliefs: Luke, for example, simply records that 'Jesus increased in wisdom', a claim that can hardly be reduced to a mere change in Jesus' professions or actions.

The dual-psychology interpretations of Morris and Swinburne, although *prima facie* plausible when explicated using analogies drawn from computing and psychology, must be judged on closer analysis to be indefensible—at least with respect to their purported avoidance of paradox. No amount of qualification or distinction can overcome the basic problem faced by non-kenotic Chalcedonian christologies, namely, that of attributing logically incompatible mental states to a single person.[99] Even if such treatments are successful in reconciling other divine and human attributes, I suggest that they face insurmountable conceptual difficulties with regard to those attributes pertaining to personal states of consciousness. Dual-psychology interpretations of the doctrine of the Incarnation ultimately disappoint in their promise to supply a non-paradoxical explication of Chalcedonian orthodoxy.[100]

---

99 It might be objected that the conclusions of Strawson's transcendental argument apply only to our concepts of *human* personhood, consciousness, belief states, and so forth; as such, they should not be pressed into use when speaking of *divine* personhood, consciousness, belief states, etc. Even if correct, such a reply would put defenders of a 'two minds' model in an equally undesirable predicament, for it would imply an equivocation in every key statement regarding Jesus' divine and human minds. Indeed, it would no longer be accurate to speak of it as a 'two minds' model, since we would not be distinguishing two things of the same kind at all!

100 A further defence of a dual-psychology interpretation can be found in Sturch, *The Word and the Christ*, 121-41. In my judgement, Sturch does not escape the objections I have raised against Morris and Swinburne. He appeals to the notion of a 'central self', according to which God the Son is aware that the human experiences of Jesus of Nazareth are also 'his own' experiences. But his account fails to alleviate the more fundamental problem of how one unified subject or 'central self' can possess seemingly contradictory mental states (e.g., awareness of X and lack of awareness of X) in the first place. It will not do to say that God the Son 'owns' Jesus' knowledge but not his ignorance! It is somewhat telling that Sturch appears to waver between a two-person christology and outright incoherence in later remarks on Jesus' divine self-awareness: 'Jesus the man cannot of Himself know that He is God in kenosis, even if He is; but others can. God the Son can, for one. (He cannot say "I am God in kenosis", but He can say, "This man is I, the Son, in kenosis".)' Sturch, *The Word and the Christ*, 259.

3.3.3 Concessions to Paradox

The kenotic and dual-psychology interpretations are without doubt the two most popular approaches to developing a non-paradoxical explication of the doctrine of the Incarnation along conservative lines. However, not all defenders of Chalcedonian christology have felt compelled to avoid paradox at all costs. In this last section, I review a selection of such writers.

No discussion of the paradoxicality of the Incarnation would be complete without reference to the work of the Scottish theologian, Donald Baillie. In his influential book *God Was In Christ*, Baillie states provocatively that the Incarnation 'presents us indeed with *the supreme paradox*, and I do not believe that we can ever eliminate from it the element of paradox without losing the Incarnation itself.'[101] For Baillie, paradox is inevitable in theological discourse 'because God cannot be comprehended in any human words or in any of the categories of our finite thought.'[102] Accordingly, he considers there to be multiple paradoxes in the Christian faith, although the paradox of God becoming man is the 'supreme' and 'central' instance.[103]

One finds in Baillie a striking example of a conservative Christian theologian emphatically and unashamedly affirming the paradoxicality of the doctrine of the Incarnation. However, it would be premature to appropriate his work as support for the apparently contradictory character of Chalcedonian christology, for two reasons: first, because Baillie does not locate the paradox in the same place as the other writers discussed in this chapter, viz. the seeming impossibility of one individual possessing both divine and human attributes; and second, because Baillie's own christology is arguably non-Chalcedonian.

For Baillie, the paradox of the Incarnation ultimately arises from *another* paradox in the Christian faith, namely, the 'paradox of

---

See also Richard Sturch, 'Inclusion and Incarnation: A Response to Bayne', *Religious Studies* 39.1 (2003), 103-6; Tim Bayne, 'Inclusion and Incarnation: A Reply to Sturch', *Religious Studies* 39.1 (2003), 107-9.

101 Baillie, *God Was In Christ*, 106, emphasis added.

102 Baillie, *God Was In Christ*, 108-9.

103 Baillie, *God Was In Christ*, 106, 110. Baillie's understanding of the term 'paradox' accords with the sense used throughout this thesis, namely, an apparent contradiction. Baillie makes clear that paradox arises 'not because the divine reality is self-contradictory' but because of the limitations of our human thought and language—a stance which accords with the model of paradox I defend in later chapters.

grace'.[104] The essence of this paradox 'lies in the conviction which a Christian man possesses, that every good thing in him, every good thing he does, is somehow not wrought by himself but by God.'[105] In short, the paradox is that on the Christian view, God takes full credit for our good deeds (even though we perform them freely and responsibly) while we are wholly culpable for our wrongdoings. How then does the paradox of the Incarnation derive from the paradox of grace? Just in this: Baillie wishes us to see Jesus Christ, the God-man, as the *supreme manifestation* of the paradox of grace—for in Christ, whose life consisted entirely of good deeds, the paradox of grace is lived out in a human being 'at the absolute degree'.[106]

Whatever the merits of Baillie's conception of the 'paradox of grace' and its relationship to the paradox of the Incarnation, it should be clear that he does not see the latter paradox as arising from the same theological constraints as those I identified earlier (for example, the biblical witness to the simultaneous omniscience and partial ignorance of Christ). Moreover, that Baillie's christology is at odds with Chalcedon should also be evident from his suggestion that the uniqueness of Christ among those in whom God works lies not in a difference of *kind* (i.e., that Jesus, unlike us, was essentially a *divine* person) but one of *degree* (i.e., that Jesus, unlike us, lived a perfect life and thus perfectly manifested the paradox of grace). If nothing else, the fact that John Hick—a persistent critic of Chalcedonian christology—considers his own 'metaphorical' view of the Incarnation to be of the same basic type as Baillie's should alert us to the questionable orthodoxy of his analysis of the person of Christ.[107]

Despite these problems, Baillie's interpretation of the doctrine of the Incarnation is far from irrelevant to the issues at hand. His discomfort with the traditional doctrines of *anhypostasia* and *enhypostasia*, and his embracing what ultimately amounts to a two-

---

104 Somewhat confusingly, Baillie explicates his notion of the 'paradox of grace' in a section entitled 'The Central Paradox'—despite having previously spoken of the Incarnation as the 'central' paradox of Christianity.

105 Baillie, *God Was In Christ*, 114.

106 Baillie, *God Was In Christ*, 129.

107 Hick, *The Metaphor of God Incarnate*, 106-10; see also Brown, *The Divine Trinity*, 234-39. The fundamental point of difference between Baillie and Chalcedon concerns the *personal identity* of Jesus of Nazareth and God the Son. As a result, Baillie's christology is closer in the final analysis to Nestorianism than to Chalcedonian orthodoxy, despite his disavowal of the former. Baillie, *God Was In Christ*, 89-91, 145, 152.

person view of Christ, further supports the argument of the previous section regarding the conceptual problem of reconciling a divine consciousness and a human consciousness in one person.[108]

Baillie fails to provide a genuine example of a theologian conceding the inevitable presence of paradox in Chalcedonian christology, but there are other writers who do represent such a stance. I have already noted the statement of Stephen Davis that the 'classical' interpretation of the Incarnation involves paradox. The biblical scholar, Charles Moule, in dialogue with the authors of *The Myth of God Incarnate*, admits that the biblical picture of Jesus Christ taken as a whole may well require the acceptance of paradox by the orthodox:

> Language which seems to recognize in Christ both the human and the divine may seem to constitute a threat to a fully personal conception of the relation of God to man; but if the data seem positively to require the recognition of a transcendent figure in Paul's experience, and the identification of this transcendent figure with the historical Jesus, *it may be that the paradox has to be accepted.*

> In the last analysis, this conflict concerns the question whether a fully theistic position does not necessitate a decisive distinction between the Creator and the created, and whether (despite this) the evidence from the beginnings of Christianity does not necessitate *a Christ who, paradoxically, is on both sides of that distinction.* It is a painful conflict. ... True, there is no merit in paradox for its own sake. True, paradox is sometimes grandly invoked when straight nonsense ought to be admitted to. It is a sacred duty for any thinking person to try to eliminate paradox. *But if the data refuse to let us escape a paradox, it may be necessary to entertain it.*[109]

Whilst not employing the specific term 'paradox', Karl Barth admits that the christology of Chalcedon faces apparently irresolvable logical difficulties:

---

108 One might wonder why Baillie should take such a rationalistic stance here, effectively rejecting traditional Chalcedonian christology on logical grounds, when he later enthusiastically embraces paradox in theology over against the 'rationalization' of Christian doctrines. Cf. Baillie, *God Was In Christ*, 131, 142, 144, 155.

109 Charles Moule, 'Three Points of Conflict in the Christological Debate', in Michael Goulder (ed.), *Incarnation and Myth: The Debate Continued* (London: SCM Press, 1979), 134, 140, emphasis added.

It is apparent at once that divine and human essence cannot be united as the essence of one and the same subject. Offence at the statement that Jesus Christ is the One who is of divine and human essence, in whom the two are united, is quite unavoidable. However we may define divine and human essence, unless we do violence either to the one or the other we can only define them (with all the regard we may have for the original divine reference of human essence) in a sharp distinction and even antithesis. *The statement that Jesus Christ is the One who is of divine and human essence dares to unite that which by definition cannot be united.*

Offence at the statement about the union of the two natures in Jesus Christ is unavoidable only for a thinking which is unconditionally bound by certain general presuppositions. This unconditional binding, whether by Church dogma or *general logic and metaphysics*, is not proper to *recta ratio*, to a thinking which is basically free. *Recta ratio* is reason as it is ready for the realism demanded of it in face of this object, and therefore free reason— free in relation to this object.[110]

Karl Rahner, meanwhile, maintains that the hypostatic union is one of the three *mysteria stricte dicta* of the Christian faith:

It is simply contradictory that something should belong completely to the order of creation, by being created, and still belong to the strictly divine order, by being strictly supernatural. Supernatural reality and reality brought about by a divine self-communication of quasi-formal, not efficient type, are identical concepts. Hence the possibility of such self-communication of God to the creature is what constitutes the theological mystery ... [It is a *mysterium stricte dictum*] because it is only through revelation (understood as salvific event and word in an indissoluble unity) that we can know that such a thing is actual and possible.[111]

Brian Hebblethwaite, commenting on the debate over *The Myth of God Incarnate*, does not shy away from talk of paradox:

It is certainly difficult, indeed paradoxical, to suppose that a human life lived out within the framework of first-century Jewish consciousness could actually be the incarnate life of God himself in one of the modes of his infinite and eternal being. ... [A]nd so it should be, if human words are to be used to precipitate our minds

---

110 *CD*, IV/1, 60-61, emphasis added. Barth treats the terms 'essence' and 'nature' as equivalent.

111 Karl Rahner, 'The Concept of Mystery in Catholic Theology', in *Theological Investigations*, Vol. 4 (London: Darton, Longman & Todd, 1966), 67.

beyond the natural into thought of the transcendent. ... It is not a matter of rejoicing in straight contradiction at the single mundane level of talk about two human individuals. The paradoxes are a sign that we have to stop thinking anthropomorphically; and they are a tool for thinking theologically about the one who cannot be 'comprehended' with clear-cut univocal terms.[112]

Similar admissions can be found in other writers.[113] The conviction that the doctrine of the Incarnation expressed in the ecumenical creeds is paradoxical and defies consistent formalisation is not restricted to its foes, but finds favour among its friends as well.

3.4 Conclusion

My aim in this chapter has been to assess whether the Christian doctrine of the Incarnation, interpreted in an orthodox fashion, is paradoxical in the sense that its metaphysical affirmations *appear* to be logically contradictory. After reviewing the historical development of the orthodox doctrine of the Incarnation, as expressed particularly in the Definition of Chalcedon and the Athanasian Creed, I concluded that deep-seated logical difficulties arise when these standards of orthodoxy are interpreted in light of the theological convictions of those who originally formulated them and the writings from which their phraseology is derived. I then turned to consider contemporary interpretations of the doctrine of the Incarnation from writers for whom alignment with credal orthodoxy was a significant concern, arguing that those interpretations purporting to avoid both paradox and heterodoxy inevitably fail on at least one of the two counts. Finally, I cited a selection of conservative theologians who concede that the doctrine of the Incarnation is a paradox.

At the end of the previous chapter, I invoked the image of a law court to underline the situation faced by orthodox trinitarianism. I

---

112 Brian Hebblethwaite, *The Incarnation: Collected Essays in Christology* (Cambridge: Cambridge University Press, 1987), 45-47.

113 Hazelton, 'The Nature of Christian Paradox', 326; Austin Farrer, *Saving Belief* (London: Hodder & Stoughton, 1964), 75-76; John Knox, *The Humanity and Divinity of Christ: A Study of Pattern in Christology* (Cambridge: Cambridge University Press, 1967), 99-100, 103-4; Dahms, 'How Reliable is Logic?', 272-73; Bloesch, *Essentials of Evangelical Theology*, 126-27, 134; Bartel, 'Why the Philosophical Problems of Chalcedonian Christology Have Not Gone Away'; John Macquarrie, *Christology Revisited* (Harrisburg: Trinity Press International, 1998), 17-21; Evans, 'The Self-Emptying of Love: Some Thoughts on Kenotic Christology', 272.

suggested that if the doctrine were to be placed in the dock and charged with the crime of apparent contradiction, each of the theologians considered during that investigation—despite their own expressed opinions on the guilt of the defendant—might well be called as a witness for the prosecution, for each one would testify (with good reason) that opposing interpretations of the doctrine are either theologically deficient, or apparently contradictory, or both. My assessment of the doctrine of the Incarnation in its historical development, credal definitions, and contemporary interpretations, indicates that it would face a comparable scenario were it to be put on trial for the same crime.

The kenotic theorists summoned to give testimony would charge defenders of dual-psychology interpretations with incoherence, while the latter would retort that the kenoticists had stepped outside the boundaries of orthodoxy. At the same time, numerous advocates of a traditional Chalcedonian interpretation would endorse *both* of these complaints, while the added testimony of various liberal scholars would leave the members of the jury with little doubt left in their minds.

As with the Trinity, so with the Incarnation. There appears to be no option for the Christian theologian but to grasp one or other horn of the dilemma: to abandon orthodoxy or to embrace paradox and thereby face the charge of irrationality. In the next chapter, I examine various strategies for handling such a dilemma.

CHAPTER 4

Responding to Paradox

4.1 Introduction

I have argued thus far that the Christian doctrines of the Trinity and the Incarnation are paradoxical; that is, they make claims which, taken in conjunction, appear to be logically inconsistent. This in itself is not a novel thesis. Others writers have made the same observation, many of whom have claimed as a consequence that Christians are irrational to believe these doctrines and other similarly paradoxical ones. In Part II, I will explicate and defend a model for Christian doctrinal belief according to which Christians can be rational in holding to doctrines such as these, their paradoxicality notwithstanding. Before doing so, however, it is incumbent upon me to consider various alternative approaches to dealing with the problem of paradoxes in Christian doctrine. I do not propose anything so ambitious as to refute decisively every alternative as a viable option; that would be an exceptional feat indeed in the arena of philosophical theology. Rather, I hope to explain why each approach is unattractive or problematic in important ways and therefore unsatisfactory as a general solution to the problem of theological paradox. If nothing else, this should prime the reader for a sympathetic consideration of the solution to be advocated later on, for my argument in the long run will be that this solution is less problematic than its competitors and thus to be preferred.

Before turning to consider each approach, it will be helpful to identify those logical and linguistic factors which give rise to the charge of irrationality in the first place. It will then be possible to categorise the various approaches I consider below according to (i) the factor or factors each one attempts to modify or eliminate so as to resolve the paradox, and (ii) how the proposed modification or elimination proceeds. By grouping strategies in this way, I hope to ensure that all relevant bases are being covered in my treatment of proffered solutions.

What factors combine to give rise to a genuine contradiction? The word 'contradict' derives from the Latin *contradicere*: literally, to *speak against* or *deny*. Naturally, there is nothing objectionable *per se* about speaking against or denying some proposition or claim; what is deemed unacceptable is for some person to speak against or deny some proposition *whilst also affirming* that same proposition. Such a practice is invariably viewed as the height of irrationality. This widespread conviction is expressed in the second of the three classical laws of thought, the principle of non-contradiction: no statement can be both true and false.[1] Accordingly, if S claims (or believes) that some proposition is both true and false (or alternatively, that some proposition and its negation are both true) then S is guilty of flagrant irrationality; likewise, any body of teaching which contains such a contradiction is deemed to be defective in that regard.

Although the basic concept of contradiction is straightforward, it is less clear that the doctrines treated in the previous chapters are guilty of contradiction in quite so blatant a manner. None of the ancient creeds state anything like 'There is only one God and there is not only one God' or 'Jesus Christ is fully divine and Jesus Christ is not fully divine'. Indeed, it is hardly plausible to think that the Christian faith would have endured and flourished to this day had it authorized such patently illogical statements of doctrine. It is therefore important to distinguish between three *types* of contradiction: *explicit* contradiction, *formal* contradiction, and *implicit* contradiction.[2] An *explicit* contradiction arises when one affirms both a proposition and its logical negation (e.g., 'The cat is on the mat' and 'It is not the case that the cat is on the mat'). A *formal* contradiction occurs when one affirms some set of propositions that includes no explicit contradiction but from which an explicit contradiction may be logically deduced (e.g., 'Harry is a Labrador', 'All Labradors are dogs', and 'Harry is not a dog').[3] Finally, a set of propositions is *implicitly* contradictory if and only if the addition of

---

1   Irving M. Copi and Carl Cohen, *Introduction to Logic* (Upper Saddle River, NJ: Prentice Hall, 10th edn, 1998), 389.

2   Alvin Plantinga, *God, Freedom and Evil* (London: Allen and Unwin, 1975), 12-16. Cf. Alvin Plantinga, *The Nature of Necessity* (Oxford: Clarendon Press, 1974), 164-65.

3   In this context 'logical deduction' would typically be taken as inferences validated by first-order logic with identity, although the choice of deductive system is rather a matter of convention. The division between cases of formal contradiction and cases of implicit contradiction is therefore not strictly defined.

one or more necessary truths yields a formal contradiction (e.g., 'The ball is red all over' and 'The ball is green all over').[4]

With these distinctions in mind, consider the two theological paradoxes on which I have focused. Although there are no *explicit* contradictions in the doctrines of the Trinity and the Incarnation, one might think that the doctrine of the Trinity seems to constitute a *formal* contradiction, since the statements involved in articulating it appear to yield an explicit contradiction merely on application of first-order logic with identity: for example, from 'The Father is God' and 'The Son is God' one can deduce 'The Father is the Son' (provided the copula in each case is interpreted as numerical identity).[5] Nevertheless, the trinitarian creeds nowhere state *explicitly* that numerical identity holds between the Godhead and each of the Father, Son, and Spirit (or, for that matter, that numerical non-identity holds between each pair of divine persons). My claim has been merely that numerical identity (or something very close) *seems* to be required between each *hypostasis* and the divine *ousia* when the creeds are interpreted so as to rule out heterodox views such as subordinationism and tritheism.

I suggest therefore that the type of contradiction, apparent or otherwise, involved in paradoxical Christian doctrines is best characterised as *implicit* contradiction. The problem is that certain statements of Christian doctrine seem to imply further claims that in turn explicitly contradict *other* statements of Christian doctrine (or certain natural implications of those statements). For example: while the Definition of Chalcedon may not explicitly state that Jesus *was* aware of everything (including the date of the Parousia) and also that Jesus *was not* aware of everything, it nonetheless appears to *imply* those very claims by virtue of the balanced christology its authors sought to articulate.

Given this understanding of the sense in which such doctrines are contradictory, it is obvious that one of the factors which invites the broader charge of irrationality is therefore *logic*: specifically, the logical law of non-contradiction and any other principles of inference that allow us to deduce further propositions from statements of Christian doctrine. Such laws of logic are considered to be canons of rationality: it is irrational to affirm sets of propositions that do not abide by those laws. However, in order to determine

---

4   In this example, the necessary truth would be something like, 'Nothing can be both red all over and green all over.'

5   Cf. Martinich, 'Identity and Trinity'; Richard Cartwright, 'On the Logical Problem of the Trinity', in *Philosophical Essays* (Cambridge, MA: MIT Press, 1987), 187-200; Tuggy, 'Trinitarian Theorizing'.

whether a contradiction has *in fact* arisen, one also needs to grasp just *what* propositions are being affirmed; in other words, the presence of a contradiction depends not only on logic but also on the *meaning* of the statements under consideration. For any set of doctrinal statements, one interpretation of those statements could involve an implicit contradiction whilst another interpretation might not.[6] The question of whether credal statements regarding the Trinity and the Incarnation are logically consistent thus depends on what one believes (or *ought* to believe) that those statements affirm.

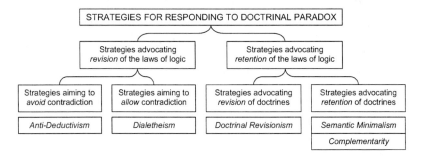

Figure 4.1

Given these paradox-generating factors, it is possible to distinguish two basic types of strategy for avoiding the charge of irrationality levelled at paradoxical Christian doctrines. The first type advocates some revision in our understanding of those *laws of logic* normally assumed to be canons of rationality. The second type, in contrast, assumes that all is well with logic and focuses instead on the *meaning* of the doctrinal statements in question. Moreover, these two basic types may be further subdivided. Within the first, there are strategies that aim to *avoid* contradiction and others that advise us to *allow* contradiction. Within the second, there are strategies that advocate *revision* of the doctrines in question (having accepted that the traditional interpretations are logically problematic) while others favour *retention* of those doctrines by arguing that traditional interpretations of the doctrinal statements do not mean anything that *necessarily* implies a contradiction. In the remainder of the chapter, I will examine examples of each of these four types of

6   For example, social trinitarians such as Cornelius Plantinga and Richard Swinburne claim that their interpretation of the Athanasian Creed is logically consistent, where other interpretations (e.g., the Augustinian reading) are not.

strategy for deflecting the charge of irrationality. (For an overview of the divided field, see Figure 4.1.) Before doing so, however, I wish to consider another type of approach altogether—one that both accepts the classical laws of logic *and* grants that some Christian doctrines do indeed violate these laws, but maintains nonetheless that this should be no cause for concern.

4.2 Theological Anti-Realism

The notion that objects of human experience and discourse—birds, bicycles, bridges, and the like—genuinely exist and have the properties they do independently of what we *think* or *state* about their existence and properties is commonly referred to as *realism*. This view is contrasted with *anti-realism*, which holds that the way the world exists actually depends, in some essential way, on our conceptualisation of the world.[7] In fact, anti-realists advise that talk of 'the real world' or 'the world as it actually exists' is altogether misguided, for the very notion is incoherent; the only reality to which we have epistemic access is one shaped and supported by the concepts and structures of our own thought and language.

Anti-realism of this type may be held either globally, with respect to *all* objects of thought or discourse, or more modestly, with respect to some particular domain of objects. Thus, a *scientific* anti-realist might hold that the kinds of entities referred to by physical theories (e.g., 'quarks') should not be thought of as enjoying any 'reality' or 'existence' other than that presupposed by the conventions of the language with which those theories are expressed. According to this position, when a quantum theorist states that 'a proton consists of three quarks', her words should not be taken to imply that such things as protons and quarks 'really exist'. Rather, the statement should be understood in a way that makes no 'naïve' ontological assumptions; perhaps something like, 'in the language of *quantum theory*, which physicists employ to describe and systematise the phenomena under their study, the sentence "a proton consists of three quarks" evaluates to *true*.'

Along similar lines, a *theological* anti-realism would hold that statements employing terms such as 'God' should not be thought of

---

7   The form of anti-realism I am considering here may be more precisely termed *alethic* realism so as to distinguish it from *metaphysical* realism. Used with respect to some type of entity (e.g., numbers, properties, propositions), the latter refers to the view that entities of that type really exist. Cf. William P. Alston, *A Realist Conception of Truth* (Ithaca, NY: Cornell University Press, 1996), 65-73.

as referring to some entity existing independently of our thought or language; *a fortiori* they should not be understood as ascribing certain properties or actions to any such entity. On the contrary, such talk serves quite another purpose: to express one's commitment to a certain community or way of life, perhaps, or to verbalise an attitude of worship. Anti-realism with respect to religious language has been advocated by a number of prominent contemporary theologians and has generated considerable interest and debate.[8]

It might be thought that theological anti-realism can offer a straightforward answer to the problem of paradox. Suppose that adherence to the Christian faith involves the affirmation of certain statements of doctrine that are implicitly contradictory. Why, given an *anti-realist* view of doctrine, should this be thought a serious problem? In making such statements Christians would not thereby be affirming that there 'really exists' some entity, God, who is both one and three in some inherently incompatible sense. They would not be making the metaphysical claim that some objective state of affairs, independent of our human minds, both obtains and does not obtain. In short, Christians would not be guilty of suggesting that some feature of reality is *actually contradictory*—for the simple reason that within the domain of theological language the idea of 'reality' being 'actually' anything is misguided from the outset.[9] On this view, the creeds and doctrines of Christianity are not making metaphysical claims at all; they serve quite another purpose altogether, such as providing an identifying badge for a particular community or set of religious practices.

---

8   For examples of a theologically anti-realist stance, see Don Cupitt, *The Sea of Faith* (London: BBC, 1984), 20, 265, 269; D. Z. Phillips, *Religion without Explanation* (Oxford: Blackwell, 1976), 100, 150, 169-81. Arguably the postliberalist school of thought, associated primarily with the work of Hans Frei and George Lindbeck, reflects an anti-realist (or at least *non*-realist) interpretation of Christian doctrine. According to such thinkers, doctrine is best thought of as the 'grammar' of Christian discourse; rather than making first-order truth claims about God, the world, etc., Christian doctrines make second-order claims about religious language, dictating what is and is not an acceptable way for the church to verbalise the gospel. For a typical exposition of this view, see Gerard Loughlin, 'The Basis and Authority of Doctrine', in Colin Gunton (ed.), *The Cambridge Companion to Christian Doctrine* (Cambridge: Cambridge University Press, 1997), 41-64.

9   As Phillips puts it, 'the confusion [of religious realism] resides in equating metaphysical and religious beliefs.' Phillips, *Religion without Explanation*, 100.

Although this route might seem attractive to some, it suffers from some serious drawbacks. First of all, it is not clear that it actually addresses the problem of paradox as I have constructed it. As I noted earlier, a contradiction pertains to a set of *statements*, not to *objects* or *states of affairs* (whether construed realistically or otherwise). So even if Christian doctrinal statements ought to be interpreted along anti-realist lines, it would remain true that such statements appear to violate those norms of logic and language relevant to their interpretation. In other words, an anti-realist's contradiction is a contradiction nonetheless; and a contradiction is generally thought of as rationally unacceptable. An enterprising anti-realist (taking a cue from Wittgenstein) might insist at this point that the Christian community has its *own* logical standards, according to which *some* contradictions are rationally legitimate. Although this move is consistent with anti-realist sentiments, the idea that different communities have different laws of logic raises a whole host of problems in itself.[10] In any case, the active ingredient of this augmented response is its *advocacy of alternative logic* rather than any basic anti-realist tenet (i.e., the denial of a mind-independent or language-independent reality) and, as such, it succumbs to the difficulties I discuss later in this chapter.

Secondly, and even more seriously, the anti-realist solution suffers from a crippling implausibility.[11] If modern anti-realist theologians wish to claim that when *they* recite (say) the Nicene Creed, they are merely identifying themselves with a certain group or lifestyle rather than confessing beliefs about some thought-independent reality, I am in no position to disagree. But it is hard to believe that the same holds for the average man or woman in the pew today—let alone the Apostles, the Fathers, and Christian believers throughout the centuries. I would wager that most Christians, if questioned on this point, would give a distinctly *realist* interpretation of their beliefs and confessions; they may be right or wrong about whether their purportedly mind-independent references actually obtain, but presumably they know best just what they *mean* by their own words. Hence, if the anti-realist solution is to succeed its advocates must argue either that, contrary to first impressions, Christian doctrines have historically been understood in an *anti-realist* sense or else that Christians should now *reinterpret* those doctrines so as to reflect an

---

10   James F. Harris, *Against Relativism* (Chicago & La Salle, IL: Open Court, 1992), 27-41; Ian Markham, *Truth and the Reality of God: An Essay in Natural Theology* (Edinburgh: T. & T. Clark, 1998), 57-65.

11   For a similar line of criticism, see Stephen T. Davis, *God, Reason and Theistic Proofs* (Edinburgh: Edinburgh University Press, 1997), 50-56.

anti-realist stance. The first option seems wildly optimistic; it would require showing, among other things, that the substance of the early trinitarian and christological debates was concerned not with theological metaphysics, as the history books would suggest, but merely with what grammar Christians should use to identify and distinguish themselves (or some similar linguistic concern).[12] The second option, on the other hand, amounts to *doctrinal revisionism*—a strategy for coping with paradox that is by no means unique to religious anti-realism and which suffers from problems of its own, as I will argue in due course.

For reasons such as these, theological anti-realism fails to provide a satisfying solution to the problem of paradox in Christian doctrines. It is doubtful whether it offers a unique answer to the problem; and even if it does, it is an answer that orthodox Christians will be disinclined to embrace, on both historical and religious grounds.

4.3 Anti-Deductivism

In this section and the following, I consider two strategies which propose to address the problem of paradox by challenging our commonsense understanding of the laws of logic. The first approach, which I will refer to as *anti-deductivism*, concedes that it is irrational to affirm contradictory statements (or to hold contradictory beliefs) but maintains that no contradiction arises from paradoxical doctrines such as the Trinity and the Incarnation because it is invalid to *deduce* from one doctrinal statement the negation of another statement.[13] For example, in the case of the doctrine of the Trinity,

---

12 Sarah Coakley has raised a number of objections to Richard Norris's thesis that the Definition of Chalcedon was merely an exercise in linguistic regulation, establishing a set of 'rules of predication'. Her criticisms could be applied equally well to postliberal readings of the other early creeds. Sarah Coakley, 'What Does Chalcedon Solve and What Does it Not? Some Reflections on the Status and Meaning of the Chalcedonian "Definition"', in Stephen T. Davis, Daniel Kendall, and Gerald O'Collins (eds), *The Incarnation: An Interdisciplinary Symposium on the Incarnation of the Son of God* (Oxford: Oxford University Press, 2002), 143-63.

13 While I have encountered numerous unsophisticated expressions of anti-deductivism in Christian circles, the only published defence of this position that I have uncovered is Kenneth L. Good, *Are Baptists Reformed?* (Lorain, OH: Regular Baptist Heritage Fellowship, 1986). Good's thesis is that the principle of 'good and necessary consequence' associated with the Reformed theological tradition, which he identifies with logical deduction,

the anti-deductivist would claim that the following argument is unsound:

(1)   The Father is God and the Father is not the Son.

(2)   If *a* is *b* and *a* is not *c*, then *c* is not *b*.

(3)   Therefore, the Son is not God.[14]

It is important to note that the anti-deductivist rejects this argument specifically as *invalid*; it is unsound not because any of the premises are false, but rather because the inference of (3) from (1) and (2) is erroneous. Moreover, the invalidity is due not to an equivocation of terms but to some formal law of inference being inapplicable in this case. The likely culprit here is the classical rule of *modus ponens*: if *p* then *q*; *p*, therefore *q*. In effect, the anti-deductivist is claiming that *modus ponens* is not universally applicable; for some *p* and *q*, the truth that *p* and the truth that *p* entails *q* do not together yield the truth of *q*. Once this door is opened, a general strategy for handling theological paradox emerges: whenever logical deductions from doctrinal statements lead to an explicit contradiction, one should conclude that this is one of those instances where the rules of deduction employed do not properly apply.

This is certainly a radical solution to the problem. There are few certainties in life, still less in philosophical theology, but elementary laws of logic such as *modus ponens* are usually considered to be among the best candidates. Psychologically speaking, at least, the rule of *modus ponens* strikes us as a self-evident, necessary truth. When we reflect on it, the phenomenology of that proposition (roughly, the way it 'feels' or 'strikes' us when considered) is indistinguishable from any other commonly accepted logical or mathematical truism; we cannot see how it could ever be false,

---

is at odds with a commitment to *sola scriptura*. In his view, Christian doctrine should consist solely of propositions explicitly stated in the Bible; logically deducing further propositions from that stock is tantamount to a rejection of the sufficiency of Scripture. The lack of enthusiasm for anti-deductivism among serious theologians is reflected in the relative brevity of my treatment here.

14   In these statements, each of the capitalized terms is a proper noun and the copula thus signifies the relation of numerical identity (the operative assumption being that while the relationship between each divine person and the divine essence may not be *equivalent* to that relation, it at least appears to *imply* such a relation). This interpretation of the doctrine of the Trinity accords with the conclusions of Chapter 2.

regardless of what propositions are represented by p and q.[15] Given the strength with which most people who have considered the matter hold *modus ponens* to be a necessary truth, not to mention the central role it plays in much of our everyday reasoning, it is hard to imagine any rational grounds strong enough to warrant abandoning that belief. So what grounds does the anti-deductivist propose? They are presumably twofold: (i) the necessary falsity of explicit contradictions and (ii) the truth of the doctrinal statements in question. Regarding the first, it is hard to see why it shouldn't be thought arbitrary to reject one apparent necessary truth on the basis of another apparent necessary truth. Why wouldn't one be as well to reject the necessary truth of the law of non-contradiction instead of the necessary truth of *modus ponens*, since both are known *a priori* if known at all and each exhibits much the same doxastic phenomenology as the other when reflected upon? Still more dubious, however, is the rejection of *modus ponens* in favour of (ii). Even granting a strong view of divine revelation through Scripture or tradition, it stretches credibility to breaking point to suppose that one's belief in Christian doctrines could be warranted to such a degree as to compel one to reject otherwise impeccable laws of deduction. If this approach could ever be justified, it must surely be considered a last resort.

Abandoning *modus ponens* would not come without a price. Laws of inference, being necessary truths, are known *a priori* if known at all.[16] Moreover, we are reassured about our belief in *modus ponens* by its phenomenology; all other considerations aside, it strikes us on reflection as being a necessary truth. Yet if we were to decide to reject its necessary truth, then the necessary truth of other propositions with the same phenomenology could easily be cast into doubt.[17]

---

15 For a discussion of the phenomenology of *a priori* necessary truths, see Alvin Plantinga, *Warrant and Proper Function* (Oxford: Oxford University Press, 1993), 103-8.

16 Necessary truths such as these cannot be known *a posteriori*, since no amount of 'positive confirmations' based on experience could ever warrant the judgement that some proposition is true *of necessity* rather than merely contingently. For a defence of *a priori* knowledge of necessary truths, see Laurence BonJour, *In Defense of Pure Reason: A Rationalist Account of A Priori Justification* (Cambridge: Cambridge University Press, 1998).

17 I am not suggesting that our knowledge of *a priori* truths is based upon their phenomenology, i.e., that they are justified or warranted via inference from some kind of doxastic experience. On the contrary, I hold that such beliefs are held basically, not inferentially. My point is a psychological one:

Furthermore, one might well wonder how far the exceptions to *modus ponens* extend. The anti-deductivist could insist that such exceptions are restricted to the domain of *theological* propositions, yet once the necessary truth of this rule of inference has been brought into question, it is difficult to see how one could justify such a restriction. Even on the assumption that it does, the validity of religiously significant inferences such as the following could no longer be taken for granted:

(4)   Whoever believes in the Son of God has eternal life.

(5)   I believe in the Son of God.

(6)   Therefore, I have eternal life.

Clearly the anti-deductivist needs to identify some principled way of distinguishing between valid and invalid inferences from theological propositions: between cases where *modus ponens* applies and cases where it does not, etc. Of course, any argument put forward for some particular criterion must scrupulously avoid begging the question by applying *modus ponens* (or its revised substitute) in an indiscriminate way.[18] Perhaps such a project can be accomplished. Nevertheless, its *prima facie* difficulty only serves to reinforce the conclusion that this strategy for defending paradox is altogether unappealing.

4.4 Dialetheism

The first of the two identified strategies for resolving the problem of paradox by revising our laws of logic—namely, the rejection of deductive rules such as *modus ponens*—does not seem at all promising. The second option is to reject the law of non-contradiction: the principle that no statement can be both true and false. Understandably, this approach is not a popular one among

---

assuming that I could bring myself to abandon belief in *modus ponens*, if I were thereafter to realise that its phenomenology had provided no assurance of its necessary truth then my assurance about the necessary truth of *other* beliefs with the same phenomenology would tend to be eroded, with potentially disastrous cognitive consequences.

18   Imagine that such an argument takes the following form: 'If X is the case, then *modus ponens* does not apply to propositions of type T. X is indeed the case; therefore, *modus ponens* does not apply to propositions of type T.' The argument itself employs *modus ponens*, either (a) in an unrestricted manner or (b) in the restricted form advocated by the anti-deductivist. But the anti-deductivist rejects (a) and cannot appeal to (b) without begging the question.

those attempting to address the problem of paradox in Christian theology, particularly those with a professed concern to preserve both rationality and orthodoxy. The comments of Thomas Morris typify the disdain of scholars for this escape route:

> It should, however, be clear that the strategy of defending the doctrine [of the Incarnation] by devaluing the status of logical consistency has very little to be said for it from a philosophical perspective. It is just a desperation move which embraces incoherence to avoid its sting.[19]

Even so, despite widespread disapproval the approach has been advocated by a handful of writers.[20] A relatively recent example is provided by John Dahms in an article challenging the 'unlimited applicability' of logic.[21] Dahms' article is of particular relevance because its author claims that his stance is motivated, at least in part, by the paradoxicality of certain central Christian doctrines. In what follows, I will explain why Dahms' specific proposal is

---

19 Morris, *The Logic of God Incarnate*, 25.
20 The most famous of which is often said to be Søren Kierkegaard. However, it is questionable whether Kierkegaard understood the paradoxes of the Christian faith to be actual logical contradictions. See C. Stephen Evans, *Faith Beyond Reason* (Edinburgh: Edinburgh University Press, 1998), 80-83. A more recent example may be provided by David Cunningham, who contends that theology 'should not be drawn into that realm of enterprises that must conform to the true/false dichotomies of Boolean logic.' Cunningham, *These Three are One*, 35-36. Elsewhere in the same volume, Cunningham seems inclined toward a form of anti-realism, suggesting as he does that while the Trinity is problematic in 'conceptual worlds such as arithmetic, formal logic, and analytic philosophy', there are nonetheless alternative conceptual schemes in terms of which threeness and oneness are not incompatible. Cunningham, *These Three are One*, 127. This suggests that there is no objective fact of the matter regarding the logicality of the Trinity; it all depends on how one thinks about it. I will not attempt to disentangle Cunningham's position here, since I argue that both anti-realism and dialetheism are inadequate responses to the trinitarian paradox; thus whichever approach Cunningham means to endorse, it is misguided.
21 Dahms, 'How Reliable is Logic?'. See also Norman L. Geisler, '"Avoid... Contradictions" (1 Timothy 6:20): A Reply to John Dahms', *Journal of the Evangelical Theological Society* 22.1 (1979), 55-65; John V. Dahms, 'A Trinitarian Epistemology Defended: A Rejoinder to Normal Geisler', *Journal of the Evangelical Theological Society* 22.2 (1979), 133-48; Norman L. Geisler, 'Avoid *All* Contradictions: A Surrejoinder to John Dahms', *Journal of the Evangelical Theological Society* 22.2 (1979), 149-59. My analysis of Dahms' thesis differs in significant respects from Geisler's.

unsatisfactory before turning to assess the general philosophical view that contradictions can be true.

Dahms introduces his case by explaining what he means by the term 'logic':

> The basic laws or principles of logic are commonly said to be three in number: the law of identity, the law of contradiction and the law of excluded middle. ... [T]hese three are at least the foremost of the laws of thought. Moreover, though the other two apparently cannot be derived from it, writers often mention the law of contradiction when they have logic generally in mind.[22]

Dahms notes that 'orthodox thinkers commonly believe that logic is of unlimited applicability'; for example, they believe that for *every* proposition *p*, it is not the case that *p* is both true and false.[23] In the remainder of his article, Dahms focuses primarily on the law of non-contradiction and argues, first, that there are good *non*-theological grounds for holding that the law is limited in its applicability, and second, that from a Christian perspective there are also good theological grounds for granting the truth of some contradictions.

Concerning the non-theological grounds for rejecting the unlimited applicability of logic, Dahms cites five reasons: (i) the problem of irrational numbers; (ii) Zeno's paradox of Achilles and the tortoise; (iii) apparent exceptions to the principle that 'according to logic the whole is equal to the sum of the parts'; (iv) the ethical problem according to which a virtuous action must be 'both determined and free, which is a contradiction'; and (v) apparent exceptions to logic in the realm of aesthetics (e.g., 'harmonic discord' in music).[24] Whether any of these amount to good reasons for rejecting the law of non-contradiction is debatable at best.[25] But

---

22 Dahms, 'How Reliable is Logic?', 369.

23 Dahms expresses the law of non-contradiction in terms of *things* rather than *propositions* or *statements*, e.g., 'nothing can be both *A* and not-*A*'. This difference does not affect my analysis, however, since on realist assumptions it follows from Dahms' characterisation that the statement '*X* is *A*' cannot be both true and false.

24 Dahms, 'How Reliable is Logic?', 370-72.

25 Indeed, Dahms' reasoning here seems plagued by confusions. For example, in his first argument he confuses *irrational* numbers (i.e., those which cannot be expressed as the division of one natural number by another) with *imaginary* numbers (i.e., those which can be expressed as the square root of a negative real number)—and in any case, the concept of irrational numbers has nothing to do with logical violations. Dahms thus fails to show why accepting irrational (or imaginary) numbers forces us to concede exceptions to any of the three classical laws of logic.

rather than engaging in a detailed critique of this part of Dahms' case, I propose instead to focus on his discussion of contradictions within *Christian theology*; for even if Dahms were right about accepting contradictions in *non*-theological areas, it would not immediately follow that he has offered a satisfactory solution to the problem of doctrinal paradox.

Turning to matters theological, Dahms writes:

> It is especially surprising that orthodox Christians should hold to the universal applicability of logic. Various doctrines of the faith provide problems for such a view.[26]

He cites four examples: (i) the fall of Satan (according to which, evil must derive from good); (ii) the biblical view of the cross (according to which, human sin is necessary to God and therefore ultimately good); (iii) the doctrine of the Incarnation; and (iv) the doctrine of the Trinity. In each case, Dahms suggests, the Christian who affirms these doctrines must thereby implicitly affirm some contradictory truth. Thus, 'it ought to be quite clear that the doctrines of historic Christianity are not always compatible with the law of contradiction.'[27]

I will not contest Dahms' claim that these four Christian doctrines are paradoxical (i.e., at least *apparently* contradictory); indeed, I have already indicated substantial agreement regarding his third and fourth examples. The relevant question is whether Dahms' recommendation that Christians revise their understanding of the law of non-contradiction constitutes a satisfactory solution to the problem. A number of objections immediately suggest themselves.

First, as I observed in the preceding section, elementary principles of logic are intuitively held to be necessary truths with a high degree of certainty: *psychological* certainty, at the very least, if not *rational* certainty (as many epistemologists would insist). As with *modus ponens*, so with the law of non-contradiction: it lacks plausibility to claim that doctrinal statements, however well supported, could be warranted to such a degree as to justify abandoning belief in these intuitive laws of logic. Dahms might counter that the Christian's policy for belief revision should be contextualized by the particular religious convictions and faith commitments of the church community; but whether or not this line would persuade Christian scholars, it hardly satisfies as a response to the extra-mural charge that orthodox Christian beliefs are irrational.

---

26 Dahms, 'How Reliable is Logic?', 372.
27 Dahms, 'How Reliable is Logic?', 375.

Secondly, it might be objected that Dahms' position is self-refuting since, as he himself concedes, he has *assumed* the laws of logic by way of *arguing* for their limited applicability:

> It is to be emphasized that we have not stated that logic is valueless, only that it is not always applicable. Logical argumentation is frequent in the Bible. Logic was one of the things that made it possible to put men on the moon. We have used logic in this paper.[28]

Although this objection might initially seem decisive, matters are not so straightforward. For while Dahms has clearly assumed *some* logical principles—he would presumably insist that his arguments are valid and his stated conclusions about the use of logic are not both true and false—it is difficult to show that he has assumed the *unlimited applicability* of the laws of logic. However suspicious, it is entirely consistent with Dahm's thesis to maintain that logic applies to the statements contained within his article, but not to certain other statements.[29] One might then object that it is incumbent on Dahms to provide and justify some set of criteria, which can be reliably and concretely applied, so as to distinguish those instances where logic is applicable from those where it is not. As it turns out, Dahms anticipates this obligation and proposes the following rule of demarcation:

> It would appear that [logic] is thoroughly reliable when dealing with the nominal (being) but not when dealing with the verbal (becoming) or the aesthetic. Our reliance on logic in this paper is justified by the fact that we only use it of the existential and the aesthetic when we are considering them in the abstract.[30]

It is not wholly clear what distinctions Dahms means to draw with his categories of 'nominal', 'verbal', and 'aesthetic'. The idea seems to be, roughly, that the following claims hold:

(7) Logic is always applicable to statements describing some *static* state of affairs (e.g., 'God is good') but not to statements describing some *dynamic* state of affairs (e.g., 'the Spirit proceeds from the Father') or expressing some *aesthetic* judgement.

---

28 Dahms, 'How Reliable is Logic?', 375.
29 Indeed, this is Dahms' own defence against Geisler's charge of self-defeat. Dahms, 'A Trinitarian Epistemology Defended', 141-42.
30 Dahms, 'How Reliable is Logic?', 378.

(8) Logic is always applicable to statements concerned with any of these three areas *in the abstract*—in other words, statements about the statements referred to in (7).

Regardless of how Dahms' distinctions cash out, his position (and variations on the same theme) can be expressed more generally as follows:

(9) The law of non-contradiction applies to all statements except those concerned *non-abstractly* with subject matter *M*.

The qualifier *non-abstractly* is essential to avoid self-refutation. Although (9) itself is concerned with subject matter *M*, it is only concerned with *M* in the abstract. One who affirms (9) is not thereby committed to holding that the law of non-contradiction does not apply to (9) and hence is not vulnerable to the objection that the *negation* of (9) cannot be excluded.

This general position on the limited applicability of the law of non-contradiction may be immune to a straightforward *reductio ad absurdum*, but I suggest that it is untenable because the criterion it recommends cannot be applied in practice. If the stance expressed by (9) is to be viable, then it must be possible for one to judge, for any statement *S*, whether or not *S* is concerned non-abstractly with subject matter *M* (whatever *M* may be). However, in order to determine that *S* is concerned non-abstractly with *M*, one must also be able to judge whether or not claims of the following two forms are true (where *X* identifies some non-linguistic, non-conceptual item, e.g., Socrates, the Atlantic Ocean, or my favourite shirt):

(10) *S* is about *X*.

(11) *X* falls under subject matter *M*.

It should be evident, however, that if both (10) and (11) *are* true, then they are both concerned non-abstractly with subject matter *M* (since they are both direct statements about *X*). Therefore, according to (9), it is possible for (10) to be both true and false and likewise for (11). But if that is so, then one cannot make a reliable judgement about whether (10) and (11) are true or not—and thus one cannot make a reliable judgement about whether or not *S* is concerned non-abstractly with *M*.

If we consider Dahms' position as a specific instance of (9), we can see how this cashes out in practice. Consider the claim, 'Madrid is in Spain.' Does the law of non-contradiction apply to this statement? As a precondition of answering this question, it must be possible in principle to judge (i) that the statement is about Madrid and (ii) that

Madrid falls under either the verbal or the aesthetic.[31] Yet if Madrid *does* fall under either the verbal or the aesthetic then, on Dahms' view, judgements (i) and (ii) are not subject to the law of non-contradiction, in which case they could be false as well as true. And if one cannot establish that both (i) and (ii) are not false, then one could never *in principle* determine that the law of non-contradiction is not applicable to the claim 'Madrid is in Spain'—or to any other non-abstract claim.

It appears that Dahms' thesis that logic applies only to statements concerned with particular subject matters cannot be observed in practice, even if correct in theory. Nevertheless, the general thesis that some contradictions can be true, irrespective of subject matter, has been seriously considered and competently defended by a number of philosophers in the last two decades. This view, dubbed *dialetheism* by Graham Priest and Richard Routley, holds that there are true contradictions; that is, there are statements that are both true and false.[32] The paradigm example of a *dialetheia* is the so-called Liar paradox:

(12) This sentence is not true.

Is (12) true or not? If it is *true*, then (by its own testimony) it must be *not true*; but if it is *not true*, then it must be *true* (since what it says to be the case *is* the case). The Liar paradox has proven remarkably resistant to explanations as to why it does not force us to concede that some statements are both true and false (and thus that some contradictions are true).[33] Self-referential paradoxes of this kind have been taken by some philosophers as a compelling reason for embracing dialetheism.[34]

---

31 I am not claiming that these judgements must always be consciously made when evaluating the applicability of logic to the target statement; my claim is merely that if these judgements could not be reliably made *in principle* then neither can the overall evaluation of the target statement.

32 Graham Priest, Richard Routley, and Jean Norman (eds), *Paraconsistent Logic: Essays on the Inconsistent* (Munich: Philosophia Verlag, 1989), xx. This neologism is a compound of the Greek words for 'two' and 'truth'. A *dialetheia* is thus a 'two-way truth': a statement that evaluates to both true and false.

33 For an analysis of attempts to resolve the Liar paradox and its close relatives, see R. M. Sainsbury, *Paradoxes* (Cambridge: Cambridge University Press, 2nd edn, 1995), 107-29; Rescher, *Paradoxes*, 193-215.

34 Sainsbury, *Paradoxes*, 135; Priest, Routley, and Norman (eds), *Paraconsistent Logic*, 503-10. Dialetheism has also been advocated on the basis of *theological* considerations; in this respect, Dahms is preceded by Peter Damiani,

Dialetheism itself is surprisingly difficult to refute, not least because attempted refutations frequently presuppose the principle they purport to prove, viz. that no statement can be both true and false. Similarly, objections based on the principle that anything whatsoever can be inferred from a contradiction (*ex contradictione quodlibet*, as the Scholastic maxim put it) fail to unseat the dialetheist since they merely take for granted a classical rule of inference which (as Priest has shown) can be rejected without any intolerable consequences. The persistent dialetheist will cheerfully advocate a paraconsistent logic in place of classical logic so as to avoid the spectre of 'logical explosion'.

Another argument sometimes raised against dialetheism runs as follows. A statement is only meaningful if it rules something out; but if the law of non-contradiction does not hold, then no statement automatically rules out its negation or, *a fortiori*, any other statement; therefore, the meaningfulness of language presupposes the law of non-contradiction. In reply, the dialetheist can point out that the statement 'everything is true' is clearly meaningful (even if obviously false) and yet it rules nothing out (by virtue of ruling everything in).

After sympathetically considering the various objections levelled at dialetheism, R. M. Sainsbury laments:

> With some distress, I come to the conclusion that none of the objections I review ought to force a resourceful rational dialetheist to admit defeat.[35]

However distressing this conclusion, it would seem to be a fair assessment of the debate. As such, it would be foolhardy for me to attempt a decisive refutation of dialetheism *simpliciter*, when others better equipped and more determined have failed. Nevertheless, it should not be thought that this concession thereby opens the door to embracing dialetheism as a satisfactory solution to the problem of paradox in Christian theology. On the contrary, I suggest that there are at least three good reasons for rejecting this *application* of dialetheism: two are of considerable weight, while the third is weightier still.[36]

Meister Eckhart, and Nicholas of Cusa. Priest, Routley, and Norman (eds), *Paraconsistent Logic*, 18-20.

35 Sainsbury, *Paradoxes*, 136.

36 It should be noted that all three points count also against the 'limited applicability' thesis of Dahms, in addition to the specific objections raised earlier.

The first is simply this: theological dialetheism has the odd consequence that God believes some falsehoods (about God, no less) and invites us to do likewise. This criticism may not be decisive, but it seems hard to reconcile this outcome with the biblical emphasis on promoting truth and eschewing untruth (e.g., Ps. 52:3; Eph. 4:25; 1 John 4:6).

The second reason is the observation, made several times previously, that the law of non-contradiction enjoys considerable *prima facie* support by way of the phenomenology and ubiquity of belief in it. If nothing else, this indicates that a rejection of the law should serve only as a last resort in attempting to address the problem of paradox. Moreover, this solution is likely to endear itself only to those standing *within* the Christian faith (and even then will be deemed a bitter pill). As a defensive strategy to counter the charge of irrationality levelled at Christian doctrines, it lacks plausibility and smacks of special pleading.

The third argument for rejecting theological dialetheism runs as follows. If dialetheism were to be adopted by Christians as a response to the problem of paradox in doctrines such as the Trinity and the Incarnation, then presumably the desire to preserve an orthodox interpretation of those doctrines would feature as a significant motivation. After all, if one were unconcerned about maintaining orthodoxy, then one would be more inclined to revise or reject the problematic doctrines themselves than the laws of logic. Yet for believers such as these, embracing dialetheism would have a direct and quite unacceptable consequence, namely, that *one could no longer object to heterodox theological statements*. For example, an orthodox explication of the doctrine of the Trinity would likely include the following statements:

(13) The Father is God.

(14) The Son is God.

(15) The Father is not the Son.

The paradox arises because on the most natural interpretation, the conjunction of (13) and (14) implies the *negation* of (15). Now, the Christian dialetheist would presumably concede this entailment but would argue that affirming (13), (14) and (15) is not irrational because *some* contradictions are *true*—including, one assumes, the following contradictory statement:

(16) The Father is not the Son and the Father is the Son.

However, even on a paraconsistent logic such as that preferred by the dialetheist, one can logically infer from (16) this heterodox modalist claim:[37]

(17) The Father is the Son.

The problem is obvious: advocating dialetheism in order to preserve orthodoxy ironically ends up making its preservation *irrelevant,* since it involves the joint affirmation of both orthodox and heterodox theological claims. It should go without saying that this solution would hardly have appealed to those Christian thinkers who were responsible for forging statements of orthodox doctrine in the fires of the trinitarian and christological controversies. It follows on a theological dialetheist view that these debates were all so much wasted breath: Athanasius and Arius should simply have concluded that they were *both* right about the deity of Christ, in spite of the logical incompatibility of their views; likewise Cyril and Nestorius on the relationship between Jesus and the Logos. As a solution to the problem of paradox, dialetheism only saves rationality at the expense of trivialising orthodoxy.

4.5 Doctrinal Revisionism

As a solution to the problem of paradoxical Christian doctrines, revising the laws of logic—either standard rules of inference such as *modus ponens* or classical laws such as the principle of non-contradiction—is a highly unsatisfactory strategy. If justifiable at all, it must remain a last refuge. This conviction appears to be shared by the considerable majority of theologians and philosophers. In the remainder of this chapter, I therefore turn to consider instances of the second basic type of strategy: responses to paradox which focus on the *meaning* of doctrinal statements, rather than the logical relations obtaining between them. The first of these strategies, which I will call *doctrinal revisionism,* maintains that the best response to the problem of paradox is to revise the offending doctrines so as to avoid all discernible elements of logical contradiction. This revision involves not merely a *clarification* or a *refinement* of the traditional statements of the doctrine, but rather a *rejection* of at least some of those statements (as originally intended) in favour of alternative statements.[38]

---

37 The rule of inference in question, one shared by classical and paraconsistent logics, is the 'Rule of Simplification': p and q, therefore q.

38 For typical examples of doctrinal revisionism with respect to the doctrines of the Trinity and the Incarnation, see Buzzard and Hunting, *The Doctrine of*

For those Christian theologians and philosophers who acknowledge the charge of contradiction levelled at Christian doctrines and attempt to defend the rationality of those doctrines without questioning the laws of logic, doctrinal revisionism is not easily embraced. Across the board, there is a desire to retain where possible the traditional formulations and interpretations of doctrines, especially those stated in the ecumenical creeds and considered historically to express the boundaries of orthodoxy.[39] What accounts for this sentiment? It is due in part, one suspects, to the conserving principle that tradition should be respected and given the benefit of the doubt. This tendency is not merely a psychological phenomenon, nothing more than a consequence of peer pressure and the natural human inclination to avoid attracting alienating labels such as 'heterodox' or 'heretical'. On the contrary, this is a perfectly rational policy, generally speaking, since tradition is precisely that which has been considered worth handing down (Latin: *traducere*) from one generation to the next because it represents the culmination of the wisdom of our predecessors. If certain beliefs or claims have survived the scrutiny of previous scholars within one's religious community, then they arguably merit *prima facie* acceptance. Given this perspective on the rationality of retaining traditions, it follows that the classical doctrines of the Christian faith ought not to be abandoned unless there is very good reason to do so.

Still, it is also eminently reasonable to suppose that the logical incoherence of traditional doctrines is just the sort of good reason that *would* warrant revision of those doctrines. The bare fact that

the Trinity: *Christianity's Self-Inflicted Wound*, and Hick (ed.), *The Myth of God Incarnate*. In a recent article on the Trinity, Dale Tuggy makes a plea for doctrinal revision in the face of paradox: Tuggy, 'Trinitarian Theorizing', 178-80. (Cf. Tuggy, 'Tradition and Believability', 454-55, where he argues that the Athanasian Creed should not be endorsed by Christians on account of its apparent self-contradiction.) To be fair, Tuggy thinks that his recommended revision is compatible with Scripture and a certain reading of the Nicene Creed. For a direct response to his proposal, see James N. Anderson, 'In Defence of Mystery: A Reply to Dale Tuggy', *Religious Studies* 41.2 (2005), 145-63.

39 Examples include Davis, *Logic and the Nature of God*, 1-3, 118; Hill, *The Three-Personed God*, xi-xii; Morris, *The Logic of God Incarnate*, 16, 44; Plantinga, 'The Threeness/Oneness Problem', 40-41; Swinburne, *The Christian God*, 180-91; van Inwagen, 'And Yet They Are Not Three Gods But One God', 245-46; Peter van Inwagen, 'Not by Confusion of Substance, but by Unity of Person', in Alan G. Padgett (ed.), *Reason and the Christian Religion* (Oxford: Clarendon, 1994), 205-7.

those doctrines are part of a religious tradition is not *in itself* sufficient to overturn the force of sheer logic. Nevertheless, I wish to argue that there are two weighty reasons—considerations that arguably go hand in hand with the notion of tradition—for Christians to strongly resist the temptation to revise paradoxical doctrines and to seek instead a less radical solution to the problem.

The first reason pertains to the question of *authority*. Christian doctrines, particularly those featuring in the ecumenical creeds, are normally thought—by Christian believers, at any rate—to enjoy some kind of authority: if not a *moral* authority (e.g., 'It is obligatory to believe X') then at least a significant degree of *epistemic* authority (e.g., 'It is reasonable to believe X').[40] The details of how such authority arises diverge across denominational lines, but the issue is invariably tied up with the notion of divine revelation through some specified channel or channels.[41] Protestants have historically held that the authority possessed by Christian creeds and other doctrines is a *derivative* one: a particular creed or teaching is deemed to be authoritative insofar as it faithfully expresses the affirmations of Scripture, which is itself taken to be supremely authoritative by virtue of being divinely inspired. For Roman Catholics, the relevant authority is invested supremely in the church (specifically the papacy and the council of bishops) as the preserver and interpreter of Scripture and tradition,[42] while in Eastern Orthodoxy the authority of the church's doctrines ultimately resides in various forms of ecclesiastical tradition (pre-eminently the Bible, the Niceno-Constantinopolitan Creed, and the decrees of the ecumenical councils).[43] According to Catholicism and Orthodoxy, the authority possessed by certain doctrines (such as those of the Trinity and the Incarnation) is not derivative but original, arising by virtue of the ecclesiastical source of the teaching. Whatever the differences here, however, it is clear that the notion of religious authority, grounded in divine revelation, stands behind the formulation and propagation of Christian doctrines throughout the history of the church. As a

---

40 As examples of the stronger claim of moral authority, consider (i) the first and last statements of the Athanasian Creed and (ii) canons 750-754 of the 1983 Code of Canon Law (*Codex Iuris Canonici*).

41 To use the Scholastic terminology: there is agreement across all traditions regarding the *principium essendi*, but fundamental disagreement between traditions over the *principium cognoscendi*.

42 J. L. Allgeier, 'Teaching Authority of the Church (Magisterium)', in *New Catholic Encyclopedia*, Vol. 13 (New York: McGraw-Hill, 1967), 959-65.

43 Ware, *The Orthodox Church*, 196-97.

consequence, the credibility of those doctrines is inextricably bound up with the credibility of the religious authority in question.

This situation poses a considerable problem for the doctrinal revisionist. Suppose a certain traditional doctrine *D* is deemed to be unacceptable due to apparent logical contradiction and therefore replaced with another doctrine *D'* (presumably close to the original but substantially modified so as to eliminate the logical difficulties). This is not merely a matter of adjusting one doctrine among many so as to improve the overall epistemic health of one's belief system. On the contrary, the abandonment of the original doctrine *D* will have serious ramifications for the status of *other* doctrines—perhaps for all of them. For if *D* was previously held on the basis of some religious authority, then the *rejection* of *D* amounts to bringing that authority into question, thereby bringing into question every other doctrine held on the basis of that same authority. Thus, for example, if a Protestant believer were to hold that the Niceno-Constantinopolitan doctrine of the Trinity is authoritative because it faithfully expresses God's self-revelation in Scripture, but later were to reject that doctrine on account of its apparent incoherence, she ought to conclude that Scripture is in some sense defective and misleading as a channel of God's self-revelation; moreover, the authority of every other doctrine held on the basis of its biblical support would subsequently be subject to doubt.[44]

In addition to the questioning of the religious authority on which the traditional (but paradoxical) doctrines are based, the doctrinal revisionist must also be asked on what basis the *revised* doctrines should be considered authoritative—if at all.[45] If no adequate alternative ground can be provided, one might as well conclude that eschewing doctrine altogether is the most reasonable course. Now perhaps an adequate religious authority *can* be found as an alternative to that on which the traditional Christian doctrines are based; my claim here is not that the task is impossible but that it is

---

44 The alternative, of course, would be for her to abandon the belief that the ecumenical creeds are a faithful expression of scriptural revelation. But this hardly alleviates matters, since it raises further questions about biblical perspicuity and ecclesiastical identity (see below).

45 Natural reason might be considered one such basis. Swinburne, for example, has formulated an *a priori* argument for the doctrine of the Trinity (given the truth of theism). Swinburne, *The Christian God*, 170-80. Even so, he acknowledges the tentativeness of his conclusions, and in any case, it is hardly plausible to suggest that *all* of the orthodox doctrines of the Christian faith could be established in this manner.

surely a tall order, which thus explains the unattractiveness of doctrinal revisionism.

A second reason why the revision of orthodox Christian doctrines should be avoided if possible concerns the *identity* of a religious body or community. The Christian church is a society—a very special society, no doubt, but a society nonetheless. As such, it possesses a certain identity and there must be corresponding criteria by which it can (at least in principle) be identified and recognised to be the same society as one existing previously. Indeed, the basic contention of any present-day claimant to the title of 'Christian church'—be it Protestant, Roman Catholic, Eastern Orthodox, or otherwise—is that it stands at the end of a historical line of continuity, defined in terms of societal identity, which can be traced back to the original institution established by Christ and the apostles.

What then are the criteria by which a society may be identified? Swinburne plausibly argues that there are two: continuity of *aim* and continuity of *organization*.[46] Moreover, with respect to *ecclesiastical* identity, fulfilment of the first criterion 'is dictated by continuity of doctrine.'[47] Substantial continuity of doctrine, with respect to the apostolic church, is therefore a necessary condition for a present-day religious body being considered part of the Christian church: 'The teaching of a body wildly out of line with the teaching of all earlier Christian bodies with which it can claim any continuity of organization cannot be the Church.'[48]

Clearly not just *any* doctrinal discontinuity is sufficient to disqualify a religious body from claiming continuity with the apostolic church. If a local congregation were to modify its statement of belief on some relatively minor point of eschatology, say, it would not thereby cease to be part of the Christian church. However, matters are rather more serious when the discontinuity in question concerns those teachings that have historically been held as central to the faith—in particular, those expressed in the early creeds—and

---

46 Richard Swinburne, *Revelation: From Metaphor to Analogy* (Oxford: Clarendon Press, 1992), 120-22.

47 Swinburne, *Revelation*, 123. Alister McGrath makes essentially the same point: 'Doctrine defines communities of discourse, possessing a representative character, attempting to describe or prescribe the beliefs of a community. ... Doctrine may thus be provisionally defined as communally authoritative teachings regarded as essential to the identity of the Christian community.' Alister E. McGrath, *The Genesis of Doctrine: A Study in the Foundations of Doctrinal Criticism* (Oxford: Basil Blackwell, 1990), 10-13.

48 Swinburne, *Revelation*, 124.

evidently this presents a difficulty for the doctrinal revisionist. Would a religious body that opts to revise the orthodox doctrine of the Trinity still qualify as part of the 'one holy catholic and apostolic church'? Would a denomination that resolves to reject the orthodox doctrine of the Incarnation in favour of a less logically problematic alternative still be entitled to label itself 'Christian'? If the answer to such questions is yes, then one has to question whether doctrine should be thought to play any role *at all* in the identity of the church.

Perhaps, though, there is some room for manoeuvre even with respect to such central Christian doctrines as the Trinity and the Incarnation. A believer standing in the Protestant tradition might argue, for instance, that the creeds are valuable but fallible, being always subject to revision in the light of Scripture.[49] In any case, the two objections I have raised here, however significant, should not be extrapolated into the dogmatic claim that any ecclesiastical body rejecting the interpretations of Christian doctrine defended in the previous two chapters clearly stands outside the boundaries of the Christian church. But the point should be clear: one does well to avoid pushing the envelope of Christian orthodoxy. Doctrinal revisionism is a path over unstable ground, theologically speaking, and its advocates should be prepared to accept that their proposals could well involve nothing less than a change of religious identity.

I conclude that doctrinal revisionism, whilst perhaps a suitable strategy for dealing with paradox in more peripheral doctrines, is far from satisfactory as a wholesale solution. It may offer a last resort for those who privilege logical orthodoxy over theological orthodoxy, but any approach that promises to preserve *both* desiderata is naturally to be preferred.

4.6 Semantic Minimalism

For those reluctant to abandon a traditional Christian doctrine on account of its paradoxicality, a more attractive option might be to argue instead that even on an orthodox interpretation the doctrine need not *necessarily* involve actual logical contradiction. There are several ways of mounting such an argument; in this section, I assess a particular strategy that I will call (for want of a better label)

---

49 For those standing in the Roman Catholic and Eastern Orthodox traditions, matters are somewhat more restrictive. Even so, the overwhelming consensus within the Protestant tradition has been that the trinitarian and christological doctrines expressed in the ecumenical creeds are indeed accurate expressions of the biblical witness.

semantic minimalism.[50] According to the semantic minimalist, the interpretations of the doctrines of the Trinity and of the Incarnation for which I have argued in the previous two chapters are *excessively meaningful*; they attribute too much semantic content to the doctrinal statements in question and in so doing needlessly give rise to implicit logical contradictions. Rectifying the problem is thus straightforward: the proper policy of the Christian theologian should be to ascribe only the *minimum* of semantic content to those doctrinal statements, so as to avoid inviting the charge of apparent contradiction in the first place. No more content should be ascribed to statements of Christian orthodoxy, such as the Nicene Creed and Athanasian Creed, than is absolutely necessary to maintain their functions *as* statements of orthodoxy. On this view, if a certain doctrine of the Christian faith appears contradictory to some person then the fault lies with the person, rather than the doctrine, for investing excessive meaning in the statements of that doctrine.

Before considering various ways in which a semantic minimalist view might be articulated, I should specify just what it might mean, in the present context, to ascribe 'too much' semantic content to a statement. For the purpose of characterising (and later criticising) the response of the semantic minimalist, we can explicate the meaning or content of a doctrinal statement in terms of *possible world semantics.*[51] A possible world may be defined as a *maximally consistent state of affairs*, that is, a state of affairs to which no further state of affairs can be conjoined without logical inconsistency.[52] Expressed in terms of possible worlds, the content of a doctrinal statement can be thought of as the set of worlds in which that statement is *true* and the set of worlds in which it is *false.*[53] So, for example, the content of the statement 'God created the world' is defined as the set of possible worlds in which God created the world

---

50 While I have encountered variations of this position in conversation with Christian academics, I can find no scholarly defence of the strategy in print. Nonetheless, I believe that it has a *prima facie* plausibility that makes it worth acknowledging and assessing here. Sarah Coakley seems to gesture in this direction, with her defence of a moderate apophatic reading of the Definition of Chalcedon and her suggestion that defenders of the coherence of the Incarnation (such as Morris, Brown, and Swinburne) who are concerned to take the Definition 'literally' may have read too much into its statements. Coakley, 'What Does Chalcedon Solve and What Does it Not?'.

51 Cf. Sainsbury, *Paradoxes*, 137.

52 Cf. Plantinga, *The Nature of Necessity*, 44-45.

53 On the assumption that dialetheism is false, these two sets will always be disjoint. Sainsbury, *Paradoxes*, 137.

along with the set of possible worlds in which he did not (because in those worlds either God does not exist, or the world does not exist, or both exist but the latter is not created by the former).

One important qualification is in order, however. The notion of consistency employed in our definition of a possible world must be that associated with *strict* or *narrow* logical consistency, rather than *broad* logical consistency;[54] in other words, it must be a consistency defined in terms of formal logic alone without any reference to *metaphysical* necessities or possibilities (if indeed there are such things). Otherwise, all doctrinal statements deemed to express metaphysically necessary truths—for example, claims about God's triunity—would, on this understanding of content, have *identical* content (namely, the set of all possible worlds paired with the empty set).

With this scheme in hand, it is a relatively easy task to explicate the notion of 'excessive semantic content': to ascribe too much content to a doctrinal statement would be to suppose that the first set of worlds (those in which that statement evaluates to true) is *smaller* than it really is and that the second set is *larger* than it really is. It amounts to supposing that the statement 'rules out' more states of affairs than it actually does.[55]

Let us now turn to consider some ways in which doctrinal semantic minimalism might be plausibly expressed. A first candidate would be something akin to the theological method of *apophasis*—a view of religious language with a respectable historical pedigree—according to which our statements about God can only assert what he *is not* and never what he *is*. As traditionally understood, apophasis is primarily concerned with predicating qualities of God, such as 'wisdom' and 'goodness'; thus to make statements such as 'God is wise' and 'God is good' is to do nothing

---

54 Cf. Plantinga, *The Nature of Necessity*, 1-2.

55 Readers familiar with contemporary philosophy of language will recognise that I am focusing exclusively on the *extensional* aspects of declarative content and ignoring any *intensional* aspects. As an analysis of statement meaning in general, this understanding of content is deficient inasmuch as it ascribes the same content to all analytically true statements and to all analytically false statements. However, since the doctrinal statements being considered here are rarely (if ever) thought of as being *analytically* true (i.e., true by definition), this deficiency does not affect my analysis. Moreover, while I grant that intension is an important and irreducible component of sentential meaning, the focus on extension is appropriate in this discussion given that the extensional content of a set of statements is *sufficient* to determine whether that set is logically consistent.

more than to *deny* that God is foolish and evil. However, there is no immediate reason why this theological sentiment could not be extended to cover *all* doctrinal statements. For example, on this view the trinitarian monotheistic tenet 'There is only one God' should be understood only as a *denial* that there exist *multiple* divine beings, not as a positive assertion about anything.

How would such a view avoid the problem of paradox? Presumably just in this: the apophatic semantic minimalist will claim that because doctrinal statements such as those enshrined in the early creeds are only denying, and not affirming, that certain things are the case, they cannot be properly charged with contradiction. After all, a contradiction only arises when one both *affirms* and *denies* the very same thing. In order to contradict oneself, one must affirm at least *something*—yet the creeds and other statements of Christian theology do no such thing.

While inventive, this strategy hardly stands up to scrutiny. In the first place, it is far from clear that doctrinal statements such as 'The Father is God' or 'Jesus Christ is fully human' should only be understood in a negative sense, as merely denying some state of affairs.[56] Moreover, it seems obvious that contradictions can arise from denials alone. For example, if one were to deny both of the following statements, one would normally be thought of as guilty of logical contradiction:

(18) There are some coins in the bag.

(19) There are no coins in the bag.[57]

The reason behind this charge is simply that the denial of some state of affairs is usually taken to imply the affirmation of the *negation* of that state of affairs (which is itself a state of affairs). Indeed, this natural understanding of declarative language is encapsulated in the notion of semantic content explicated above: the content of a doctrinal statement concerns not only the set of worlds in which the statement is *false*, but also the set of worlds in which it is *true*. One cannot make a meaningful doctrinal statement without thereby affirming that some states of affairs obtain.

---

56 Sellers, for one, is insistent that the Definition of Chalcedon makes positive metaphysical assertions. Sellers, *The Council of Chalcedon*, xii-xiv, 210, 350.

57 The assumption made here, of course, is that the bag referred to in these statements actually exists. If the bag were thought not to exist, then denying both statements would not involve any contradiction. This qualification does not affect my point. No apophatic theologian is likely to claim that his position is underwritten by atheism!

Thus a purely apophatic version of semantic minimalism lacks plausibility and flies in the face of how language is normally understood. Nevertheless, the semantic minimalist need not be so unsophisticated. For he could concede that making meaningful doctrinal statements necessarily involves affirming *some* states of affairs, yet still insist that no real contradictions need arise, by the following argument: although making some set of doctrinal statements involves affirming that *something* is the case, it does not require us to say *precisely what* is the case, only that the truth of the matter lies somewhere within a region circumscribed by the statements in question. Since the Christian who affirms a paradoxical set of doctrinal statements is under no obligation to specify the theological truth of the matter with any more precision than the creeds dictate, the charge of contradiction cannot be made to stick—at least, not conclusively. A genuine contradiction would involve simultaneously affirming and denying some particular state of affairs, but the genius of semantic minimalism is that no *particular* state of affairs is being affirmed—only the logical disjunction of a *range* of acceptable possibilities.

In assessing whether this more plausible version of semantic minimalism provides a satisfying response to the problem of paradox, it will be helpful to illustrate its understanding of doctrinal statements diagrammatically, in terms of the possible-worlds apparatus specified earlier. Figure 4.2 illustrates the situation (as the semantic minimalist sees the matter) regarding the semantic content of a set of doctrinal statements; for example, the Christian doctrine of the Trinity expressed minimally in the following three statements (none of which *in itself* involves any logical impropriety):

(20) There is only one God.

(21) The Father is God, the Son is God, and the Spirit is God.

(22) The Father is not the Son, the Son is not the Spirit, and the Father is not the Spirit.

In the diagram, the outer circle represents the entire space of *possible worlds* (in the sense defined earlier). Each of the inner lines represents the demarcation of possible-world space by one of the three doctrinal statements, and the shaded area on one side of each line represents that portion of possible-world space *ruled out* by one of the doctrinal statements (with darker shading indicating portions of possible-world space ruled out by multiple statements). The remaining *unshaded* area thus represents that portion of possible-world space in which the truth of the matter, as dictated by the entire set of doctrinal statements, must lie—which is simply to say that if the conjunction of these statements is true, then the actual world (i.e., the one possible world which actually obtains) lies somewhere in the unshaded area. Where precisely, the Christian cannot say; but then neither can the critic who charges the Christian with contradiction.

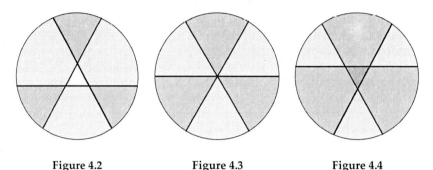

Figure 4.2   Figure 4.3   Figure 4.4

If Figure 4.2 were to represent accurately the situation faced by orthodox trinitarians, then this stance would appear to have considerable promise. As it is, however, things are not so fortunate, because this diagram simply fails to capture the paradoxicality of the doctrines in question. It is crucial to realise that the very reason the doctrinal statements are deemed paradoxical in the first place is because they appear to exclude *every possible world*.[58]

As such, Figure 4.2 should be replaced with something like Figure 4.3 — or, even more damningly, Figure 4.4. Recall the interpretation of the doctrine of the Trinity established in Chapter 2. On this interpretation, (20) apparently rules out all possible worlds in which there are no deities or there are multiple deities; (21) apparently rules out all possible worlds in which one (or more) of the persons of the Trinity is not numerically identical with a deity; and (22) apparently rules out all possible worlds in which two (or three) of the persons of the Trinity are numerically identical. Paradox therefore arises because taken together, and in orthodox fashion, these theological statements seem to rule out the *entirety* of possible-world space. The semantic minimalist defence, to the effect that the doctrinal statements leave some ambiguity regarding the *precise* truth of the matter, thus rings hollow; for these three statements appear to leave no room for there to be *any* truth of the matter, precise or otherwise. Concisely put, the problem is this: to insist on

---

58   This is true whether the conception of logical possibility in view is 'narrow' (as I have taken it here) or 'broad' (as it is commonly taken).

the minimum semantic content required to exclude heterodox views such as modalism, polytheism, and subordinationism (and thus to preserve orthodoxy) is to grant content that is *not minimal enough to avoid the appearance of contradiction.*

I have taken the doctrine of the Trinity as an example in explaining why semantic minimalism is inadequate as a solution to the problem of paradox. The same difficulties apply *mutatis mutandis* with respect to the doctrine of the Incarnation and indeed to any other similarly paradoxical doctrine. In general, semantic minimalism may well represent a responsible approach to interpreting Christian creeds and confessions, insofar as it serves to reign in both unwarranted speculation and unnecessary exclusion. But as a response to the charge of irrationality levelled at paradoxical doctrines, it takes us no further forward.

4.7 Complementarity

Small comfort though it may be, theologians have not been alone in suffering perplexity at the hands of paradoxes. Ever since the pre-Socratics, philosophers (of all religious persuasions) have also wrestled with a wide range of puzzles raised by sets of seemingly impeccable statements from which contradictory or otherwise absurd conclusions can be deduced.[59] Such difficulties may strike the non-philosopher as somewhat contrived and unreal, detached from the concrete, empirical facts of our experience and merely illustrative of the hazards of philosophical abstractions. One might therefore imagine that the realm of modern science is happily free from the sort of conceptual conundrums that have plagued philosophers and theologians through the centuries. However, even a cursory knowledge of twentieth-century science is sufficient to dispel this notion.[60] The dawning of post-Newtonian physics, of relativity theory and quantum mechanics, has given rise to a number of new paradoxes, the most prominent of which appear to be solidly

---

59 Rescher lists over 130 different philosophical paradoxes. Rescher, *Paradoxes*, xvii-xx.

60 It is worth noting that science could not function without relying on mathematics, and there are no shortage of mathematical paradoxes; thus, science is no more immune to paradox than the mathematical relations and principles on which it relies. Nonetheless, mathematical paradoxes still have an air of contrivance about them that many would consider so far removed from the unproblematic practice of *applied* mathematics as to cause no undue discomfort. Whether this confidence is well placed is an interesting question, but one beyond the scope of this book.

grounded in experimental results and thus cannot be simply dismissed as idle speculation and irrelevant extrapolation.

One of the most infamous of such paradoxes is the apparent dual nature of light (and electromagnetic radiation in general). Prior to the twentieth century, light was generally considered to behave in an unambiguously wave-like manner.[61] As a matter of fact, in many experimental situations it does; for example, it can be shown to exhibit those interference patterns that characteristically arise from the interaction of waves. Scientists are now well aware, however, that in other circumstances light appears to behave like a stream of discrete particles, as illustrated by the scattering of X-rays on collision with electrons. Conversely, electrons and other subatomic entities, hitherto treated as simple particles, are now understood to exhibit wave-like behaviour under certain experimental conditions. In short, a wealth of empirical data supports the conclusion that the fundamental building blocks of our physical world can be described either *as waves* or *as particles*, depending on the manner in which their behaviour is observed; indeed, there are even cases in which quantum entities exhibit wave-like properties and particle-like properties *at the same time*.[62]

This characterization of quantum physical entities is counterintuitive at best and arguably incoherent. It is extremely difficult to see how one and the same entity can exist both as a wave and as a particle, since these two types of entity have apparently incompatible properties: for example, a particle is located at a point in space, whereas a wave is distributed throughout space (e.g., between two points). Yet the fact remains that electrons and other quantum objects behave as if they were *both*, such that descriptions of their behaviour in terms of 'waves' and 'particles' are inevitably paradoxical.

The striking parallel between this modern scientific paradox and one ancient theological paradox—the doctrine of the Incarnation— has not escaped notice. In both cases, one thing is said to exhibit two seemingly incompatible natures: just as an electron exhibits a 'wave-particle duality', so Jesus Christ exhibits a 'God-man duality'. Yet despite the apparent logical difficulties, physicists have learned to accommodate the paradoxical character of quantum entities by

---

61 Immediately prior, that is. Earlier still, light was understood in particle terms. For an overview of the historical development of the wave-particle duality thesis, see John Gribbin, *In Search of Schrödinger's Cat* (London: Black Swan, 1997).

62 Yutaka Mizobuchi and Yoshiyuki Ohtaké, 'An "Experiment to Throw More Light on Light"', *Physics Letters A* 168.1 (1992), 1-5.

appealing to the notion of 'complementarity': descriptions of such objects in terms of 'waves' and 'particles' are deemed to be *complementary* rather than *contradictory* and can be affirmed in such a way that no norms of rationality are violated.[63] Once this parallel has been noted, an obvious question arises. Could not this notion of complementarity offer a solution to the problem of *theological* paradoxes as well?

In the remainder of this chapter, I will address this question by assessing the contributions of two writers who have tried to apply the same concept of complementary used in physics to logical problems in the theological domain. After discussing Christopher Kaiser's application of complementarity to the specific problem of the christological paradox, I will examine Donald MacKay's influential explication of complementarity and consider whether it can be fruitfully applied to the paradoxes of the Trinity and the Incarnation.[64]

In his article 'Christology and Complementarity', Kaiser begins by remarking that the notion of complementarity has been used by some writers to express the relation between God and the world. [65] This is misguided, Kaiser suggests, because Christians have traditionally insisted on a fundamental ontological distinction between the Creator and the creation; yet as Bohr understood and explicated the term, complementarity 'can only properly be applied to different modes, or "levels", of being that pertain to *one and the same object* and are coreferential.'[66] However, this coreferentiality

---

63 The first use of the term 'complementary' in this technical sense is credited to Niels Bohr.

64 A third attempt to address the problem of theological paradoxes via the notion of complementarity can be found in the writings of William Austin. However, of the two particular paradoxes on which I am focusing, Austin considers only the doctrine of the Incarnation and concludes that orthodoxy would *not* be satisfied by treating 'God' and 'man' as complementary models for speaking of Jesus Christ in the same way that 'wave' and 'particle' are treated as complementary models. William H. Austin, *Waves, Particles, and Paradoxes* (Rice University Studies: Houston, TX: William Marsh Rice University, 1967). Cf. Austin, 'Complementarity and Theological Paradox'. See also James L. Park, 'Complementarity without Paradox: A Physicist's Reply to Professor Austin', *Zygon* 2 (1967), 382-88; Christopher B. Kaiser, 'Waves, Particles, and Paradoxes', *Scottish Journal of Theology* 25 (1972), 94-95.

65 Christopher B. Kaiser, 'Christology and Complementarity', *Religious Studies* 12 (1976), 37-48.

66 Kaiser, 'Christology and Complementarity', 37.

condition suggests that the principle of complementarity might be more suitably applied in the area of christology:

> [T]he central doctrine of Christian theology affirms that man is one mode of a 'higher being' in Christ. That is, Christ is both man and God as man is both body and mind, as body is both atom and organism, as atom is both wave and particle. Therefore, the most natural area in which to compare Bohr's principle of complementarity with theology is not the God-world relation, but the relation of the two 'natures' in Christ. Christ is said to be one single being, one *hypostasis*, in a way that God and the world are not, so the problem of 'one-ness' would not militate against an application of complementarity to Christology as it does against the parallel application to general providence.[67]

Kaiser notes the parallels between the problems faced by the disciples of the first century and the physicists of the twentieth. Both groups were confronted with a 'new thing' in their experience, incommensurable with traditional concepts. Both were warranted in applying each of two different categories to that 'new thing', despite the fact that those categories were previously assumed to be 'incompatible (i.e. non-coreferential) concepts'. Consequently, both were faced with the prospect of communicating their discoveries (at least initially) in 'seemingly paradoxical language.'[68] Given these common experiences and difficulties, the potential utility of the complementarity concept for reducing the sting of the christological paradox is evident.

Kaiser continues his discussion by explicating Bohr's idea of complementarity in the original context of wave-particle duality:

> In Bohr's view, then, the classical concepts of 'wave' and 'particle' must be applied to atomic objects in order to communicate their unique character. On the other hand, the very act of applying classically incompatible terms to a single new reality entails a radical shift in their meaning. In their common application to an atomic object, the terms 'wave' and 'particle' become positively related to each other in an unprecedented manner. They are no longer strictly incompatible, but coreferential and 'complementary'. Hence, there is a semantic displacement of the two terms. They retain their classical senses, which are incompatible, in order to allow communicability (and not to become 'dead metaphors'), but they also take on new significance

---

67 Kaiser, 'Christology and Complementarity', 38.
68 Kaiser, 'Christology and Complementarity', 39-42.

by virtue of their application to one and the same object in quantum theory.[69]

He then proceeds to explain how an 'uninitiated enquirer' is able to gain an understanding of the nature of quantum entities by means of the complementary concepts of 'wave' and 'particle':

> He can 'get a handle on' the new discovery by understanding the terms 'wave' and 'particle' in their classical senses, but then he must 'see' and 'see through' the resulting paradox by allowing the meanings of the two terms to shift as they enter a new relation, a relation of 'complementarity', to each other in their coreferential application to atomic objects.[70]

Thus, when physicists apply the terms 'wave' and 'particle' to quantum entities in a complementary sense, the meaning of those terms is a *modification* of their classical senses (indeed, a *radical* modification, according to Kaiser).[71] According to these new senses of the terms, certain properties that would be ascribed to quantum entities by the classical senses are *not* to be ascribed; moreover, certain other properties *not* associated with the classical senses *are* to be ascribed to the entities described by the terms in their modified, complementary senses.[72] In other words, the terms are employed *analogically* in their quantum-mechanical senses; there is commonality (so as to allow communicability) but also disparity (so as to allow coreferentiality).

Note then the following crucial features of Kaiser's explication of the complementarity relation, as used in the context of quantum physics:

- The concepts denoted by the terms 'wave' and 'particle' in their *classical* senses are strictly incompatible and therefore cannot be coreferential.

- The concepts denoted by the terms 'wave' and 'particle' in their *complementary* senses are not strictly incompatible and therefore can be coreferential.

- The complementarity senses of the terms involve a significant modification of their classical senses; as such, some of the properties ascribed to an object under the

---

69 Kaiser, 'Christology and Complementarity', 40.
70 Kaiser, 'Christology and Complementarity', 40.
71 The application is 'quasi-metaphorical', as Kaiser puts it.
72 Kaiser, 'Christology and Complementarity', 40-41.

classical senses are not ascribed under the complementary senses and vice versa.

It is not my intention here to evaluate whether applying the complementarity principle is successful in resolving the paradoxes of quantum mechanics; for the sake of argument, I shall assume that it is. The important question is whether the complementarity approach can be applied in the same way toward a resolution of the paradox of the Incarnation: whether the Chalcedonian claim that one person is both 'God' and 'man' can be treated in the same way as the Bohrian claim that one quantum object is both 'wave' and 'particle'.

It should be evident from the three features listed above that this approach faces some formidable objections. According to the complementarity principle, Christians who claim that Christ is both 'God' and 'man' would *not* be using those terms in any classical or literal sense, but rather in novel analogical senses.[73] Moreover, those new senses would, in one way or another, be deliberately stripped of any attributive entailments which appear to preclude coreferentiality; thus *whatever* the terms 'God' and 'man' connote when used in a new and complementary sense, they *cannot* ascribe (say) simultaneous omniscience and ignorance to Jesus. Indeed, the very purpose of employing the classical terms in modified complementary senses is so as to *eliminate* paradoxes such as these.[74]

---

73 Cf. James Park's response to Austin's treatment of complementarity: 'Contemporary physicists who have pondered these matters at all realize that such experiments do not mean, as Austin suggests, that an electron, for example, must be regarded as some kind of dialectical entity torn between being impossibly both a wave and a particle. On the contrary, the electron is not *both*; it is *neither*.' Park, 'Complementarity without Paradox', 383. If this understanding of complementarity were to be carried over directly into christology, the Christian would be forced to say that, strictly speaking, 'Jesus is not *both* God and man; he is *neither*.' Incidentally, it is not altogether clear that Austin is guilty of the error Park ascribes to him; for example, he acknowledges that 'if we are going to mix the two models, we need some entity which will function as a sort of compromise, combining approximations to the features of both. Such entities exist; they are called "wave packets."' Austin, 'Complementarity and Theological Paradox', 370.

74 This is certainly how Park sees the matter: 'Present-day quantum mechanics, including its philosophical structure of complementarity, contains no paradoxes. To believe otherwise is to misunderstand complementarity.' Park, 'Complementarity without Paradox', 383. In other words, complementary descriptions properly understood should not involve even the *appearance* of contradiction.

Against this construction, there is no evidence that when the authors of the Definition of Chalcedon used the phrase 'truly God and truly man' they acknowledged a radical shift in the meaning of the terms 'God' and 'man'. On the contrary, every indication is that those words were understood to carry something very close to, if not identical with, the classical senses of those terms at that point in time—not least because so much theological weight was hanging on that very fact. Modern physicists have no particular interest in preserving the traditional senses of quantum theoretical terms and the property ascriptions associated with those senses, provided the terms are useful for consistently expressing and communicating the empirical results characterised and predicted by quantum theory. But for the theologians involved in the early christological debates, it was effectively a given that the crucial concepts involved were *not* susceptible to substantial revision and manipulation. If anything, it was a dogmatic commitment to understanding the ascriptions 'divine' and 'human' in the conventional way that kept the debates fired for so long. Moreover, the notion that one or more of the attributes or characteristics traditionally thought essential to 'divinity' or 'humanity' could simply be dropped or modified in order to allow their co-exemplification in one person was evidently not given serious consideration by the Fathers as a resolution to the problem.[75] As Kaiser explicates the principle of complementarity, the use of the terms 'God' and 'man' in a *complementary* sense would be designed to avoid, rather than accommodate, anything approaching a *literal* ascription of omniscience and ignorance to Christ. Yet as I argued previously, it is the theological rationale for making that very ascription (among others) which gives rise to the paradox in the first place. The complementarity strategy thus understood does not provide a way of reconciling orthodoxy with logical perspicuity; on the contrary, it self-consciously sides with the latter at the expense of the former.

---

75   This strategy is effectively that advocated by kenotic theorists and critiqued in §3.3.1. It might be objected that the Alexandrian scholars did in fact advocate a concept of 'humanity' which lacked properties associated with it by the Antiochenes (specifically, possession of a distinct human soul). However, is not at all clear that the Alexandrians took themselves to be advocating the application of a *new* concept of 'humanity' over against the *traditional* concept; more plausibly, they held (contra the Antiochenes) that Christ's being literally human *did not in fact require* possession of a distinct human soul. In other words, there is no indication that either party understood themselves to be advocating anything other than the regular senses of the key terms.

Kaiser appears reluctant to acknowledge this point. In considering the application of complementarity to the Incarnation he suggests that the disciples, given their paradoxical experiences of Jesus, were faced with a choice. On the one hand, they could have opted to 'discard the categories of "God" and "man" and devise an entirely new terminology'; but this would have made the task of *communicating* those novel experiences all but impossible. The alternative, in Kaiser's view, parallels the course plotted by the quantum theorists:

> So for the purposes of communication, if nothing else, the O.T. categories of 'God' and 'man' had to be retained, yet in their unprecedented application to a single individual, Jesus, they were brought into a new relationship with each other and shifted in meaning. They retained their 'classical' O.T. senses, yet they also took on new significance in the context of the Incarnation. ... As in the case of quantum theory, the uninitiated enquirer is presented with an acute problem of insight. He begins by taking the terms 'God' and 'man' in their 'classical' senses, then applies them simultaneously to Jesus, and, hopefully, comes to see them in a new light in relation to each other.[76]

It is difficult to understand what Kaiser is claiming when he states that the designations 'God' and 'man' retained their classical Old Testament senses despite the fact that they also 'shifted in meaning' and 'took on new significance'. According to Kaiser's account, one of the defining characteristics of terms used in a complementary sense is precisely that they do *not* retain their classical senses, for the very reason that they are *strictly incompatible* in those classical senses. The difficulty remains: Kaiser's complementarity approach to resolving the paradox of the Incarnation amounts to a semantic revision that strips the theological claims in question of any implications that appear to logically conflict. His attempt to draw out the historical and linguistic parallels between quantum theory and christology is provocative, but ultimately fails to provide a real alternative to the approaches to paradox considered already.[77]

Kaiser rightly comments in his article that the notion of 'complementarity' has been understood in various ways, although he chooses to focus on the version originally suggested by Bohr and

---

76 Kaiser, 'Christology and Complementarity', 42.

77 The criticisms raised here apply equally well to attempts to excuse the doctrine of the Trinity by appealing to wave-particle duality. For other objections to this line of defence, see Tuggy, 'Trinitarian Theorizing', 177-78.

endorsed by many quantum physicists today.[78] I have argued that this understanding, catered specifically towards quantum mechanics, does not satisfactorily resolve the christological paradox. Nevertheless, there exist more generic understandings of complementarity that may be better suited for the task. One influential analysis of complementarity has been promoted by Donald MacKay, who applies the concept to a number of logical problems in the interface between science and theology including the mind-brain relationship, free will and determinism, and the perceived conflict between evolutionary theory and the doctrine of creation.[79] It will therefore be worthwhile to review MacKay's understanding of complementarity and to consider whether it offers any hope for defending the rationality of paradoxical Christian doctrines such as the Trinity and the Incarnation.

The most comprehensive and relevant account of MacKay's understanding of complementarity is found in his 1974 article, '"Complementarity" in Scientific and Theological Thinking'.[80] In this essay, MacKay carefully explains and illustrates his understanding of genuinely complementary descriptions; he then clarifies how the complementarity relation applies in the specific case of quantum physics before discussing its application to three theological issues: creation, miracles, and conversion. The first notable feature of MacKay's exposition is his insistence that the concept of complementarity is a purely *logical* one and is therefore independent of any application it might enjoy in the physical sciences:

> Complementarity stands not for a physical theory, still less for a mystical doctrine, but rather it stands for a particular kind of logical relation, distinct from and additional to traditional ones like contradiction, synonymy, or independence; it demands to be considered along with others whenever there is doubt as to the connection between two statements.[81]

Descriptions taken to be complementary are never *logically independent* of one another, although the dependence relationship may be unidirectional or bidirectional:

> Complementary statements are not logically independent. By saying that they are about the same situation we mean that there is

---

78 Cf. Park, 'Complementarity without Paradox', 386-87.

79 Donald M. MacKay, *The Clockwork Image: A Christian Perspective on Science* (Christian Classics Series: Leicester: InterVarsity Press, 1997).

80 Donald M. MacKay, '"Complementarity" in Scientific and Theological Thinking', *Zygon* 9 (1974), 225-44.

81 MacKay, 'Complementarity', 226.

at least one feature of one of the statements whose alteration or absence would necessitate a change in the other(s). They show correlations, or at least what might be called "existential covariance." As logical relations go this is a weak constraint but not a negligible one. We shall see that it can sometimes be asymmetrical, in the sense that the alteration or absence of a feature in description A would necessitate a change in B, but not conversely.[82]

Thus, for example, the *physical* description of a printed page (the number and location of ink molecules, etc.) could change without its *semantic* description being affected (i.e., the message it conveys) although the reverse would not be true.

A third feature of MacKay's account is that properly complementary descriptions pertain to *one and the same referent* but obtain with respect to *different standpoints*:

> [C]omplementary views are by definition views of the same subject: In this sense complementary descriptions must have a common reference, although they need not, and in general will not, refer to the same aspects of it. ... [T]here could be no excuse for claiming that two disparate views of the same subject were complementary rather than contradictory unless in some respect (of position or time, for example) they were different in standpoint.[83]

As MacKay sees things, the difference in the standpoints of complementary descriptions arises in one of two ways: (i) by virtue of separation in terms of some dimension that does not feature in the conceptual frame of either descriptions (as in the example of the two disparate two-dimensional images that together constitute a binocular view); or (ii) by virtue of representing two or more hierarchically-arranged 'logical levels' (as in the example of an exhaustive *electronic* description of a computer and an exhaustive *mathematical* description of that same computer).[84] In the first case, the logical relationship between complementary descriptions is symmetrical; in the second, it is asymmetrical.[85]

MacKay's account of complementarity has two other important features. The first is that truly complementary descriptions of some state of affairs are not intertranslatable without loss of meaning;

---

82   MacKay, 'Complementarity', 226.
83   MacKay, 'Complementarity', 228.
84   MacKay, 'Complementarity', 227, 229-30.
85   MacKay, 'Complementarity', 232-33.

which is just to say that while such descriptions pertain to the *same object*, they do not simply *say the same things* about that object albeit with different terminology.

> I have suggested as a necessary condition (which applies both in hierarchic and nonhierarchic cases) that two (or more) descriptions must, respectively, employ terms whose preconditions of precise definition or use are mutually exclusive if they are to be termed complementary in a sharp sense. This rules out, for example, logically equivalent expressions of the same statement in different languages or idioms, for which we already have the term "synonymous."[86]

The second is that the standpoints from which the complementary descriptions are valid must be *specifiable*:

> To call two or more accounts of the same situation complementary is to imply that each becomes valid from a specifiably different logical standpoint. Chronologically, what comes first may be the discovery in brute experience that each is necessary, which then initiates attempts to specify the presumed differences in standpoint; but logically it is only those differences that legitimize any disparity between the accounts. *The apologist who invokes complementarity incurs a corresponding obligation to indicate those differences in his own case.*[87]

With these five features of MacKay's account of complementarity before us, we may summarise his understanding as follows:

- The concept of complementarity is a *purely logical one* and is not dependent on any scientific theories or observations.

- Complementary descriptions may be related *hierarchically* or *non-hierarchically*; in the former case there is an *asymmetrical* dependency relationship, while in the latter there is a *symmetrical* dependency relationship.

- Complementary descriptions refer to *one and the same object* (or state of affairs) but from *different logical standpoints*; furthermore, those different standpoints must be *specifiable* if an appeal to complementarity is to be legitimate.

- Complementary descriptions are *incommensurable*; they do not merely say the same thing but with alternative vocabulary.

---

86 MacKay, 'Complementarity', 240.
87 MacKay, 'Complementarity', 241, emphasis added.

Let us then consider what prospects this account of complementarity holds for resolving the problem of theological paradoxes. Can the rational offence of apparent contradiction be removed by claiming that conflicting statements should be thought of as *complementary* rather than *contradictory*?

Take first the doctrine of the Trinity. The immediate problem faced is that of identifying just what the relevant complementary descriptions should be. Whatever the answer here, those descriptions must (i) pertain to the same object and (ii) taken together say everything that the ecumenical creeds require us to say. The most plausible candidate for the referent of such descriptions would seem to be the Deity or Godhead, rather than any individual Person. Moreover, since the paradox arises from the difficulty of reconciling God's oneness and God's threeness, one might expect the complementary descriptions to characterise these two counterpoised aspects of the divine existence. Let us therefore take the candidate descriptions to be something like the following:

(T1) There is one God: Father, Son, and Spirit. The Father is God, the Son is God, and the Spirit is God.

(T2) God exists as three persons: Father, Son, and Spirit. The Father is not the Son, the Father is not the Spirit, and the Son is not the Spirit.

Neither of the two descriptions, taken alone, would appear to be incoherent. Considered in isolation, (T1) would tend to invite a heterodox modalist conception of the Trinity, while (T2) would likely suggest a heterodox tritheistic conception of the Trinity. Taken together, however, can (T1) and (T2) be legitimately treated as complementary, rather than contradictory, descriptions that conjointly express the whole truth of the Christian doctrine?

The first question to ask, in light of MacKay's account, is whether (T1) and (T2) represent hierarchical or non-hierarchical descriptions. This question is a difficult one to answer: there has been no majority opinion within the Christian tradition as to whether God's unity is at a 'higher logic level' than his plurality, such that the former is grounded in and emerges from the latter, or whether the reverse is true, or whether neither is in fact the case. According to MacKay, the issue can be settled by considering whether the logical dependency of the complementary descriptions is unidirectional or bidirectional; however, it is hard to see how either of (T1) or (T2) is logically dependent on the other, in the sense that if one were modified then the other would also need to be modified (in order for both to remain valid descriptions). If, as many Christian theists might hold,

(T1) and (T2) are necessarily true if true at all (because God is *essentially* triune) then there is a symmetrical logical dependence between the descriptions, but only in the trivial sense that there is such a dependence between *any* two necessary truths (e.g., *2 is the square root of 4* and *every red object is a material object*).

Even if this initial hurdle were surmountable, a greater one follows: namely, the problem of *specifying the different logical standpoints* from which (T1) and (T2) — or whatever complementary descriptions are taken to express the doctrine — are meaningful and true. The difficulty is made acute by the very nature of the trinitarian paradox: to avoid tritheism, one must insist that the relation between the Godhead and each Person is something very like numerical identity; yet to avoid modalism, one must also insist that each Person is numerically distinct from every other. It is not easy to see (and no one has thus far succeeded in showing) how one might specify different standpoints from which each description is literally true, without compromising the theological constraints on the doctrine. Unlike, for example, complementary two-dimensional descriptions of a three-dimensional object, statements involving relations of numerical identity and distinctness do not possess the conceptual wiggle room that might legitimise an appeal to complementarity over against contradiction. There is no known or imaginable 'logical dimension' in terms of which the claim that P *is numerically identical to* Q can be reconciled with the claim that P *is numerically distinct from* Q. As such, the prospects for recasting the doctrine of the Trinity in terms of MacKay's complementarity scheme are not promising.

Turning to the doctrine of the Incarnation, the initial indications are more favourable with regard to relieving the paradox with the medicine of complementarity. The common referent of any purportedly complementary descriptions would clearly be, as the Council of Chalcedon demanded, the singular person of Jesus Christ. Moreover, the two obvious candidates for complementary descriptions would be the following:

(I1) Jesus Christ is fully God.

(I2) Jesus Christ is fully human.

This much is reasonably straightforward, although clearly these two statements need to be unpacked in such a way that (i) orthodoxy is satisfied and (ii) the complementarity relationship between them is explicated. Once again, the first question to ask is whether (I1) and (I2) are related hierarchically or not. If related non-hierarchically, then there must be a two-way logical dependence between them;

accordingly, if a true description of Jesus Christ from one standpoint were to change, so would a true description from the other. Orthodox christology holds that Christ is only *contingently* human, since he existed prior to the Incarnation; moreover, his taking on a human nature did not necessitate any change in his divine characteristics.[88] Thus, if there is any *logical* dependence between the (I1) and (I2) it must be *asymmetrical*; specifically, (I2) must be logically dependent on (I1). This analysis would, in MacKay's terminology, put the affirmation of Christ's divinity at a 'higher logical level' than that of his humanity, a result that seems intuitively correct. On the other hand, however, in each of MacKay's illustrations of hierarchically-related descriptions—the physical and semantic descriptions of writing; the electronic and mathematical descriptions of a computer; the physical and mental descriptions of a person—the higher level description is true *by virtue of* the lower level description being true. In such cases, no description would be *possible* at the higher level unless there were *some* true description at the lower level. Yet this is manifestly not the case with respect to (I1) and (I2). No orthodox theologian would hold that Christ was fully God *by virtue of* being fully human and having those particular creaturely characteristics that he did have during his earthly life.[89] Determining how to construe the doctrine of the Incarnation in terms of MacKay's understanding of complementarity is evidently no easy matter. There is no obvious analogy with any of the examples MacKay gives of complementary descriptions of a single referent.

Putting aside such difficulties, and having established that (I1) and (I2) are related in a *hierarchical* complementarity relation if at all, the next question concerns the specification of the different logical standpoints according to which each description is meaningful and true. Whatever standpoints are specified, they must be such that

---

88 Kenoticists, of course, would demur. However, if kenotic theory were acceptable as an interpretation of Chalcedonian orthodoxy—and I have argued that it is not—then there would be no need to appeal to the notion of complementarity, for there would be no paradox.

89 Note that this claim, however odd, does not imply that when Christ was not human then he was not divine either; it merely implies that when Christ was *both* human and divine, his being divine was on account of his being human. If this were so, then presumably Christ's being *preincarnately* divine was on account of being *something else* (where that 'something else' must be expressible from the same logical standpoint as the description of Christ's humanity). At any rate, such implications seem hard to reconcile with the doctrine of divine aseity.

each description implies the sort of things that orthodox christology requires: for example, that from the standpoint of (I1) Christ knew all things, whereas from the standpoint of (I2) Christ did *not* know all things. One immediately appealing option is suggested by the dual-psychology models advocated by Thomas Morris and Richard Swinburne.[90] The idea would be that since Jesus Christ possessed two logically distinct levels of consciousness, the description *Christ knew all things* would be true with respect to one level of consciousness, whereas the description *Christ did not know all things* would be true from the standpoint of the other, and the two would constitute complementary descriptions of one person. However, as I argued previously, the notion of one person possessing two logically distinct minds or consciousnesses is highly problematic, if not altogether incoherent, and therefore cannot provide a plausible basis for specifying different logical standpoints for complementary descriptions.[91]

Once this avenue is abandoned, there are no other obvious candidates. As the history of christology testifies, it is extremely difficult to locate and specify two different logical standpoints from which descriptions of Christ's divine characteristics and experiences, and descriptions of his human characteristics and experiences, are conjointly true and together capture all that orthodox christology requires believers to affirm.

In light of these formidable difficulties, I suggest that even if MacKay's concept of complementarity is coherent and illuminating in some contexts (as I believe it to be), it offers little promise as a general means of articulating the paradoxical doctrines of the Christian faith in a way that is both faithful to orthodoxy and rationally digestible. In the cases of the doctrine of the Trinity and the doctrine of the Incarnation, two obstacles remain: (i) the problem of determining in each case what the complementary descriptions of the relevant subject matter should be (and whether they relate hierarchically or non-hierarchically); and (ii) the problem of specifying in each case the logical standpoints from which each description can be understood to be coherent, true, and faithful to

---

90 See §3.3.2.
91 Furthermore, it is not clear that descriptions from such standpoints would qualify as complementary in MacKay's sense, since there appears to be no logical dependence relation (either symmetrical or asymmetrical) between the two descriptions. Is it the case that any change in the description of Jesus' divine consciousness would *necessitate* a change in the description of his human consciousness, or *vice versa*, or both?

the theological concerns of credal orthodoxy (by properly excluding all heretical positions).

4.8 Conclusion

In this chapter I have considered a range of possible responses to the problem of doctrinal paradox and have argued that each is unsatisfactory on either philosophical or theological grounds. Taking refuge in anti-realism is far from appealing in light of Christian tradition and practice; in any event, it would still leave unresolved the problem of the logical impropriety of Christian discourse. Solutions that recommend revising our understanding of classical laws of logic and rules of inference either raise more philosophical problems than they answer, or clash with some of our most firmly held logical presuppositions, or else simply fail to attain the goal of protecting orthodoxy. The revisionist strategy of modifying or replacing traditional Christian doctrines so as to attain logical perspicuity amounts to waving a white flag in the face of paradox; given the troubling questions it raises about religious authority and identity, any advance it offers may be no better than a leap from frying pan to fire. The semantic minimalist claim that paradox is an unnecessary artefact arising from over-interpretation of the ecumenical statements of orthodoxy cannot be sustained in light of the conclusions reached in Chapters 2 and 3. Finally, the notion of 'complementary descriptions', despite its *prima facie* utility for defending the rationality of paradoxical doctrines, has been found unsuitable for the specific cases of the Trinity and the Incarnation; thus it cannot provide Christian theologians with a *general* solution to the problem of paradox.

Of the various strategies surveyed in this chapter, I would venture that the complementarity approach offers the greatest promise, despite its inadequacy in the final analysis. In the remaining chapters, I develop an alternative model for understanding theological paradox that is similar in several ways—for example, it advocates neither logical revisionism nor doctrinal revisionism and focuses attention on the *meaning* of the doctrinal statements—but in contrast is able to accommodate the doctrines of the Trinity and the Incarnation, along with various other doctrines often viewed as paradoxical, without sacrificing either the rationality or the orthodoxy of Christian beliefs.

PART II

The Propriety of Paradox

Returning to the analogy I used in my introduction to Part I, it would seem that the loaded question—'How are you coping with your drink problem?'—is appropriate after all. Christianity *does* have a problem: a problem with paradoxes. Two cardinal doctrines in particular, the Trinity and the Incarnation, suffer from the appearance of internal contradiction (at least implicitly) when interpreted in such a way as to clearly avoid the heresies proscribed by the early creeds and confessions. Moreover, after surveying a range of possible 'coping' strategies, I concluded that none provides a solution that is both philosophically and theologically satisfying. Thus a question mark remains over the rationality of Christian belief in such problematic doctrines: the *presence* of paradox forces us to consider the *propriety* of paradox.

The stage is therefore set for Part II of the book, in which I argue that belief in paradoxical Christian doctrines *can* be rational, contrary to received wisdom on such matters. Chapter 5 lays the epistemological foundation for the argument by explaining (with a heavy debt to Alvin Plantinga's theory of epistemic warrant) how Christian doctrines *in general* can be known to be true. Chapter 6 then sets forth a model for understanding theological paradox according to which assent to paradoxical Christian doctrines will be rational for most believers (whatever their level of intellectual sophistication) provided that the central Christian narrative is, in fact, *true*. Finally, Chapter 7 addresses various objections to the model motivated by a range of biblical, theological, and philosophical concerns.

CHAPTER 5

Warranted Christian Doctrines

5.1 Introduction

In Chapter 1, I stated that I would be working throughout with a definition of 'paradox' as *a set of claims which, taken in conjunction, appear to be logically inconsistent*. I argued in Chapters 2 and 3 that the orthodox doctrines of the Trinity and the Incarnation, as reflected in the Niceno-Constantinopolitan Creed, the Definition of Chalcedon, and the Athanasian Creed, are paradoxical in precisely this sense. Since apparent contradictions are commonly deemed an affront to reason, it is natural that Christians have explored various strategies for resolving the intellectual problem presented by doctrinal paradoxes. Six such strategies were assessed in Chapter 4. It was concluded that none of them offers a resolution that is both theologically and philosophically satisfying (at least with respect to the doctrines of the Trinity and the Incarnation).

In the second half of this book, I propose to consider whether a person can be rational in believing the doctrines of the Trinity and the Incarnation, despite the conclusions reached earlier. And the first question to address, I suggest, must be whether the component claims that together constitute such doctrines are *individually* worthy of assent. For if these individual theological claims—for example, that *there is only one God* and that *Jesus Christ is fully God*—lack any rational foundation, then the epistemic problem of paradox becomes an irrelevant sideshow. The compound claim that *the moon is made entirely of green cheese and the moon is made entirely of pink marshmallow* is a paradox, as I have defined it, but the intellectual propriety of believing the claim hardly turns on that fact, given that neither conjunct has any epistemic merit whatsoever. In this chapter, I therefore consider whether *any* Christian doctrines, paradoxical or otherwise, invite or enjoy rational assent in the first place—and if so, in what way and to what degree. By addressing this question, I will be constructing a platform from which to obtain a clear view of the consequences of paradoxicality on the rationality of belief in Christian doctrines.

Before doing so, however, one important preliminary issue must be settled in order to properly frame the question at hand. Exactly *what* positive quality is it that Christians wish to ascribe to the doctrines of their faith and that would make the problem of paradox worth examining in the first place? On the traditional assumption that doctrines are the sort of things that invite belief, the quality in view is presumably some kind of *epistemic* property such as *being rational* rather than (say) a mere psychological or historical property such as *being comforting* or *being popular*. After all, what is usually deemed problematic about paradoxical claims is that the overall phenomenon—a combination of individual credibility and mutual incompatibility—runs up against certain *epistemic* norms, certain standards for 'acceptable' or 'respectable' belief. Having thus narrowed the field to epistemic virtues, the question becomes this: precisely *which* epistemic property should we focus our attention on? As anyone familiar with contemporary epistemology will be aware, there are a whole host of candidates here, ranging from relatively weak qualities such as *credibility, plausibility*, and *rational entitlement* to stronger properties of belief such as *justification* (of which there are numerous competing conceptions),[1] *rationality* also susceptible to various understandings),[2] and *warrant* (defined as that elusive property which, in sufficient degree, distinguishes knowledge from mere true belief).[3]

For several reasons, I propose to focus primarily on the last of these candidates: *warrant*. If nothing else, targeting a relatively strong epistemic quality will make my subsequent conclusions all the more interesting—after all, many people might find certain Christian doctrines to be credible or plausible without being in the least bit inclined to go so far as to *believe* them. (As a resident of Scotland, I think it plausible that it will rain next Saturday; but I do not consider that a sufficient basis for *believing* that it will.) Secondly, since several important types of rationality turn out to be necessary conditions of warrant, it follows that if a belief is warranted then it must also enjoy these types of rationality. By focusing on warrant I will thus also be indirectly addressing various types of rationality. Thirdly, it is *prima facie* likely that the more exalted the epistemic status of Christian doctrine, the better equipped it will be to deal with epistemic challenges such as those raised by the problem of

---

1 See, e.g., William P. Alston, 'Epistemic Desiderata', *Philosophy and Phenomenological Research* 53.3 (1993), 527-51.
2 See, e.g., Plantinga, *Warranted Christian Belief*, 108-34.
3 Plantinga, *Warrant and Proper Function*, v.

paradox.[4] Finally, the epistemic quality known as warrant appears to be the one that Christians, from the earliest times, have most commonly ascribed to their beliefs and doctrines.[5] It is not that the apostles and their followers merely found *plausible* the claim that Jesus rose from the dead, or that they considered themselves *rationally entitled* to believe it. They professed to *know* that Jesus was alive again. Likewise, Christians throughout the centuries (those with any degree of confidence in their faith, at any rate) have maintained that the cardinal doctrines of the faith express things that are *known* about the nature and works of God—that God is one but exists in three persons, that Jesus Christ is both fully divine and fully human, that Christ died for our sins so as to reconcile us to God, and so forth. The heated trinitarian and christological debates of the early centuries would hardly have arisen had there not been a widespread assumption that the answers to the theological questions raised could actually be *known* by those engaged in the controversies. Why would anyone waste time and energy defending claims that, even if true, would never amount to more than weakly supported beliefs?

I will therefore be concentrating in this chapter on the question of whether Christian doctrines can be epistemically warranted; in other words, whether belief in some Christian doctrine (the principal claims of which happen to be true) can ever amount to *knowledge*. Answering this question will pave the way for discussing the narrower question with which this book is directly concerned, namely, whether belief in *paradoxical* Christian doctrines can ever be warranted. Does the paradoxicality of the doctrines of the Trinity and the Incarnation mean that belief in those doctrines *cannot* be warranted—or, less strongly, are *probably not* warranted? This latter question will be taken up in the following chapters. In addition, while I propose to focus on *warrant* in this chapter and the next, I will consider in Chapter 7 some alternative notions of rationality to assess whether the problem of paradox can be raised in other potentially troubling forms.

---

4   A non-theological illustration: even if I find the proposition that it is raining outside to be *plausible*, a report from a colleague that it is not raining will likely lead to my believing that is it *not* raining; yet if that same proposition is *warranted* for me (e.g., because I can actually see the rain through the window) then my colleague's report is very unlikely to lead me to believe otherwise.

5   For some particularly strong New Testament affirmations regarding the epistemic status of Christian teaching, see Luke 1:3-4; Acts 2:36; 1 Thess. 5:2.

5.2 What is Warrant?

My aim in this chapter is to explain how the cardinal doctrines of the faith can be *warranted* for Christian believers, where warrant is understood to be that epistemic quality enough of which transforms mere true belief into knowledge.[6] Indeed, I propose to argue that such doctrines can enjoy a substantial degree of warrant: if true, they can be *known* to be true, with considerable confidence if not with unshakable certainty. However, simply defining warrant as that which distinguishes knowledge from mere true belief sheds little light on the *criteria* for knowledge. Just what is it about knowledge that sets it apart from mere true belief? What are the necessary and sufficient conditions for warrant? Without an adequate answer to this question, one cannot begin to assess whether certain beliefs—in the present case, Christian doctrinal beliefs—can, or do, enjoy warrant. Therefore, in this section and the next, I will set out and defend a particular account of warrant that I take to be very close to the truth, if not the whole story, about what constitutes knowledge. I will thereafter assume, in this and subsequent chapters, that this particular analysis of warrant is substantially correct. Although I suspect that my conclusions about the rationality of theological paradox can be sustained on the basis of alternative accounts of warrant, it will not be my burden to argue the point here; I leave it as an exercise for interested readers who share the concerns motivating this project but find themselves inclined toward a different analysis of epistemic warrant.

Numerous competing analyses of warrant exist in contemporary epistemology and it would be foolish to attempt to reinvent the wheel in the context of a book such as this. Instead, I propose to adopt the account developed by Alvin Plantinga in his influential *Warrant* trilogy.[7] There are two good reasons for this. The first is that, as I have indicated, I consider his account of the conditions of warrant to be substantially accurate and more defensible than any competing theory. Furthermore, Plantinga has himself already applied his analysis to the debate over whether theistic beliefs in

---

6   Some epistemologists, particularly those of an internalist bent, prefer to use the term 'justification' to refer to the third necessary component of knowledge (besides truth and belief). For the sake of consistency and clarity, I will use the term 'warrant' exclusively for this purpose in the subsequent discussion.

7   Alvin Plantinga, *Warrant: The Current Debate* (Oxford: Oxford University Press, 1993); Plantinga, *Warrant and Proper Function*; Plantinga, *Warranted Christian Belief*.

general, and Christian beliefs in particular, are warranted; he concludes that such beliefs can indeed be warranted, even strongly warranted, provided one important assumption is granted (to be discussed in due course). As such, Plantinga's account is well suited for the purpose of assessing the reasonableness of paradoxical Christian doctrines. In what follows, I will review Plantinga's theory of knowledge, summarising the arguments he marshals in support of his analysis of warrant, before turning to discuss the application of his theory to theistic beliefs (e.g., that God exists and possesses certain attributes) and to specifically Christian beliefs (e.g., that Jesus Christ died to save sinners). Although much of this material will consist of a summary exposition of Plantinga's writings, I will draw attention at points to what I perceive to be ambiguities or shortcomings in his epistemology of Christian belief and attempt to remedy these problems. Moreover, as will become clear, although Plantinga purports to show how the main lines of Christian belief can be warranted, he does not supply an account of how those ecumenical doctrines *not explicitly articulated in the Bible* (such as the trinitarian and christological statements bequeathed to us by Nicea and Chalcedon) can also be warranted. I will therefore take up the task of extending Plantinga's account of warranted Christian belief to encompass this important element of the Christian tradition. Finally, in the closing section of this chapter, I introduce the topic of *epistemic defeaters*, an understanding of which will prove crucial to my treatment of paradox in the remaining chapters.

5.3 Warranted Belief

In presenting Plantinga's analysis of warrant, it will be helpful to locate his theory on the epistemological map. There are various of ways of dividing up the territory, but one fruitful approach would be to categorise Plantinga's epistemology in terms of two prominent debates in contemporary epistemology: the debate over *internalism* versus *externalism* and the debate over *coherentism* versus *foundationalism*. In fact, since Plantinga spends much of the first volume of his *Warrant* series interacting with these questions, it makes considerable sense to frame his conclusions in light of them and to examine why he comes down on the latter side in both cases.

5.3.1 *Internalism and Externalism*

According to Laurence BonJour, one well-known defender of internalism in epistemology, the distinction between internalist and externalist theories may be characterised as follows:

> The most generally accepted account of [the distinction between externalism and internalism] is that a theory of justification is *internalist* if and only if it requires that all of the factors needed for a belief to be epistemically justified for a given person be *cognitively accessible* to that person, *internal* to his cognitive perspective; and *externalist*, if it allows that at least some of the justifying factors need not be thus accessible, so that they can be *external* to the believer's cognitive perspective, beyond his ken.[8]

There are two points to note here. The first is the basic underlying conviction of internalism, which is that one can know that some proposition *p* is true only if one is in a position to identify appropriate grounds for believing that *p* is true, merely by reflecting on one's own mental states: that is, roughly, only if one can see on reflection just *why* it is reasonable or acceptable to believe that *p*.

The second point is that BonJour, in common with most internalists, inclines toward the classical analysis of knowledge as *justified true belief*, the tripartite formula dating back (so it is said) to Plato's *Theaetetus*. According to this analysis, the mere fact that a certain belief is *true* is insufficient for it to constitute knowledge, since it could be true by sheer coincidence. Genuine knowledge also requires *justification*: the believer must be able to *justify* her belief by supplying an adequate account (e.g., one or more reasons) explaining why it should be thought true.

In Plantinga's view, post-Enlightenment epistemology has been dominated (at least until very recently) by strongly internalist convictions, even if those convictions have not been self-consciously recognised and explicitly articulated. He plausibly suggests that this tradition is closely tied to the 'justified true belief' view of knowledge, and that this connection becomes especially clear when the notion of epistemic justification is construed along *deontological* lines.[9] On this understanding of what it means be justified in one's beliefs, an understanding reinforced by the connotations of the word itself, epistemic justification is primarily a matter of fulfilling certain doxastic *duties* or *obligations*. According to epistemic deontologism,

---

8   Laurence BonJour, 'Externalism/Internalism', in Jonathan Dancy and Ernest Sosa (eds), *A Companion to Epistemology* (Oxford: Blackwell, 1992), 132.

9   Plantinga, *Warrant*, 3-29; Plantinga, *Warrant and Proper Function*, v-vi.

as Plantinga characterises it, one is justified in holding some belief provided one has not flouted any relevant epistemic duties in so doing (e.g., the duty not to believe something contradicted by immediate sense experience). One is thus *permitted* or *entitled* to hold that belief; in short, one is *justified* in so believing. Plantinga finds that this deontologist theme features prominently in the epistemologies of Descartes and Locke (albeit with some important qualifications in the latter) as well as in the writings of numerous modern epistemologists.[10] Furthermore, the affinity between internalism and deontological justification is not difficult to discern. For if being justified is a matter of meeting certain epistemic obligations, it follows naturally enough that one must be *in a position* to fulfil those obligations; therefore those factors determining whether a particular belief is permissible must be *internally accessible* to the mind of the believer.

While appreciating the internal coherence of this 'triumvirate' of justification, internalism, and epistemic deontology, Plantinga finds it to be utterly inadequate as a basis for understanding warrant. In the first place, it is clear that deontological constraints do not square well with our normal epistemic practices, for belief formation and sustenance is not, in the main, under our direct control. I cannot simply *will* to believe one thing and not another. Moreover, even if such belief control were available, Plantinga argues that justification construed along these lines is nowhere near sufficient to transform mere true belief into knowledge. Deontological justification is not sufficient for warrant because even if one is doing one's level best to meet one's relevant epistemic obligations vis-à-vis some belief, that belief may still lack warrant due to *cognitive dysfunction*. Consider, for example, the poor victim of Descartes' deceiving demon, who is caused to perceive the external world in an entirely coherent and credible, yet almost wholly fictional manner. A person deceived in this way about the world may be fulfilling to the letter every epistemic obligation with respect to belief evaluation and revision, even though all of his beliefs about that world quite obviously lack warrant.[11]

Plantinga's critique of internalist epistemologies has been criticised for relying too heavily on the association of internalism

---

10 Plantinga, *Warrant*, 25-29.

11 Plantinga also argues, though with less emphasis, that justification is also not *necessary* for warrant. Plantinga, *Warrant*, 45; Plantinga, *Warrant and Proper Function*, vii. Since justification is neither necessary nor sufficient for warrant, it is misguided to make it the centrepiece of one's account of epistemic warrant.

with deontological notions of justification.[12] Internalist theories of knowledge have been defended that do not rely on any such notions; one common approach is to focus on some form of *evidentialist* requirement, e.g., that beliefs are justified only insofar as one possesses *adequate evidence* of their truth. Still, by challenging deontologism, Plantinga has certainly called into question one prominent motivation behind internalism in epistemology.[13] Moreover, as the problem of Descartes' demon illustrates, Plantinga's basic objection to the sufficiency of justification for warrant, where justification is understood in wholly internalist terms (e.g., in terms of evidence available to the believer via introspection alone), still stands. Even if some belief *B* is wholly justified with respect to *S*'s other beliefs and experiences—for example, *B* is rendered highly probable with respect to everything else *S* believes—*B* could still lack warrant on account of large-scale dysfunction in *S*'s cognitive apparatus. The important point here is that internalist factors are insufficient: there must be significant *external* constraints on warrant and some of these constraints need to address the possibility of dysfunctional belief-formation. Plantinga thus appears to be entirely correct in rejecting an analysis of warrant dominated by internalist justification, whether construed deontologically or otherwise.[14]

Nevertheless, the last decade or so has seen some convergence in the debate over internalism, which requires further comment in defence of Plantinga's position. Few self-professed internalists today would maintain (as BonJour's earlier characterisation suggests) that *every* warrant-contributing factor needs to be internally accessible to the believer—not least because of so-called Gettier counterexamples, which purport to show that external factors beyond the believer's ken can result in a justified true belief falling short of knowledge (where 'justified' is construed along typically internalist lines).[15] For

---

12 Earl Conee and Richard Feldman, 'Internalism Defended', in Hilary Kornblith (ed.), *Epistemology: Internalism and Externalism* (Oxford: Blackwell, 2001), 231-60.

13 Michael Bergmann, 'Externalism and Skepticism', *The Philosophical Review* 109.2 (2000), 159.

14 For various criticisms of Plantinga's case against internalism, along with Plantinga's response, see Jonathan L. Kvanvig (ed.), *Warrant in Contemporary Epistemology: Essays in Honor of Plantinga's Theory of Knowledge* (Lanham, MD: Rowman & Littlefield, 1996).

15 Edmund Gettier, 'Is Justified True Belief Knowledge?', *Analysis* 23 (1963), 121-23; Paul K. Moser, 'Gettier Problem', in Jonathan Dancy and Ernest Sosa (eds), *A Companion to Epistemology* (Oxford: Blackwell, 1992), 157-59.

this reason, many internalists who wish to preserve the classical picture of knowledge argue that a *fourth* condition is required for knowledge if Gettier problems are to be successfully circumvented.[16] The upshot of these recent developments is that if warrant is taken to encompass every factor required for knowledge other than truth and belief, then few contemporary epistemologists would insist that the necessary and sufficient conditions of warrant are *wholly* internal.[17] Consequently, the current debate over internalism is more usefully characterised as engaged between 'moderate' internalists who maintain that warrant *always* involves *some* significant internal component (i.e., epistemic conditions that can be evaluated by a person via introspection alone) and externalists who reject this requirement.[18]

The playing field is further complicated by the fact that some externalists, Plantinga included, grant that there is one *negative* internal constraint on warrant: specifically, that a belief *B* is warranted for *S* only if on adequate reflection *S* would *not* be aware of any sufficient reason to *reject B*.[19] Thus, while externalists of all stripes deny that there are always *positive* internal constraints on

---

16 One common account of this fourth condition involves specifying a *defeasibility* criterion, such as the following:

> (D) *S* knows that *p* only if there is no true proposition *q* such that if *S* were to believe *q*, then *S* would not be justified in believing that *p*.

A condition like (D) is clearly *not* internal, for it requires only that there *be* no justification-defeating truth; it does not require that whether or not *p* is defeasible is something that can be determined by *S* via introspective assessment of *S*'s own cognitive states. Cf. Peter Klein, 'Warrant, Proper Function, Reliabilism, and Defeasibility', and Marshall Swain, 'Warrant Versus Indefeasible Justification', in Kvanvig (ed.), *Warrant in Contemporary Epistemology*, 97-146. See also Plantinga's critique of various attempts to save the classical internalist account of knowledge by adding a fourth, externalist constraint. Alvin Plantinga, 'Respondeo', in Kvanvig (ed.), *Warrant in Contemporary Epistemology*, 308-78.

17 Even BonJour has practically conceded this point in more recent discussions. See Laurence BonJour, 'Plantinga on Knowledge and Proper Function', in Kvanvig (ed.), *Warrant in Contemporary Epistemology*, 55.

18 Michael Bergmann, 'Internalism, Externalism and the No-Defeater Condition', *Synthese* 110.3 (1997), 399-417.

19 This negative constraint on warrant is commonly referred to as a *no-defeater condition*. Bergmann, 'Internalism, Externalism and the No-Defeater Condition', 406-7. For a fuller discussion of internalist constraints in Plantinga's epistemology, see Michael C. Sudduth, 'The Internalist Character and Evidentialist Implications of Plantingian Defeaters', *International Journal for Philosophy of Religion* 45.3 (1999), 167-87.

warrant (i.e., that S must *have* introspective access to grounds for thinking B is reasonable to hold), one can distinguish 'moderate' externalists who accept that there is a negative internal constraint (i.e., that S must *lack* introspective access to grounds for thinking B is *un*reasonable to hold) from 'strong' externalists who reject even this latter condition.[20]

How then does Plantinga's analysis of warrant fare in this more refined debate between internalists and externalists? As I have noted, his conclusion that there must be *some* significant external constraints is now conceded by nearly all epistemologists, and he readily accepts the most plausible of proposed internal constraints on warrant (the negative condition mentioned above). The remaining question concerns whether he is correct to hold (against the 'moderate' internalists) that the necessary conditions of warrant do not include any *positive* internal constraints. Suffice it here to say that claims made in support of such constraints are controversial and typically open to counterexample. Furthermore, Michael Bergmann has recently developed a powerful argument against moderate internalism, by showing that any epistemology which places one or more positive internal constraints on warrant either faces infinite regress problems (thus implying that knowledge is impossible) or else offers no advantage over an externalist epistemology which rejects those constraints.[21] It seems therefore that Plantinga is on firm ground in advocating, as he does, a moderate externalist analysis of warrant.

5.3.2 Coherentism and Foundationalism

The second debate in epistemology addressed head-on in Plantinga's *Warrant* series is that between coherentism and foundationalism. Foundationalism, as Plantinga characterises it, is the view that (i) some of our beliefs are held *basically*, that is, not on the evidential basis of *other* beliefs, and (ii) basic beliefs can (at least in principle) be held *rationally* or with *warrant*. On a foundationalist picture of our noetic structures, warranted beliefs are either held basically (thus serving as the 'foundations' of our knowledge) or by way of *warrant transfer* from other warranted beliefs (e.g., on the basis of deductive or inductive inference).[22] One important feature of

---

20 Bergmann, 'Internalism, Externalism and the No-Defeater Condition', 408.
21 Michael Bergmann, *Justification without Awareness: A Defense of Epistemic Externalism* (Oxford: Oxford University Press, 2006), 3-24.
22 Plantinga, *Warrant*, 67-77.

foundationalism is its rejection of *circular reasoning*: a belief cannot be warranted by virtue of warrant transfer *alone*.[23]

Plantinga's analysis of coherentism is initially confusing in that, as he explicates the two competing views, coherentism turns out to be a 'special case' of foundationalism.[24] Coherentism arises from the conviction that no belief is an island; beliefs can enjoy warrant only by virtue of their relation to *other* beliefs (and ultimately to the overall coherence of a person's belief system). However, Plantinga takes pains to explain that, contrary to prevalent opinion, coherentists need not be committed to the implausible idea that circular reasoning is a source of warrant (provided the circle is sufficiently large). Rather, coherentism is most charitably defined as holding (i) that the basic source of warrant is *coherence itself* and (ii) that coherence is the *only* source of warrant in a person's noetic structure.[25] This thesis is quite compatible with a distinction between basic and non-basic beliefs and therefore with epistemic foundationalism (as Plantinga defines it). The important point is that for coherentists, basic beliefs can enjoy warrant *only* by virtue of their coherence with a person's overall belief system; for non-coherentist foundationalists, basic beliefs can be warranted in other ways as well.[26]

Although Plantinga maintains that coherentism cannot be summarily dismissed by charging it with an untenable reliance on circular reasoning, he still considers it to be 'clearly mistaken.'[27] The root of the problem is that it suffers from the same inadequacy as the theories of warrant based on internalist notions of justification: in each case, the favoured epistemic property is neither *necessary* nor *sufficient* for warrant. Plantinga marshals a battery of counterexamples to establish both points; I will repeat only one here, since it is particularly illuminative with respect to Plantinga's later

---

23 For example, S's belief that propositions p, q and r are true cannot be warranted solely on the grounds that p is good evidence for q, q is good evidence for r, and r is good evidence for p.

24 Plantinga, *Warrant*, 80.

25 Plantinga, *Warrant*, 77-80.

26 Plantinga notes that we can further distinguish between 'pure' coherentism, which rejects the idea of warrant transfer altogether (and therefore takes *all* beliefs to be basic), and 'impure' coherentism, which allows that beliefs can be warranted either directly, by way of coherence, or indirectly, by way of transfer from other warranted beliefs. Either way, the defining axiom of coherentism remains that coherence *alone* is the ultimate source of warrant in a person's noetic structure.

27 Plantinga, *Warrant*, 80.

conclusions about warrant.[28] To show that coherence alone can never be sufficient for warrant, Plantinga invites us to consider the 'Case of the Epistemically Inflexible Climber'. This individual, we are to imagine, is enjoying the sensuous experience of scaling a rock-face in the Grand Tetons. His beliefs, grounded in his present experiences, are entirely coherent and thoroughly warranted. Unfortunately, the climber

> is struck by a wayward burst of high-energy cosmic radiation. This induces a cognitive malfunction; his beliefs become fixed, no longer responsive to changes in experience. No matter what his experience, his beliefs remain the same.[29]

Having been rescued from the mountain, a friend tries to shake the climber out of his chronic belief-fixity by taking him to an opera, yet despite fully experiencing the music and atmosphere, his *beliefs* are still those he formed on the basis of his earlier climbing experiences. Plantinga's point is clear: although his beliefs are now no less *coherent* than when they were first formed, they are surely no longer *warranted*. Coherentism not only severs the connection between beliefs and experiences,[30] it also fails to account for lack of knowledge due to *cognitive dysfunction*. Plantinga continues his critique of coherentism by turning from 'coherentism *überhaupt*' to consider two sophisticated versions of coherentism—the theory of knowledge defended by Laurence BonJour and a model for rational belief regulation based on Bayesian probability—but finds that both suffer, as one might expect, from the same shortcomings as generic coherentism.

Plantinga thus rejects coherentism in favour of a less restrictive foundationalism according to which basic beliefs can obtain their warrant by a variety of means, not merely by way of coherence with other beliefs.

It would be a mistake, however, to think that Plantinga therefore endorses the narrow form of foundationalism that seeks to ground all human knowledge on a platform of indubitable and indisputable truths—an optimistic project launched by Enlightenment thinkers but now treated with almost universal scepticism (if not outright scorn) by modern philosophers. On the contrary, Plantinga utterly repudiates what he refers to as 'classical foundationalism': the thesis

---

28 Plantinga, *Warrant*, 81-84.
29 Plantinga, *Warrant*, 82.
30 'This is the source of a fatal consequence: on the coherentist view, a belief acquires no warrant by virtue of its relation to experience.' Plantinga, *Warrant*, 80.

that basic beliefs must be either self-evident, or incorrigible, or immediately evident to the senses, in order to be rationally acceptable.[31] On this view, most of our commonsense, everyday beliefs turn out to be unwarranted; more embarrassing still, so does the belief that classical foundationalism is true.

5.3.3 Reliabilism and Proper Function

Plantinga's analysis of warrant leads him to reject both internalism and narrow forms of foundationalism, such as coherentism and 'classical' foundationalism. Moreover, for each of the theories considered thus far, Plantinga enlists the notion of cognitive dysfunction to show that some necessary component of warrant has been overlooked. After an analysis of John Pollock's theory of knowledge—'a sort of uncomfortable halfway house, an uneasy compromise between internalism and externalism'[32]—Plantinga turns to consider various unashamedly externalist epistemologies. He assesses the theories of William Alston, Fred Dretske, and Alvin Goldman, each of which is form of *reliabilism*, according to which (roughly) a belief is warranted if and only if it is formed by a reliable belief-forming mechanism or process.[33] The difference between the theories of these three externalists lies in the way in which the central reliability constraint is spelled out. While Plantinga believes reliabilism is heading in the right direction—it avoids the misdirection of internalism (especially in its deontologist incarnations) and goes some way toward accounting for the commonsense view that our memory beliefs and perceptual beliefs can be both basic and warranted—it still does not give us the whole truth about warrant. One relatively minor problem is presented by the fact that warrant comes in *degrees*. Some beliefs are more warranted than others, even among beliefs of the same basic type (such as memory beliefs), but difficulties arise when trying to account for this doxastic feature simply in terms of what type of cognitive process or faculty is responsible for producing or sustaining those beliefs.

---

31 Plantinga first set his sights on this species of foundationalism in 'Reason and Belief in God', in Alvin Plantinga and Nicholas Wolterstorff (eds), *Faith and Rationality* (Notre Dame, IN: University of Notre Dame Press, 1983), 16-93.

32 Plantinga, *Warrant*, 162-81; Plantinga, *Warrant and Proper Function*, vii.

33 Plantinga notes that while reliabilism is the 'new boy on the block' in contemporary epistemology, its roots can be traced to the writings of Aristotle, Thomas Aquinas, and Thomas Reid.

More seriously though, no matter how one construes the reliability condition, the mere fact of a belief originating from a cognitive source that is reliable (with regard to producing *true* beliefs) is not sufficient for that belief to be warranted. Plantinga argues this point by way of a barrage of counterexamples to reliabilist accounts. The most illuminative one (and surely the best named) is the 'Case of the Epistemically Serendipitous Lesion', a version of which he employs for each of the three varieties of reliabilism in order to highlight its inadequacy.[34]

The basic form of this counterexample runs as follows. Suppose that S is suffering (unbeknown to him or to anyone else) from a rare type of brain lesion. The pathology of this lesion is such that it induces a number of belief-forming processes in the cognitive apparatus of S. While most of the beliefs thus formed are absurdly false, one of these processes results (by ironic coincidence) in the belief that S suffers from a brain lesion. Now, this process (we may stipulate) is a *reliable* one: the resulting beliefs are predominantly *true*. Moreover, a causal connection (often included in reliabilist accounts of warrant) is also present: the belief that S suffers from a brain lesion is caused by S's suffering from a brain lesion. Nonetheless, S's true belief hardly amounts to knowledge. The reason for this, Plantinga suggests, is obvious: the belief-forming process is only reliable *by accident*, by sheer dumb luck. The process itself is a consequence of cognitive *dysfunction* and therefore cannot be a source of warranted beliefs.

The Case of the Epistemically Serendipitous Lesion can be thought of as just one illustration of a general recipe for generating counterexamples to reliabilist accounts of warrant.[35] All that is required to reveal the insufficiency of the proposed reliabilist conditions of warrant is to concoct a scenario in which a belief-forming process is instigated or substantially affected by some cognitive dysfunction yet the resultant beliefs turn out, by happy accident, to be predominantly true. The conclusion is clear: reliability may be a necessary condition of warrant, but it is far from sufficient.[36]

---

34 A precursor of the Case of the Epistemically Serendipitous Lesion appears in the discussion of Alston's reliabilism. Plantinga, *Warrant*, 192. It is formally introduced as a counterexample to Dretske's reliabilist account, and modified versions are then enlisted against Goldman's earlier and later reliabilism. Plantinga, *Warrant*, 195, 199, 207.

35 Cf. Plantinga, *Warrant*, 192.

36 Plantinga refines his critique of reliabilism, as a response to William P. Alston, 'Epistemic Warrant as Proper Function', *Philosophy and*

Plantinga's central strategy in his critique of the various contemporary accounts of warrant is to show, by way of counterexample, that the proposed conditions of knowledge are either not necessary, or not sufficient, or both.[37] Moreover, whatever the other failings of each account, Plantinga emphasises that the notion of *cognitive dysfunction* can be introduced to secure its downfall. Thus, in the various counterexamples he marshals against internalism, deontologism, coherentism, and reliabilism, this element proves to be a recurring theme — whether due to a Cartesian demon, interfering Alpha Centaurian scientists,[38] brain envatment,[39] disruptive cosmic radiation,[40] pathological obsession or gullibility,[41] or epistemically serendipitous brain lesions. The conclusion Plantinga draws from this pattern is that the notion of *proper function* in our belief-forming faculties or processes must be an essential element of a satisfactory account of warrant. Any account that lacks this feature will inevitably fall foul of the sort of counterexamples that Plantinga wields.[42]

In *Warrant and Proper Function*, Plantinga turns from the negative task of identifying the deficiencies in existing accounts of warrant to the positive task of developing his own account of warrant, centred on the notion of proper function. According to this account, a belief is only warranted if it results from a cognitive faculty or process that is functioning properly. The notion of proper function leads naturally to the concept of a *design plan*: a 'blueprint' for our cognitive apparatus in terms of which any particular belief-forming faculty may be judged to be functioning properly or otherwise.[43]

Phenomenological Research 55.2 (1995), 397-402, in Alvin Plantinga, 'Reliabilism, Analyses and Defeaters', *Philosophy and Phenomenological Research* 55.2 (1995), 427-64. Whereas Plantinga had only targeted specific versions of reliabilism in *Warrant*, here he argues that *generic* reliabilism falls short as an account of warrant.

37 Cf. Plantinga, *Warrant and Proper Function*, v-x.
38 Plantinga, *Warrant*, 42, 44-45, 59, 61, 63, 81, 111, 130-31.
39 Plantinga, *Warrant*, 27.
40 Plantinga, *Warrant*, 210.
41 Plantinga, *Warrant*, 191.
42 Plantinga, *Warrant*, 212-15. For a defence of proper function as a necessary component of epistemic justification, see Bergmann, *Justification without Awareness*, 109-51.
43 Plantinga remarks that the concept of design here can be taken literally, as might a theist, or analogically (perhaps in terms of evolutionary goals), so that no controversial metaphysical questions are being begged. Plantinga, *Warrant and Proper Function*, 13. This might be thought somewhat misleading, since he later argues (194-215) that there are no naturalistic

Moreover, for any particular belief produced by cognitive faculties in accordance with the design plan, the relevant portions of the design plan must be *aimed at truth*. It is conceivable that beliefs might be formed in order to support some other goal than truth-attainment (e.g., survival or psychological comfort) but such beliefs would not be *warranted* (since warrant is an epistemic concept and thus aligned with truth-conducivity). Furthermore, the design plan must be a *good* one; those faculties geared toward furnishing us with true beliefs must, on the whole, do just that in practice. This amounts to a 'reliabilist constraint on warrant' corresponding to 'the important truth contained in reliabilist accounts of warrant.'[44] Among other things, the design plan will also include one or more 'defeater systems', which govern how beliefs will be accepted or revised in light of truth-relations with other beliefs.[45]

Beside these factors internal to the cognitive apparatus of the knower, there are also external constraints on warrant: specifically, the need for belief-forming faculties to operate in an environment conducive to their proper function. For example, if I perceive a red object in normal lighting, and form the belief that there is a red object before me, that belief would be warranted. Yet if I perceive the object illuminated (unbeknown to me) by red lighting, that same belief would *not* be warranted. It is not that my belief-forming faculties are *malfunctioning* in the second case; it is merely that the reliability of the beliefs produced is contingent on certain environmental factors.[46] Combining these internal and external constraints, Plantinga presents the following basic analysis of warrant:

> According to the central and paradigmatic core of our notion of warrant (so I say) a belief *B* has warrant for you if and only if (1) the cognitive faculties involved in the production of *B* are

---

accounts of proper function available that would satisfy the conditions of warrant. Although the matter cannot be pursued here, it is worth noting that these arguments, conjoined with the arguments for a proper function account of knowledge, provide the resources for an intriguing piece of natural theology.

44 Plantinga, *Warrant and Proper Function*, 17. Plantinga has pointed out, however, that his account should not be thought of as merely 'reliabilism plus'. The extent to which a belief-producing faculty needs to be reliable will depend on the details of the design plan and its execution. See Plantinga, 'Reliabilism, Analyses and Defeaters', 428, n. 2.

45 Plantinga, *Warrant and Proper Function*, 40-42. For more on epistemic defeaters, see §5.8.

46 Plantinga, *Warrant and Proper Function*, 6-7.

functioning properly (and this is to include the relevant defeater systems as well as those systems, if any, that provide *propositional* inputs to the system in question); (2) your cognitive environment is sufficiently similar to the one for which your cognitive faculties are designed; (3) the triple of the design plan governing the production of the belief in question involves, as purpose or function, the production of true beliefs (and the same goes for elements of the design plan governing the production of input beliefs to the system in question); and (4) the design plan is a good one: that is, there is a high statistical or objective probability that the belief produced in accordance with the relevant segment of the design plan in that sort of environment is true.[47]

One further detail is required in order to account for the fact that warrant comes in *degrees*: while I may know many things, some of my beliefs are more warranted than others. On Plantinga's account, then, 'the degree of warrant is given by some monotonically increasing function of the strength of S's belief that B.' As such, warrant depends on a certain psychological feature, viz. the firmness with which a belief is held. Even if a true belief satisfies all of Plantinga's conditions (1) through (4), if it is not held with enough conviction it will not be *sufficiently* warranted to constitute knowledge.

Armed with this basic paradigm, Plantinga explores in some detail the various *kinds* of knowledge that we are normally thought to possess—self-knowledge, memorial knowledge, perceptual knowledge, testimonial knowledge, *a priori* knowledge, inductive knowledge—and argues that each can be plausibly understood in terms of the proper function of cognitive faculties.

In later publications, Plantinga has refined his account of warrant in response to objections and alleged counterexamples.[48] Most notably, he has recognised the need to distinguish between cognitive *maxi*environments (i.e., broad or 'global' environmental conditions) and *mini*environments (i.e., narrow or 'local' circumstances, of which the believer is likely unaware) in order to handle certain Gettier-type examples involving 'accidentally' true beliefs.[49] Despite these adjustments, however, the basic contours of Plantinga's analysis of warrant remain, and it is this account that he carries forward to his lengthy treatment of theistic and Christian belief in *Warranted Christian Belief*.

---

47 Plantinga, *Warrant and Proper Function*, 194.
48 Plantinga, 'Reliabilism, Analyses and Defeaters'; Plantinga, 'Respondeo'.
49 Plantinga, *Warranted Christian Belief*, 156-61.

5.4 Warranted Theistic Belief

From the late 60s to the early 80s, Plantinga invested considerable effort in defending the thesis that belief in God (as traditionally conceived by theists) can be *properly basic*; that is, theistic belief can be rationally held without relying on evidential support from other, more fundamental beliefs. In *God and Other Minds*,[50] he critiqued the classical arguments for God's existence and a selection of contemporary arguments against God's existence, concluding that there are no compelling arguments either for or against theism.[51] The most promising is the teleological argument, he suggests, although it still falls short of providing adequate inferential support for belief in God.

However, in a ingenious move Plantinga proceeded to argue that belief in the existence of *other minds* (human or otherwise) is in precisely the same predicament, there being no compelling arguments to support or contradict it. The best hope in this case is some form of *analogical* argument, but such an argument suffers from the same difficulties afflicting the teleological theistic argument. Nonetheless, few people would seriously contend that belief in other minds is less than rational. Plantinga thus arrived at the following parity thesis: 'if my belief in other minds is rational, so is my belief in God. But obviously the former is rational; so, therefore, is the latter.'[52]

In his later essay 'Reason and Belief in God',[53] Plantinga developed this line of thinking by taking aim at what he dubbed the *evidentialist* objection to theism, according to which belief in God is irrational because there is insufficient evidence to support it.[54] Plantinga suggested that this objection is invariably motivated by a commitment (indigenous to both medieval and modern epistemology) to a *classical foundationalist* epistemology. Classical foundationalism maintains that in order to be rationally acceptable, beliefs must either be held on the evidential basis of other (rationally acceptable) beliefs or else be *properly basic*, where properly basic beliefs are either self-evident, evident to the senses, or incorrigible.

---

50 Alvin Plantinga, *God and Other Minds* (Ithaca, NY: Cornell University Press, 1967).
51 Plantinga later judged this verdict to be unnecessarily harsh. See the preface to the 1990 reedition of Plantinga, *God and Other Minds*.
52 Plantinga, *God and Other Minds*, 271.
53 Plantinga, 'Reason and Belief in God'.
54 Bertrand Russell, when asked what he would say if he were brought into God's presence and asked why he had not been a believer, is reported to have replied, 'Not enough evidence, God! Not enough evidence!'

But as Plantinga explains in his devastating critique, while classical foundationalism may condemn belief in God as irrational, it also rules as epistemically deficient a whole range of commonsense beliefs (such as the belief that the world has existed for longer than five minutes). Worse still, belief in classical foundationalism is *itself* irrational, by its own lights. Plantinga concluded that the criteria for properly basic belief must be far less narrow than classical foundationalism would have us believe and, moreover, that there is no good reason to assume belief in God would not fall into this category—in which case, the evidentialist objection quite misses the mark. Furthermore, this suggestion is by no means original to Plantinga; in fact, something close to the idea that theistic belief is properly basic featured in the theology of John Calvin and the subsequent Reformed tradition. The essay closed with a consideration of various objections to this basicality thesis, none of which Plantinga found compelling.

In *Warranted Christian Belief*, the third volume of his *Warrant* series, Plantinga's defence of the rationality of theistic belief reaches its most mature form. The main question he proposes to consider is whether or not classical Christian belief is 'intellectually acceptable'—even for 'educated and intelligent people living in the twenty-first century, with all that has happened over the last four or five hundred years'.[55] This is the *de jure* question of Christian belief (concerning whether such belief is rationally acceptable, epistemically respectable, warranted, etc.), to be distinguished from the *de facto* question (concerning whether such belief is *true*). Since Christian belief involves belief in God, it follows that if generic theistic belief is not rationally acceptable then neither is *Christian* theistic belief.

Plantinga therefore begins by addressing the *de jure* question with respect to theism *simpliciter*. After rebutting some Kantian and neo-Kantian objections to the very possibility of having beliefs about God, let alone rational ones, Plantinga considers various notions of rationality and asks in each case whether theistic belief could be 'rational' in the sense in question. He rehearses and extends his earlier rebuttal (in 'Reason and Belief in God') of the 'classical picture' of justification: the evidentialism, classical foundationalism, and deontologism typified by the writings of John Locke.[56] A more forgiving conception of justification, cashed out in terms of fulfilling one's epistemic duties, fails to provide any philosophically

---

55 Plantinga, *Warranted Christian Belief*, viii.
56 Plantinga, *Warranted Christian Belief*, 67-99.

interesting *de jure* question; a Christian could be wildly mistaken in her beliefs, yet without falling foul of any relevant epistemic obligations.[57] Other assorted versions of rationality—Aristotelian rationality, proper function rationality, compatibility with the deliverances of reason, means-end rationality, William Alston's 'practical rationality'—suffer a similar fate: none provides an interpretation of the *de jure* challenge with which the Christian should be at all troubled.[58]

From all this analysis Plantinga draws the conclusion that the truly interesting *de jure* question must be framed in terms of *warrant*—and that understood in terms of properly functioning cognitive faculties. This interpretation of the *de jure* objection to Christian belief accords well with criticisms typically levelled by sceptics of the Marxian and Freudian schools: the former claim that belief in God is a type of delusion (and is thus attributable to cognitive *dysfunction*); the latter contend that belief in God amounts to something like wish-fulfilment (and thus results from cognitive faculties functioning so as promote some psychological benefit, such as emotional well-being, but not *aimed at truth*).[59]

The interesting question, then, is whether the Christian's beliefs about God are *warranted*: whether they are produced by cognitive faculties functioning properly in a congenial epistemic environment according to a design plan successfully aimed at truth. Plantinga approaches the question by offering a model, inspired by Aquinas and Calvin, according to which theistic belief is indeed warranted, even to a high degree. According to this A/C model, human beings are by nature endowed with 'a kind of faculty or a cognitive mechanism, what Calvin calls a *sensus divinitatis* or sense of divinity, which in a wide variety of circumstances produces in us beliefs about God.'[60] These triggering circumstances would include such things as

---

57 Plantinga, *Warranted Christian Belief*, 99-102.

58 Plantinga, *Warranted Christian Belief*, 108-32. In his discussion of rationality in terms of proper function, Plantinga here restricts himself to considering the notion of irrationality as *pathological dysfunction*, i.e., the kind of cognitive malfunction that involves 'clinical psychoses.' In this sense, Plantinga remarks, most Christians are surely *not* irrational. Plantinga, *Warranted Christian Belief*, 110-13. Subtler forms of cognitive malfunction are considered, naturally enough, in Plantinga's later discussion of epistemic warrant.

59 Plantinga, *Warranted Christian Belief*, 135-63.

60 Plantinga, *Warranted Christian Belief*, 172.

the marvelous, impressive beauty of the night sky; the timeless crash and roar of the surf that resonates deep within us; the majestic grandeur of the mountains (the North Cascades, say, as viewed from Whatcom Pass); the ancient, brooding presence of the Australian outback; the thunder of a great waterfall.[61]

Similarly, the beauty, delicacy, and intricacy of living organisms could also induce the same response, as might certain common human experiences, such as guilt over wrongdoing or intense fear in the face of grave danger. Whatever the details, the point is that in a broad range of circumstances, typically experienced by all human beings at some time or other, this *sensus divinitatis* functions to generate beliefs such as that God exists, that he is powerful, good, transcendent, just, and so forth. Furthermore, because (according to the A/C model) the *sensus divinitatis* has been placed in us by a God who possesses the aforementioned attributes, these theistic beliefs are produced by a cognitive faculty functioning properly in a congenial epistemic environment according to a design plan successfully aimed at truth; which is just to say, they are *warranted* beliefs.[62] In accordance with Plantinga's earlier contentions, these beliefs are also *properly basic*: they are held with warrant, though not by way of inference from other beliefs.[63]

According to the A/C model, then, theistic beliefs can be warranted to a degree sufficient for knowledge. But is the model *true*—or at least close to the truth? The question of whether theistic beliefs *are* warranted ultimately depends on whether those beliefs

---

61   Plantinga, *Warranted Christian Belief*, 174.
62   Some reviewers have questioned whether Calvin conceived of the *sensus divinitatis* as a faculty or disposition toward true belief in God or as the resultant knowledge of God itself. See K. Scott Oliphint, 'Epistemology and Christian Belief', *Westminster Theological Journal* 63.1 (2001), 151-82; Michael C. Sudduth, 'Plantinga's Revision of the Reformed Tradition: Rethinking Our Natural Knowledge of God', *Philosophical Books* 43.2 (2002), 81-91. These criticisms are probably justified. However, this is partly a matter of terminology and partly a matter of tweaking the model. Plantinga's main contention—that theistic beliefs can easily meet the conditions of warrant— is substantially unaffected.
63   Plantinga, *Warranted Christian Belief*, 178-79. Since warrant requires that two important types of rationality be exemplified—external rationality (that is, proper function with respect to the formation of experience, whether sensuous or doxastic) and internal rationality (that is, the proper function of all belief-forming processes 'downstream from experience')—it follows that warranted theistic beliefs also enjoy external rationality and internal rationality. Plantinga, *Warranted Christian Belief*, 110, 179.

are *true*. If theism is *false*, then it goes without saying that human beings do not possess anything like a *sensus divinitatis*; in which case, theistic beliefs are unlikely to be warranted. But on the assumption that theism is *true*, it is entirely natural to suppose that God has equipped us with cognitive faculties designed to furnish us with true beliefs about our Creator; in which case, our beliefs about God (at least, those produced via such faculties) will normally be warranted.[64] This analysis leads Plantinga to a very significant conclusion, namely, that the *de jure* question concerning belief in God (i.e., whether theistic belief is justified, rational, warranted, etc.) is not logically independent of the corresponding *de facto* question (i.e., whether theistic belief is true). Furthermore, an important corollary of this thesis is that one cannot object to the *rationality* of theism without also objecting to its *truth*. As Plantinga puts it:

> [Atheologians] can't any longer adopt the following stance: "Well, I certainly don't know whether theistic belief is *true*—who could know a thing like that?—but I do know this: it is irrational, or unjustified, or not rationally justified, or contrary to reason or intellectually irresponsible or ..." There isn't a sensible *de jure* question or criticism that is independent of the *de facto* question. There aren't any *de jure* criticisms that are sensible when conjoined with the *truth* of theistic belief; all of them either fail right from the start (as with the claim that it is unjustified to accept theistic belief) or else really presuppose that theism is false.[65]

Despite the many virtues of Plantinga's A/C model, its logical cogency and the support it enjoys from certain streams of Christian tradition, one objection immediately presents itself. How does all this square with the phenomenon of widespread disagreement about God and even outright unbelief? Is this not compelling evidence against the existence of a *sensus divinitatis* (or at least, against its proper function or successful design)? Plantinga has a ready response: according to the A/C model, while all humans possess a faculty aimed at producing basic theistic beliefs, the actual operation of the faculty can be hindered, or even halted, by the presence of *sin* in a person's life. Among other things, sin involves an element of 'cognitive disease' that affects (to one degree or another) the operation of the *sensus divinitatis*.[66] Consequently, for any particular person the faculty may produce true beliefs but with insufficient strength, or fail to produce those beliefs at all, or even produce some

---

64   Plantinga, *Warranted Christian Belief*, 186-90.
65   Plantinga, *Warranted Christian Belief*, 191.
66   Plantinga, *Warranted Christian Belief*, 184-86.

false beliefs. Either way, the result will be a lack of true beliefs with warrant sufficient to constitute knowledge of God. This appeal to the controversial notion of sin, however, anticipates Plantinga's extension of the A/C model so as to cover not only *theistic* beliefs, but also specifically *Christian* beliefs—to which subject I now turn.

5.5 Warranted Christian Belief

The basic A/C model supplies an account of warranted belief in God. Christian belief, however, involves considerably more than mere belief in God (or beliefs about God); among other things, it includes beliefs about the spiritual state of human beings, about God's response to the human predicament, and about a historic individual, Jesus of Nazareth. Plantinga's goal is to show that even these more specific beliefs can be warranted to a degree adequate for knowledge; but rather than concern himself with controversial denominational views (e.g., convictions about the meaning and application of the sacraments) he proposes to restrict himself just to those ecumenical Christian beliefs expressed in the early creeds and confessions (or what C. S. Lewis dubbed 'mere Christianity').[67] To accomplish this, Plantinga develops an *extended* A/C model, according to which these beliefs are no less warranted than the theistic beliefs of the basic A/C model.

Reflecting Plantinga's own approach, I will sketch out the extended model before focusing in on the details. First of all, the extended A/C model posits those propositions affirmed by the basic Christian narrative, just as the basic A/C model posits the existence of God (as the author of the *sensus divinitatis*). According to the extended model, God created us in his own image, as persons possessing both intellect and will, endowed with the *sensus divinitatis* and therefore enjoying knowledge of God. We are also capable of affections and were originally made so as to share *God's* affections; to love what God loves and to hate what God hates.[68] However, 'we human beings have fallen into sin, a calamitous condition from which we require salvation—a salvation we are unable to accomplish by our own efforts.' This sin affects not only our relationship with God, but also our *knowledge* of God; in particular, 'the *sensus divinitatis* has been damaged and deformed [and furthermore] sin induces in us a *resistance* to the deliverances of the *sensus divinitatis*'. But there is also good news:

---

67 Plantinga, *Warranted Christian Belief*, 200-3.
68 Plantinga, *Warranted Christian Belief*, 204.

God ... has provided a remedy for sin and its ruinous effects, a means of salvation from sin and restoration to his favor and fellowship. This remedy is made available in the life, atoning suffering and death, and resurrection of his divine Son, Jesus Christ. Salvation involves among other things rebirth and regeneration, a process (beginning in the present life and reaching fruition in the next) that involves a restoration and repair of the image of God in us.[69]

Such are the basic theological contours of the extended A/C model; nothing that ought to prove controversial for any orthodox Christian believer. However, the extended model also makes some more specifically cognitive claims. In order to inform human beings of his scheme of salvation, God has specially inspired a collection of human writings, the Bible, in such a way as to be its principal author.

Furthermore, he has commissioned the Holy Spirit, in accordance with the promise of Christ, to produce *faith* in us, by which we are enabled to grasp and induced to believe 'the truth of the central Christian affirmations.' While faith is certainly a cognitive affair—it involves belief and assent to propositions—it is also a matter of the will and the affections. Most significantly, the way in which this faith arises has important implications for the epistemic status of the beliefs involved:

> In giving us faith, the Holy Spirit enables us to see the truth of the main lines of the Christian gospel as set forth in Scripture. The internal invitation of the Holy Spirit is therefore a source of belief, a cognitive process that produces in us belief in the main lines of the Christian story. Still further, according to the model, the beliefs thus produced in us meet the conditions necessary and sufficient for warrant; they are produced by cognitive processes functioning properly (in accord with their design plan) in an appropriate epistemic environment (both maxi and mini) according to a design plan successfully aimed at truth; if they are held with sufficient firmness, these beliefs qualify as *knowledge*, just as Calvin's definition of faith has it.[70]

Such is the essential structure of the extended A/C model. After introducing its basic contours, Plantinga proceeds to discuss at length the noetic effects of sin: the implications of our fallen state for our knowledge both of God and of the world. The details of his

---

69 Plantinga, *Warranted Christian Belief*, 205.
70 Plantinga, *Warranted Christian Belief*, 206.

exposition on this subject need not detain us here. Instead, I wish to turn immediately to Plantinga's exposition of how, according to the extended model, specifically *Christian* beliefs come to enjoy warrant and precisely what role the Bible plays in that process, for this will serve as the foundation for my later discussion of Christian *doctrines*.

Plantinga recognises that the extended model he proposes is one prompted by a particular Christian tradition, namely, that of Calvin and the Reformers. Nevertheless, he maintains that alternative models can be constructed, in accordance with other traditions, for which Christian belief turns out to be just as warranted as on his favoured model.[71] As Plantinga explains, according to his own model there are three main elements involved in a person coming to know 'the great things of the gospel' (as Jonathan Edwards put it):

> First, he arranged for the production of *Scripture*, the Bible, a library of books or writings each of which has a human author, but each of which is also specially inspired by God in such a way that he himself is its principal author. Thus the whole library has a single principal author: God himself. In this library, he proposes much for our belief and action, but there is a central theme and focus (and for this reason this collection of books is itself a book): the gospel, the stunning good news of the way of salvation God has graciously offered. Correlative with Scripture and necessary to its properly serving its purpose is the *second* element of this three-tiered cognitive process: the presence and action of the Holy Spirit promised by Christ himself before his death and resurrection, and invoked and celebrated in the epistles of the apostle Paul. By virtue of the work of the Holy Spirit in the hearts of those to whom faith is given, the ravages of sin (including the cognitive damage) are repaired, gradually or suddenly, to a greater or lesser extent. Furthermore, it is by virtue of the activity of the Holy Spirit that Christians come to grasp, believe, accept, endorse, and rejoice in the truth of the great things of the gospel. It is thus by virtue of this activity that the Christian believes that "in Christ, God was reconciling the world to himself in Christ, not counting men's sins against them" (2 Corinthians 5:19).[72]

While the first two elements are *external* to the believer, the third is *internal*:

> According to John Calvin, the principal work of the Holy Spirit is the production (in the hearts of Christian believers) of the third

---

71 Plantinga, *Warranted Christian Belief*, 242.
72 Plantinga, *Warranted Christian Belief*, 243-44.

element of the process, *faith*. ... Faith therefore involves an explicitly cognitive element; it is, says Calvin, *knowledge*—knowledge of the availability of redemption and salvation through the person and work of Jesus Christ—and it is revealed to our minds.[73]

As Plantinga describes things here, it appears that the role of Scripture is to supply the *content* of belief—the propositions to be believed—while the role of the Holy Spirit is to *produce* the belief itself (as a component of faith) in the mind of the Christian.[74] Moreover, the propositional content in question is considerably less than the totality of scriptural teaching. It is restricted to 'the main lines of the Christian gospel': the content of faith is 'just the central teachings of the gospel'.[75] On this view, the formation of Christian belief is decidedly unnatural; indeed, it is *super*natural:

> These beliefs do not come to the Christian just by way of memory, perception, reason, testimony, the *sensus divinitatis*, or any other of the cognitive faculties with which we human beings were originally created; they come instead by way of the work of the Holy Spirit, who gets us to accept, causes us to believe, these great truths of the gospel. These beliefs don't come just by way of the normal operation of our natural faculties; they are a supernatural gift.[76]

With this tri-partite process in hand, Plantinga sketches the typical scenario by which a person comes to believe the gospel through an encounter with Scripture:

> We read Scripture, or something presenting scriptural teaching, or hear the gospel preached, or are told of it by parents, or encounter a scriptural teaching as the conclusion of an argument (or conceivably even as an object of ridicule), or in some other way encounter a proclamation of the Word. What is said simply seems right; it seems compelling; one finds oneself saying, "Yes, that's right, that's the truth of the matter; this is indeed the word of the Lord." I read, "God was in Christ, reconciling the world to

---

73 Plantinga, *Warranted Christian Belief*, 244.
74 Cf. Plantinga's comparison of his model with the account of Christian belief suggested by Aquinas: 'Here we have (embryonically, at any rate) the same trio of processes: there is *belief*, there is the *divine teaching* (as given in Scripture) which is the object of that belief, and there is also special divine activity in the production of the belief ("the inward instigation of the divine invitation").' Plantinga, *Warranted Christian Belief*, 249.
75 Plantinga, *Warranted Christian Belief*, 248.
76 Plantinga, *Warranted Christian Belief*, 245.

himself"; I come to think: "Right; that's true; God really was in Christ, reconciling the world to himself!" And I may also think something a bit different, something *about* that proposition: that it is indeed a divine teaching or revelation, that in Calvin's words it is "from God." What one hears or reads seems clearly and obviously true, and (at any rate in paradigm cases) seems also to be something the Lord is intending to teach.[77]

Two things should be observed at this point. The first is that Plantinga's model allows for the production not only of first-order beliefs about the gospel (for example, that Christ died for our sins) but also of second-order beliefs *about* those first-order beliefs (for example, that the belief that Christ died for our sins comes to me by way of the very teaching of God). The second point to note is that, on the basis of Plantinga's exposition thus far, it appears that the reading or hearing of Scripture is needed only to provide (i) the propositional *content* of Christian belief and (ii) the *occasion* of coming to believe that content. The idea seems to be that on encountering the biblical declaration that 'God was in Christ reconciling the world', a person *entertains* (presumably in a natural way) the proposition expressed by that claim; the Holy Spirit may then affect the mind of the person so as to induce *belief* in that proposition. This understanding of the role of Scripture in Plantinga's model seems to be confirmed by the following passage:

> This process can go on in a thousand ways; in each case there is presentation or proposal of central Christian teaching, and by way of response, the phenomenon of being convinced, coming to see, forming of a conviction. There is the reading or hearing, and then there is the belief or conviction that what one reads or hears is true and a teaching of the Lord.[78]

If this interpretation of Plantinga's model is correct, then I suggest that many would find this account of Christian belief somewhat at odds with Christian tradition. For the Bible has usually been understood by believers to serve not merely as a conduit for true propositions, but also as a *testimony* to their truth. Indeed, this appears to be the view promoted by Christ and by Scripture itself:

> 'You diligently study the Scriptures because you think that by them you possess eternal life. These are the Scriptures that testify about me, yet you refuse to come to me to have life.'[79]

---

77 Plantinga, *Warranted Christian Belief*, 250.
78 Plantinga, *Warranted Christian Belief*, 251.
79 John 5:39-40.

> This is the disciple who testifies to these things and who wrote them down. We know that his testimony is true.[80]

> But now a righteousness from God, apart from law, has been made known, to which the Law and the Prophets testify.[81]

> To the law and to the testimony! If they do not speak according to this word, they have no light of dawn.[82]

However, according to the model as presented thus far by Plantinga, even if Scripture *is* a testimony to God's plan of salvation through Christ, this feature seems to play *no role* in the formation of Christian belief. As such, God might equally well have used a set of writings with no testimonial value whatsoever—for example, documents that were written in ignorance, in jest, or as an inspiring work of fiction— but which just so happened to express (unbeknown to the authors and contrary to their intentions) the true propositions of the gospel.[83] Furthermore, not only is this traditional characteristic of the Bible neglected by Plantinga's exposition to this point, it even appears to be explicitly ruled out, because according to Plantinga's earlier statement Christian belief does not come by way of any of our normal cognitive faculties, including those devoted to the acceptance of testimony.[84]

The apparent exclusion of the testimonial value of Scripture is a surprising aspect of Plantinga's opening discussion of the formation of warranted Christian beliefs. Still more surprising is that Plantinga suddenly changes tack at this point in his treatment and affirms that the Bible *is indeed* testimony, as if this were in fact an important feature of the extended A/C model:

> According to the model, this conviction [that what one reads or hears is true and a teaching of the Lord] comes by way of the activity of the Holy Spirit. Calvin speaks here of the internal 'testimony' and (more often) 'witness' of the Holy Spirit; Aquinas, of the divine 'instigation' and 'invitation'. On the model, there is both Scripture and the divine activity leading to human belief. God himself (on the model) is the principal author of Scripture. Scripture is most importantly a message, a communication from

---

80 John 21:24.
81 Rom. 3:21.
82 Isa. 8:20.
83 Of course, scriptures with such origins would introduce myriad other problems. The point here is only that they would be equally adequate in supplying the *content* and *occasion* of Christian belief.
84 Plantinga, *Warranted Christian Belief*, 245.

God to humankind; Scripture is a word from the Lord. But then this just is a special case of the pervasive process of testimony, by which, as a matter of fact, we learn most of what we know. From this point of view, Scripture is as much a matter of testimony as is a letter you receive from a friend. What is proposed for our belief in Scripture, therefore, just *is* testimony—divine testimony. So the term 'testimony' is appropriate here. However, there is also the special work of the Holy Spirit in getting us to believe, in enabling us to see the truth of what is proposed.[85]

Continuing on this theme, Plantinga writes:

So Scripture is, indeed, testimony, even if it is testimony of a very special kind. First, the principal testifier is God. It also differs from ordinary testimony in that in this case, unlike most others, there is both a principal testifier and subordinate testifiers: the human authors. There is still another difference: it is the instigation of the Holy Spirit, on this model, that gets us to see and believe that the propositions proposed for our beliefs in Scripture really *are* a word from the Lord. This case also differs from the usual run of testimony, then, in that the Holy Spirit not only writes the letter (appropriately inspires the human authors) but also does something special to enable you to believe and appropriate its contents. So this testimony is not the usual run of testimony; it is testimony nonetheless. According to the model, therefore, faith is the belief in the great things of the gospel that results from the internal instigation of the Holy Spirit.[86]

I suggest that the picture painted in these latter passages of the way in which Christian beliefs arise is substantially different from the one presented by Plantinga in his earlier exposition. On this latter view, Scripture contributes more than mere propositional content. It actually functions as testimony. Even so, this is insufficient in itself to bring about Christian belief in accordance with God's plan; thus, the additional intervention of the Holy Spirit is required in order to *enable* and *encourage* belief in the central gospel message. Just how much of the belief production is to be attributed to the testimony of Scripture and how much to the witness of the Spirit is unclear (and perhaps unimportant). The point, however, is that on this latter picture the testimonial value of Scripture *does* play some role in the appropriation of its truth.

---

85 Plantinga, *Warranted Christian Belief*, 251.
86 Plantinga, *Warranted Christian Belief*, 252.

How should this ambiguity regarding the role of Scripture in Plantinga's exposition be resolved? Before attempting to address it, I wish to introduce into the discussion another potential problem in his account—a problem that, as it turns out, suggests a way of resolving this curious ambiguity along with the problem itself.

On Plantinga's model, Christian belief arises by way of the 'internal instigation of the Holy Spirit' (IIHS)—that is, the supernatural operation of the Holy Spirit, the third Person of the Trinity, on the cognitive and volitional faculties of a person so as to bring about belief in the testimony of Scripture (at least regarding 'the great things of the gospel'). Plantinga characterises this belief formation as a *process*, rather than in terms of the operation of a *faculty*. He does so primarily, it would seem, because of the crucial contribution of the Holy Spirit: because the Spirit is not part of the cognitive apparatus of the Christian, the IIHS cannot be straightforwardly thought of as either a faculty or the operation of a faculty.[87] Thus it seems more accurate to speak of it as a *process* of belief-formation.

But there is a difficulty here. For while it makes sense to speak of a *faculty* as 'functioning properly', it is rather less clear that it makes equal sense to speak of a *process* as 'functioning properly'. A process *qua* process is just not the sort of thing that intrinsically possesses a function; *a fortiori*, it is not the sort of thing that can be said to function properly. The freezing of water, for example, is a process. But what sense does it make to ask whether this process *as such* is functioning properly or not? Richard Gale has identified and commented on the problem as follows:

> In regard to basic religious beliefs that are internally instigated by the Holy Spirit, it is obvious that the notion of proper functioning could have no application to them since they are supernaturally caused directly by God. Such instigation, furthermore, is not a faculty but a process and thus cannot be said to have any function and therefore cannot be said to malfunction or be subject to a pathology; for there is no correct way for God to supernaturally cause worldly occurrences. Plantinga recognizes this difficulty: "A *caveat*: as Andrew Dole points out in 'Cognitive Processes, Cognitive Faculties, and the Holy Spirit in Plantinga's Warrant Series' (as yet unpublished), it is not obvious that one can directly transfer necessary and sufficient conditions for warrant from

---

87 Recall Plantinga's earlier comment that Christian beliefs do not come by way of any of our natural cognitive faculties. Plantinga, *Warranted Christian Belief*, 245.

beliefs produced by *faculties* to beliefs produced by *processes*." (257) Plantinga gives no response to this caveat, nor do I think one can be given.[88]

Although I would take issue with Gale's claim that 'there is no correct way for God to supernaturally cause worldly occurrences' — after all, proper function is a *teleological* notion rather than a *nomological* one — his basic criticism is justified. Unlike faculties, processes *as such* do not have functions. Plantinga appears to be aware of this, but he does nothing to address it.

I suggest that there are at least two ways for Plantinga to resolve this issue.[89] The first would be to treat the combination of the cognitive apparatus of the believer and the action of the Holy Spirit as a *system* of belief-formation: a system intended or designed to bring about that *process* of belief-formation which Plantinga labels the 'internal instigation of the Holy Spirit'. While not every system is a faculty,[90] a system is nonetheless the sort of thing that can be naturally thought of as having a function. Moreover, there seems to be nothing objectionable about viewing the action of the Holy Spirit on the mind of a human being as part of a system by which

---

88 Richard Gale, 'Alvin Plantinga's *Warranted Christian Belief*' (2001). A similar complaint is raised by Pierre Le Morvan and Dana Radcliffe, 'Plantinga on Warranted Christian Belief', *The Heythrop Journal* 44.3 (2003), 345-51.

89 A third solution, proposed by Andrew Dole, involves 'a readjustment of the central paradigm for knowledge' along self-consciously theistic lines. Andrew Dole, 'Cognitive Faculties, Cognitive Processes, and the Holy Spirit in Plantinga's *Warrant* Series', *Faith and Philosophy* 19.1 (2002), 34-46. According to Dole, God's knowledge provides the paradigm for human knowledge, leading to a deeper analysis of warrant in terms of the 'epistemic credentials' of the source of a belief. Divine beliefs, naturally enough, have maximally good epistemic credentials. Human beliefs, however, ultimately depend on divine knowledge for their credentials and consequently on the way in which those beliefs are produced: either *immediately*, by the direct supernatural operation of the Holy Spirit, or *mediately*, by way of cognitive faculties functioning according to a divine design plan (as in Plantinga's account of warrant). Dole's basic point about epistemic credentials seems plausible, but I do not adopt his solution here because it fails to incorporate the testimonial aspect of Scripture. By his own admission, on his view the Bible is only essential to Christian knowledge to the extent that God decides to make the reading of Scripture the *occasion* of Christian belief. Dole, 'Cognitive Faculties', 43-44.

90 As Plantinga uses the term 'faculty', the reverse is true: cognitive faculties are systems (or perhaps *sub*systems) of belief production.

Christian beliefs are produced.[91] If this system is designed in such a way as to bring about a preponderance of true beliefs in a congenial epistemic environment, then beliefs produced in such circumstances would appear to meet Plantinga's conditions of warrant.

Although this response would seem to address Gale's objection, it does nothing to resolve the ambiguity in Plantinga's account of the role of Scripture and tends to reinforce the notion that the testimonial value of Scripture does not contribute to the warrant of Christian beliefs. For this reason, I think another solution is preferable. In the earlier stages of Plantinga's discussion, although the testimonial aspect of Scripture passes without mention, neither is it explicitly denied; yet in his later comments, as we have seen, it is explicitly affirmed. It seems therefore that while there is an element of inconsistency here, on the whole Plantinga *does* mean to acknowledge that the testimonial aspect of the Bible is an important component of his extended A/C model. If so, it would be natural to assume that the model should involve, at least in part, the operation of those human cognitive faculties designed for the formation of belief based on *testimony*. Following Thomas Reid, Plantinga defends these faculties at length in *Warrant and Proper Function*, arguing that testimony 'is the source of an enormously large proportion of our most important beliefs'; that we are 'dependent upon testimony for most of what we know'; and that testimony is 'a crucially important part of our noetic arsenal'.[92] It is a key feature of the design plan of our cognitive faculties that we naturally form beliefs on the basis of the testimony of others; thus, according to a proper function account, testimonial beliefs can be warranted to a degree sufficient for knowledge.

How then might these faculties play a role in the extended A/C model? Various plausible options present themselves. One possibility is that Christian beliefs are formed in the same basic way as other testimonial beliefs on encountering the witness of Scripture, but the Holy Spirit acts so as to considerably *strengthen* these beliefs (which would otherwise lack the *degree* of warrant required for knowledge). The regenerative work of the Holy Spirit might well

---

91   As far as I can tell, there is nothing incoherent about treating an intentional agent as a component of a system, designed to bring about a certain result. For example, the UK Passport Service has a system for producing passports that includes both human agents and non-intentional elements (such as computers and printing presses). It makes perfect sense to speak of this system, *as a whole*, functioning properly—that is, operating according to a good design plan aimed at reliable passport production.

92   Plantinga, *Warrant and Proper Function*, 77-78, 87.

play a key role here: no doubt the presence of sin in our own lives and those of others has caused us generally to treat testimony with greater scepticism; perhaps therefore the Spirit acts so as to overcome this subversive and (in the case of divine testimony) inappropriate doubtfulness.

Alternatively, the activity of the Holy Spirit might be thought of as bringing about a *congenial epistemic environment* for the formation of testimonial beliefs based on Scripture. On this view, the natural recognition and acceptance of divine testimony is actually part of the proper operation of our cognitive faculties, although its operation (like that of the *sensus divinitatis*) has been affected by the human sin and the correlative withdrawal of the divine presence in our lives.

A third, but similar account could treat the recognition and acceptance of divine testimony as part of the *original* design plan for human cognition, where that testimony is associated with a range of identifying phenomena. This faculty has been rendered inoperative by sin, yet the Holy Spirit graciously acts so as (i) to repair the faculty (at least to the extent that beliefs in the 'great things of the gospel' are formed) and (ii) to fortify the beliefs produced in this manner. In fact, this belief-producing component need not be part of an original cognitive design plan at all, but could be implemented by way of the supernatural modification or adaptation of *existing* faculties (primarily, one would assume, those involved in the formation of testimonial beliefs). As Plantinga elsewhere explains, beliefs can be warranted according to *new* design plans as well as original ones. Provided that beliefs are formed in accordance with the relevant segments of a *current* design plan successfully aimed at true belief production, such beliefs can still be warranted.[93]

---

93 Plantinga, *Warrant and Proper Function*, 26. Prior to the publication of *Warranted Christian Belief*, it appears that Plantinga envisaged just such a scenario: '[I]n *Warranted Christian Belief*, the third and (I devoutly hope) last in the Warrant series, I follow John Calvin and much of the rest of the Christian tradition in arguing that Christian faith is produced by way of the Internal Testimony of the Holy Spirit; I also mean to hold, of course, that Christian faith so produced can constitute knowledge. ... What happens in this case, we can suppose, is that there is a smallish revision in the design plan governing the relevant parts of my cognitive architecture, as well as the architecture of will and what Jonathan Edwards calls "affections," in particular the *religious* affections. *The relevant cognitive powers are, so to say, mildly redesigned, and they work properly according to his new design plan.*' Plantinga, 'Respondeo', 337-38, final emphasis added.

Perhaps the best option here will incorporate aspects of several of the above. Indeed, just such a multifaceted view is suggested by what the *Westminster Larger Catechism* has to say on the matter:

> The Scriptures manifest themselves to be the Word of God, by their majesty and purity; by the consent of all the parts, and the scope of the whole, which is to give all glory to God; by their light and power to convince and convert sinners, to comfort and build up believers unto salvation: but the Spirit of God bearing witness by and with the Scriptures in the heart of man, is alone able fully to persuade it that they are the very word of God.[94]

Here the natural faculties concerned with the acceptance of testimony are involved, yet there are also features unique to Scripture that indicate its divine origin; moreover, the work of the Holy Spirit is needed to internally enable, induce, and strengthen the resultant beliefs. Whatever the details here, the basic picture is clear enough:

- those natural faculties normally involved in the formation of testimonial beliefs are also involved in the formation of Christian belief;
- the gracious activity of the Holy Spirit is nevertheless essential for those beliefs to be formed at all (because of the noetic effects of sin) and with sufficient psychological firmness as to meet the conditions of knowledge, such that Christian faith may rightly be deemed a divine gift;
- all of this proceeds in accordance with a divine design plan and thus involves human cognitive faculties functioning properly (i.e., operating as intended), well aimed at truth, and in a congenial epistemic environment.

As such, Christian beliefs meet all of the conditions of warrant and can be warranted to a degree sufficient for knowledge. I suggest that this second solution, by casting matters in terms of *faculties*, avoids the objections invited by talk of 'properly functioning processes'; moreover, unlike the first solution, it also nicely accommodates the traditional Christian recognition of the testimonial value of Scripture.

One final point is worth noting with regard to Plantinga's extended A/C model. It might well be asked why this relatively elaborate scheme, with its appeal to supernatural intervention, should be required in order for Christian beliefs to be warranted. Could these beliefs not simply be warranted through normal historical investigation into the reliability of the biblical documents?

---

94 *Westminster Larger Catechism*, Question 4.

Is it not possible to build a solid *evidential* case for the basic claims of the Christian gospel—that Jesus of Nazareth was the divine Messiah, that he was crucified for our sins but rose from the dead, that he founded the church and commissioned the writing of the New Testament, and so on—along the lines proposed by Richard Swinburne? Plantinga's answer is, first of all, that such methods are beyond the grasp of the average believer; yet the Christian faith is surely not the property of intellectual sophisticates.[95] Moreover, a predominantly inferential strategy could never deliver the goods in any case. Its inevitable failure is due to the 'principle of dwindling probabilities': each stage in the evidential argument will only be *probable* with respect to the conclusions of the preceding stage, and the probability of the final conclusion must be calculated by *multiplying* the probabilities involved in each stage. Thus, for an argument of any complexity (as this one would indeed be) the overall probability will be rather lower than 0.5—in other words, the target propositions will turn out to be less probable than their denial with respect to any uncontroversial stock of background knowledge.[96] For this reason, Plantinga contends, a model in which warranted Christian beliefs are formed in a basic way is to be preferred—and, as a matter of historical fact, *has* been preferred among thinkers in the Reformed tradition.

5.6 Revelation, Scripture, and Doctrine

I have thus far explicated and defended Plantinga's extended Aquinas/Calvin model for warranted Christian beliefs. By Plantinga's own admission, the model does not cover every teaching of Scripture: beliefs formed by way of the IIHS concern only 'the

---

95 Cf. Matt. 11:25; 1 Cor. 1:26-27. William Alston, also advocating an externalist view of religious knowledge, makes a similar point: 'Even at the most optimistic estimate the average person in the pew, or even the average sophisticated theologian or religious philosopher, would be hard pressed to *show* that the Bible contains revelations from God that carry a divine guarantee of truth, or that the church is guided by the Holy Spirit in its doctrinal pronouncements. At least any claims to be able to show this will be highly controversial. Thus from an internalist justification approach to knowledge, prospects do not look good for satisfying necessary conditions for religious knowledge.' William P. Alston, 'On Knowing That We Know: The Application to Religious Knowledge', in C. Stephen Evans and Merold Westphal (eds), *Christian Perspectives on Religious Knowledge* (Grand Rapids, MI: Eerdmans, 1993), 22.

96 Plantinga, *Warranted Christian Belief*, 268-80.

main lines of the Christian story.'[97] Concerning his use of the label 'Christian' in the description of his project, and the beliefs he associates with it, Plantinga makes the following claims:

> However we propose to use that term, my project is to inquire into the epistemological status of a certain set of beliefs: the ones embodied, say, in the Apostle's [sic] Creed and the Nicene Creed. (Alternatively, we could identify the beliefs in question as belonging to the intersection of those expressed in the creeds of more specific Christian communities [the New Catholic Catechism, the Heidelberg Catechism, the Augsburg Confession, the Westminster Catechism, and so on].)[98]

> [T]he propositional object of faith is the whole magnificent scheme of salvation God has arranged. To have faith is to know that and how God has made it possible for us human beings to escape the ravages of sin and be restored to a right relationship with him; it is therefore a knowledge of the main lines of the Christian gospel. The content of faith is just the central teachings of the gospel; it is contained in the intersection of the great Christian creeds.[99]

> I've argued that Christian belief—the full panoply of Christian belief, including trinity, incarnation, atonement, resurrection—can, if true, have warrant, can indeed have sufficient warrant for knowledge, and can have that warrant in the basic way. There are no cogent philosophical objections to the notion that these beliefs can have warrant in this way. It is easily possible to work out an account—for example, the extended Aquinas/Calvin (A/C) model—of how it is that beliefs of these sorts do indeed have warrant.[100]

Despite Plantinga's claims, however, the extended A/C model does *not* cover belief in the Trinity and the Incarnation—at least, not if we understand that to involve assent to the orthodox doctrines of the Trinity and the Incarnation formulated in the fourth and fifth centuries. The model does *not* include belief in 'the intersection of the great Christian creeds' if by that phrase Plantinga means to include at least (as one would reasonably assume) the Nicene-Constantinopolitan trinitarian statements and the Chalcedonian christological statements. The reason for this is clear: such doctrines are not *explicitly stated* in the Bible, even if they nonetheless faithfully

---

97   Plantinga, *Warranted Christian Belief*, 206.
98   Plantinga, *Warranted Christian Belief*, 202.
99   Plantinga, *Warranted Christian Belief*, 248.
100 Plantinga, *Warranted Christian Belief*, 357.

express biblical teaching. If the text of Scripture were such that belief in the doctrines of the Trinity and the Incarnation could arise just as the extended A/C model suggests, there would have been no need for such creeds to be formulated in the first place. As such, Plantinga's account of warranted Christian beliefs does not go so far as to explain how Christian *doctrines* can also be warranted. It will therefore be necessary to explain how the extended A/C model might reasonably be developed so as to cover these 'higher level' articles of the Christian faith.

There is considerable disagreement, of course, among professing Christians as to the epistemological foundation of doctrines such as those of the Trinity and the Incarnation. There exist disparate views in competing traditions about the relationship between Scripture and doctrine, the historical development of doctrine, the criteria of doctrinal criticism, and so forth. These issues cannot be treated in great detail here. Instead, I propose to briefly outline four influential perspectives on Christian doctrine, and to select one of the four to provide the basis of a model for warranted Christian doctrines, giving reasons for that choice. These four perspectives may be distinguished with respect to their understanding of *divine revelation* and the consequent relationship of revelation to doctrine.[101] I should emphasise that by focusing on this aspect of doctrine (i.e., the source and ground of its content) I do not mean to suggest that Christian doctrine is nothing more than summary statements of the theological beliefs of the church. Clearly doctrine serves other important functions, such as establishing the identity of a religious community (as I noted in Chapter 4) and providing an interpretive framework

---

101 There is a fifth view, which I do not include here, but which certainly needs to be acknowledged given its recent popularity. This is the so-called *postliberal* account, associated primarily with the work of George Lindbeck (*The Nature of Doctrine*, 1984), according to which doctrines are not so much statements about an extra-linguistic reality as claims about how Christian discourse ought to be conducted. On this view, doctrinal statements are better understood as second-level statements about other statements, rather than first-level statements about non-linguistic entities; in short, they function as the 'grammar' of Christian theology. As I remarked earlier, in my judgement this view effectively adopts an anti-realist (or at best *non-*realist) stance with respect to Christian doctrinal claims and is therefore subject to the difficulties raised in Chapter 4. Regardless of its other merits or demerits, it fails to provide a satisfactory solution to the problem of theological paradox. For a fair-minded critique of Lindbeck's thesis, see McGrath, *The Genesis of Doctrine*, 14-34.

for the church's experiences and *praxis*.[102] My concern here, however, is with a specific epistemological issue, which can be distilled into two questions: given that Christian doctrines do affirm certain propositions about God and his actions within human history, what is the *source* of the propositions expressed in those doctrines and how could anyone come to *know* that those propositions are true?

5.6.1 Four Perspectives on Christian Doctrine

By far the majority opinion within the church has been that the content of Christian doctrines is grounded in divine revelation—this belief being motivated by a firm conviction that if finite human beings are to know anything about their transcendent Creator then that knowledge must come by way of God graciously *revealing* himself to us by some means or other, rather than through our own unaided investigations.[103] This much is generally agreed; the disagreement concerns the precise *character*, *location*, and *appropriation* of this divine revelation. I propose to consider four broad camps in the debate: (1) the 'Reformed' perspective; (2) the 'Catholic' perspective; (3) the 'Neo-Orthodox' perspective; and (4) the 'Liberal' perspective.

As a first candidate, there is the Reformed perspective on doctrine associated with Calvin and the Protestant tradition and encapsulated in the Reformation slogan '*sola scriptura*'. On this view, God reveals

---

102 Alister McGrath has argued that as a matter of historical fact, Christian doctrine has been understood as exhibiting four major dimensions: (1) doctrine as social demarcator; (2) doctrine as interpretation of the Christian narrative; (3) doctrine as interpretation of Christian experience; and (4) doctrine as truth claim. McGrath, *The Genesis of Doctrine*, 35-80. In light of the specific epistemological question being addressed in this section, I am focusing only on the second and fourth dimensions: given that Christian doctrines make truth claims, my concern is to give an account of how those truths might be *known* by way of the Christian narrative (i.e., Scripture).

103 'For the first eighteen centuries of the Christian era, while there were certainly different understandings of the precise nature and intermediate sources of revelation, and while revelation itself as a source and norm for theology was various correlated with other relevant factors, there was nonetheless general agreement that "revelation" was both a necessary and a central feature of the religious and theological encounter with God. God was to be "known", that is to say, and subsequently spoken of only as and when God rendered the form and substance of such "knowing", establishing humans in a knowing relationship otherwise inaccessible to them.' Trevor Hart, 'Revelation', in John Webster (ed.), *The Cambridge Companion to Karl Barth* (Cambridge: Cambridge University Press, 2000), 37.

himself (indeed, God *speaks*) through the text of the Bible, by way of inspiring the human authors to write just those things he wishes to communicate.[104] Since the Bible is the only collection of human writings inspired by God, so the thinking runs, true Christian doctrine should derive from the teaching of Scripture alone. Representing the Reformed school, the *Westminster Confession of Faith* affirms:

> The Supreme Judge, by which all controversies of religion are to be determined, and all decrees of councils, opinions of ancient writers, doctrines of men, and private spirits, are to be examined, and in whose sentence we are to rest, can be no other but the Holy Spirit speaking in the Scripture.[105]

A second candidate deserving due consideration is the Catholic perspective on doctrine.[106] This view shares with the Reformed tradition an affirmation of propositional revelation through Scripture,[107] but differs from it by locating this revelation not only in the Bible but also in extra-biblical church tradition. According to this perspective, the total content of special revelation (and therefore the basis for Christian doctrine) is either (a) found partly in the teaching of the Bible and partly in oral traditions passed down from the apostles (the *partim-partim* or *two-source* view) or (b) found wholly in the teaching of the Bible but only *appropriated* when the biblical text is properly interpreted in the light of an extra-canonical body of apostolic tradition (the *material sufficiency* or *one-source* view).[108] Either way, the divine revelation on which Christian doctrines are

---

104 The Reformed tradition also affirms a limited knowledge of God through *general* revelation—a form of revelation taken up, of course, in Plantinga's defence of the *sensus divinitatis*. For a robust defence of the idea that God can speak, and indeed *has* spoken in Scripture, see Nicholas Wolterstorff, *Divine Discourse: Philosophical Reflections on the Claim that God Speaks* (Cambridge: Cambridge University Press, 1995).

105 *Westminster Confession of Faith*, 1.10.

106 The general view of the character and location of revelation expressed under this heading, and the consequent view of the basis of doctrine, is shared by the Eastern Orthodox tradition, although there is considerable difference of opinion over just *which* ecclesiastical traditions and bodies serve as the conduits of divine revelation.

107 Likewise, it affirms a general revelation through nature.

108 Avery Dulles, 'Revelation, Fonts of', in *New Catholic Encyclopedia*, Vol. 12 (Detroit, MI: Thomson/Gale Group, 2nd edn, 2003), 190-93. Debate persists over which view, if either, the Council of Trent meant to endorse in opposition to the Reformers, but more recent pronouncements (e.g., *Dei Verbum*) deliberately allow for both.

grounded is to be found in the conjunction of Scripture and ecclesiastical tradition; moreover, the latter enjoys a degree of priority over the former insofar as the Bible is to be interpreted in accordance with that tradition, under the teaching authority of the Roman Magisterium. Thus, according to the Second Vatican Council:

> [I]t is not from Sacred Scripture alone that the Church draws her certainty about everything which has been revealed. ... Sacred tradition and Sacred Scripture form one sacred deposit of the word of God, committed to the Church. ... [S]ince Holy Scripture must be read and interpreted in the sacred spirit in which it was written, no less serious attention must be given to the content and unity of the whole of Scripture if the meaning of the sacred texts is to be correctly worked out. The living tradition of the whole Church must be taken into account along with the harmony which exists between elements of the faith. ... For all of what has been said about the way of interpreting Scripture is subject finally to the judgment of the Church, which carries out the divine commission and ministry of guarding and interpreting the word of God.[109]

A third account of the relationship between revelation and doctrine is represented by the Neo-Orthodox perspective, associated primarily with the theology of Karl Barth. Although it has much in common with the traditional Reformed perspective, there are some notable differences. According to this view, the divine revelation that roots Christian doctrine is to be identified with *the person of Christ*, who is the Word of God in the flesh;[110] more generally, God has revealed his character, plans and will in the events that constitute the redemptive ministry of Jesus Christ. The Christian believer appropriates this revelation by way of the Bible, which is given by God to serve as an authoritative *witness* to those events. As such, there is no straightforward identity between revelation and Scripture, since the Bible is *in itself* merely a collection of human writings. Nonetheless, the Bible is unique in being a human book graciously used by God to communicate to us the revelation of Jesus Christ. Whereas in the traditional Reformed and Catholic perspectives, Scripture is intrinsically both the word of man and the Word of God—it is literally authored by God, regardless of whether anyone comes to know or experience it as such—in the Barthian perspective the Bible is not the Word of God *per se*; rather, it *becomes*

---

109 *Dogmatic Constitution on Divine Revelation: Dei Verbum* (1965), 9, 10, 12.

110 'Revelation in fact does not differ from the person of Jesus Christ, nor from the reconciliation accomplished in Him. To say revelation is to say "The Word became flesh."' *CD*, I/1, 119.

the Word of God for a particular individual when that person encounters the living God through faith (where that faith is, in deference to Reformed tradition, a supernatural gift of the Holy Spirit). Any identity between the Bible and the Word of God is merely *indirect* and strictly *occasional*. As Barth puts the matter:

> The Bible is God's Word to the extent that God causes it to be His Word, to the extent that He speaks through it. ... The Bible, then, becomes God's Word in this event [of faith], and in the statement that the Bible is God's Word the little word "is" refers to its being in this becoming. It does not become God's Word because we accord it faith but in the fact that it becomes revelation to us.[111]

Neo-orthodoxy thus favours a 'dynamic' view of revelation through Scripture, in contrast to what it sees as the 'static' view of traditional orthodoxy—a preference motivated in part by a concern to uphold at all costs the *absolute freedom* of God in revelation.[112] Despite these differences, however, in practice the formulation of doctrine proceeds in much the same way, given the fact that God's self-revelation is mediated by Scripture: Christian doctrines such as those of the Trinity and the Incarnation, though not explicitly stated in the Bible, are nonetheless to be grounded in what it teaches implicitly about God revealed in Christ.[113]

Finally, we may note the so-called Liberal perspective on doctrine inspired by Friedrich Schleiermacher. Although Schleiermacher was raised in a devoutly Protestant family, and is considered by some to represent an alternative Reformed tradition which restores a neglected emphasis on personal piety, his approach to theology is more plausibly construed as a deviation from the orthodox tradition. A reaction to the critical philosophy of Kant, the conclusions of which seemed to rule out both natural theology and divine revelation in history, this fourth perspective differs radically from

---

111 *CD*, I/1, 109-10.

112 Klaas Runia, *Karl Barth's Doctrine of Holy Scripture* (Grand Rapids, MI: Eerdmans, 1962), 189-205.

113 While I take this to be a fair summary of the general position of Barth and his followers, I recognise that there are many further subtleties in each of their discussions of revelation and Scripture. For more detailed treatments of Barth's understanding of this subject, see Runia, *Karl Barth's Doctrine of Holy Scripture*; Bromiley, *An Introduction to the Theology of Karl Barth*, 3-53; Colin Brown, *Karl Barth and the Christian Message* (Eugene, OR: Wipf and Stock Publishers, 1998), 30-76; Hart, 'Revelation'; Francis Watson, 'The Bible', in John Webster (ed.), *The Cambridge Companion to Karl Barth* (Cambridge: Cambridge University Press, 2000), 57-71.

the other three by locating revelation not in inspired texts (either by identity or by mediation) but in the subjective experience of the religious believer.[114] Christian doctrine is thus not the elucidation of propositional truths revealed in Scripture, but rather the human verbal expression of God-consciousness, manifested in that community known as the Christian church. In essence, 'Christian doctrines are accounts of the Christian religious affections set forth in speech.'[115] In Schleiermacher's own exposition of this perspective on revelation and doctrine, the primary emphasis is placed on the self-consciousness of 'absolute dependence' on some being which *transcends* the self. Countless variations on this basic liberal theme have been propounded in the last two centuries; my purpose here is simply to acknowledge this as one perspective on doctrine that has enjoyed some currency among Christian theologians.

5.6.2 Evaluating the Four Perspectives

Which of these four basic perspectives on divine revelation and its relationship to doctrine would be most suitable as a basis for extending Plantinga's account of basic Christian belief? It ought to be evident that the Liberal perspective is the least promising of all, given its proposal to ground doctrine in the subjective experience of the church rather than in Scripture. On this view, the Bible is at best a flawed record of other people's experiences of God (even if that domain includes the consciousness of one unusually enlightened Jewish individual), which may indirectly provide data in support of certain doctrines. It is certainly not to be treated as a divinely authored set of writings intended to furnish us with (among other things) propositional content for Christian beliefs. Hence, it is hard to see how this perspective could accommodate, or be accommodated by, Plantinga's extended A/C model.

Consider next the Neo-Orthodox perspective. This account might be thought more suitable inasmuch as it attributes a central and exclusive role to the teaching of Scripture and, furthermore, insists that the illuminative activity of the Holy Spirit is necessary for Christian faith. Even so, on this account Scripture is not divine testimony *as such*; it is merely human testimony to divine revelation, however privileged. In this regard it does not square immediately

---

114 In fact, it may be legitimately questioned whether Schleiermacher held to anything like 'divine revelation' in the traditional Christian sense. Hart, 'Revelation', 39-40.

115 Friedrich Schleiermacher, *The Christian Faith* (trans. H. R. Mackintosh and J. S. Stewart; Edinburgh: T. & T. Clark, 1928), 76.

with the extended A/C model, in which Scripture is treated as divine testimony *prior to* and *independent of* the internal instigation of the Holy Spirit (which is the closest thing in Plantinga's account to the Barthian 'encounter with the living God'). It might be argued in response that according to the Neo-Orthodox perspective the biblical text certainly *becomes* divine testimony at the point of faith, and therefore the extended A/C model could be modified so as to fit this scheme. Perhaps so, but this would reintroduce the problem of the redundancy of our normal cognitive faculties in the formation of Christian belief.

Moreover, a further difficulty arises from the neo-orthodox denial of the infallibility of Scripture (based on the insistence that the biblical texts are, as such, only human testimony and therefore susceptible to error at any point).[116] In its refusal to endorse even a qualified doctrine of infallibility, according to which Scripture is at least (say) wholly reliable in matters of faith and practice,[117] one suspects that such a stance cannot support an account of warranted Christian doctrines according to which belief in the doctrines of the Trinity and the Incarnation, based on objective exegesis of the biblical texts, can be warranted to a high degree. It may well be that the Barthian *in practice* treats every Scripture passage on the assumption that it reliably conveys God's self-revelation when expounding and defending these doctrines, but this assumption is hardly in accord with his conception of the Bible as a flawed human witness to divine revelation. It is one thing to suppose that God could use selected statements from a set of fallible human writings as a vehicle for essential Christian beliefs (i.e., those basic beliefs covered by Plantinga's extended A/C model and required for saving faith); but it is quite another to maintain that God could use the entirety of those fallible human writings as a foundation for warranted Christian doctrines, when those writings are

---

116 'The prophets and apostles as such, even in their office, even in their function as witnesses, even in the act of writing down their witness, were real, historical men as we are, and therefore sinful in their action, and capable and actually guilty of error in their spoken and written word.' *CD*, I/2, 528-29. See also Runia, *Karl Barth's Doctrine of Holy Scripture*, 57-80; Bromiley, *An Introduction to the Theology of Karl Barth*, 37, 43; Brown, *Karl Barth and the Christian Message*, 59-62, 146.

117 Cf. Stephen T. Davis, *The Debate about the Bible: Inerrancy versus Infallibility* (Philadelphia, PA: Westminster Press, 1977); Bloesch, *Essentials of Evangelical Theology*, 64-70; Jack B. Rogers and Donald K. McKim, *The Authority and Interpretation of the Bible: An Historical Approach* (San Francisco, CA: Harper & Row, 1979).

acknowledged by the Christian believer (at least in theory) to be an inseparable mixture of truth and error about their subject matter.[118]

Compounding matters further, it appears Barth would have us suppose that God freely (but conveniently) chose for Scripture to *become* the Word of God for him, and therefore divine testimony, just as often as he sat down to write the exegetical sections of the *Church Dogmatics*—and likewise for every other Christian theologian's exposition of biblical doctrine. But if the exegete can count on acts of divine inspiration with this degree of stability and predictability, one has to wonder whether the celebrated contrast between a 'dynamic' and a 'static' understanding of revelation is anything more than rhetoric. In practice, the Barthian must choose between his commitment to 'absolute' divine freedom and the possibility of authoritative and reliable exegetical theology—for he cannot consistently accommodate both.

For reasons such as these, I suspect that the extended A/C model would require considerable modification in order to accommodate the Neo-Orthodox view of Christian faith; and even then, it is not clear that the model could be successfully extended to account for warranted Christian doctrines.

Of the remaining two views, it is not difficult to see that *ceteris paribus* the Reformed perspective offers a simpler basis than the Catholic perspective for extending Plantinga's model of warranted Christian belief. This is hardly a surprising observation, since it is precisely this tradition with which Plantinga aligns himself and from which he has drawn considerable inspiration in developing the epistemology expounded earlier in the chapter. The additional complexity that would be required in order to extend the model to accommodate the Catholic perspective is reason enough to favour the first position over the second, given that both traditions purport to reach the same conclusions regarding the orthodox doctrines of the Trinity and the Incarnation (i.e., concurrence with the ecumenical statements). Among other concerns, Roman Catholic and Eastern Orthodox qualms about the private interpretation of Scripture do not sit comfortably with Plantinga's model of warranted beliefs formed in a basic way on reading the biblical text alone, independent of any ecclesiastical teaching. Nevertheless, it is plausible to suppose that an alternative model for warranted Christian beliefs and doctrines *could* be developed on the basis of

---

118 Runia notes that Barth rejects outright any attempt by the exegete to separate the divine wheat from the human chaff. Runia, *Karl Barth's Doctrine of Holy Scripture*, 122-23.

Plantinga's proper function epistemology yet in accordance with the Catholic commitment to both Scripture and tradition as essential components in the appropriation of propositional revelation. I therefore tentatively suggest that if my defence of the rationality of paradoxical doctrines is successful, then a parallel defence based on an alternative Catholic model for warranted Christian doctrines would likely also be successful. However, it is the traditional Reformed perspective on doctrine that I propose to adopt in the remainder of this book.

5.7 Warranted Christian Doctrine

So then, according to that stream of Christian tradition represented by the Reformers and their heirs, Christian doctrines (including those expressed in the ecumenical creeds and confessions) are only warranted insofar as they are grounded on God's special revelation through the Holy Spirit speaking in Scripture alone. I noted earlier the view expressed by the Westminster Divines, whose convictions on this point mirror the earlier remarks of Calvin:

> Let this be a firm principle: No other word is to be held as the Word of God, and given place as such in the church, than what is contained first in the Law and the Prophets, then in the writings of the apostles; and the only authorized way of teaching in the church is by the prescription and standard of his Word.[119]

> I should not seem too quarrelsome because I insist so strongly that the church is not permitted to coin any new doctrine, that is, to teach and put forward as an oracle something more than the Lord has revealed in his Word.[120]

Regarding the Christian's warrant for believing (and the church's warrant for teaching) the doctrines of the Trinity and the Incarnation, as formulated by the early councils, Calvin's position is quite clear:

> [W]henever a decree of any council is brought forward, I should like men first of all diligently to ponder at what time it was held, on what issue, and with what intention, what sort of men were present; then to examine by the standard of Scripture what it dealt with—and to do this in such a way that the definition of the

---

119 John Calvin, *Institutes of the Christian Religion* (trans. Ford Lewis Battles; London: Collins, rev. edn, 1960), IV, 8.8.
120 Calvin, *Institutes*, IV, 8.15.

council may have its weight and be like a provisional judgment, yet not hinder the examination which I have mentioned. ...

Thus councils would come to have the majesty that is their due; yet in the meantime Scripture would stand out in the higher place, with everything subject to its standard. In this way, we willingly embrace and reverence as holy the early councils, such as those of Nicaea, Constantinople, Ephesus I, Chalcedon, and the like, which were concerned with refuting errors—in so far as they relate to the teachings of faith. For they contain nothing but the pure and genuine exposition of Scripture...[121]

Likewise, the Belgic Confession recognises that knowledge of God can come via both general revelation in nature and special revelation in Scripture, but contends that the latter alone functions as the source and standard of Christian doctrine:

> We know [God] by two means: First, by the creation, preservation, and government of the universe, since that universe is before our eyes like a beautiful book in which all creatures, great and small, are as letters to make us ponder the invisible things of God: his eternal power and his divinity, as the apostle Paul says in Romans 1:20. ... Second, he makes himself known to us more openly by his holy and divine Word, as much as we need in this life, for his glory and for the salvation of his own.

> We include in the Holy Scripture the two volumes of the Old and New Testaments. They are canonical books with which there can be no quarrel at all.

> We receive all these books and these only as holy and canonical, for the regulating, founding, and establishing of our faith. And we believe without a doubt all things contained in them—not so much because the church receives and approves them as such but above all because the Holy Spirit testifies in our hearts that they are from God, and also because they prove themselves to be from God.[122]

How then might Plantinga's extended A/C model be further extended, in line with this Reformed perspective, so as to account for warranted belief in Christian doctrines? The first point to recognise is surely this: if doctrines such as those of the Trinity and the Incarnation are epistemically warranted by virtue of being affirmed by Scripture, either explicitly or implicitly, it follows that a person must be warranted in believing that *whatever is affirmed by Scripture is true* (or something close) in order to be warranted in believing the

---

121 Calvin, *Institutes*, IV, 16.8.
122 *Belgic Confession* (1618), Articles 2, 4, 5.

doctrines themselves. Plantinga himself suggests that this belief could be warranted in various ways, each of which is consistent with the extended A/C model and all of which involve a person coming to believe that the Bible *as a whole* is God's Word (and not merely that certain individual claims are of divine origin).[123]

One typical way in which this belief *could* be warranted is 'by way of ordinary teaching and testimony': thus, Reverend Green tells his Sunday School class that the Bible is a book from God and young Timothy consequently believes it.[124] However, the warrant of beliefs based on testimony is strictly *derivative*. Such beliefs cannot be any more warranted than the corresponding beliefs of the testifier.[125] It cannot therefore be the case that *every* Christian's belief that Scripture is divinely inspired is warranted by way of testimony—at least, not by way of *human* testimony. Still, this need be no great obstacle, for a proper function epistemology conjoined with Christian theism allows for this belief to be warranted in various other ways. Plantinga notes two in particular, both of which are suggested by the fifth article of the Belgic Confession:

> The first is that the Holy Spirit testifies in our hearts that this book is indeed from God; the Holy Spirit doesn't merely impel us to believe, with respect to a given teaching of this book, that it is from God but impels us as well to believe that the Gospel of John itself is from God. The second is that the book "proves itself" to be from God. Perhaps here the idea is that the believer first comes to think, with respect to many of the specific teachings of that book, that they are, indeed, from God; that is, the Holy Spirit causes her to believe this with respect to many of the teachings of the book. She then infers (with the help of other premises) that the whole book has that same status.[126]

According to the first option, the belief arises by way of the internal instigation of the Holy Spirit in much the same manner as belief in 'the great things of the gospel'.[127] On this view, the Spirit induces a

---

123 Plantinga, *Warranted Christian Belief*, 375, 380.

124 Plantinga, *Warranted Christian Belief*, 376.

125 Plantinga, *Warrant and Proper Function*, 35-36.

126 Plantinga, *Warranted Christian Belief*, 380.

127 Although Plantinga rightly notes that the inspiration of Scripture 'is not an essential element of Christian belief'—that is, it is not part of the propositional content of saving faith—it is arguably so fundamental for Christian doctrine and practice, and so ubiquitous a conviction among Christians throughout the history of the church, that belief in it would most likely be warranted by way of the IIHS if it were to be warranted at all.

person reading the Bible (perhaps over a period of time, but not necessarily) to the belief that it is God's Word. Although Plantinga does not say so, this would most plausibly be occasioned by the reading of particular claims that the Bible makes about itself (e.g., 2 Tim. 3:16; 2 Peter 1:21), thus involving those cognitive faculties normally concerned with the acceptance of testimony (albeit in a supernaturally enhanced way).[128] On the second view, a person comes by way of the IIHS to believe with warrant that many individual teachings of the Bible are of divine origin and thereafter infers that the entire Bible is of divine origin. This could involve a straightforward inductive inference, perhaps bolstered by premises such as, for example, *God would be unlikely to inspire only some parts of the Bible (or of a book of the Bible) rather than inspiring the whole* (especially given that God has apparently provided no extracanonical means of distinguishing inspired teachings from uninspired teachings). Even if this would otherwise be a weak inductive conclusion, provided that the belief is formed in accordance with a design plan aimed at truth, with the added impulsion of the Holy Spirit, it could still be warranted to a high degree.[129]

There are further possibilities beyond these two.[130] One scenario involves the perception (perhaps in a way analogous to normal sense perception) of certain characteristics of Scripture, or phenomena encountered upon reading it, that are indicative of divine inspiration. As the *Westminster Confession of Faith* has it:

---

128 Note that this does not involve the believer reasoning in a vicious circle (e.g., *the Bible claims to be divinely inspired, therefore the Bible is true*) because the believer here does not *infer* the inspiration of Scripture from any of its teachings; rather, the belief is formed in a basic way on the occasion of reading those teachings.

129 As Plantinga elsewhere notes, according to a proper function theory of knowledge there is no simple relationship between warrant and the *general* reliability of a belief-forming process: '[O]n a rough and ready version of reliabilism, a belief has warrant only if it is produced by reliable cognitive faculties or processes; on my view, however, it is possible that a belief have warrant even if it isn't produced by a reliable faculty: if, for example, it is produced by a faculty that is unreliable overall (overall produces too few true beliefs), but has an area of operation in which it functions reliably and in which it is aimed at the production of true beliefs. *What really counts is not the reliability of the faculty or process involved, but the specific module of the design plan governing the production of the belief in question*.' Plantinga, 'Reliabilism, Analyses and Defeaters', 428, n. 2, emphasis added.

130 Plantinga adds two other suggestions to those I mention here: Plantinga, *Warranted Christian Belief*, 380.

[T]he heavenliness of the matter, the efficacy of the doctrine, the
majesty of the style, the consent of all the parts, the scope of the
whole (which is to give all glory to God), the full discovery it
makes of the only way of man's salvation, the many other
incomparable excellencies, and the entire perfection thereof, are
arguments whereby it doth abundantly evidence itself to be the
Word of God; yet, notwithstanding, our full persuasion and
assurance of the infallible truth and divine authority thereof, is
from the inward work of the Holy Spirit, bearing witness by and
with the Word in our hearts.[131]

This spiritual perception of the inspiration of Scripture need not
involve any *inference*, as if the Christian were to reason like this: *the
Bible displays X, X is indicative of divine authorship, therefore the Bible is
the Word of God.* Rather, it may only involve a certain distinctive
phenomenology associated with the *occasion* of belief in the
inspiration of Scripture, according to a divine design plan for belief
formation. In this respect, the belief would parallel other types of
beliefs (e.g., memory beliefs and *a priori* beliefs) that come packaged
with a distinctive phenomenology, but are warranted in a basic way
and not via a dubious inference *from* that phenomenology.[132]

In any event, the precise details are not crucial to the argument
here and the best model may involve a combination of some or all of
the above possibilities. The important point is simply this: there
appears to be no good reason to doubt that, given the truth of
Christian theism, the belief that Scripture is God's Word, furnishing
the believer with information about God and his works, could be
formed by human cognitive faculties functioning properly in
accordance with a design plan successfully aimed at truth. Thus
there is no reason to suppose that the belief could not be warranted.
Indeed, given God's purposes in arranging for the Bible to be
written, it is most likely that this belief *would* be warranted in normal
cases and to a considerable degree.

I have argued to this point that if the basic contours of the
Christian narrative are correct then biblical teaching can indeed
function as the basis for warranted belief in Christian doctrines. It
remains for me to explain how individual Christians would be
warranted in believing, for example, the statements of the Nicene

---

131 *Westminster Confession of Faith*, 1.5.

132 Plantinga, *Warrant and Proper Function*, 57-64, 103-8. Consider too the
     parallel with Plantinga's view of the *sensus divinitatis*: theistic beliefs are
     properly formed on the occasion, but not the inferential basis, of the
     experiences in question. Plantinga, *Warranted Christian Belief*, 173-77.

Creed or the Definition of Chalcedon. I propose that there are, broadly speaking, *four paradigmatic ways* in which doctrinal beliefs can be warranted. In practice, the boundaries between these cases are somewhat blurred, and individual believers may reflect the characteristics of more than one case; some doctrines will be warranted in one fashion, some in another, still others by a mixture of means. Moreover, the way in which an individual Christian's doctrinal beliefs enjoy warrant is liable to shift over time, as that person matures both intellectually and spiritually. Such qualifications aside, I maintain that these four paradigm cases cover the ground well enough.

In the first paradigm case, which provides the epistemic foundation for the other three, a Christian with a warranted belief in the inspiration of the Bible carefully studies its teachings, accurately interpreting its texts, and comes to the warranted conclusion that a certain set of propositions, corresponding to the content of some Christian doctrine, is affirmed by Scripture and therefore true.[133] No doubt the Holy Spirit can graciously assist in the process—if nothing else, to counter the sinful tendency to reject divine truth and to fortify those true beliefs that will prove of greater importance to the ongoing spiritual life of the individual and the church—but otherwise the reasoning involved in reaching these conclusions goes by way of the normal operation of the believer's cognitive faculties.

Moreover, although the Reformed perspective holds that only those truths revealed in Scripture should provide the *propositional basis* of Christian doctrines, it does not follow that additional background knowledge—lexicons, textual critical data, other ancient documents, liturgy, church tradition, historical research, scholarly commentaries, personal experience, logic textbooks, and the like—cannot provide appropriate assistance in determining the overall teaching of Scripture on any particular topic. Indeed, the greater the quantity (and quality) of available background knowledge adduced and employed, the more warranted the doctrinal conclusions are likely to be, just as in any other scholarly discipline.

On a similar note, the idea that the content of doctrine is fundamentally derived from and warranted by the biblical text does not demand that the relationship between the formulation of doctrine and the interpretation of Scripture be thought of as simple and unidirectional; on the contrary, it must be acknowledged that

---

133 Of course, the person in question need not be *aware* that the propositions in question constitute some Christian doctrine; this would be the case, at the very least, for those who initially discover and formulate doctrines.

there will be a significant element of 'epistemic feedback' to the degree that doctrine is used as an interpretive framework in the reading of the Bible.[134] The presence of a hermeneutical spiral need in no way diminish the warrant of the exegetical conclusions reached, provided the process of interpretation is appropriately self-conscious and self-critical—after all, a ball-bearing cast into a funnel can be directed just as accurately as one dropped through a pipe. It could be argued, in fact, that the critical attention (directed toward both text and interpreter) invited by this dynamic relationship will ultimately tend to *increase* the warrant of doctrinal conclusions.[135] Likewise, the warrant of those conclusions can be further enhanced through interaction with other believers engaged in the same project, even when those conclusions are challenged—for if the challenge is met, then potential warrant defeaters will have been eliminated.[136] This first paradigm case, then, corresponds principally to those great minds of the Christian church that have contributed to the recognition and development of central Christian doctrines.

One relevant issue to raise briefly at this point concerns the precise logical relationship of properly interpreted biblical affirmations to those doctrinal beliefs reached in the way described above. Is the relationship one of logical entailment or is it merely probabilistic? Drawing guidance from the *Westminster Confession* once again, we find the following principle expressed:

> The whole counsel of God, concerning all things necessary for his own glory, man's salvation, faith, and life, is either expressly set down in Scripture, or by good and necessary consequence may be deduced from Scripture...[137]

According to this principle, even if the Nicene-Constantinopolitan doctrine of the Trinity is not explicitly stated in Scripture, it may still be known to be true if it can be *logically deduced* from biblical teaching. This certainly seems sensible and provides an effective constraint on speculative theology. It may, however, be needlessly restrictive. If I know that there is a one-in-a-million chance of my winning the lottery, my belief that I will not win the lottery (despite having bought a ticket) can be warranted to a very high degree even though that belief cannot be *deduced* by anything I know prior to the

---

134 McGrath, *The Genesis of Doctrine*, 55-61.

135 Compare, in this regard, Vanhoozer's proposal for a 'hermeneutic of humility and conviction'. Kevin J. Vanhoozer, *Is There a Meaning in This Text?* (Leicester: Apollos, 1998), 455-68.

136 The topic of epistemic defeaters is discussed in more detail in §5.8.

137 *Westminster Confession of Faith*, 1.6.

draw. It is therefore reasonable to add that some doctrines could be warranted on the basis of *probabilistic* reasoning—by either inductive or abductive inference—from the direct affirmations of the Bible. Moreover, even if many Christian doctrines do turn out to be deducible from the teaching of Scripture, a modest probabilistic factor will be introduced inevitably by way of the interpretive process of reading the texts. In other words, although the belief that Scripture explicitly affirms p and q may be warranted to a very high degree, that belief will never enjoy the same certainty as a belief in some logical or conceptual truth (e.g., that there are no married bachelors). Consequently, any deductive belief from p and q that Scripture implicitly affirms r will inherit that limitation. Just the same, doctrines secured by logical deduction will still be more warranted (all else being equal) than those reached by a probabilistic inference. But most doctrines, of course, will rely on a combination of the two.

According to the first paradigm case, then, a person may form warranted beliefs corresponding to cardinal Christian doctrines by way of the scholarly study of biblical texts, under the guidance of the Holy Spirit. Such a person will be in a position to state and explain to others the reasoning by which his conclusions were reached; for example, to defend Calvin's contention that the affirmations of Nicea and Chalcedon 'contain nothing but the pure and genuine exposition of Scripture.'

This observation provides a foundation for the second paradigm case of warranted belief in Christian doctrines. In this instance, a Christian with a warranted belief in the inspiration of the Bible is presented with an exposition of some doctrine, detailing its scriptural basis, by someone falling into the first case (or even this second case). On careful reflection, with a sufficient understanding of the reasoning involved, the Christian forms a warranted belief in that doctrine. This manner of obtaining warranted beliefs is a common one and by no means unique to this scenario. To take an example from another discipline: while I almost certainly lack the cognitive ability (let alone the patience) to have discovered Gödel's incompleteness theorems myself, I am nonetheless able to understand and appreciate a well-reasoned exposition of those theorems and can thereby be warranted in believing them. In much the same way, by comprehending a well-reasoned exposition of the exegetical basis for the doctrine of the Trinity, I can be warranted in believing that Scripture implicitly teaches the doctrine; coupling this with a warranted belief that the Bible is divinely inspired, I can be warranted in believing that the doctrine is *true*. Furthermore, as in the first case the *degree* of warrant may be enhanced—and the hindrance of spurious warrant defeaters arising from sinful psychological tendencies may be countered—by the consolidating activity of the Holy Spirit.

The third paradigm case, though still dependent on instances of the first, is simpler still: a Christian with a warranted belief in the inspiration of the Bible accepts on the basis of trustworthy testimony (e.g., the teaching of a parent, professor, or church leader) that a certain doctrine is taught in Scripture and thereby infers that the doctrine must be true. As I noted earlier, the warrant of beliefs formed by way of testimony is derivative of the warrant of the corresponding beliefs of the testifier. But provided the testimony comes from someone whose *own* doctrinal beliefs are warranted, and there is no reason to doubt the reliability of that testimony, a person may thereby gain a warranted belief that the doctrine in question is true.[138] Once more, the influence of the Holy Spirit may be determinative in both the initial acceptance of doctrines and the strength with which the relevant beliefs are held; to the extent that all of the belief-inducing factors form part of a divinely-instituted cognitive design plan aimed at the production of true beliefs about God and his redemptive work, they can only contribute to the warrant of the resultant beliefs.

The fourth and final paradigm case is the simplest of all. In this scenario, a Christian accepts that some doctrine is true purely on the basis of reliable testimony from another Christian who believes (with warrant) that same doctrine. Here the belief is held basically, without inference from any other beliefs (including beliefs about Scripture), but it is warranted nonetheless. This case would be most applicable to young children for whom even inferences of the form *the Bible teaches X, the Bible is God's Word, therefore X* would not come naturally and confidently enough to secure warranted beliefs. If

---

138 Although testimony plays a crucial role in this case and the following one, basic beliefs formed by way of testimony will also play a significant part in the first two cases, by way of the contribution of expert opinion. In the first case, testimonial beliefs come into play in the use of scholarly reference works such as lexicons and commentaries; in the second case, the person will be relying to some extent on the testimony of the one supplying the argument for the doctrine in question (e.g., that their appeals to reference works are appropriate). As Plantinga notes, the extent to which we rely on testimony to some degree or other for most of our beliefs is rarely appreciated. Plantinga, *Warrant and Proper Function*, 77-82.

such persons are able to believe Christian doctrines with warrant at all, it will be by way of straightforward catechizing.[139]

These four paradigm cases can be summarised as follows:

WD1: S's belief in doctrine D is warranted via personal scholarly study of the biblical texts, coupled with warranted belief in biblical inspiration.

WD2: S's belief in doctrine D is warranted via understanding and agreement with a scholarly exposition and systematisation of biblical teaching, coupled with warranted belief in biblical inspiration.

WD3: S's belief in doctrine D is warranted via reliable testimony that Scripture teaches D, coupled with warranted belief in biblical inspiration.

WD4: S's belief in doctrine D is warranted via reliable testimony that D is true.

WD1 is the foundational case, of course; instantiation of the other cases will be dependent on instances of lower-level cases. I suggest that these four cases taken together account for the principal ways in which warranted beliefs in Christian doctrines are formed, on the assumption that belief in the divine inspiration of Scripture is also warranted. Other than this assumption (which I have argued is very likely, given the truth of Christian theism) and the warrant-strengthening activity of the Holy Spirit, there is nothing novel about the warrant-conferring factors to which I have appealed in each of the four cases. In principle, they could apply equally well to any summary statement taken to be representative of the central claims of a written text: say, the 'doctrine' of transcendental idealism expressed in Kant's *Critique of Pure Reason*. Some people believe that Kant taught this doctrine on the basis of their own personal scholarly study of his seminal tome; others believe it on the basis of arguments put forward by the first group; still others believe it simply on the basis of testimony, having read neither the *Critique* nor

---

139 Consider, for example, an excerpt from the Westminster-based *Catechism for Young Children*: 'Q6. Are there more gods than one? A. There is only one God. Q7. In how many persons does this one God exist? A. In three persons. Q8. What are they? A. The Father, the Son, and the Holy Ghost.' Of these three statements, only the first finds explicit affirmation in the Bible (e.g., Rom. 3:30). Nevertheless, it is plausible to suppose that with sufficient explanation a child could form some true (albeit rudimentary) trinitarian beliefs; if those beliefs were formed on the basis of testimony, then they would also be warranted.

any analytical commentary on it; and some might even believe the doctrine itself purely on the testimony of a trusted professor. The main difference between this analogous scenario and my proposed model for warranted belief in Christian doctrines is, of course, that the biblical text has the considerable advantage of being divinely inspired (though some Kant enthusiasts might demur). Moreover, knowledge of this fact arises by way of a combination of natural and supernatural belief-producing factors in order to secure a high degree of warrant.

I therefore conclude that if fundamental Christian beliefs can be *prima facie* warranted according to Plantinga's extended A/C model, then so in principle can more sophisticated Christian doctrinal beliefs such as those expressed in the Nicene Creed and the Definition of Chalcedon. As for the question of whether the orthodox doctrines of the Trinity and the Incarnation *are* in fact taught in Scripture, albeit implicitly, I do not propose to reproduce here the supporting arguments developed over the course of two millennia. Representative expositions can be found, among other places, in the works of the great systematic theologians of the Reformed tradition.[140]

5.8 Epistemic Defeaters

In the preceding sections I have explicated and defended Plantinga's proper function epistemology and his extended Aquinas/Calvin model for warranted Christian beliefs. According to this model, if the basic contours of the Christian narrative are *true*, then there is good reason to suppose that the Christian's beliefs are *warranted*, in an epistemically basic way, and to a degree more than sufficient for knowledge. I have further argued that the model can be naturally developed to encompass belief in higher-level Christian doctrines not explicitly stated in Scripture, such as the doctrines of the Trinity and the Incarnation. Given the same proviso—that the central propositions of the Christian narrative are true—belief in such doctrines can be warranted in a variety of ways, depending on the intellectual sophistication of the believer, and warranted to a degree quite sufficient for knowledge.

---

140 In Chapter 7, however, I will draw attention to those biblical passages I consider supportive of the paradoxical interpretations defended in Chapters 2 and 3 when I discuss various biblically-motivated concerns about the model for theological paradox set out in the next chapter.

Plantinga recognises, however, that his defence of the *prima facie* rationality of Christian beliefs does not say all that needs to be said about whether most Christians living in the twenty-first century actually *are* warranted in their beliefs—especially those whom Philip Quinn designates the 'intellectually sophisticated adults in our culture'.[141] The problem is that while Christian beliefs might be initially or potentially warranted in the way Plantinga describes, such beliefs may nonetheless face *epistemic defeat* by other beliefs that are likely to be formed in today's intellectual climate; in fact, many would suggest that they nearly always *will* be defeated in any rational noetic structure. As Plantinga explains:

> Someone might put it like this: "Well, perhaps these [Christian] beliefs can indeed have warrant, and perhaps (if they are true) even warrant sufficient for knowledge: there are circumstances in which this can happen. Most of us, however—for example, most of those who read this book—are not in those circumstances. What you have really argued so far is only that theistic and Christian belief (taken in the basic way) can have warrant, *absent defeaters*. But defeaters are not absent." The claim is that there are serious defeaters for Christian belief: propositions we know or believe which make Christian belief—at any rate, Christian belief held in the basic way and with anything like sufficient firmness to constitute knowledge—*irrational* and hence unwarranted.[142]

The relevance of this issue to the foregoing discussion should be clear. If warranted Christian beliefs face the prospect of epistemic defeat, then so do warranted Christian doctrines. Moreover, the paradoxicality of certain Christian doctrines is exactly the sort of feature that might be thought to serve *as* a defeater for belief in those doctrines; in other words, even if Christian doctrines could *in principle* be believed with warrant, those that apparently involve logically irreconcilable claims are open to the objection that they *cannot* be rationally believed for precisely that reason. Indeed, I suggest that this is precisely how the problem of theological paradox ought to be framed: even granting that *some* Christian doctrines can be rational or warranted, how can *paradoxical* Christian doctrines be

---

141 Philip L. Quinn, 'On Finding the Foundations of Theism', *Faith and Philosophy* 2.4 (1985), 469-86. See also Alvin Plantinga, 'The Foundations of Theism: A Reply', *Faith and Philosophy* 3.3 (1986), 298-313; Philip L. Quinn, 'The Foundations of Theism Again: A Rejoinder to Plantinga', in Linda Zagzebski (ed.), *Rational Faith: Catholic Responses to Reformed Epistemology* (Notre Dame, IN: University of Notre Dame Press, 1993), 14-47.

142 Plantinga, *Warranted Christian Belief*, 357-58.

rational or warranted, given that their logical difficulties seem to function as obvious defeaters? As Plantinga himself notes, Frege might have been rational to believe the conclusions of his *Foundations of Arithmetic* prior to Russell's letter pointing out the contradiction at the heart of his axiomatic system, but once apprised of this fatal flaw the rational course of action was for him to acknowledge the defeater and abandon some of his prior beliefs.[143] Does not the same go for belief in the paradoxical doctrines of the Trinity and the Incarnation? In Chapters 6 and 7, I will attempt to address this problem by arguing that contrary to initial suspicions, the paradoxicality of these doctrines need not provide a defeater for belief in them. Before doing so, however, it will be necessary to say something about different *kinds* of defeaters and to establish *which* kind of defeater theological paradox is alleged to be.

A warrant *defeater* is essentially something that precludes, removes, or at least substantially reduces the warrant of a belief. Defeaters commonly arise in the form of *other* beliefs, but need not always be doxastic in character. For example, a defeater can be introduced by way of a person's immediate experiences or his cognitive environment, the latter being *external* to his cognitive apparatus.[144] To take up a well-worn example: suppose I look at the mantelpiece clock and form the belief that it is 3:24pm. Unbeknown to me, the clock stopped days ago; yet by sheer coincidence, the time *is* 3:24pm. In this situation, my belief is *rational*—since I am not flouting any epistemic duties and all the relevant cognitive faculties involved in the production of the belief are functioning properly. Furthermore, the belief is *true*. But it is clearly not *warranted* and I therefore lack knowledge. The malfunction of the clock serves as a warrant defeater for my belief.

Other non-doxastic defeaters can be due to cognitive malfunction within the believer with respect to the formation of experience. Consider Robert, who suffers from a rare type of brain lesion one of the effects of which is that whenever he hears the doorbell ring it appears to him quite vividly that there is a fly buzzing in front of his nose. On one particular occasion, the doorbell rings and Robert forms the belief, in response to his experience, that there is a fly in the room; moreover, it just so happens that there is indeed a fly in the room (though resting in a corner out of Robert's sight and hearing). Even though Robert's belief is true, and rational insofar as

---

143 Plantinga, *Warranted Christian Belief*, 361.
144 Recall that according to Plantinga's analysis, the presence of a conducive cognitive environment is a necessary condition of warrant.

it is based on his experience in the appropriate way, it is not warranted.[145] The interference of the lesion amounts to a warrant defeater for Robert's belief that there is a fly in the room.

If the phenomenon of paradox is a warrant defeater for belief in Christian doctrines, then it is not a defeater in either of the two ways described above. For if there is any irrationality involved in such belief, it will not be due to elements in the believer's cognitive environment or to pathology in those parts of her cognitive apparatus involved in the formation of experience.[146] Rather, it will be doxastic in nature: it will present in the form of some other belief (or conjunction of beliefs). In Plantinga's terminology, beliefs that defeat the warrant for other beliefs are known as *rationality* defeaters:

> [G]iven belief in the defeating proposition, you can retain belief in the defeated proposition only at the cost of irrationality. ... A defeater for a belief *b*, then, is another belief *d* such that, given my noetic structure, I cannot rationally hold *b*, given that I believe *d*.[147]

Rationality defeaters can be either rebutting or undercutting.[148] A *rebutting* defeater is a belief that is inconsistent with some other belief, thereby giving reason to think the latter belief false. For example: Susan believes on the basis of testimony that her friend will be arriving from Paris this evening but then hears a report that all flights from Paris today have been cancelled due to a security threat. In this case, the latter belief (that the flights have been cancelled) serves as a rebutting defeater for the former.

In contrast, a belief will be an *undercutting* defeater if it reveals the grounds or reasons supporting some other belief to be inadequate.

---

145 In terms of Plantinga's distinction between *internal* and *external* rationality, noted earlier, Robert's belief is internally rational (which requires proper function 'downstream from experience') but not externally rational (which requires the proper function in *sources* of experience).

146 It would be a mistake to argue, as some might be tempted to do, that the *necessary falsehood* of paradoxical doctrines (entailed by their logically incoherence) amounts to an external warrant defeater, for two reasons. First, it begs the question against the model I will present in the next chapter, according to which those doctrines are not *really* contradictory. Second, the mere fact that some belief is false (though that fact is, strictly speaking, external to the believer) cannot count as a warrant defeater for that belief, for otherwise warranted but false beliefs would be impossible *in principle*. (Examples of warranted but false beliefs can be easily generated.)

147 Plantinga, *Warranted Christian Belief*, 359, 361.

148 This distinction can be traced to John L. Pollock, *Contemporary Theories of Knowledge* (Totowa, NJ: Rowman & Littlefield, 1986), 38-39.

Consider Professor Hamilton, who believes that one of her students is extremely gifted based on the essays he has submitted over the course of two terms. In the third term, however, she receives an essay from the student which she realises is the product of blatant plagiarism. In this case, the belief that the student has been cheating all along is not *incompatible* with the belief that he is a bright spark, but it nonetheless undermines the evidential connection between that belief and the quality of his submitted work, rendering her earlier conclusion unwarranted.

In both of these examples, rationality demands that some of the person's beliefs be given up once a defeater has been acquired. However, in some cases epistemic disharmony within the person's noetic structure can be avoided by rejecting the potential *defeater*, instead of the potential *defeatee*. Take Archie, who has been married for several years and believes, with good reason, that his wife is completely faithful. One day, to his great surprise, he happens to see her in a restaurant holding the hand of some dark, handsome stranger. Archie can respond in at least two ways here: he can either believe the proposition that his wife is having an affair on the basis of his perceptual experiences (with the consequence that his former belief is defeated) or he can reject that proposition on the basis of his knowledge (as he sees things) that his wife is faithful, believing instead that there must be some other alternative explanation for what he has seen. Just which of these is the *rational* course will ultimately depend, according to a proper function account of warrant, on those parts of Archie's cognitive design plan relevant to the production and revision of the beliefs in question (in conjunction with the precise details of Archie's noetic structure, experiences, cognitive environment, etc.) and the extent to which those parts are aimed at *true belief* (rather than, say, psychological comfort).

Although a detailed blueprint of our cognitive design plan is not in our possession, in most cases the rational response to potential defeaters (i.e., what proper function would require in any particular instance) is intuitively clear and uncontroversial. For example, if I come to believe (due to absentmindedness) that I parked my car on the left side of the street, but return to find it parked on the opposite side, it would hardly be rational of me to conclude that someone must have moved it while I was away, particularly if I am well aware of being prone to lapses of memory. The portion of the design plan covering the 'defeater system' will thus place a premium on those sorts of qualities, such as coherence and simplicity, which normally accompany true beliefs. In some cases, however, precisely what proper function rationality requires with respect to belief revision will not be entirely obvious.

One further point should be mentioned. Beliefs can still function as defeaters if those beliefs are themselves *irrational*—and the resultant relinquishing of defeated beliefs may still be considered rational in a qualified sense. Imagine a man suffering from paranoia, utterly convinced that everyone is trying to do him great harm. Due to his illness, this belief simply seems as obvious as that the sky is blue (it exhibits, as Plantinga puts it, a great deal of 'doxastic experience').[149] Reminiscing one afternoon, he recalls a time several years ago when a relative apparently did him a good turn. Although he believed at the time that the deed was genuine, this belief is now defeated by his far stronger belief that everyone has always had it in for him and so he concludes instead that the relative was simply trying to lure him into a false sense of security. In this scenario, the defeat considered *alone* is quite rational, for his belief revision is precisely that which should occur *if* the defeating belief were warranted. The problem, of course, is that this defeater is far from warranted; neither therefore is the resultant set of beliefs. In such cases the distinction between internal and external rationality is crucial: the paranoiac is internally *rational*—his defeater system is functioning properly with respect to the beliefs he forms and the strength with which they are held—but he is externally *irrational*, due to the dysfunction in the way his beliefs form in response to experience. Since warrant requires both internal and external rationality, his beliefs about his relative's apparent kindness ultimately lack warrant.

After discussing the nature and varieties of defeaters, Plantinga devotes the final chapters of *Warranted Christian Belief* to addressing four alleged defeaters for Christian belief: projective theories of religious belief, the results of so-called higher biblical criticism, postmodernist theory and religious pluralism, and the problem of evil and suffering. He concludes that none of these 'presents a serious challenge to the warrant Christian belief can enjoy if the [extended A/C] model, and indeed Christian belief, is, in fact, true.'[150] In other words, these potential defeaters would only function as *actual* defeaters on the prior assumption that Christian belief is false (in which case, it is unlikely to be warranted even in the absence of defeaters). One potential warrant defeater that Plantinga does not address, however, is the problem of theological

---

149 Plantinga, *Warranted Christian Belief*, 111.
150 Plantinga, *Warranted Christian Belief*, 499.

paradox—and it is the burden of this book, in part, to fill that lacuna.[151]

How then should the alleged defeat of doctrinal beliefs by the phenomenon of paradox be characterised in light of the distinctions identified above? I have already indicated that the problem of paradox involves a purported *rationality* defeater, that is, a belief that defeats other beliefs. The belief in question would be something like *the propositions affirmed by doctrine D are implicitly contradictory* or *the propositions affirmed by doctrine D appear to be implicitly contradictory*.[152] Furthermore, the alleged defeater would be better categorised as a rebutting one rather than an undercutting one, for the apparent incoherence of the relevant doctrines does not merely indicate that the putative grounds or reasons for believing the doctrine are in fact inadequate (leading to the conclusion that belief is unwarranted but may still be true) but suggests that the doctrine is *false* (leading to the conclusion that outright *dis*belief is warranted).[153]

Thus the objection to paradoxical Christian doctrines amounts to this:

> Even if the component claims of a paradoxical doctrine can be individually warranted for S according to a proper function epistemology, once S grants that the doctrine seems to involve a logical contradiction, even an implicit one, proper function rationality will require that S not believe that doctrine—indeed, S ought thereafter to consider it (at least partly) false.

---

151 Plantinga does twice briefly acknowledge the charge that certain Christian doctrines are incoherent, but not in the context of warrant defeaters. Plantinga, *Warranted Christian Belief*, viii-ix, 115. In the first instance, he notes it as a potential *de facto* objection to Christian belief without further comment. In the second, it is mentioned as a potential *de jure* objection to the rationality of Christian belief (where rationality is here construed as consistency with the 'deliverances of reason'). In this latter passage, Plantinga responds by claiming that formulations of the doctrines of the Trinity and the Incarnation are available that 'clearly are not inconsistent.' This is certainly true; but as I contended in Chapters 2 and 3, these formulations only secure consistency at the expense of orthodoxy. In my judgement, Plantinga's cursory response does not adequately address the challenge of doctrinal paradox.

152 As I will argue in Chapter 6, these two beliefs are by no means equivalent, nor do they enjoy the same epistemic status.

153 Recall the example of Russell's letter to Frege. Russell's observation about Frege's axioms was a rebutting defeater: the rational conclusion for Frege was not that the axioms were merely inadequately supported, but that at least one of them must be *false*.

Now it goes without saying that for the problem of paradoxical doctrines to be of any epistemological interest, the potential defeater must *itself* be held rationally.[154] I have argued in Chapters 2 and 3 that it is indeed reasonable to believe that the doctrines of the Trinity and the Incarnation, interpreted in an orthodox manner, are paradoxical. In the next chapter, I present a model for understanding theological paradox according to which this belief remains warranted, but nevertheless fails to provide a rationality defeater for belief in the doctrines themselves.

---

154 If the belief that the doctrines of the Trinity and the Incarnation are apparently contradictory were merely a product of (say) mental illness or drug ingestion, then the problem of paradox would be better addressed by psychiatrists (or policemen) than by philosophical theologians.

CHAPTER 6

A Model for the Rational Affirmation of Paradoxical Theology

6.1 Introduction

'It is wrong always, everywhere, and for anyone, to believe anything upon insufficient evidence,' insisted William Clifford.[1] This robust evidentialist dictum has been brought into question by recent writers, many of whom are motivated (at least in part) by Christian convictions.[2] One gets the impression, however, that an equally robust *rationalist* dictum still holds sway among many contemporary Christian thinkers: *It is wrong always, everywhere, and for anyone, to believe anything that appears contradictory.* A. P. Martinich typifies this mindset in his analysis of the doctrine of the Trinity:

> Reason and revelation seem to have engaged forces in civil war. Reason cannot accept revelation's seeming contradiction, while revelation cannot allow reason to abandon any article of faith. In deciding which side to support, one must consider that, if faced with the alternatives of being a heretic and asserting a contradiction, the rational person will always choose heresy and trust himself to the mercy of God. A rational man can put no faith in contradiction.[3]

I have argued that the doctrines of the Trinity and the Incarnation, as expressed in the ecumenical creeds, do indeed present us with seeming contradictions (and I have intimated that other Christian

---

1   William K. Clifford, 'The Ethics of Belief', in Louis J. Pojman (ed.), *Classics of Philosophy, Volume 2: Modern and Contemporary* (Oxford: Oxford University Press, 1998), 1047-51.

2   Alvin Plantinga and Nicholas Wolterstorff (eds), *Faith and Rationality* (Notre Dame, IN: University of Notre Dame Press, 1983); Peter van Inwagen, 'It Is Wrong Everywhere, Always, and for Anyone to Believe Anything upon Insufficient Evidence', in Ruth J. Sample, Charles W. Mills, and James P. Sterba (eds), *Philosophy: The Big Questions* (Oxford: Blackwell, 2003), 87-98.

3   Martinich, 'Identity and Trinity', 172. Note that according to Martinich, reason cannot accept even a *seeming* contradiction.

doctrines may well share this feature). None of the models of the Trinity and the Incarnation proposed to date—social trinitarianism, kenoticism, 'two minds' christology, and so on—have proven successful in reconciling orthodox convictions with logical perspicuity. Even if belief in biblical doctrines can be warranted absent defeaters, as I argued in the last chapter, many would take it as a given that only doctrines free from any appearance of logical conflict can be ultimately warranted. Accordingly, doctrines that exhibit seeming contradiction must either be modified so as to eliminate these logical difficulties or else be deemed rationally untenable and abandoned altogether. In this chapter I intend to challenge this view by presenting a model for understanding theological paradox according to which Christians can be entirely rational in believing certain apparently contradictory doctrines. This model for rational affirmation of paradoxical theology (hereafter, the RAPT model) will involve claims about the character and origin of theological paradox, as well as the epistemic circumstances in which it would be legitimate to affirm, and rational to believe, a paradoxical doctrine. I will defend the model against a range of objections that might be levelled against it in Chapter 7.

Before setting out the model, I ought to say a few things about models in general and to clarify what is and is not being claimed about the model presented here. In the last chapter I explicated and defended Plantinga's 'extended Aquinas/Calvin model' for warranted Christian beliefs: belief in God and in the basic tenets of the Christian story. The construal of theological paradox I propose to develop and defend here is a model in precisely the same sense as Plantinga's extended A/C model. (Indeed, it may be taken as a *further* extension of this extended model, although it could also be adapted for use with other models of warranted Christian belief.) Plantinga explains his use of the term as follows:

> The rough idea is this: to give a model of a proposition or state of affairs S is to show *how it could be* that S is true or actual. The model itself will be *another* proposition (or state of affairs), one such that it is clear (1) that it is possible and (2) that if it is *true*, then so is the target proposition. From these two, of course, it follows that the target proposition is possible.[4]

For the model I develop here, then, the target proposition or state of affairs may be taken as: *Christians who affirm paradoxical doctrines (such as the Trinity and the Incarnation) are normally warranted and rational in so doing.*

---

4   Plantinga, *Warranted Christian Belief*, 168.

Plantinga makes four further claims about his extended A/C model: (1) that it is *epistemically* possible, that is, its constituent propositions are consistent with everything else we think we know; (2) that there are no *cogent objections* to the model, or at least none that are not also objections to the truth of Christian theism itself; (3) that the model is not merely possible, but close to the *truth* of the matter; and (4) that there are a range of different but similar models for warranted Christian belief, at least *one* of which is correct (on the assumption that Christian theism is true).

I wish to make parallel claims about the RAPT model. I maintain: (1) that the model is epistemically possible, consistent with what we otherwise know;[5] (2) that there are no cogent objections to it that are not also objections to Christian doctrines *as such*; (3) that the model (or something close) describes how things actually stand with regard to paradoxical Christian doctrines; and (4) that this model is one of a family of similar models, one member of which will be true if (i) the central claims of Christianity are also true and (ii) some essential Christian doctrines are indeed paradoxical.

There is an important correlative to these claims: just as Plantinga contends that there are no good objections to the *warrant* of Christian belief that are independent of its *truth*, I maintain that there are no good objections to the *warrant* of Christian doctrines (based on their paradoxicality) that are independent of their *truth*. In other words, there are no grounds for arguing along these lines: 'Well, perhaps God *is* a Trinity, and maybe God the Son *did* become fully human, but it's irrational nonetheless to *claim* or *believe* that such things are the case, just so long as they appear to be logically contradictory.'[6]

Before proceeding, it will also be worth listing the *desiderata* for such a model. Ideally: (i) the model should avoid denying or revising the law of non-contradiction or any other classical rules of logic; (ii) it should obviate the need to abandon the orthodox interpretations of central Christian doctrines; (iii) it should not conflict with other traditional Christian doctrines; (iv) better still, it

---

5   Following Plantinga, 'what we know' should be understood as restricted to what all (or most) of the participants in the discussion agree on. It would be question begging, of course, for someone to object to the RAPT model on the grounds that (say) Christianity is known to be false.

6   Cf. Plantinga, *Warranted Christian Belief*, 191. '[Atheologians] can't any longer adopt the following stance: "Well, I certainly don't know whether theistic belief is *true*—who could know a thing like that?—but I do know this: it is irrational, or unjustified, or not rationally justified, or contrary to reason or intellectually irresponsible or ..." There isn't a sensible *de jure* question or criticism that is independent of the *de facto* question.'

should derive positive support from other Christian doctrines; (v) it should spell out the circumstances in which it would be rational to affirm paradoxical doctrines; and (vi) it should uphold a robust distinction between orthodoxy and heterodoxy, such that the distinction (and its application to specific doctrines) can be articulated and defended. I trust it will be clear after reading this chapter and the next that the RAPT model satisfies all of the above.

6.2 The Character of Paradox

In Chapter 4, I distinguished two basic types of strategy for deflecting the charge of irrationality aimed at certain Christian doctrines: the first recommends revising our conception of the classical *laws of logic*—either the law of non-contradiction or some other basic principle of deduction—while the second approach eschews any tinkering with logic and focuses instead on the *meaning* of the statements that together comprise the doctrines of the Trinity and the Incarnation. I examined representative strategies of each type, arguing that none comes close to offering a wholly satisfactory solution (with most being highly unsatisfactory). Nevertheless, I suggested that the second type of approach offers greater promise than the first; and furthermore that the complementarity strategy, which purports to retain the orthodox interpretation of doctrines, is the most promising of all, even though it ultimately fails to provide a workable solution—either in general or with respect to the Trinity and the Incarnation. The model I propose here shares a number of features with the complementarity approach, but the criteria it specifies for rational belief in paradox are more amenable toward these two doctrines. It also draws on elements of other Christian doctrines, thereby offering a more integrated and coherent approach to the phenomenon of theological paradox.

6.2.1 Apparent Contradiction

I have argued that the doctrines of the Trinity and the Incarnation, interpreted in such a way as to satisfy orthodox convictions, at least *appear* to be contradictory. On the one hand, Christians want to affirm the strict monotheism of the Old Testament (and indeed the New Testament); on the other, they want to confess that Christ is no less than God whilst maintaining that he is *distinct* from the divine individual whom he called 'Father'. But after ruling out polytheism, subordinationism and modalism, what logical space is left for orthodoxy? Similarly, while confessing the undiminished divinity of

Christ along with his undivided personhood, Christian believers want to do justice to scriptural claims regarding Jesus' genuine humanity: his weakness, his limitations, his ignorance, his suffering. Yet if docetism, kenoticism, Apollinarianism, Eutychianism, and Nestorianism are all deemed unacceptable, what possibilities remain? For both doctrines, the joint denial of all heterodox alternatives seems to lead inevitably to logical inconsistency.

In my earlier discussion of these doctrines, I scrupulously restricted my conclusions to claims about the *appearance* of contradiction. I did so in order to avoid begging the question as to whether these doctrines, properly understood, are *really* contradictory or not—and thus, in the eyes of those who (rightly) take consistency to be one of the hallmarks of truth, to avoid begging the question as to whether the doctrines are *false* or not.

Now the distinction between *apparent* contradiction and *real* contradiction is both intelligible—as evidenced by the fact that you, the reader, presumably grasped the point expressed in the previous paragraph—and is crucial to the model I develop here. Moreover, as later discussion will show, this is no empty or trivial distinction. For the appearance of contradiction does not *entail* the actuality of contradiction any more than, say, the appearance of contrition entails the actuality of contrition. Taking the point further, it is worth reminding ourselves that appearances are always in the eye of the beholder: what appears contradictory to one person might not appear contradictory to another. Just how things appear to a person will depend on an array of factors such as background knowledge, comprehensional ability, prior experience, preconceptions, and so forth.[7]

If a genuine distinction can be made between apparent contradiction and real contradiction, it follows that one can be made between *apparent-and-real* contradiction and *apparent-but-not-real* contradiction. Let us refer to an instance of the latter as a *merely* apparent contradiction (MAC). If certain Christian doctrines appear contradictory (as they do) but the notion that they involve real contradiction is logically and theologically anathema (as it is) then the only acceptable option for Christians is to treat these doctrines as MACs. Whether they are rational in doing so is a question to be tackled in due course. For now, I wish to explore what this view

---

7   Some writers on theological paradox have made a point of denying the distinction between apparent contradiction and real contradiction—or at least denying that it is of any utility. I will address this objection in Chapter 7.

would entail and how the phenomenon of apparent contradiction might arise in the first place.

How should one construe a doctrinal MAC? By virtue of what, precisely, is the contradiction merely apparent? Aristotle famously stated that something cannot be both X and non-X at the same *time* and in the same *sense*. The temporal qualifier is surely of no utility in this context: no one wants to claim, for example, that sometimes only the Father is God and at other times only the Son is God, or that Christ was non-divine during the period he lived on earth as a human.[8] We are therefore left with the semantic qualifier. Aquinas (doubtless inspired by Aristotle) famously stated that when one is faced with a contradiction, one should make a distinction. Of course, when one *can* make the appropriate distinctions, one should do so; but one may not always be in a position to specify those distinctions. Nevertheless, knowing that the relevant distinctions could *in principle* be articulated and explicated is sufficient grounds for distinguishing a MAC from a genuine contradiction. MACs of this kind are thus accounted for by the presence of *unarticulated equivocation* among key terms involved in the claims. For brevity's sake, I will hereafter refer to an instance of this phenomenon as a MACRUE (Merely Apparent Contradiction Resulting from Unarticulated Equivocation).[9]

It will be best to introduce some examples at this point to establish that the notion of a MACRUE is unobjectionable in principle and of general utility quite apart from any association with paradoxical Christian doctrines. Consider first the following two claims:

(A1)   I am concerned about my wife's operation.

(A2)   I am not concerned about my wife's operation.

These statements certainly appear to be contradictory. Yet if you were to have overheard me making both claims within a short space of time you might well have thought (if you took me to be an honest, straightforward fellow) that there must be some alternative explanation for this contradiction than that I was speaking falsely on

---

8   It has been claimed, of course, that this is in effect what the kenotic solution advocates. Swinburne, *The Christian God*, 233; Donald MacLeod, *The Person of Christ* (Downers Grove, IL: InterVarsity Press, 1998), 205. Still, no kenoticist would want to express it in such terms.

9   It is important to note from the outset that not all equivocation is *mere* equivocation (as between 'bank' referring to a financial institution and 'bank' referring to a river's border). Analogy and metaphor are also forms of equivocation, but involving a substantial element of meaning-commonality.

one or other occasion. You might thus have concluded that the contradiction is merely apparent, even if you could not immediately see why. And you would have been correct, too, because both (A1) and (A2) were true but involved an unarticulated equivocation on the term 'concerned': I was *concerned* in the sense that I care about my wife's welfare, but I was *not concerned* in the sense that I was not anxious about the outcome (since I knew that the operating surgeon is one of the best in the world). Naturally, once the distinction is articulated and grasped the appearance of contradiction vanishes; yet both of my original claims were true, despite the seeming inconsistency.

As a second example consider the case of Harry, a Christian layman who has been invited by a friend to attend a lecture given by an eminent Continental theologian. Due to a combination of factors—a previous late night, the stuffiness of the lecture theatre, the monotony of the speaker's voice—Harry's attention drifts in and out during the course of the presentation. At one point, he hears the following claim:

(B1)   God's kingdom has arrived.

Soon afterwards, he dozes off—only to awaken to catch this second claim:

(B2)   God's kingdom has not arrived.

Harry's immediate thought is that the lecturer has flatly contradicted himself. Still, being a charitable chap by nature, and working on the assumption that an eminent Continental theologian would be unlikely to exhibit such flagrant illogicality, he quickly concludes that the speaker has in mind a distinction according to which God's kingdom has arrived *in one sense* but has not arrived *in another sense*. Having tuned out for most of the lecture, Harry lacks the information needed to specify just *what* distinction is operative here, but nonetheless he is justified in believing *that* some distinction is operative and therefore that this is a MACRUE. He reasons that the crucial distinction *could* be explicated (by the source of the claims if by no one else) and the appearance of inconsistency thereby removed.

One final, subtler example. Reflect on the situation faced by Susan, who is presented with the following two claims about one and the same human individual:

(C1)   Jamie has an XY chromosome pair.

(C2)   Jamie is an attractive teenaged girl.[10]

Although (C1) and (C2) do not explicitly conflict in the way illustrated in the previous two examples, there is nonetheless an appearance of contradiction: an *implicit* contradiction. (C1) implies that Jamie is male, while (C2) implies that Jamie is *not* male. Yet if the source of the claims were someone who knew Jamie well and in the relevant respects (e.g., Jamie's family doctor), and Susan had good reason to believe that this person intended to speak truthfully, then she would be justified in taking this to be a MACRUE.

The actual state of affairs lying behind claims (C1) and (C2) is this: there exists a rare medical condition known as *male pseudohermaphroditism* in which an embryo with an XY genotype nonetheless develops physiologically as a female.[11] Thus the apparent contradiction can be fully resolved once it is understood that there are various distinct senses in which a person can be male or female. In this case, Jamie is 'genotypically' *male* but 'phenotypically' *not male*. Nevertheless, Susan need not be aware of this phenomenon (let alone have any medical understanding of how it occurs) to believe with good reason that (C1) and (C2) constitute a MACRUE.

There are two further points to recognise about a person S who finds herself in a cognitive situation such as this, the relevance of which will become evident later on. First, it does not follow from the fact that (C1) and (C2) appear to contradict (albeit implicitly) that these statements are meaningless for S. Secondly, the appearance of contradiction arises from the fact that S's concepts of *being male* and *being female* are not sufficiently discriminating to enable her to resolve the contradiction: the relatively 'coarse' concept of gender applied by S in her everyday thinking does not distinguish, but rather subsumes, the more 'refined' notions of *genotypic* gender and *phenotypic* gender (which turn out to be only contingently coincident, even if ubiquitously so). As S sees things, then, *being male* implies *having an XY chromosome pair* and also *not being a girl*. Moreover, this

---

10 The adjective 'attractive' is intended to convey that there is nothing in Jamie's physical appearance that would suggest any abnormality, while the adjective 'teenaged' is meant to exclude the possibility of Jamie having undergone gender reassignment treatment. Both of these constraints could have been specified explicitly so as to bring out more acutely the phenomenon of apparent contradiction, albeit at the expense of simplicity and rhetorical impact.

11 T. W. Sadler, *Langman's Medical Embryology* (Baltimore, MD: Williams & Wilkins, 5th edn, 1985), 273-76. At present, the aetiology of this condition is only partially understood.

limitation in *S*'s conceptual palette does not affect in the slightest her ability to interact appropriately with family and friends in the course of everyday life or prevent her from passing an introductory course in human biology.

These examples show that the notion of a merely apparent contradiction resulting from unarticulated equivocation is cogent and applicable in a range of plausible scenarios. I now turn to consider how this notion can be applied to the phenomenon of theological paradox.

6.2.2 Equivocation: Unarticulated and Articulated

At the heart of the RAPT model is the claim that the paradoxical doctrines of the Trinity and the Incarnation are best treated as merely apparent contradictions resulting from unarticulated equivocation. Indeed, I suggest that *all* genuinely paradoxical Christian doctrines should be construed along these lines. These doctrines are rarely stated in such a way that the seeming contradiction is explicit (e.g., 'Christ is omniscient and Christ is not omniscient'), though in some cases may be expressed so as to present a formal contradiction (as with certain formulations of the doctrine of the Trinity). Generally speaking, however, the perceived contradiction will be merely implicit—but no less awkward for that.[12] Moreover, these apparent contradictions in the expression of Christian doctrines are the product of theological theorizing from source data that also strikes us as implicitly contradictory. For the Bible nowhere makes any explicitly or formally contradictory statements about God's triune nature or the hypostatic union, but rather supplies copious data about God and Jesus Christ from which we *infer* the sort of neat, succinct set of claims which serves as a formal statement of orthodox belief such as the Athanasian Creed or Definition of Chalcedon. Furthermore, these doctrinal inferences are not conducted in an epistemic vacuum, so to speak; they draw on a considerable amount of extra-biblical background knowledge and prior experience about the concepts and categories employed by the

---

12 Recall that an explicit contradiction arises when some statement and its negation are both affirmed; a formal contradiction arises when a set of statements is affirmed from which an explicit contradiction can be *logically deduced* (typically via first-order logic with identity); and an implicit contradiction is a set of propositions to which some necessary truth(s) may be added so as to yield a formal contradiction. I contended earlier (§4.1) that the doctrines of the Trinity and the Incarnation are best construed as giving the appearance of *implicit* contradiction.

biblical text, including natural intuitions about conceptual entailments and metaphysical necessities. As we will see, this has significant epistemic consequences.

So what implications follow for our doctrinal statements if paradoxical doctrines are construed as MACRUEs? By way of example, suppose that a particular expression of the doctrine of the Trinity includes the following two statements—or, more plausibly, either includes or *implies* these statements:[13]

(T1)   God is one divine being.

(T2)   God is three divine beings.

According to the RAPT model, these two statements must involve an equivocation on one or more of the terms employed: 'God', 'one', 'three', 'is', 'divine', or 'being'.[14] This being the case, the apparent contradiction is *merely* apparent; and furthermore, it follows that equivalent but formally consistent expressions of trinitarian theology can be constructed simply by *articulating* distinctions between one or more terms. For example:

(T1A)   God is$_1$ one divine being.

(T2A)   God is$_2$ three divine beings.

Or:

(T1B)   God is one divine$_1$ being.

(T2B)   God is three divine$_2$ beings.

Or:

(T1C)   God is one divine being$_1$.

(T2C)   God is three divine beings$_2$.

Simple examples such as these serve to illustrate the principle, but more sophisticated and informative strategies are available for augmenting our terminology so as to render the concealed equivocation explicit and thereby permit formally consistent expressions of trinitarian doctrine. We could, for instance, reconfigure our notion of *identity* so as to accommodate the 'exceptional' cases raised by the metaphysics of divine personhood. This could be accomplished by either (a) qualifying our concept of identity to allow for exceptions to the transitivity principle with

---

13   Arguably, the first of these claims is implied by statements 3 and 16 of the Athanasian Creed, the second by the conjunction of statements 4, 5, and 15.

14   In the case of 'one' and 'three', the equivocation would be with respect to a natural deduction from either (T1) or (T2): 'God is not three divine beings' or 'God is not one divine being', respectively.

respect to the divine essence and the divine persons, or (b) bifurcating the identity relation so as to distinguish two distinct *species* of identity (which turn out to be conflated by our intuitive notion of numerical identity): one species (call it 'ousia-identity') obtaining between the divine persons, the other (call it 'hypostasis-identity') *not* obtaining. If the second route were taken, the doctrine of the Trinity could be expressed symbolically, and entirely consistently, along the following lines:

(1) $f =_o g$ [read: the Father is *ousia*-identical to God]

(2) $s =_o g$ [read: the Son is *ousia*-identical to God]

(3) $h =_o g$ [read: the Holy Spirit is *ousia*-identical to God]

(4) $\sim(f =_h s)$ [read: the Father is not *hypostasis*-identical to the Son]

(5) $\sim(f =_h h)$ [read: the Father is not *hypostasis*-identical to the Holy Spirit]

(6) $\sim(s =_h h)$ [read: the Son is not *hypostasis*-identical to the Holy Spirit]

The crucial point with regard to systematic consistency is that according to this 'Trinitarian Calculus' the following rule of inference does *not* hold:

$$(x =_o y) \rightarrow (x =_h y)$$

On the other hand, the following rules *do* hold:

$$(x =_h y) \rightarrow (x =_o y)$$
$$(x =_o z) \wedge (y =_o z) \rightarrow (x =_o y)$$
$$(x =_h z) \wedge (y =_h z) \rightarrow (x =_h y)$$

Consequently, deductions such as the following (which presumably captures the crucial Nicene *homoousios* claim) are entirely valid:

(7) $f =_o s$ [read: the Father is *ousia*-identical to the Son]

A full explication of this approach would require a corresponding adaptation of Leibniz's Law, so as to accommodate a distinction between *ousia*-properties (aseity, eternality, omnipotence, etc.) and *hypostasis*-properties (begottenness, procession, etc.). Note also that the resultant propositional apparatus will be perfectly capable in principle of expressing everything we want to say about 'regular' identity relations between *non*-divine things, on the understanding that our intuitive notion of identity (symbolized by '=') effectively conflates *ousia*-identity and *hypostasis*-identity. Put formally:

$$(x = y) \rightarrow (x =_o y) \wedge (x =_h y)$$

The apparatus is thus better thought of as a *refinement* of first-order logic with identity, tailored to handle the sensitivities of revealed trinitarian metaphysics, than an alternative to it. Hence with one formalism we can accommodate not only the claim that 'Hesperus is Phosphorus' but also the Athanasian Creed—and all without formal contradiction.

Alternatively, and perhaps still more profitably, we could reconfigure our notion of *numerical oneness* (and thus our enumerative procedures) so as to handle the oddities of trinitarian theology. Inspired by supervaluationist solutions to paradoxes of vagueness,[15] we could introduce the notion of *superone*: something is superone with respect to some sortal F just in case it can be enumerated as both one F and three Fs (following typical definitions of 'one' and 'three' expressed in first-order predicate logic with identity). It would then be a matter of adapting our enumerative terminology—our definitions of 'one', 'two', 'three', etc.—so as to accommodate the biblical conviction that God is *superone* divine being, such that numerical claims about divinity ('there is one omniscient being', 'there are three omniscient beings', 'there are ten omniscient beings', etc.) evaluate to true or false as appropriate. We would thus have at our disposal a vocabulary in terms of which we could (i) express trinitarian monotheistic orthodoxy (and exclude heterodoxy) without formal contradiction and (ii) still say all that we normally want to say about counting *non*-divine things, without having to tinker with any laws of logic in the process.[16] Among other virtues, this approach would seem to enjoy some Patristic support. Basil of Caesarea, for one, appears to have accepted that our enumerative procedures need to be attuned for service in trinitarian theorizing:

> In delivering the formula of the Father, the Son, and the Holy Ghost, our Lord did not connect the gift with number. ... But, O wisest sirs, let the unapproachable be altogether above and beyond number, as the ancient reverence of the Hebrews wrote the unutterable name of God in peculiar characters, thus endeavouring to set forth its infinite excellence. *Count, if you must; but you must not by counting do damage to the faith. Either let the ineffable be honoured by silence; or let holy things be counted consistently with true*

---

15   See, e.g., Kit Fine, 'Vagueness, Truth and Logic', *Synthese* 30 (1975), 265-300.
16   Arguably the numerical definitions resulting from this procedure would merely systematize the way most Christians *already* speak and think about God and the persons of the Trinity. I am grateful to David Byron for suggesting this scheme to me in correspondence.

religion. There is one God and Father, one Only-begotten, and one Holy Ghost. We proclaim each of the hypostases singly; and, when count we must, we do not let an ignorant arithmetic carry us away to the idea of a plurality of Gods.[17]

Whatever the nuts and bolts of such strategies, the underlying point is straightforward enough: if the doctrine of the Trinity is taken to be a MACRUE then a formally consistent statement of the doctrine can be generated by explicitly articulating appropriate distinctions within whatever terminology is used to express the doctrine.

A question naturally arises at this point. Between just *which* terms should these distinctions be articulated? Which of the formulations suggested above (or further alternatives) properly captures the truth about God's triunity by locating the crucial distinctions on the correct terms? At the very least, we can say that if we are warranted in taking the doctrine to be a MACRUE then at least *one* of these formally consistent statements must be correct. (Whether we *are* warranted in taking the doctrine this way is a question to be taken up in due course.) This implication alone is sufficient to deflect the anti-trinitarian charge of falsity due to logical inconsistency; for if the doctrine is a MACRUE then it must *in the nature of the case* be susceptible to formally consistent expression.[18]

---

17 Basil of Caesarea, *On the Spirit*, 18.4, emphasis added; in *NPNF2*, Vol. 8. Contemporary philosopher Timothy Mahoney gestures toward the same conclusion in his treatment of trinitarian orthodoxy: 'Christians do not claim "One God is Three Gods," or "One Person is Three Persons." Rather Christians claim God is one in one respect and three in a different respect. Nonetheless, although formal contradiction is avoided, we cannot understand how what is expressed can be true. In other words, the Trinity does not so much violate logic as it transcends logic. In both our experience and natural conceptual schemes if there are three persons, then there are three beings, three instances of the same nature. Likewise, if there is one being, then there cannot be more than one person. The Trinity fractures these categories of thought in irremediable ways.' Timothy A. Mahoney, 'Christian Metaphysics: Trinity, Incarnation, and Creation', *Sophia* 8.1 (2002), 79-102.

18 This dialectical move is one frequently employed in defences of the coherence of Christian theism, i.e., arguing that at least one logically consistent model can be constructed for the claims in question, but withholding judgement on whether that particular model is in fact correct. For example, consider Plantinga's claim, as part of his Free Will Defence, that the mere *possibility* of all natural evil being due to the free actions of non-human spirits is sufficient to rebut the deductive atheistic argument from evil. One need not be committed to the *truth* of that proposition, only to its possibility. Plantinga, *The Nature of Necessity*, 192-93. So with defences

It may be possible to take matters further, however, should there turn out to be philosophical or exegetical grounds for rationally preferring one formulation over against another. Moreover, it is plausible to suppose that some formulations will be materially equivalent to others. By way of analogy, consider this geometric example of a merely apparent contradiction:

(S1)   The object O is shaped triangularly.

(S2)   The object O is not shaped triangularly.

Given that the object in question is a three-dimensional cone, the resolution of this apparent contradiction is obvious (see Figure 6.1). However, the statements (S1) and (S2) can be rendered formally consistent in (at least) two ways:

(S1A) The object O is shaped$_1$ triangularly.

(S2A) The object O is not shaped$_2$ triangularly.

Or:

(S1B) The object O is shaped triangularly$_1$.

(S2B) The object O is not shaped triangularly$_2$.

In each case, the meaning of one term is refined so as to remove any inconsistency between the two statements. Hence, 'shaped$_1$' will convey something like the meaning '*horizontally*-shaped' while 'shaped$_2$' will signify something like '*vertically*-shaped'; likewise, 'triangularly$_1$' will convey something like the meaning '*horizontally*-triangularly' while 'triangularly$_2$' will signify something like '*vertically*-triangularly'. It thus turns out that the semantic distinction (which is grounded in a real geometric dimension) can be cashed out in multiple ways: the conjunction of (S1A) and (S2A) effectively captures the same facts about the object as the conjunction of (S1B) and (S2B). Accordingly, if a dimensionally-impoverished Flatlander were to receive a trustworthy revelation from a Spacelander that included the statements (S1) and (S2) about some 'transcendent' object O, he might reasonably conclude that (S1) and (S2) amount to a *merely* apparent contradiction and might render them formally consistent as *either* (S1A) and (S2A) *or* (S1B) and (S2B).[19] It seems to me that something parallel may well hold for alternative formulations of

---

of the Trinity and the Incarnation: the Christian need not argue that any *particular* consistent formulation of the doctrine is correct, only that a consistent formulation is *possible*. The burden is shifted to the naysayer, who must argue that this is false, i.e., that there *could not be* such a formulation.

19   Edwin Abbott, *Flatland* (Penguin Classics: London: Penguin Books, rev. edn, 1998).

trinitarian doctrine; at any rate, I see no reason to suppose it could not.

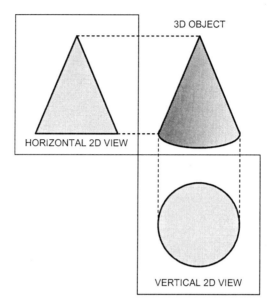

Figure 6.1

I have focused here on the doctrine of the Trinity, but the principles apply equally to other paradoxical doctrines. Consistent expressions of the doctrine of the Incarnation and its implications can be likewise generated by formally articulating distinctions which are, by default, concealed:

(I1)   Christ was aware$_1$ of the date of the Parousia.

(I2)   Christ was not aware$_2$ of the date of the Parousia.

Conundrums raised by the Reformed tradition's robust view of providence, coupled with well-grounded biblical convictions about human culpability for sin, can be treated in similar fashion by drawing appropriate distinctions within our intuitive notion of *causal determination*:

(P1)   God determined$_1$ that the people would conspire to have Jesus killed.[20]

---

20   Cf. Acts 2:23; 4:27-28.

(P2)   God did not determine₂ that the people would conspire to
        have Jesus killed.[21]

On a closely related point, the Reformed distinction between God's
decretive will and God's *preceptive* will arguably exemplifies precisely
the strategy advocated here: positing distinctions that are not
articulated in the biblical text itself, so as to resolve the apparent
contradiction between sets of scriptural statements regarding divine
volition (e.g., Rom. 9:19 and Eph. 1:11 contrasted with Rom. 12:2 and
1 Thess. 4:3; 5:16-18).[22]

One final remark before moving on. By claiming that paradoxical
Christian doctrines construed as MACRUEs can be rendered
formally consistent by the systematic augmentation of the
terminology with which they are expressed, I am not at all
suggesting that this strategy should be implemented in every
expression of those doctrines. I hardly wish to recommend, for
example, that henceforth the Athanasian Creed be printed with
subscripted numbers on key terms or that it be prefaced with a
system of numerical definitions according to which its claims are
formally consistent. Religious vocabulary, just as in any other
domain of discourse, should be tailored toward the contexts in
which it is employed and the purposes to which it is directed. In
some circumstances, where the demands of the analytic mind are
uppermost, precision of expression will be a priority. On the other
hand, when dealing with (say) liturgy and catechism, where
simplicity and intuitive appeal are of greater value, it is better by far
to leave the formal distinctions unarticulated and thereby avoid
fruitless complication. In each case the terminology used, and the
thoughts induced, will be adequate for the ends intended. The point
is simply this: one can dance, and one can rock-climb, and one can
do both well; but one cannot do both at the same time.

---

21 A deduction from the fact that those who conspired against Jesus freely
    chose to do so and were morally culpable for their actions.
22 Francis Turretin, *Institutes of Elenctic Theology*, Vol. 1 (trans. George
    Musgrave Giger; ed. James T. Dennison, Jr.; Phillipsburg, PA: Presbyterian
    & Reformed, 1992), 220-22; John Piper, 'Are There Two Wills in God?
    Divine Election and God's Desire for All to be Saved', in Thomas R.
    Schreiner and Bruce A. Ware (eds), *The Grace of God, the Bondage of the Will*,
    Vol. 1 (Grand Rapids, MI: Baker Books, 1995), 107-31.

6.2.3 Paradox and the Doctrine of Analogy

The understanding of paradoxical doctrinal statements advocated above raises another question. If such doctrines are to be construed as MACRUEs, does this not imply that at least some of the terms in our theological statements about the Trinity and the Incarnation are not being employed in their regular senses? Quibbles about what constitutes linguistic regularity aside, the short answer here is: *yes*, it does. If one were to claim (to take a simplistic example) that there is 'one' divine being yet also 'not one' divine being, while maintaining that there is an unarticulated equivocation on the term 'one', it would follow that *at least one* of the instances of the term 'one' does not carry precisely the same sense as it does in the sentence, 'There is one clock on the mantelpiece.' Even so, for most traditional Christian theists this implication should not be too bitter a pill to swallow—in principle, at least. On the contrary, it comports nicely with what believers have traditionally wanted to say about religious language, inspired by the biblical theme that God so far transcends the creation in his perfection and profundity that no comparison with any created thing can capture his divine qualities without some residual imprecision. As the Book of Isaiah rhetorically puts it: 'To whom will you compare me or count me equal? To whom will you liken me that we may be compared?'[23]

This conviction about God-talk finds its theological expression in the linguistic version of the doctrine of analogy. According to its most famous proponent, Thomas Aquinas, words predicated of creatures (such as 'good') cannot be applied *univocally* to God on account of the vast ontological difference between the Creator and the creation; consequently, while objects in the natural order reflect the likeness of their transcendent cause, they do so only imperfectly—and *very* imperfectly. Thus when we affirm that 'Socrates is wise' and 'God is wise' we do not employ the predicate 'is wise' in precisely the same sense. Among other differences, the quality said to be exemplified by Socrates exists *independently* of him—for there could have been wisdom even if Socrates had never existed—yet the same cannot be said of God's wisdom.[24] But neither are these words used in a 'purely equivocal' sense, for then we could say nothing meaningful about God. All reasoning from the creation to the Creator would commit the logical fallacy of equivocation. The solution here is to adopt a *via media*: words are used of God in *analogous* senses, such that there is both commonality and

---

23 Isa. 46:5; cf. 40:18, 25.
24 *ST*, 1a.13.5.

divergence of meaning. When we affirm that 'God is wise', the predicate 'is wise' is *analogous* to that in the affirmation 'Socrates is wise'; there is both similarity and difference of meaning, since Socrates' wisdom resembles God's wisdom in some respects but by no means all.

Although Aquinas's explication of the doctrine of analogy has intuitive appeal, few philosophical theologians today would wish to endorse his classical theory without substantial modification, encumbered as it is with questionable metaphysical and psychological theses (e.g., the Thomistic doctrine of the analogy of *being*).[25] However, sophisticated contemporary versions of the doctrine have been developed which avoid such unappetizing attachments. Prominent among them is the account developed by James Ross, who argues persuasively that analogy is a ubiquitous linguistic phenomenon, explicable independent of any theological or metaphysical theories, which is best understood as 'adaptation of meaning to contrast of context and environment.'[26] Differentiation of meaning between identical terms arises in a law-like way based on two principles underlying the structure of language: the principle of *linguistic inertia*, according to which the same words 'recur in the same meanings if nothing differentiates them,' and the principle of *linguistic force*, according to which 'words resist concatenating into unacceptable expressions by making step-wise meaning-adaptations, comparative to other occurrences, to avoid doing so.'[27] In short, words and sentences make the best sense that they can, given the forces exerted by the linguistic corpus in which they occur; among other things, meanings naturally adapt so as to avoid inconsistency and contradiction, to the extent that a 'hard-core' contradiction will only arise if the linguistic environment *mandates* it.[28]

According to Ross, every word in a sentence stands in a *meaning matrix*: roughly, a pattern of affinities ('is entailed by', 'is a type of', etc.) and oppositions ('is the contrary of', 'is precluded by', etc.) of meaning to other words. Whenever a term is used in an analogous sense with respect to some other instance of that term, there will be regions of both commonality and divergence between the meaning

---

25 For some incisive criticisms of the classical theory, see James F. Ross, *Portraying Analogy* (Cambridge: Cambridge University Press, 1981), 17-32.
26 James F. Ross, 'Religious Language', in Brian Davies (ed.), *Philosophy of Religion: A Guide to the Subject* (London: Cassell, 1998).
27 Ross, *Portraying Analogy*, 3, 9-11.
28 Ross, *Portraying Analogy*, 79, 172.

matrices of those terms.[29] Consequently, the statements 'Socrates is wise' and 'God is wise' will share certain patterns of implication ('Socrates is no fool' and 'God is no fool') but not others ('Socrates is fortunate' and 'God is fortunate') in light of everything else we take to be acceptably or unacceptably attributable to Socrates and to God.

Ross's general theory of analogy accounts for meaning differentiation between terms that feature both in ordinary discourse and also in some specialist domain of discourse—whether medicine, mathematics, or metaphysics—and thus it naturally supplies an account of analogous usage in the domain of *religious* language.[30] Consider then the application of Ross's analysis to the phenomenon of paradoxical doctrines construed as MACRUEs. With respect to the statements (T1) and (T2) discussed above, we can say something along these lines: whatever meaning ought to be conveyed by the same terms between which distinctions are articulated—'is', 'divine', 'being', etc.—those terms will be such that (i) there remains substantial commonality of meaning with same terms used in ordinary discourse and yet (ii) there is difference of meaning at least in those regions where genuine contradiction would otherwise arise with respect to all the *other* things we want to say about God's nature—most fundamentally, with respect to the things *God* says about himself in Scripture.

Thus, to take one example, when Christians affirm with the Athanasian Creed that 'there are not three gods but one God', each of the words exhibits substantial similarity (and in some cases identity) of meaning with the same word used in other contexts, such that the statement can be approximately paraphrased using near-synonyms (e.g., 'there exists not a triple of deities but a single deity'), yet there is sufficient differentiation of meaning that one cannot properly infer from this statement (in conjunction with other biblical data) that God the Father took on flesh and bore our sins. The analogous senses of the relevant terms will not permit such a conclusion to be deduced; indeed, it is just *because* the conclusion is denied by Christians that terms are to be considered analogous and not univocal.[31] Similarly, it is just because genuine contradictions are

---

29 Ross, *Portraying Analogy*, 107, 170-71.

30 Ross, *Portraying Analogy*, 158-78. Ross refers to ordinary discourse as *unbound* discourse: discourse that is not bound (with respect to the acceptability conditions of utterances) to the practice of some 'craft' (such as medicine, law, or theology). Ross, *Portraying Analogy*, 165-67.

31 In fact, the analogy involved in our systematic formulations of trinitarian doctrine is *derivative* of analogy (or approximation) found in Scripture itself, on the assumption that God is the primary author of the biblical corpus and

unacceptable that some pairs of same terms within formal statements of the doctrine of the Trinity (or the implications thereof) are to be understood as related analogously *to one other*.

Parallel conclusions follow with respect to other paradoxical Christian doctrines. The central point here is that while construing such doctrines as MACRUEs entails that some of the words involved in the expression of those doctrines are used equivocally with respect to their use in ordinary discourse, the meaning differentiation involved is not that of *mere* equivocation but *analogy*—and the notion that much (if not all) of what is said about God employs terms analogously is something that Christians have historically embraced rather than eschewed. If analogy can be explicated as meaning adaptation controlled by linguistic forces exerted through the context and domain of discourse, then the model of theological paradox presented here fits hand-in-glove with at least one contemporary exposition of the Christian doctrine of analogy in religious language.[32]

God cannot contradict himself. For whatever meaning is conveyed by the affirmation, 'The Lord our God, the Lord is one' (Mark 12:29; cf. Rev. 4:11), it cannot be such as to contradict (whether taken alone or conjoined with other biblical statements) the affirmation, 'There is but one God, the Father ... and there is but one Lord, Jesus Christ' (1 Cor. 8:6). The same principle applies for all biblical data adduced in support of paradoxical doctrines.

32   Dan Stiver notes that while a univocal paradigm dominated the philosophy of language until the early twentieth century, subsequent to the later Wittgenstein's influential contributions there has been an increasing appreciation of the ubiquity of analogy and metaphor in *all* domains of discourse. He comments: 'In terms of the philosophy of religious language, language philosophy in general is moving from a univocal paradigm toward an analogical or even equivocal paradigm. Whereas the analogical has been dominant in the Western religious tradition, the univocal has been dominant in terms of language in general. An interesting kind of "merger" is occurring with important implications for the relationships between the two. One implication is that less suspicion about religious language, with its mystery and inexactitude, should exist since all language is pervaded by similar dynamics.' Dan R. Stiver, *The Philosophy of Religious Language: Sign, Symbol, and Story* (Oxford: Blackwell, 1996), 200. Perhaps it is too much to hope that such developments can provide a philosophical atmosphere in which the RAPT model proves plausible to the non-religious as a defence of the rationality of Christian doctrines.

6.3 The Origin of Paradox

In the previous section, I introduced and defended the notion of a merely apparent contradiction resulting from unarticulated equivocation and discussed what it would mean to construe paradoxical Christian doctrines along such lines. But given that some doctrines *are* paradoxical, why should Christians construe them in this way? Three reasons have already been indicated: it avoids the inherent irrationalism of denying classical laws of logic; it provides the groundwork for a defence of the logical possibility of such doctrines; and it comports with the traditional doctrine of analogy. Still, a further question arises as to just what might *account* for the presence of such paradoxes in Christian theology. Is there any aspect of orthodox Christianity that might lead us to *expect* such a phenomenon? Indeed there is: the doctrine of divine incomprehensibility. In this section, I outline the doctrine and some of its implications before discussing its significance for the RAPT model.

6.3.1 The Doctrine of Divine Incomprehensibility

With a few notable exceptions, Christians traditionally have wanted to maintain that God is *apprehensible*: that is, we humans can attain genuine knowledge of God. This certainly seems to be the consistent conviction of the biblical writers, who speak frequently and emphatically about the importance of seeking knowledge of God, apparently taking for granted that this endeavour is not in vain, and who just as often claim to possess such knowledge themselves. In the last chapter, I defended the claim that Christians can know things about God and can systematically formulate doctrines on the basis of that knowledge.

However, Christian believers have also insisted (notably, with *no* notable exceptions) that God is *incomprehensible*: although God can be known in part, he cannot be known fully and exhaustively.[33] This conviction, expressed emphatically at various places in Scripture,[34] is hardly controversial when stated in this basic form, although Christian thinkers have differed in their interpretations of the

---

33 It is worth noting that the doctrine of incomprehensibility presupposes that God is *apprehensible*, for it suggests that we know enough about God to recognise that he cannot be comprehended. The orthodox conviction that God is apprehensible yet incomprehensible is neatly expressed in Isa. 40:28.

34 Ps. 145:3; Job 11:7-9; 36:26; 37:5; Isa. 55:8-9; Rom. 11:33-36; 1 Cor. 2:10-11; Phil. 4:7.

doctrine. Pseudo-Dionysius and John Scotus Erigena maintained that we can have no *positive* knowledge of God, that is, we can only know what God is *not* and never what God actually *is*. Aquinas contended that our positive knowledge of God (at least in this life) is restricted to knowledge of his *effects* within nature; we cannot know God's *essence*, God *in se*.[35] Moreover, even if the divine nature may be apprehended by a human intellect in the hereafter, it can never be perfectly *comprehended* on account of God's infinitude.[36] John Calvin concurs, writing that God's 'essence is incomprehensible; hence, his divineness far escapes all human perception.' It is futile, he suggests, to try to penetrate God's inner being with our puny creaturely minds.[37] Karl Rahner takes matters further still: considering the doctrine of divine incomprehensibility to be 'obvious in itself' as well as 'dogmatically assured', he insists that not only is God permanently and inherently incomprehensible, but also that an unhindered perception of divine incomprehensibility is an essential aspect of the beatific vision (rather than merely a limitation upon it).[38]

Such divergences regarding the scope of the doctrine merit careful consideration, but rather than endorse a particular construal of the doctrine I propose to explicate its central conviction in a way that ought to be plausible to Christians of all theological traditions. The notion that God is incomprehensible—that he cannot be known perfectly and exhaustively—follows straightforwardly from the classical conception of the divine attributes and the recognition that we are mere creatures. To comprehend God one would have to know everything there is to know about God, which in turn would require knowing everything that God knows. Since only God is omniscient, it follows that no one but God can comprehend God.[39] A

---

35 *ST*, 1a.12.11.

36 *ST*, 1a.12.7.

37 Calvin, *Institutes*, I.5.1, I.5.9. Some interpreters have taken Calvin to be using the term 'incomprehensible' in a sense more akin to *inapprehensible* and thus they read him as making the stronger claim that nothing *at all* can be known about God's essence. No doubt Calvin had a robust view of divine incomprehensibility, but charity would suggest that it stopped short of self-referential absurdity.

38 Rahner, 'The Concept of Mystery in Catholic Theology', 41. Rahner effectively treats incomprehensibility as a divine *attribute*; thus he takes it to be a consequence of divine simplicity that God is *identical* with his incomprehensibility (which explains his remarks about its place in the beatific vision).

39 Cf. 1 Cor. 2:10-11.

full understanding of God's power would require knowledge of every possible state of affairs that God is able to bring about; something clearly beyond human ken. Similarly, on the assumption that God's actions are constrained by his goodness, a perfect comprehension of God's nature would involve knowing what God would or would not do in any given situation. As the Psalmist concedes, 'Such knowledge is too wonderful for me, too lofty for me to attain.'

Of course, the doctrine of divine incomprehensibility is as much a teaching about us as about God.[40] It asserts that by nature the human intellect is ill equipped to attain perfect and exhaustive knowledge of God. While our present ignorance may result in part from our sin,[41] it is also a consequence of our finitude; even redeemed and glorified creatures are creatures nonetheless. The inherent limitations in our knowledge of God are certainly *quantitative*: however much we might learn about God in the short span of our lives, there will always remain a incalculable number of facts about him that elude us. But it makes sense to suppose that there are also considerable *qualitative* constraints on our understanding. For example, although we might have *some* grasp of God's goodness, the concept of goodness that each of us applies to God will surely be limited and imperfect at points; indeed, the fact that many Christians disagree about what God's goodness entails suggests that most, if not all, suffer from qualitative conceptual inaccuracies. Furthermore, to have a perfect grasp of divine goodness would require one to have a *maximally precise* concept of goodness, such that one could accurately deduce what God's goodness would entail in any context whatsoever; and likewise for God's power, wisdom, love, knowledge, transcendence, perfection, and every other divine quality. While our concepts of such qualities are may be entirely adequate for the knowledge of God (and of the creation) that he

---

40 Cf. Rahner on Aquinas's version of the doctrine: 'Any interpretation of the Thomist doctrine of the incomprehensibility of God should not overlook the fact that this doctrine is *primarily a statement about man*, about his finite nature and its positive quality.' Karl Rahner, 'An Investigation of the Incomprehensibility of God in St. Thomas Aquinas', in *Theological Investigations*, Vol. 16 (London: Darton, Longman & Todd, 1979), 252, emphasis added.

41 For treatments of the noetic effects of sin, cast in a contemporary epistemological context, see Plantinga, *Warranted Christian Belief*, 199-240; Stephen K. Moroney, *The Noetic Effects of Sin: A Historical and Contemporary Exploration of How Sin Affects Our Thinking* (Lanham, MD: Lexington Books, 2000).

intends for us to acquire, they are relatively 'coarse' nonetheless.[42] Cognitive realism, coupled with Christian theism, implies that human concepts are *approximations* to those concepts (or whatever the divine analogue may be) by which God comprehends himself. Indeed, it is reasonable to presume that we lack altogether some of the concepts required in order to perfectly comprehend God's essence and his relationship with his creation. The doctrine of divine incomprehensibility thus suggests that our minds are limited in terms of both *epistemic capacity* and *conceptual accuracy*: considered both quantitatively and qualitatively, our cognitive apparatus is simply not on a par with God's.

Divine incomprehensibility, as I have teased it out here, has obvious implications for our doctrines of revelation and Scripture. According to Christian tradition, God is the primary author of the Bible; nevertheless, God has spoken by means of *human* authors, in *human* language, employing (whether by affirmation or negation) the very concepts and categories by which we cognize our experiences of one another and the natural world around us. Hence whatever information God might reveal to us about himself and his activities and purposes, it will be revealed in a manner accommodated to our human limitations. This does not at all imply that what is revealed is not *true*, any more than Newton's laws of force should be thought untrue in light of post-Einsteinian physics. It merely indicates that what is revealed is not the *whole* truth; while adequate for our needs, it will inevitably lack precision to a greater or lesser degree.[43] Furthermore, if we interpret the concepts and expressions Scripture uses with inflexible univocality then we will

---

42 As Plantinga points out, however good the design plan for our cognitive faculties may be, it will inevitably involve trade-offs and compromises. Even if the designer's overall aim is that of producing true and accurate beliefs, there will also be other desiderata (such as efficiency and material realizability) that will impose constraints on the design. Plantinga, *Warranted Christian Belief*, 38-40.

43 Klaas Runia comments: 'As to the *extent* of the knowledge of God, the view generally held was that God, although he can be known, remains incomprehensible, not only as to his innermost being but also in his revelation itself. This incomprehensibility of God is due to our human limitations on the one hand, and to the nature of revelation on the other. ... The inadequacy of all our knowledge of God does not mean, however, that this knowledge is not true or trustworthy.' Klaas Runia, 'Knowledge of God', in Sinclair B. Ferguson and David F. Wright (eds), *New Dictionary of Theology* (Leicester: InterVarsity Press, 1988), 370.

invite, rather than inhibit, doctrinal error. As Calvin famously remarked:

> For who even of slight intelligence does not understand that, as nurses commonly do with infants, God is wont in a measure to 'lisp' in speaking to us? Thus such forms of speaking do not so much express clearly what God is like as accommodate the knowledge of him to our slight capacity. To do this he must descend far beneath his loftiness.[44]

Such observations naturally lead us back to the doctrine of analogy, pointing to an appealing internal coherence in the model for rational theological paradox proposed here.[45]

6.3.2 Divine Incomprehensibility and Paradox

How then does this modest construal of divine incomprehensibility contribute to the RAPT model? Just in this: the doctrine of divine incomprehensibility should lead us to *anticipate* paradox in some of our theological knowledge. As such, Christians ought not to be in the least surprised to find MACRUEs arising in their systematic theorizing about God—and particularly so when enquiring into realms as profound as God's triune nature and the incarnation of God the Son. The reasoning here runs as follows. The doctrine of incomprehensibility informs us that our understanding of God is limited by the finitude and imprecision of our human conceptual apparatus; the concepts and categories by which we acquire partial knowledge of God are strictly speaking *approximations* of those

---

44 Calvin, *Institutes*, I.13.1.
45 According to G. L. Prestige, the Western pioneers of trinitarian doctrine recognised this connection between paradox, analogy, and divine incomprehensibility. 'They owned that there was something paradoxical in the attempt, necessary as it was, by finite human intellects to give expression to the nature of the infinite mystery of God. This recognition enabled them to grasp that any doctrine of God is only a human allegory, true enough in so far as it presents a faithful picture of the revelation disclosed by God for man's practical apprehension, but quite inadequate to convey a complete account of what God is in His own perfect nature. On this understanding, they were ready to allow that two different definitions of the being of God might well be equally true to fundamental divine fact. Both were based upon analogy, and analogies must not be pressed in detail beyond the points which they are intended to cover.' Prestige, *God in Patristic Thought*, 236-37. The two different definitions mentioned here are, in effect, characterizations of God as 'one divine individual' and as 'three divine individuals'.

perfect concepts and categories required to accommodate comprehensive and maximally precise knowledge of God. It is therefore likely that at certain points in our reasoning about God the concepts we employ, though precise enough when applied in our logical analysis of created things, will be insufficiently refined to support those distinctions required to render our theological theorizing free from all appearance of logical conflict. For while we can *formally articulate* the existence of such distinctions, as discussed earlier, we still lack the conceptual precision to be able to clearly grasp the *content* of those subtle distinctions: to see just *how* God can be F in one respect but not-F in another respect.

Some of the examples employed in my earlier discussion of MACRUEs can serve as helpful analogies here. Recall the case of Jamie, statements about whom seemed to imply that Jamie is both *male* and *not male*. To a person holding an unsophisticated, indiscriminating notion of gender—a notion that simply subsumes the finer notions of 'genotypic gender' and 'phenotypic gender'—the claims made about Jamie will be paradoxical, even though that person may still reasonably conclude that this is an instance of MACRUE. Of course, such a person will usually be susceptible to education on this topic; they will be able to grasp the relevant distinctions and to understand how, in exceptional cases, an individual can be *male* in one respect and *not male* in another respect. But the point here is simply one of *conceptual precision*: when applying insufficiently discriminating concepts in one's analysis of some state of affairs, apparent contradictions can arise. Whether or not one is in a position to *attain* a grasp of the requisite distinctions is another matter.

Returning to a second example, consider an inhabitant of Flatland, who utterly lacks the concepts of *depth* and *volume*. Given that he conducts his life exclusively within a two-dimensional realm, we may suppose that he is simply not cognitively equipped to accommodate such notions—nor does he need to be, for all practical purposes. Thus, if he were to receive a revelation from Spaceland concerning a three-dimensional object such as a cone he would inevitably conceptualise this revelation in two-dimensional terms; and depending on the extent of revelation, this may well lead to paradox in the Flatlander's theorizing about transcendental conic reality. In this example, unlike the previous one, the prospects for conceptual refinement are slim: on a theistic view, the Flatlander has been created to live in Flatland and unless the Creator has specifically intended for him to attain (or to have the capacity to attain) a perspicuously consistent understanding of cones, he will never do so, however much he may desire it.

Divine incomprehensibility does not give us reason to think that *most* of our theorizing about God and his interaction with the world will be paradoxical, nor does it *entail* paradox in our theology, but it does give us reason to think that *some* of our theorizing might well be indissolubly paradoxical. We could be confident in presuming that our noetic apparatus is adequate for us to systematize God's self-revelation in a manner free from all seeming contradiction only if that fact had been divinely revealed to us. But we have no such revelation and thus we have no reason to presume that things stand so. In the absence of such a guarantee, we should treat matters on a case-by-case basis. Where we are able to express Christian doctrines without generating any logical oddities and without twisting or neglecting any revelational data, we can reasonably conclude that our creaturely minds are equipped to that end; where we are not able to do that, we must rest (at least provisionally) with paradox.[46]

Two further points may be briefly made. First, any paradoxes that might arise when systematizing revelational data concerning an incomprehensible divine reality will be paradoxes incipient in that very source; for as I have noted, it is not only our doctrines derived from revelation, but also revelation itself that is accommodated for human cognition. Secondly, the reasoning spelled out above suggests that the presence and location of doctrinal paradoxes (i.e., at what points in our theological theorizing they arise) will be a function of (i) the specifications of our cognitive apparatus and (ii) the scope and content of revelation (i.e., what subject matters God wishes to reveal to us and to what extent).

---

46 In defending Kierkegaard against the charge of irrationalism, Stephen Evans endorses a similar analysis to the one recommended here: 'A paradox is an apparent contradiction. In general the discovery of a paradox is the result of an encounter with a reality which our concepts are inadequate to deal with, a reality that ties us in a conceptual knot. When we try to understand it we find ourselves saying self-contradictory things, but of course this does not mean that the reality we have encountered is itself self-contradictory. It means that there is a problem with our conceptual equipment.' Evans, 'Is Kierkegaard an Irrationalist?', 353. If Evans' interpretation of Kierkegaard is correct, then perhaps the epistemological model I develop here could be renamed the 'extended A/C/K (Aquinas/Calvin/Kierkegaard) model'!

6.4 The Rationality of Paradox

The term 'mystery' has often been employed by Christians to describe the doctrines of the Trinity and the Incarnation, as well as various other important doctrines. Peter van Inwagen remarks that the Trinity 'has always been described as a mystery, as something that surpasses human understanding,' while Stephen Davis concedes that the doctrine is indeed a 'mystery'.[47] Karl Barth insists that care must be taken to ensure 'the *mysterium trinitatis* remains a mystery.'[48] John Calvin uses the term with reference to both the Trinity and the Incarnation, as does Karl Rahner, while Donald Baillie declares that 'the mystery of the Incarnation is the climax of all the Christian paradoxes.'[49] Other theologians have gone even further in their ascription of mystery to theological theorizing: 'Mystery is the vital element of Dogmatics,' insists Herman Bavinck, before explaining that Christian doctrine is 'concerned with nothing but mystery, for it does not deal with finite creatures, but from beginning to end raises itself above every creature to the Eternal and Endless One himself.'[50]

Since my project here is to explicate and defend the notion of theological paradox, it will come as no surprise that I propose to carry on this venerable terminological tradition. I concur that doctrines such as the Trinity and the Incarnation are mysterious; but I wish to go further by arguing that the mystery at the heart of these doctrines, rather than *threatening* the rationality of Christian belief in the doctrines, actually helps to *explain* their rationality. A central claim of the RAPT model is that the Christian's affirmation of paradoxical doctrines can be warranted via an *appeal to mystery*. In this section, I specify the precise sense of 'mystery' intended before explaining the role it plays in the model.

6.4.1 Mystery Defined

The term 'mystery' has been employed in theological discussions with a variety of senses. Some of those usages are incompatible with

---

47 Van Inwagen, 'And Yet They Are Not Three Gods But One God', 242; Davis, *Logic and the Nature of God*, 141.
48 *CD*, I/1, 368.
49 Calvin, *Institutes*, I.13.7, II.14.1; Rahner, *The Trinity*, 46ff; Rahner, 'The Concept of Mystery in Catholic Theology', 64ff; Baillie, *God Was In Christ*, 110.
50 Herman Bavinck, *The Doctrine of God* (trans. William Hendriksen; Edinburgh: Banner of Truth Trust, 1977), 13.

others, while some carry implications that I wish to avoid rather than endorse. It is important therefore that I make quite clear what is meant when I speak of theological 'mystery'.

In a recent and highly pertinent article by Dale Tuggy, in which he assesses (unfavourably, as it turns out) the prospects for defending the orthodox doctrine of the Trinity via an appeal to mystery, five different senses of the term are identified: (i) the New Testament sense, that of 'a truth formerly unknown'; (ii) 'something that we don't completely understand, something whose entire essence we can't grasp'; (iii) some fact that we can't fully or adequately explain; (iv) an unintelligible doctrine whose meaning we can't begin to grasp; and (v) a truth which one ought to believe 'even though it seems, even after careful reflection, to be impossible and/or contradictory'.[51] Now which of these types of 'mystery' do I have in mind? At first glance, the last appears most appropriate: I maintain that the doctrine of the Trinity is an apparent contradiction (though the contradiction is *merely* apparent) but is true nonetheless and ought to be believed. However, this does not quite get to the root of the matter. For as I have indicated, if the doctrine is a 'mystery' in the *fifth* sense it is due to the presence of a 'mystery' in something like the *second* sense (a species of mystery that Tuggy himself takes to be ubiquitous even within the created universe). The doctrines of the Trinity and the Incarnation are mysterious because they appear to be logically inconsistent, but this phenomenon is merely a symptom of a deeper mystery residing in the incomprehensibility of God—in the fact that (to understate matters considerably) we lack a complete understanding of God's essence and relationship to the world and cannot even in principle attain such an understanding. The phenomenon of paradox is thus a consequence both of what *God* is and of what *we* are. Combining these two senses, then, I propose to adopt the following definition of 'mystery':

A mystery is a metaphysical state of affairs the revelation of which appears implicitly contradictory to us on account of present limitations in our cognitive apparatus and thus resists systematic description in a perspicuously consistent manner.[52]

---

51 Tuggy, 'Trinitarian Theorizing', 175-76.
52 Note that this definition deliberately avoids any claim about the permanency, or otherwise, of mystery. The RAPT model leaves open the possibility that any doctrine that is paradoxical for S at time t_1 may be non-paradoxical for S at some later time t_2. For all I know, the doctrines of the Trinity and the Incarnation may be less mysterious post-mortem or post-glorification.

This definition thus draws together two threads commonly found in discussions of theological mysteries: the appearance of logical conflict and the inherent limitations of human cognition. Note that on this definition it is the *subject matter* of certain doctrines (e.g., the Trinity or the Incarnation) that is mysterious, rather than the doctrines themselves. If any Christian doctrine is said to be a 'mystery' then this is meant in a derivative sense, strictly speaking: the doctrine is mysterious by virtue of *describing a mystery*.

6.4.2 Defeaters Revisited: Defeater-Defeaters and Defeater-Insulators

At the close of the last chapter I suggested that the problem of theological paradox is best understood as the presence of a purported *rationality defeater* for belief in certain Christian doctrines: a belief that would diminish, or remove altogether, any warrant that such Christian doctrinal beliefs might otherwise enjoy. As I explained, this defeater is of the rebutting kind, for it allegedly gives one reason to *disbelieve* the doctrines in question (or at least elements of those doctrines). It remains for me to explain, therefore, how the RAPT model construes the relationship between divine mystery and this purported defeater. To do that, I will need to briefly augment my earlier overview of epistemic defeaters by introducing two further concepts: *defeater-defeaters* and *defeater-insulators*.[53]

A defeater-defeater, as the name suggests, is a belief that defeats a defeater for some *other* belief. Suppose that D is a defeater for person S of some belief B, giving S reason to abandon B or at least to hold B less firmly. A further belief D^* will be a defeater-defeater for S if D^* gives S reason to think that B is *not* defeated by D. Just as D may defeat B by way of either undercutting or rebutting, so D^* may defeat D's defeat of B by either undercutting or rebutting. Note, however, that strictly speaking it is *the defeat of B by D* that is eliminated or brought into doubt by D^* rather than the belief D itself. For while D^* *may* provide reasons for abandoning D, it need not do so; it need only reveal that the rationality of B is compatible with belief D. Thus, D^*'s being a defeater-defeater for D may be consistent with S rationally believing D as well as D^* and B.

---

53 For a fuller discussion of these concepts in the context of Plantinga's epistemology, see Sudduth, 'The Internalist Character and Evidentialist Implications of Plantingian Defeaters'; Michael C. Sudduth, 'Proper Basicality and the Evidential Significance of Internalist Defeat: A Proposal for Revising Classical Evidentialism', in Godehard Brüntrup and Ronald K. Tacelli (eds), *The Rationality of Theism* (Dordrecht: Kluwer Academic Publishers, 1999), 215-36.

Some examples will make things clear. Suppose I believe my car is parked in the street outside my house, because I parked it there myself earlier in the day. Answering a knock at the door late in the afternoon, I am told by a policeman that my car has just been found abandoned and burned out in a ditch several miles away. Naturally enough, I form the belief that my car is *not* in the street outside; my earlier belief B has been defeated (specifically, rebutted) by a belief D that I am the victim of a joy-rider, formed on the basis of the policeman's testimony. Suddenly, however, a smirk breaks out on the man's face and he confesses all; it turns out that he is not a real policeman but the employee of a friend who has been enlisted to play a cruel practical joke on me. I now have a new belief D* that this fellow is a prankster, and this belief acts as a defeater-defeater with respect to D, such that my belief B is restored. In this case, D* functions as a defeater-defeater by *defeating D itself*, so that D can no longer serve as a defeater for B.

Contrast this with a second example. Suppose again that I believe my car is parked in the street outside. Later in the day, I happen to look out of the kitchen window and notice that the vehicle is no longer there; consequently, my belief B that the car is parked in the street outside is defeated by my belief D that I cannot see it any more (and I may even form the new belief that it has been stolen). Just at that moment, the front door opens and my wife enters. She quickly explains to me that having spotted a band of pigeons with malicious intent perched on a cable above the car, she moved it to a space further down the street (and just out of view from the kitchen window). At this point, my belief that the car has been reparked functions as a defeater-defeater D* with respect to D, and the original belief B is restored. Moreover, in this case the original defeater D is not *itself* defeated by D*, for I still believe (rightly) that I cannot see the car. What has changed is that in light of new information, D no longer functions to defeat B.

The existence of defeater-defeaters suggests a certain constraint on the rationality of our beliefs, namely, that a belief B will only be rational for S if any defeaters S has for B are *themselves* defeated. Recalling that belief-revision in the face of defeaters is governed by the operation of one's defeater system,[54] and furthermore that the rationality of such belief-revision is determined in a proper function epistemology by the *design plan* for one's defeater system, this defeater-defeater requirement can be expressed as follows:

---

54 See §5.3.3.

(DD) A person S who acquires an undefeated defeater D for a
       belief B at some time t_1 is rational in holding B at some
       later time t_2 (when D is at least accessible fairly readily
       upon reflection) only if S has a defeater-defeater D^* for D
       at t_2.[55]

Let us turn now to the closely related concept of defeater-
insulators, the character of which can be best explained by
contrasting it with defeater-defeaters. Return to the first example
above, but suppose instead that just before the knock at the door I
receive a phone call from another (better) friend, forewarning me of
the imminent prank. As a result, I form the belief D^* that someone
will very soon try to trick me into thinking something unpleasant
has happened. Consequently, when I am presented with the theft
story by the man dressed in uniform, my belief B that my car is
outside is *not* defeated by a potential defeater D (i.e., a belief that my
car has been stolen). D^* functions here to *insulate* my belief B from a
certain range of potential defeaters, such that my belief B is never
actually defeated (and thus never relinquished).

Now consider an alternative version of the second example, in
which my wife arrives home and tells me of her pigeon-thwarting
measures *before* I look out of the window and form the belief D that I
cannot see the car any longer. In this scenario, the belief D^* that the
car has been moved further down the street does not function as a
defeater-*defeater*, since my original belief B is not subject to defeat.
Rather, D^* *insulates* B from defeat by D. Because I believe D^*, I realise
that D does not give me reason to doubt B, even though I believe D
nonetheless. Moreover, if it were not for my holding D^* in advance,
B *would* have been defeated by D.

The notion of defeater-insulators leads to the recognition of a
constraint on rationality to parallel that suggested by the concept of
defeater-defeaters. This defeater-insulator requirement may be
expressed thus:

(DI) A person S who acquires a potential defeater D for a
       belief B at some time t is rational in holding B at t (when
       D is at least accessible fairly readily upon reflection) only
       if S has a defeater-insulator D^* for D at t.

One further point should be noted before I turn to apply these
concepts to the topic of paradoxical doctrines. There is an important
sense in which most warranted beliefs function as defeater-

---

55 Cf. Sudduth, 'The Internalist Character and Evidentialist Implications of
    Plantingian Defeaters', 174-75.

insulators against their *own* potential defeat by certain other beliefs. Put another way, such beliefs are *intrinsically* insulated, to a certain degree, against defeat. By way of example, consider Plantinga's 'Case of the Disappearing Letter':

> I apply for a National Endowment for the Humanities fellowship; realizing I am not really qualified, I offer you five hundred dollars to write a glowing if inaccurate letter of recommendation. Perhaps, as they say, everyone has a price; as it turns out, yours is definitely more than five hundred dollars. You indignantly refuse, and write a blistering letter to the chair of my department. The letter mysteriously disappears from her office. One of the most respected members of the department, however, reports having seen me apparently trying to enter her office through a second story window. I have means, motive, and opportunity. Further, I am known to have done this sort of thing before. But *I* clearly remember being on a solitary hike in the mountains the entire afternoon during which the letter disappeared. I believe that I did not remove that letter, and that belief has warrant for me.[56]

The point here is that while there may be considerable evidence *against* the proposition that Plantinga did not steal the letter — and Plantinga may himself accept that this evidence cumulatively renders his guilt more probable that not, objectively speaking — he is nonetheless warranted in believing that he is innocent, the reason being that his memory belief is sufficiently warranted as to be insulated from defeat by these other beliefs.[57] Whether or not a belief *B* is insulated against defeat by some potential defeater *D* will depend on such factors as *how* the belief is warranted, to what *degree* it is warranted, the evidential relation of *D* to *B*, the presence of other defeater-insulators, and so forth. And the interaction of all these factors in the process of rational belief maintenance and

---

56 Plantinga, *Warranted Christian Belief*, 371. The example was first introduced by Plantinga in his exchange with Philip Quinn concerning defeaters for theistic belief. Plantinga, 'The Foundations of Theism: A Reply'. Plantinga speaks in this context of 'intrinsic defeater-defeaters'. Michael Sudduth has suggested that such terminology is misleading, given that no defeat actually occurs; he therefore recommends that such scenarios be characterized in terms of defeat 'insulation', as I have done here. Sudduth, 'The Internalist Character and Evidentialist Implications of Plantingian Defeaters', 182.

57 It does not follow, however, that Plantinga's belief in his innocence is absolutely *immune* to defeat. For example, he may be presented with compelling evidence that his memory has played tricks on him on several occasions in recent months.

revision will ultimately depend on the design plan for one's defeater system.

6.4.3 Mystery as Defeater-Defeater and Defeater-Insulator

With the concepts of defeater-defeat and defeater-insulation in hand, let us finally consider how such matters bear on the rationality of belief in doctrines such as the Trinity and the Incarnation. I have argued that these doctrines exhibit *merely* apparent contradiction, but it is apparent contradiction nonetheless. Can it *ever* be rational to believe a set of claims that strike one as logically inconsistent, even after long and careful reflection, even if those claims turn out to be *true*?

Stephen Davis suggests that a seemingly contradictory set of theological statements can be rationally believed provided that two criteria are met: first, there must be good reason for thinking the contradiction to be *merely* apparent; and second, there must be strong, independent reasons for believing the component statements (considered apart from the question of their coherence when taken jointly).[58] Dale Tuggy essentially agrees with Davis, although he reverses the order of the criteria:

> It seems to me that one can [reasonably believe an apparent contradiction] if two somewhat hard-to-specify conditions are met. First, one must have very strong grounds for believing the claim or claims in question. Second, one must have some reason to suspect that the contradiction is only apparent. Unless these two conditions are met, one ought not believe any apparent contradiction, for what is apparently contradictory is for that reason apparently false.[59]

I concur with the Davis-Tuggy line on the necessary conditions for rationally embracing a paradox, but would add that arguably one of these conditions may be fulfilled (at least in part) by way of the other. After all, if I have very strong grounds for believing *each member* of a set of claims that seem inconsistent then I *thereby* have good reason to suspect that the inconsistency is merely apparent. This principle is certainly supported by the examples of MACRUEs I

---

58 Davis, *Logic and the Nature of God*, 142-43.

59 Tuggy, 'Trinitarian Theorizing', 176. The agreement between Davis and Tuggy on this point is noteworthy given that while both conclude that the orthodox doctrine of the Trinity involves an apparent contradiction, Davis maintains that it *is* rational to believe the doctrine while Tuggy maintains that it *is not* rational to believe it.

offered earlier.[60] In each case, the one to whom the statements appear to conflict is nonetheless warranted in believing them to be jointly true, given that each statement is individually warranted to a substantial degree. I argued in Chapter 5 that belief in the component claims of central Christian doctrines derived from biblical revelation may be warranted in a number of ways; in favourable circumstances, such doctrines may enjoy a high degree of warrant. If this is the case, then these doctrinal beliefs will be intrinsically insulated against defeat by certain other beliefs: for instance, a warranted belief that the universe was created *ex nihilo* may be insulated against defeat by the intuition that something cannot be created out of nothing.

It is therefore quite plausible to suppose that warranted beliefs in the doctrines of the Trinity and the Incarnation are *intrinsically* insulated against defeat by the belief that these doctrines seem logically inconsistent when systematically formalised. Now it might be objected that the appearance of contradiction is such a formidable potential defeater that no belief could be intrinsically insulated against it (at least to the degree necessary to withstand defeat) but it is difficult to see how a compelling argument could be made to support this claim. After all, whether or not defeat is the rational outcome here will be determined by the design plan of the believer's defeater system,[61] and according to Christian theism, the author of this design plan is God. There is thus an intriguing dialectical circle at work here: for if Christianity is true, then (i) the doctrines of the Trinity and the Incarnation are also true, even if apparently contradictory, and (ii) our cognitive faculties will most likely have been designed so that beliefs in these doctrines are normally rational and warranted, which will in turn entail a design plan for our defeater systems such that these doctrinal beliefs ought not to be defeated by the mere appearance of contradiction. As such, one cannot prove that the doctrines of the Trinity and the Incarnation are *irrational* (because defeated by their seeming inconsistency) without thereby assuming that the doctrines are *false*. We are confronted here with a close relative of Plantinga's thesis that the *de jure* question regarding Christian belief is not independent of the *de facto* question.[62] Any disagreement on this point boils down to a clash of

---

60 See §6.2.1.
61 Plantinga, *Warrant and Proper Function*, 40-42. Cf. Bergmann, *Justification without Awareness*, 170-71.
62 Plantinga, *Warranted Christian Belief*, 190-91.

intuitions about a particular case of defeat—and appeals to intuition in such controverted areas are notoriously inconclusive.

Nevertheless, let us suppose for the sake of argument that no matter how strongly warranted the doctrines of the Trinity and the Incarnation might be for a Christian, that alone will not be enough (epistemically speaking) to stave off defeat by the belief that these doctrines are extremely difficult, if not impossible, to logically harmonise. Are there other considerations that might be taken into account? Indeed there are: namely, the considerations raised by the doctrine of divine incomprehensibility as discussed above. As both Davis and Tuggy suggest, one can be rational in believing a paradoxical set of claims provided one has grounds for thinking that the contradiction is *merely* apparent. Careful reflection on these doctrines certainly provides grounds for the belief that they are apparently contradictory; it follows from this belief that the conflict in question is either *apparent-and-real* or *apparent-but-not-real*. All else being equal, one is normally warranted in concluding from *X appears to be the case* that *X is really the case*. But if one has adequate grounds for doubting the reliability of this inference, then the rational course is to *withhold* the inference. Furthermore, if one has positive grounds for denying that *X really is the case* then one ought to conclude that *X merely appears to be the case*. This is precisely how things stand regarding paradoxical Christian doctrines, I propose, because the doctrine of divine incomprehensibility should lead us to *expect* that certain revelational truths about God may strike us as difficult, even impossible, to conceptualize and systematize in a perspicuously consistent manner. It thereby serves to undermine any inference from the *appearance* of contradiction to the *actuality* of contradiction (and thus falsehood).[63]

With these considerations in mind, consider two concrete examples. Until recently, Sam believed that Jesus Christ was both fully God and fully man, having been taught it in Sunday school as a child and never having reflected on his christological beliefs to any great degree since then. However, a sceptical colleague has lent him

---

63 Peter van Inwagen comes close to making this point in his analysis of apparent contradiction in the doctrine of the Trinity. 'The world may abuse us for believing in God and revelation if it will, but I think the world should admit that once we have accepted something as a revelation, it is reasonable for us to retain it even if we cannot answer all the intellectual difficulties it raises; or at least the world should admit this if the subject matter of the putative revelation is one that it is plausible *a priori* to suppose we should find it very difficult to understand.' Van Inwagen, 'And Yet They Are Not Three Gods But One God', 244.

a copy of *The Myth of God Incarnate* and on reading it Sam realises that there are grave logical difficulties in explicating this central Christian claim. For one thing, the claim that Jesus was fully divine implies that he was omniscient, yet the Gospels record that he professed ignorance on some subjects. Sam thus comes to believe that the Chalcedonian doctrine of the Incarnation appears implicitly contradictory; he consequently infers that it is likely to be false for that reason and thereby acquires a defeater for his original set of beliefs. (Let us suppose that he relinquishes the belief that Jesus was literally and fully God rather than that he was authentically human.) Shaken, Sam turns to prayer—and in so doing, he finds himself reflecting in humility on the limitations of his human understanding in the face of a divine reality that he can only begin to grasp. He reasons that if a transcendent, illimitable deity *were* to take on a human nature and live among us, it is more than likely that aspects of that state of affairs would far surpass our comprehension and might even strike us as logically irreconcilable on account of limitations in our cognitive apparatus. In short, it would hardly be surprising if that remarkable event were a *mystery* (in the sense defined earlier) and thus resisted our attempts to comprehend it and express it without some residue of apparent systematic inconsistency. Sam thus acquires a *defeater-defeater* with respect to his defeated belief in the full divinity of Christ and his original belief in the orthodox doctrine is restored and warranted once again.[64] Sam's belief that the doctrine seems contradictory will remain, but will no longer function as a *defeater*.

Sam's friend Helen, on the other hand, has always had a healthy sense of epistemic humility. Although she has never read any theological treatise on the doctrine of divine comprehensibility, she realised early on in her Christian life that there would always be elements of her knowledge of God that she might find difficult to reconcile either with other teachings of Scripture or with her natural intuitions about what is possible. Furthermore, she has read some introductory texts on basic Christian doctrine and is persuaded that the orthodox doctrine of the Trinity faithfully reflects the testimony of Scripture about God the Father, Son, and Holy Spirit. In the course of her studies, however, she becomes aware that there is something logically perplexing about the doctrine. How can it be that the Father is God and the Son is God but the Father is not the

---

64 Indeed, it may even be more warranted than before, since the confidence with which one holds some belief *B* may be increased as intellectual challenges to *B*'s truth or rationality are understood and overcome.

Son? An entry on 'perichoresis' in a theological dictionary increases her appreciation of the unity of the Godhead, but ultimately only accentuates the paradoxicality of it all. Still, she reasons that the doctrine must be true nonetheless—after all, it follows from the clear teaching of God's self-revelation in Scripture—and that any appearance of contradiction must reside merely in the eye of the beholder, given her cognitive situation vis-à-vis her Creator's. In this case, Helen's belief that the doctrine of the Trinity describes a divine mystery functions as a *defeater-insulator* and thus her belief in the doctrine is never actually defeated. The warrant enjoyed by this belief depends both on its initial warrant (with any *intrinsic* defeat-insulation that might entail) and also on the rudimentary doctrine of incomprehensibility that she holds as a prior belief.

These illustrations show that the recognition of theological mystery can serve as a defeater-defeater, or better still as a defeater-insulator, in the face of the intellectual challenge posed by the paradoxicality of various Christian doctrines. In a similar way, objections to the rationality of adhering to these doctrines can be deflected by appealing to mystery and thereby undercutting the objector's inference from the appearance of contradiction to the actuality of contradiction. In fact, I believe an illuminating parallel can be drawn between the reasoning employed here and recent responses by Christian philosophers to the problem of evil. According to the evidential (or inductive) atheological argument from evil, there are instances of suffering in the world which certainly *appear* to be gratuitous; we cannot begin to imagine what morally sufficient reason God could have for allowing such suffering. On the assumption that appearances are not normally deceptive, it follows from the *appearance* of gratuitous evil that probably there *is* gratuitous evil; ergo, probably no omnipotent and omnibenevolent deity exists (since such a being would not allow evil of this kind without good reason). A popular and effective line of response to this argument has been to undermine the inference from appearance to reality by appealing to *other* features of theism.[65]

---

65   Stephen J. Wykstra, 'The Humean Obstacle to Evidential Arguments from Suffering: On Avoiding the Evils of "Appearance"', *International Journal for Philosophy of Religion* 16 (1984), 73-94; William P. Alston, 'The Inductive Argument from Evil and the Human Cognitive Condition', in James E. Tomberlin (ed.), *Philosophical Perspectives 5: Philosophy of Religion* (Atascadero, CA: Ridgeview Publishing, 1991), 26-67; Peter van Inwagen, 'The Problem of Evil, the Problem of Air, and the Problem of Silence', in James E. Tomberlin (ed.), *Philosophical Perspectives 5: Philosophy of Religion*

Given the vast epistemic disparity between God and us, should we expect that for any particular instance of evil God's reasons for allowing it would likely be evident to *us*? Is our understanding of good and evil so extensive that we are aware of every kind (or at least most kinds) of greater good, not to mention every way (or at least most of the ways) in which evil can be permitted for a greater good? Surely not. On the contrary, we ought not to be in the least bit surprised to discover that some of God's reasons for allowing evil and suffering elude us.

I contend that something similar applies with respect to paradoxical Christian doctrines. The appearance of gratuitous evil is often taken to be a defeater for theism, while the appearance of contradiction is frequently thought to be a defeater for belief in the Trinity and the Incarnation. Yet both conclusions are mistaken, because both inferences are unwarranted. Just as acknowledging the epistemic distance between Creator and creature undercuts any inference from the *appearance* of gratuitous evil to the *actuality* of gratuitous evil, so it also undercuts any inference from the *appearance* of contradiction (among claims based on special revelation about God's transcendent nature or incarnational status) to the *actuality* of contradiction. According to the RAPT model, where paradoxical doctrines are construed as MACRUEs originating in divine mystery, if adherence to such doctrines is warranted absent defeaters (by being grounded in divine revelation) then it can also *remain* warranted even in the face of potential defeat by the recognition of paradox.

After discussing the role of defeater-defeaters in the preservation of rational Christian belief (with particular reference to the utility of natural theology), Michael Sudduth concludes:

> Among other things, I should think that the defeater-defeater requirement permits a broad range of considerations both external and *internal* to the Christian tradition to count as potential defeater-defeaters. In this way, the positive epistemic status of theistic and Christian belief can plausibly be viewed as often depending on evidential considerations drawn from within the tradition itself. The Christian doctrines of creation, the fall, and

---

(Atascadero, CA: Ridgeview Publishing, 1991), 135-65; Plantinga, *Warranted Christian Belief*, 465-81.

redemption provide potentially rich resources for reasons that can defeat putative defeaters against theistic and Christian belief.[66]

This is a valuable insight, for there are indeed rich resources within the Christian tradition for neutralising potential defeaters to Christian belief. This has certainly proved to be the case with respect to the problem of evil. I have argued that similar considerations can and should be acknowledged when handling the problem of paradox.

6.4.4 Warranted Belief in Paradoxical Christian Doctrines

Let us pause momentarily and take stock. According to the RAPT model, paradoxical Christian doctrines are merely apparent contradictions resulting from unarticulated equivocation in our systematic formulations of special revelation. These doctrinal paradoxes originate in genuine theological *mysteries*, that is, metaphysical states of affairs the revelation of which strikes us as contradictory on account of present conceptual limitations in our cognitive apparatus (thus resisting systematic description in a perspicuously consistent manner). By drawing on a proper function account of warrant, and building on Plantinga's extended Aquinas/Calvin model of warranted Christian belief, the RAPT model also indicates how belief in Christian doctrines *in general* can be known (on the assumption that Christian theism is in fact true). Furthermore, since the component claims of two central paradoxical doctrines—the doctrines of the Trinity and the Incarnation—are well supported by biblical teaching, beliefs in these claims can be warranted to a high degree for Christians. It is plausible to suppose that for many Christians these beliefs are warranted in such a manner as to be *intrinsically* insulated from defeat by the belief that they give the appearance of contradiction. Precisely which course of belief-maintenance or belief-revision would be the rational one in such a situation will be governed by the design plan of one's defeater system (a plan shaped primarily by the designer's concern for truth-directedness). But even if this were not enough to preserve the rationality of belief in these doctrines, any Christian holding a modest doctrine of divine incomprehensibility will possess a defeater-defeater or defeater-insulator against defeat by the appearance of contradiction. Thus the rationality of adhering to a

---

66 Sudduth, 'Proper Basicality and the Evidential Significance of Internalist Defeat: A Proposal for Revising Classical Evidentialism', 231, emphasis original.

paradoxical doctrine can be defended via an appeal to theological mystery, drawing on other elements of Christian theological tradition that enjoy substantial biblical support.

The foregoing examples of Sam and Helen illustrate two ways in which warranted belief in a paradoxical doctrine might be typically instantiated. However, not only are there various different ways in which doctrinal beliefs may be warranted, but there are also a range of stances a Christian might take with respect to the paradoxicality or otherwise of some particular doctrine. Let us therefore consider the most likely permutations of doxastic stance and determine in each case how things cash out vis-à-vis the epistemic status of the doctrinal beliefs.

I outlined earlier four paradigm cases of warranted belief in a Christian doctrine:[67]

WD$_1$: *S*'s belief in doctrine *D* is warranted via personal scholarly study of the biblical texts, coupled with warranted belief in biblical inspiration.

WD$_2$: *S*'s belief in doctrine *D* is warranted via understanding and agreement with a scholarly exposition and systematisation of biblical teaching, coupled with warranted belief in biblical inspiration.

WD$_3$: *S*'s belief in doctrine *D* is warranted via reliable testimony that Scripture teaches *D*, coupled with warranted belief in biblical inspiration.

WD$_4$: *S*'s belief in doctrine *D* is warranted via reliable testimony that *D* is true.

In the following analysis, I assume that the Christian believer takes a *realist* stance with respect to whatever doctrine is affirmed and I consider only those cases in which a paradoxical interpretation of the doctrine is held (e.g., with respect to the doctrines of the Trinity and the Incarnation, those interpretations defended in Chapters 2 and 3).

Consider then the following possibilities. Any person *S* who believes paradoxical doctrine *D* will fall into one of these four categories:

Category I: *S* believes that *D* involves *no* apparent contradiction.

Category II: *S* believes that *D* involves a *merely* apparent contradiction.

---

67   See §5.7.

Category III: *S* believes that *D* involves an apparent contradiction but withholds judgement on whether this is due to a real contradiction.

Category IV: *S* believes that *D* involves a real contradiction.[68]

Treating the options in reverse order, I suggest that Category IV can be swiftly dealt with: I take it as obvious that if *S* believes that some *genuinely* contradictory state of affairs obtains, then *S* is irrational in so believing. Category III can be handled with comparable efficiency, as follows: if *S* withholds judgement on whether *D* describes some genuinely contradictory state of affairs, then *S* must (at least) withhold judgement on whether genuinely contradictory states of affairs can obtain *in principle*. But surely withholding belief in such an irreproachable metaphysical axiom cannot be considered rational (even if it is psychologically possible, which is doubtful). Epistemically speaking, it is on a par with withholding belief in one's own existence or belief in other minds.

Leaving II aside for the moment, consider now Category I. *D* is *ex hypothesi* a paradoxical doctrine; properly understood it involves an apparent contradiction, yet *S* does not believe that this is so.[69] Is *S* irrational here? It might seem so at first glance, but this is not necessarily the case. Perhaps *S* has not reflected on *D* long enough and carefully enough to *see* the logical difficulty; even so, cognitive proper function need not *require* that *S* do this. Prior to Russell's famous letter, Frege was unaware that a contradiction lay at the heart of his axiomatic system, but it would be harsh to suggest that Frege was thereby irrational in thinking his theory to be consistent and substantially correct at that point in time. Of course, it was a different matter after the problem was *shown* to him. If he had grasped Russell's objection but continued to believe firmly that his system avoided any hint of inconsistency, that belief would likely not have been warranted. Similar considerations stand with respect to paradoxical doctrines: if *S* is presented with a cogent case for the paradoxicality of *D*, *S* may thereafter be irrational if he stubbornly persists in believing it to be clearly consistent.

---

68 Strictly speaking, for completeness one might also consider the case in which *S* withholds judgement on whether *D* involves an *apparent* contradiction. However, this stance seems unlikely to arise in practice simply because appearances, by virtue of their immediacy, are not normally the sort of things about which one can withhold judgement; either it appears to me that something is the case or it does not so appear.

69 That is, *S* either (a) disbelieves it or (b) neither believes nor disbelieves it.

In summary: the rationality of S's belief that D is non-paradoxical will depend on the extent to which S has reflected on D and also the extent to which S has been exposed to evidence for D's paradoxicality. Where there has been limited reflection and exposure, the cognitive design plan may well be such that S is proper function rational in believing D at that juncture.

Turn lastly to Category II, where S takes the contradictory aspects of D to be *merely* apparent. Here some consideration must be given towards the manner in which the component doctrinal beliefs are warranted. I have already explained that S's warrant for treating the inconsistency as merely apparent, and thus not relinquishing belief in D, may be supplied simply by way of S's warrant for believing the individual component claims of D. In each of the four paradigm cases of warranted doctrinal beliefs, S's epistemic situation may be sufficiently favourable that these beliefs are warranted (absent defeaters) to a high degree. (Recall that according to a proper function epistemology, if a belief meets the basic conditions of warrant—roughly, it has been produced by properly functioning truth-directed cognitive faculties operating in a conducive epistemic environment—the *degree* of warrant will depend on the firmness with which the belief is held. In the case of Christian beliefs, the internal instigation of the Holy Spirit will play an important role in determining the degree of warrant.) If the component claims of D are adequately warranted, S's belief in D can be insulated against defeat by the appearance of contradiction. As I noted above, the rational course for S will be determined by the design plan for S's defeater system; thus if D is *true* (and assuming it is important in the divine scheme of things for D to be believed by S) then it is highly probable that this design plan will favour *non*-defeat in these circumstances.

Beyond these considerations, there is the question of the role played by some notion of divine mystery in S's reasoning. If S's belief in D is warranted according to WD$_1$ or WD$_2$, commensurate with an average or advanced degree of theological sophistication, it is likely that S will also hold to at least a modest version of the doctrine of divine incomprehensibility. If this is the case, and if S reflects on the implications of divine incomprehensibility for the systematic formulation of Christian claims about God derived from biblical revelation, then S may well conclude that D expresses a *mystery* (in roughly the sense defined earlier). S will thereby acquire a further defeater-insulator (or a defeater-defeater, depending on the chronology of S's beliefs) against defeat by S's belief that D is paradoxical.

What about WD₃, where S's belief in D is warranted in a less sophisticated manner? It would be quite wrong to assume that the degree to which a belief is warranted is proportioned according to the complexity of reasoning employed in forming the belief; indeed, the opposite principle may often hold. (Consider: the person who believes in the existence of the moon by seeing it in the sky will be more warranted than the person who holds the same belief purely on the basis of a scientific theory explaining tidal movements.) Even so, since the doctrinal beliefs of Christians in WD₃ depend on human testimony derived from WD₁ and WD₂, S's belief in D will not normally enjoy *greater* warrant than in these foundational cases. Still, whatever warrant it *does* possess may nonetheless be sufficient to insulate S's belief in D against defeat by S's belief that D seems logically inconsistent.

As for the contribution made to S's epistemic situation by an appreciation of mystery, it is likely that any notion of divine incomprehensibility embraced by S will be more rudimentary than that entertained by Christians falling into WD₁ and WD₂. Nevertheless, my impression is that those with a simpler approach to doctrinal commitment often possess a greater sense of the incomprehensibility of God than many theological sophisticates. Accordingly, it is entirely plausible to construe such believers as typically thinking along the following lines:

> Well, doctrine D is certainly a head-scratcher and I don't pretend for a moment that I can spell it out in a way that shows it to be logically consistent. But doesn't the Bible say that God's ways are far beyond our human understanding? So wouldn't it be quite presumptuous for me to think that I could get my head around *every* doctrine in such a way that it makes perfect logical sense — not least those doctrines concerned with God's inner being and the way he relates to his creation? Perhaps this is just one case in which we don't know (and maybe *can't* know) enough about heavenly matters to grasp and explain just *how* these things can be so. For all I know, God alone is in a position to see how it all fits together logically. Yet it seems clear to me that D faithfully expresses the teaching of Scripture, so it must be true nonetheless and I'll continue to believe it so far as my limited understanding allows.

Now where, I would ask, is the irrationality in that?[70]

---

70 Note that, despite the informality and lack of technical terminology, all of the important components are present: (i) a conviction that D is warranted by scriptural testimony; (ii) an acknowledgement that D is apparently

This leaves us only WD₄ to consider in conjunction with Category II. This fourth case concerns those who hold their doctrinal beliefs purely on the basis of reliable testimony, without any inference involving beliefs about Scripture. This is how things typically go, I suggested, for young children and those with limited intellectual ability (albeit sufficient to possess a rudimentary appreciation of the doctrines in question). For such believers, the notions of formal and implicit contradiction will not normally be well understood, let alone the distinction between apparent and real contradiction; and since the paradoxical doctrines I have been considering do not involve *explicit* contradiction, a certain degree of critical reflection on these doctrines is required in order to recognise the logical difficulties involved and the implications thereof. Such reflection is not characteristic of Christians in WD₄ and therefore I doubt that many (if any) of these doctrinal adherents would fall into Category II. Most will fall into Category I and thus the epistemic status of their beliefs would depend on the factors indicated above. Of those who *are* cognizant of the paradoxicality of the doctrines they confess, should any such exist, the best we can say is that they could *in principle* be rational in their doctrinal beliefs; for it is at least possible that such beliefs would be intrinsically insulated from defeat by the recognition of apparent contradiction.

I therefore conclude that no matter how S's beliefs in the component claims of a paradoxical doctrine obtain warrant, provided that S believes the doctrine does not constitute a *real* contradiction (i.e., does not posit a genuinely contradictory state of affairs) then it is likely that S's belief will not be defeated on account of the doctrine's paradoxicality. Of course, it does not follow that S's doctrinal belief cannot or will not suffer defeat from *other* potential rationality defeaters—but that is a topic for another occasion.

---

contradictory; (iii) a presupposition that real contradiction entails falsehood, thus any appearance of contradiction must be *mere* appearance; (iv) an appreciation of biblical support for a doctrine of divine incomprehensibility; (v) a recognition that divine incomprehensibility would likely lead to the phenomenon of doctrinal paradox; (vi) a realisation that the state of affairs described by D could well be a divine mystery; (vii) an implicit inference that if D is true then it is consistent and hence that warrant for believing D to be true is also warrant for believing it to be consistent when fully comprehended; and (viii) a self-conscious conclusion that belief in D should therefore not suffer epistemic defeat on account of its paradoxicality.

6.5 Conclusion

In this chapter I have set out what I take to be a viable model for rational belief in paradoxical Christian doctrines. In the next chapter I will complete my case by addressing a range of objections and anxieties invited by the model, but I conclude this chapter by summarising why the RAPT model should be preferred over each of the approaches to the problem of paradox discussed in Chapter 4.

Among those strategies taking a *theologically realist* approach to doctrine, I distinguished two types: (i) those that recommend abandoning or revising standard rules of logic (either the law of non-contradiction or principles of deduction) and (ii) those that prefer to focus on the meaning of doctrinal claims. Questioning strongly intuitive logical principles (the upshot of *anti-deductivism* and *dialetheism*) is not a promising strategy and threatens to derail the projects of theological definition and exploration. Fortunately, the RAPT model offers a way of honouring orthodoxy without relying on such drastic moves. At the other extreme, *doctrinal revisionism* sacrifices orthodoxy on the altar of received rationality, but the RAPT model shows that a Christian can be epistemically warranted (and therefore rational) in believing a set of theological claims even when those claims give the appearance of inconsistency. The refuge of *semantic minimalism* has superficial appeal but ultimately glosses over the constraints placed on trinitarian and christological orthodoxy; in contrast, the model proposed here frankly acknowledges the presence of paradox and tackles it head on. Lastly, the *complementarity* solution has much to recommend it (since it purports to avoid both logical and theological deviance) and comes closest to the approach I defend, but it either turns out to be too restrictive in its criteria to accommodate the doctrines of the Trinity and the Incarnation or else winds up advocating some form of doctrinal revisionism. While the RAPT model also places constraints on what types of paradox may be deemed rational (as I explain in the next chapter), it nonetheless avoids the pitfalls faced by the complementarity route.

CHAPTER 7

The Model Defended

7.1 Introduction

The orthodox Christian doctrines of the Trinity and the Incarnation are paradoxical, so I have argued. Nevertheless, Christians who believe these doctrines (even conceding their paradoxicality) are not necessarily—or even typically—irrational in so believing, because epistemic models can be developed according to which such doctrinal beliefs can be warranted to a degree sufficient for knowledge despite the logical tension between component claims. In Chapter 6, I set out a plausible explication of one such model, which I dubbed the RAPT (Rational Affirmation of Paradoxical Theology) model. According to this model, paradoxical doctrines do not involve real contradiction, that is, they do not posit logically impossible states of affairs. Rather, they are instances of merely apparent contradiction resulting from unarticulated equivocation between terms employed when formalising and explicating the doctrines. This phenomenon is, moreover, a consequence of divine incomprehensibility: our cognitive apparatus is limited in such a way that we lack the concepts and categories of thought that would enable us to grasp (as God does) precisely *how* the metaphysical states of affairs affirmed by these doctrines can obtain. Furthermore, if a Christian is warranted in believing the component claims of the doctrines (by way of, e.g., the inspired testimony of Scripture and the internal witness of the Holy Spirit) and implicitly accepts a modest doctrine of divine incomprehensibility, then her beliefs need not suffer epistemic defeat on account of the paradoxicality of the doctrines. In short, if she has good epistemic grounds for taking those doctrines to be revelational MACRUEs, she can be rational in affirming them.

Following the lead of Plantinga's extended Aquinas/Calvin model for warranted Christian beliefs, I maintain that the RAPT model (or a close relative) is probably true given the truth of Christian theism, and, correlatively, that there are no good objections to the model that do not require the objector also to argue that one or more of the central tenets of the Christian faith are *false*. In this chapter, I attempt to make good on this claim by addressing a range of objections to the model and concerns about its viability. Some of these are drawn from writings which speak directly to the issue of paradox and mystery in Christian doctrines, particularly with reference to the Trinity and the Incarnation. Others I have attempted to anticipate in advance; my rebuttals here may be thought of as pre-emptive strikes. For want of a better structure, I have arranged the objections into three categories. In the first place, there are several *biblical* concerns. How does the model fare in light of Scripture and how does Scripture fare in light of the model? Secondly, there are a number of *theological* concerns. What implications does the model have for theological theorizing and doctrinal development? Does the model have implications that conflict with other beliefs about God typically held by Christians? Finally, I consider an array of *philosophical* concerns: analytical objections to the cogency or plausibility of the model that do not depend (at least, not overtly) on any specific religious convictions. The responses I provide in this chapter could be developed in greater detail, if space permitted, but I am confident nonetheless that they are sufficient to establish the viability of the RAPT model and to counter any suggestion that it is implausible or obviously wrong.

There is one general anxiety, however, that should be alleviated at the outset. Since I have argued that it can be perfectly rational to believe paradoxical claims, some readers may be concerned that this offers *carte blanche* to all manner of doctrinal nonsense. In advocating the RAPT model, do I not run the risk of opening a Pandora's box of contradictory and irrefutable religious claims? If we allow that Christians can be warranted in believing that God is both one divine being and three divine beings, and that Jesus Christ exhibited both divine omniscience and human ignorance, what basis for objection remains when someone claims, for example, that God is both identical to the world and distinct from the world?

Others may harbour a related concern that the RAPT model sanctions facile solutions to difficult exegetical and theological problems. Take the alleged discrepancies between the Gospel accounts. If one can rationally believe that the number of divine beings is both one and three, why cannot one rationally believe that the number of angels attending the empty tomb was both one and two?[1] Similarly, it might be argued that just any doctrinal dispute can be trivially resolved by treating it as a paradox. Perhaps five

---

1   Mark 16:5; Luke 24:4.

hundred years of Protestant-Catholic polemics have been so much wasted ink; Christians should simply conclude that, paradoxically, we are justified by faith alone yet also *not* justified by faith alone. If this is how things stand, it would seem that appealing to mystery in defence of paradoxical religious claims is a recipe for ecumenism on a unparalleled scale!

Were these genuine implications of the RAPT model, it would have little to recommend it. Yet it ought to be evident even from what has been already said that the model does not licence belief in just *any* paradoxical doctrine or set of claims. The thrust of my argument has been that *provided certain conditions are met*, an apparently contradictory set of claims can be warranted. What is needed then is a set of criteria for distinguishing genuine paradoxes such as the Trinity and the Incarnation, for which an appeal to mystery is warranted, from spurious paradoxes such as the following:

(P1) God is identical to the world and God is distinct from the world.

(P2) There was exactly one angel at the tomb and there were exactly two angels at the tomb.

(P3) We are justified by faith alone and we are not justified by faith alone.

Let me therefore spell out what I take to be the criteria for a legitimate appeal to mystery, based on the claims of the RAPT model. Consider a formulation of some doctrine D, consisting of a set T of component claims $(C_1, C_2, \ldots C_n)$ which appear to be logically inconsistent—typically, some members of T taken in conjunction seem to imply the falsity of one or more of the remaining members. If the rationality of affirming D is to be defended via an appeal to mystery (in the sense defined in Chapter 6) then, above all else, every member of T must be individually warranted; more specifically, according to the RAPT model, warranted by way of special revelation (i.e., grounded in the testimony of Scripture and the witness of the Spirit).[2] The rationale for this requirement is clear enough: if God alone is in a position to know how some state of affairs X that strikes *us* as metaphysically impossible is nonetheless possible (and indeed actual) then only an

---

2   As I noted earlier, although I have explicated the RAPT model in line with one particular perspective on how Christian doctrinal claims are warranted (the Reformed tradition), alternative models could be developed in accordance with other perspectives.

implicit assurance from God to that effect could warrant the belief that *X* is a mystery rather than an absurdity. Only divine revelation has the epistemic authority to 'trump' our natural intuitions about what is metaphysically possible and what is not.

Moreover, the claims in question must be warranted to a significant degree: at a minimum, to a degree sufficient for knowledge. Crucially, there must be available no alternative, *non-paradoxical* set of claims *T** derived from an interpretation of the revelational data that is of comparable plausibility (linguistically speaking) to the paradoxical reading from which *T* is derived.

Now these revelational constraints clearly rule out an appeal to mystery in defence of (P1) above. Scripture teaches unambiguously that God is *not* identical to the world and offers no support for the opposite view. Rejecting (P3) on the same basis may not be quite so straightforward, but a good case can be made that the New Testament affirmations about justification harmonize in ways that satisfy linguistic norms of grammar, semantic range, context, and so forth. In short, Christians can appeal to non-paradoxical interpretations of the data that avoid doing hermeneutical violence to the inspired text.[3]

Beyond the basic requirement of substantial revelational warrant, there is a second criterion for legitimate appeals to mystery. As I discussed in Chapter 6, the RAPT model draws on the doctrine of divine incomprehensibility in explaining how the phenomenon of paradox can arise; it follows that an appeal to mystery in defence of some paradoxical doctrine *D* will only be legitimate if the appearance of contradiction can be plausibly attributed to divine incomprehensibility. In general, this suggests that the relevant component claims of *D* ought to involve metaphysical affirmations about *God*: his nature, his actions, his relationship to the creation, and suchlike. This additional constraint on appeals to mystery explains why (P2) should not be considered a genuine paradox— defenders of biblical inerrancy must look elsewhere for a solution. It also casts further doubt on the credentials of (P3), for it is difficult to

---

3   See, e.g., Douglas J. Moo, *The Letter of James: An Introduction and Commentary* (ed. Leon Morris; Tyndale New Testament Commentaries: Leicester: Inter-Varsity Press, 1985), 101-17. Solutions to the apparent contradiction between Paul's and James's statements on justification are typically resolved by arguing that the two authors employ certain terms, such as 'justified' and 'faith', in distinct senses. While these explanations involve positing equivocation between key terms, no appeal to mystery is required, since the semantic distinctions in question *can* be cognized and communicated.

see why this apparent contradiction would arise as a consequence of a metaphysically mysterious state of affairs.

Taken together, these two criteria rule out rational appeals to mystery in defence of spurious paradoxes such as (P1), (P2), and (P3), while permitting such appeals in the case of doctrines that many Christians thinkers *have* taken to be genuinely paradoxical. Thus the fear that the RAPT model throws a lifeline to any apparently contradictory set of claims whatsoever is without foundation.

7.2 Biblical Concerns

Following the example of Christ and the apostles, Christians have typically considered the Bible—that collection of historic texts deemed to be divinely inspired—to be a moral and epistemic authority of the highest order. Its teachings are generally taken as normative for Christian belief and practice. As such, it behoves any philosophical model which purports to account for the rationality of certain Christian doctrines to be consonant with the Christian view of Scripture: its character, its interpretation, and its content. In this section, I address three objections to the effect that the RAPT model falls short in this regard.

7.2.1 The Fount of Doctrinal Paradox: Creeds or Scripture?

It will not have passed notice that in my earlier arguments for the paradoxicality of the doctrines of the Trinity and the Incarnation, I focused on the credal statements of these doctrines developed by the early church rather than the biblical basis of the doctrines. According to my explication of the RAPT model, however, the warrant for believing the component claims of Christian doctrines is grounded in *Scripture* rather than in church tradition (although I suggested that alternative models could be developed in accordance with other theories of doctrinal warrant). One might therefore raise the following objection. Suppose we grant that the credal formulations *are* paradoxical; nonetheless, these classical expressions of trinitarian and christological orthodoxy are (on the Reformed view) merely fallible human restatements of biblical teaching. Is it not possible that the biblical documents *alone* do not make (or imply) any paradoxical theological claims? If so, it follows that the credal formulations can be refined or reinterpreted so as to massage away all logical tension, resulting in doctrinal expressions that are more, not less, faithful to Scripture. In sum, if the fount of doctrinal paradox is human error rather than divine revelation, then the RAPT model is redundant.

I opted to focus on credal formulations in the earlier chapters for several reasons. The Niceno-Constantinopolitan Creed, the Definition of Chalcedon, and the Athanasian Creed are rightly held in high esteem throughout the Christian church, and believers aware of their historical pedigree are understandably resistant to the idea that they are seriously flawed. Indeed, those who adhere to them normally do so on the basis of a firm conviction that they are grounded in divine revelation. For this reason, the paradoxicality of these statements is a philosophical problem in itself for the Christian community.[4] Moreover, in spite of the political and personal agendas that complicated the early theological controversies, the tacit assumption by each of the various parties in the trinitarian and christological debates was that *their* position was the one with superior biblical support and hence the debate frequently turned on the interpretation of key scriptural texts.[5] Since the controversies were driven (at least on the theological level) by a desire to be faithful to divine revelation, the very fact that these heated controversies arose in the first place, and that compromise positions had to be struck in order to resolve them, is strong evidence that the biblical documents which supplied the source data do indeed support paradoxical doctrines of the Trinity and the Incarnation.

These considerations constitute an indirect argument for the claim that doctrinal paradox originates in the biblical data and not merely in the conciliar interpretations of it.[6] Nevertheless, the same conclusion can be directly argued from Scripture (though space constraints forbid more than an outline here). Consider first the doctrine of the Trinity. It is not difficult to argue that there is strong biblical support for the following claim:

(T1)   There is more than one divine person.

---

4   As evidenced by the fact that those Christian scholars who have defended the logical consistency of the doctrines of the Trinity and the Incarnation, such as Richard Swinburne, Cornelius Plantinga, David Brown, Ronald Feenstra, Thomas Morris, and Peter van Inwagen, typically allow the ecumenical creeds to set the parameters of the problem.

5   Pelikan, *The Christian Tradition*, 173ff, 243ff.

6   At the risk of over-egging the cake, one might add an 'argument from providence'. On the reasonable assumption that God superintended the doctrinal developments of the church so as to promote correct theological beliefs among the community of the redeemed, it follows that the ecumenical declarations forged by the early church fathers are likely to be a faithful systematic interpretation of God's self-revelation in Scripture.

It goes without saying that the Bible teaches the existence of *at least one* divine person. Moreover, Jesus and the New Testament writers speak of 'the Father' and 'the Son' in a manner implying that these names denote numerically distinct persons (e.g., Matt. 11:27; 24:36; John 5:19-23; Gal. 4:6; Col. 1:12-13; 1 John 2:22-24). The Father is said to be God (e.g., John 6:27; 20:17; Rom. 1:7; Gal. 1:3; 1 Peter 1:2; Jude 1:1) and the Son is also spoken of in terms that imply deity (e.g., John 1:1; 5:18; 10:30; Rom. 9:5; Col. 1:15-20; 2:9). The additional data regarding the Holy Spirit (e.g., Matt. 28:18-20; Luke 1:35; Acts 5:3-4; 1 Cor. 2:10-12; 3:16; 6:19-20; 2 Cor. 6:16) lends further support to (T1).

Remarkably, however, there is equally strong biblical support for a second claim:

(T2)   There is only one divine person.

The consistent witness of the Old Testament is that of a *monotheistic* faith. The classic expression of this Hebrew conviction is that of the *Shema*: 'Hear, O Israel: The LORD our God, the LORD is one.' (Deut. 6:4) There is one and only one God: *Yahweh*. Yet in the same context, this one God is spoken of in explicitly *personal* terms: he self-refers with a singular personal pronoun; he issues commands; he expresses a desire for us to have a loving relationship with him. Other unequivocal Old Testament affirmations of monotheism are couched in similarly personalistic language (Deut. 32:39; 2 Sam. 7:22-24; Ps. 86:8-10; Isa. 44:6-8; 45:5-6, 21-22).[7] Such robust monotheistic convictions are carried over, as one might expect, into the New Testament (Rom. 3:30; 1 Cor. 8:6; Eph. 4:6; James 2:19).

These data alone provide sterling support for (T2), but still more striking is the fact that the New Testament writers reinforce this by apparently *identifying* Christ with 'Yahweh' of the Old Testament: Matthew 3:3 and Mark 1:3 (cf. Isa. 40:3); Luke 2:11 (cf. v. 9); John 8:58 (cf. Ex. 3:14); John 12:41 (cf. Isa. 6:1); Acts 2:21 (cf. v. 38); Romans 10:9, 12-13 (cf. Joel 2:32); Ephesians 4:8 (cf. Ps. 68:18); Philippians 2:9-11 (cf. Isa. 45:22-24); 1 Corinthians 2:16 (cf. Isa. 40:13); 1 Corinthians 10:4 (cf. Ex. 13:21); Hebrews 1:10-12 (cf. Ps. 102:25-27); 1 Peter 2:8 (cf. Isa. 8:13-14).[8] This is not identification in a weak sense (e.g., 'Jesus

---

7   Dale Tuggy makes this feature of the OT characterisation of Yahweh a central plank in a 'biblical-moral' argument against social trinitarianism, citing Deut. 6:4 (along with other texts) in support. Tuggy, 'Divine Deception, Identity, and Social Trinitarianism'.

8   Consider also Acts 20:28, Rev. 22:13 (cf. 1:8), Jer. 23:5-6, and Ezek. 34:11-24. The christological implications of the latter passage are particularly striking. Yahweh states, '*I myself* will search for my sheep and look after them. ... *I myself* will tend my sheep' (vv. 11, 15). Yet he immediately goes on to

identified himself with sinners by being baptized') but in a stronger, numerical sense: two proper names (or rigid designators, to use the Kripkean terminology) are treated as co-referential. Similarly, while Paul reaffirms the 'one Lord' creed of the Old Testament (Eph. 4:5), he feels at liberty to identify *Christ* as the 'one Lord' (1 Cor. 8:6). Indeed, the theological significance of the New Testament authors' liberal application of the title ὁ κύριος (familiar to readers of the Septuagint as the favoured translation of the Tetragrammaton) to Jesus is widely acknowledged among biblical scholars.[9]

Thus, even the briefest examination of the biblical data reveals strong support for a paradoxical doctrine of the Trinity. Similar considerations can be marshalled with regard to the doctrine of the Incarnation. One of the simplest ways to appreciate the logical tensions introduced by the biblical testimony to Christ's dual nature is by considering the claims in the Gospel accounts pertaining to the extent of Jesus' knowledge. On the one hand, there are statements that assert or imply his *omniscience* (Matt. 9:4; 12:25; 17:27; Mark 2:8; John 1:47-50; 2:24-25; 4:29; 6:64; 11:11-14; 13:19; 16:30; 21:17).[10] This direct biblical evidence thus confirms a natural inference from the extensive biblical witness to his deity.[11] Yet on the other hand, the

---

declare, 'I will place over them *one* shepherd, my servant David [i.e. Christ], and *he* will tend them … and be their shepherd' (v. 24).

9   See, e.g., Hurtado, *Lord Jesus Christ*, 108-18.

10 These texts also serve as evidence against the adequacy of kenotic models of the Incarnation. Further evidence is supplied by the author of the Epistle to the Hebrews, whose theology of Christ's eternal priesthood presupposes his ongoing *post-ascension* humanity. (As I argued in §3.3.1, the Definition of Chalcedon also reflects a commitment to Christ's post-ascension humanity.) Kenoticists must either claim that the exalted Christ *still* lacks omniscience or admit that Scripture gives no sanction to the assumption that Jesus could not be simultaneously omniscient and fully human. C. Stephen Evans considers the 'radical' option of grasping the first horn of the dilemma and rejecting the assumption that the glorified Christ must be omniscient. Evans, 'The Self-Emptying of Love'. However, even leaving aside the biblical data supporting Christ's omniscience during his earthly sojourn, this uncompromising kenoticism is difficult to reconcile with John 17:5 (which seemingly equates Christ's post-glorification status with his pre-incarnate status) and Col. 2:2-3. In the latter passage, part of Paul's defence of the sufficiency and deity of Christ in the face of proto-gnostic heresy, Christ is said to be the repository of 'all the treasures of wisdom and knowledge'. Paul's appeal would fall flat if Christ were forevermore constrained by human noetic limitations.

11 As I noted in §3.3.1, some kenoticists have maintained that omniscience *simpliciter* should not be considered an essential divine attribute; instead,

Gospel authors testify to his *lack of knowledge* on certain matters and what appear to be genuine expressions of *surprise* (Matt. 8:10; 24:36; Mark 6:6; 13:32; Luke 2:52; 7:9; 8:45). Moreover, these texts will not permit the paradox to be resolved by introducing a distinction between a divine person (God the Son) and a human person (Jesus of Nazareth) since one and the same individual is manifestly the subject in each case. As the orthodox have always insisted, Jesus Christ is *one* person, *one* individual. The biblical text thus presents us directly with paradoxical aspects of the doctrine of the Incarnation. The implicit logical tensions in the christological confessions of the church are begotten, not created.

This survey of the biblical data has been admittedly cursory, but nonetheless it casts doubt on the suggestion that the post-apostolic development of the doctrines of the Trinity and the Incarnation drifted into a paradoxicality foreign to the scriptural texts. On the contrary, it is *because* these statements of orthodox belief are well grounded in the biblical data that they exhibit the conceptual difficulties commonly attributed to them.[12]

7.2.2 Logic as a Hermeneutical Tool

Texts, religious or otherwise, cannot be interpreted in an epistemic vacuum. In order to understand an author's claims, we inevitably have to appeal to a broad range of background knowledge, which in turn suggests a set of *hermeneutical principles*: rules or guidelines to

---

the relevant divine attribute must be some suitably qualified property such as *omniscient-unless-kenotically-incarnate*. As far as I am aware, no direct biblical support has been adduced for this move. Moreover, it would seem to be contradicted by Isaiah's polemic against false gods (Isa. 41:21-23; 44:6-8; 46:9-10), in which the prophet, speaking on behalf of Yahweh, argues from the following premise: if S does not know the future, then S is not divine.

12 It might be objected that my approach to the scriptural data here is naïve, lacking sensitivity to the kind of issues raised by higher biblical criticism. In defence, I should emphasise that my purpose in this section has been merely to make a *prima facie* case that the biblical affirmations about God and Jesus Christ give rise to paradoxical implications; this requires no assumptions about the reliability or veracity of those affirmations. Furthermore, I would contend (following Plantinga) that the methodology of higher criticism typically involves epistemological assumptions (often left unargued) at odds with the model for warranted Christian beliefs defended in Chapter 5. See Plantinga, *Warranted Christian Belief*, 374-421. As an objection to the RAPT model, then, an uncritical appeal to the results of higher criticism is question begging.

which we appeal when trying to establish the meaning of a series of linguistic tokens. One of these principles, plausibly enough, is the principle of logical charity: we do well to assume that an author does not exhibit self-contradiction unless we have good reason to think otherwise. The principle is especially apt when the author in question is none other than God, as Christians have historically taken to be the case when interpreting Scripture.[13] Yet this observation gives rise to a concern about the RAPT model. How can the claim that biblical theology presents us with apparent contradictions (albeit implicit ones) be reconciled with the principle that the God who inspired the Bible does not contradict himself? David Basinger raises this objection in concluding his critique of the claim that there are genuine biblical paradoxes:

> [T]he real issue of import here is not simply one of terminology. It is hermeneutical in nature. If no real contradiction from a human level is meaningful and God would not reveal nonsense, then the primary purpose for attempting to determine whether certain Biblical statements are self-contradictory should not be, as it appears to be for the theologians of paradox, to determine the logical status of undeniable Biblical truths. It should be to attempt to identify the truth. For, given my analysis, if two seeming truths are really incompatible, then reinterpretation or suspension of judgment is necessary.[14]

In response to Basinger's concern, it must be immediately granted that the conviction at the heart of this objection—namely, that the law of non-contradiction functions as a necessary hermeneutical principle—is wholly justified. It will not do to accept that Scripture may contradict itself, not least because contradictory statements cannot both be true. Nevertheless, this principle is quite compatible with acceptance of the RAPT model. For in the first place, the model distinguishes between *real* contradictions (which it denies) and *merely apparent* contradictions (which it allows). Indeed, it is precisely because real contradictions in revelation are unacceptable that any seeming contradictions are to be deemed merely apparent.[15] One can therefore accept Basinger's claim that 'if two seeming truths

---

13 'That God does not speak in contradictions is both the most fundamental and the least controversial of the prior convictions about God's nature and purposes that the church, down through the ages, has used for interpreting divine discourse.' Wolterstorff, *Divine Discourse*, 206-7.

14 Basinger, 'Biblical Paradox', 213.

15 This principle of interpretation applies equally well to statements in other contexts, as indicated by the examples of MACRUEs offered earlier (§6.2.1).

are really incompatible, then reinterpretation is ... necessary' while maintaining that if two seeming truths are *apparently* incompatible then reinterpretation is *not* necessary (though it may be appropriate in the majority of cases).

On similar grounds, we should distinguish between the law of non-contradiction *as such* (which is a necessary truth) and our *application* of the law of non-contradiction (which is fallible). Our ability to identify a real contradiction depends on the extent to which we grasp the meaning of the sentences in question: crucially, we must have good grounds for taking it that same terms are being used univocally. Thus while Christians should certainly apply the law of non-contradiction in their interpretation of Scripture, when faced with a seeming violation of the law they should be open to the possibility of the law being *misapplied* due to the presence of unarticulated equivocation and semantic imprecision. The upshot of these considerations is that while the presumption of discernible logical consistency is an indispensable hermeneutical principle, it should not be wielded as an *absolute*; rather, it should be applied with due sensitivity to the limitations of human language and human cognition in the face of divine mystery. If a plausible alternative interpretation of the biblical data is available, all well and good. But if it becomes clear that any reinterpretation would stretch norms of vocabulary and grammar to breaking point, then resting with paradox and appealing to mystery will be the most rational course.[16]

7.2.3 Paradox as Defeater for Biblical Inspiration

Earlier I specified two necessary conditions for a warranted appeal to mystery in defence of a paradoxical doctrine D: first, the component claims of D must be strongly warranted by divine revelation; and second, the phenomenon of paradoxicality must be plausibly attributable to divine incomprehensibility. Clearly the application of the first criterion depends on the divine revelation in question being properly identified *as* divine revelation. However, one might argue that the paradoxicality of D serves as a defeater for the belief that the putative epistemic ground of D (in the RAPT model, biblical testimony) is *in fact* divine revelation. God,

---

16 Of course, it is always possible that ongoing creative reflection will shed new light on the problem and allow the paradox to be resolved. The point here is that *until* such a time, there is no intellectual shame in accepting that our best interpretation of the data points to a paradox occasioned by divine mystery.

presumably, is a paragon of truth and consistency; so if the Christian doctrines of the Trinity and the Incarnation are apparently contradictory, and these doctrines are taught in the Bible, should not one rationally conclude that the Bible (or at least those portions from which the doctrines are drawn) is not divinely inspired after all?

It is important to recognise the inferential structure of this objection, since this proves to be its undoing. I argued in Chapter 5 that the component claims of Christian doctrines can be warranted on the basis that they are taught in Scripture, coupled with a warranted belief that the Bible is divinely inspired (hereafter, BI). In such circumstances, the belief that doctrine D is *true* is normally held by way of an *inference* from the belief that D is taught in Scripture conjoined with BI.[17] The inference thus has the following form:

(1)   If doctrinal source DS is divinely inspired, and DS teaches doctrine D, then D is true.

(2) DS is divinely inspired.

(3) DS teaches D.

(4)   Therefore, D is true.   [from (1), (2), (3)]

Now if the objection above is cogent, then the conclusion it proposes (that the Bible is not divinely inspired) must *also* be reached inferentially. It is not that the paradoxicality of D is *directly* a defeater for BI. Rather, it is that the paradoxicality of D indicates the *falsity* of D, which in turn functions as a defeater for BI. Put formally:

(1)   If doctrinal source DS is divinely inspired, and DS teaches doctrine D, then D is true.

(3) DS teaches D.

(5)   If D is paradoxical, then D is not true.

(6) D is paradoxical.

(7)   Therefore, D is not true.   [from (5), (6)]

(8)   Therefore, DS is not divinely inspired.   [from (1), (3), (7)]

Set out in this way, it becomes clear that the objection begs the question against the RAPT model. For according to the model, premise (5) is unwarranted (considered as a general claim about

---

17   The main exception here is the case in which a doctrine is held non-inferentially, purely on the basis of reliable testimony. With respect to that particular case, the present objection is irrelevant; for if S does not hold D on the basis of inference from a conviction about Scripture, then S is unlikely to infer from the paradoxicality of D that such a conviction is in error.

paradoxical doctrines). The paradoxicality of D is not *necessarily* a defeater for D; and if it is not a defeater for D, then neither will it serve as a defeater for BI. Consequently, this objection to the model can only succeed by riding piggyback on some *other* objection (specifically, an objection challenging the contention at the heart of the model that in some instances the inference from apparent contradiction to actual contradiction is unwarranted).

It is worth noting that the flaw in this objection is twinned with the flaw in the previous objection from the hermeneutical role of logic. The difference is that whereas the present objection assumes that D is taught by Scripture and infers from the paradoxicality of D that Scripture is not divinely inspired, the previous objection assumes that Scripture is divinely inspired and infers from the paradoxicality of D that D is not taught in Scripture. In both cases, however, the pivotal inference begs the question against the RAPT model.

7.3 Theological Concerns

7.3.1 The Practice of Systematic Theology

Systematic theology is generally understood as that discipline which attempts to develop an orderly, coherent, comprehensive, thematically arranged exposition of Christian belief and confession. Its practitioners, moreover, usually manifest a special concern to relate the fruits of their work to contemporary issues and problems both in the church and in wider society. At any rate, whatever disagreements there might be over the aims and methods of systematic theology, it is reasonable to suppose that logical principles ought to play a central role in its practice simply by virtue of the *systematic* character of the discipline. Systematic theologians will typically be found arguing for constructions of the form 'biblical data B implies doctrine D_1', 'doctrine D_2 is incompatible with doctrine D_3', 'doctrines D_4 and D_5 lend support to doctrine D_6', and the like. It is therefore possible that the RAPT model presented here will cause offence to such scholars. If apparent violations of the laws of logic are permitted (perhaps even unavoidable) in our doctrinal formulations, how can we maintain that any doctrine should (or should not) be held on the basis of its *logical relation* to some body of revelational data or to some other doctrine? Indeed, would not acceptance of the RAPT model render altogether futile the project of developing a clear and consistent system of Christian theology?

Such anxieties are misplaced. My argument has been that *in certain epistemic circumstances* one can be rational in affirming a paradoxical doctrine; yet circumstances are liable to change, and it is always possible that one's understanding of that doctrine may improve in such a way as to allow rational penetration of the paradox (for example, by recasting it in terms of a novel conceptual framework).[18] The drive toward greater consistency and comprehension in systematic theology is no more hindered by the legitimacy of an appeal to mystery in the face of paradox than, say, the desirability of a university education is hindered by the legitimacy of an appeal to expert authority. Furthermore, even if developing a comprehensive and systematic expression of revelational data without any hint of paradox were to prove impossible, it still remains that theologians ought to strive to express their conclusions *with as much consistency, clarity, and precision as the data will reasonably permit.*

It is crucial to recognise that the RAPT model does not rule out the use of deduction and inference in theology, but merely implies certain constraints on the application of logical principles. If it were known *in advance* that no apparent contradictions should arise in our theological theorizing, then we could allow any valid inference whatsoever from propositional revelational data (or our best interpretation of that data). But if we grant that some elements of divine revelation *could* strike us as paradoxical on account of limitations in our noetic apparatus, then we can permit any valid inference from revelational data *provided its conclusion does not explicitly negate other revelational data.* By far the majority of theological inferences will be unaffected if the RAPT model is correct, but whenever we are presented with an inference from biblical data B_1 that requires a dismissal or suppression of biblical data B_2 we should be alerted to the fact that there may be more going on than meets the eye; consequently, we should be prepared to *withhold* the inference in question and to reassess our interpretation of the data overall. By withholding the inference we are not positing an exception to the laws of logic, but merely acknowledging an element of imprecision in our systematic comprehension of the data. According to the RAPT model, if we were to fully grasp (as God does) the metaphysical state of affairs represented by the data, we

---

18   While I think it is ultimately unsuccessful, the application of the Aristotelian notion of 'numerical sameness without identity' to the oneness-threeness problem of the Trinity (see §2.3.3) provides one example of innovative thinking.

would understand *why* such an inference is invalid; as it is, however, we can only understand *that* it is invalid.

By way of illustration (and offering something of a change of doctrinal scenery) consider the range of biblical statements pertaining to the divine will. According to 1 Thessalonians 4:3, for example, the following statement is true:

(9)   God wills that Christians avoid sexual immorality.

Given that adultery is a form of sexual immorality, we might well infer:

(10)   God wills that Christians avoid adultery.

Moreover, on the reasonable supposition that God's will is ethically normative for Christian behaviour, we might further infer:

(11)   Christians ought not to commit adultery.

Since there are no biblical statements that *contradict* (11), we can conclude that these inferences are entirely legitimate.

Consider now a second inference. As a matter of regrettable historical fact, numerous Christians *have* committed adultery. It is therefore tempting to deduce in conjunction with (10) that the following claim is true:

(12)   God's will is not always fulfilled.

However, the problem with this deduction is that it appears to contradict a substantial body of biblical data supporting the *unrestricted efficacy* of God's will:[19]

(13)   God's will is always fulfilled.

We are thus alerted to a complexity in the divine volition that renders invalid the inference of (12) from (10). More precisely, the inference is invalid if corresponding terms in (12) and (13) are taken *univocally*; the apparent contradiction (brought into sharp relief by the process of systematic theorizing) indicates the presence of an unarticulated equivocation. Hence an inference along these lines can only be admitted if a *distinction* is posited (at least formally) between same terms: for example, as the Reformed tradition has recommended, a distinction between God's *decretive* (or 'secret') will and God's *preceptive* (or 'revealed') will.[20] The lesson here for

---

19   A sampling of relevant texts: Job 42:2; Prov. 16:9; 19:21; 21:1; Isa. 14:24; 46:9-10; Lam. 3:37-38; Rom. 9:19-21; Eph. 1:11; James 4:15.

20   Turretin, *Institutes of Elenctic Theology*, 220-25; Paul Helm, *The Providence of God* (Contours of Christian Theology: Leicester: InterVarsity Press, 1993), 130-37. It is difficult to specify satisfactorily (i.e., in terms other than those of

systematic theologians is that whenever a potential inference from some body of revelational data leads to a conflict with some other body of revelational data (by negating it or rendering it inexplicable), either the inference should be withheld altogether or else formal distinctions should be introduced to signal the recognition of a mystery and to insulate against unwarranted interpretations and implications (for example, that it is ethically permissible to cheat on one's spouse). By observing the modest constraints on theorizing indicated above, systematic theology can make its peace with apophatic theology.

Thus it should be evident that the RAPT model does not undermine the project of theological systematization and deduction by flouting the logical principles which direct that project. On the contrary, it *presupposes* those principles, while at the same time imposing certain methodological constraints on the *process* of systematisation and deduction, with a view to accommodating the source data as faithfully as possible.

7.3.2 Defining Orthodoxy and Excluding Heterodoxy

From the inception of the church, the historical development of Christian doctrine has been driven by a conviction that *orthodoxy matters*. There are certain claims about God and his redemptive activity that are *right*, which ought to be believed and acted upon; there are also correlative claims that are *wrong* and ought to be rejected. Indeed, some instances of the latter are to be vehemently repudiated, because they involve or imply a serious distortion of the truth about God and the message of salvation through Jesus Christ. The principle established by the apostles and New Testament

---

the explanandum) just what the substantial difference is between these aspects or dimensions of divine volition, which suggests that the distinction is little more than a formal device for attaining systematic consistency. The connotations of 'decretive' and 'preceptive' are useful for indicating how one ought to draw implications and applications (e.g., ethical norms should be deduced from the latter rather than the former) but do not really shed light on how these diverse aspects of God's will can be reconciled with our intuitive notions of volition. It is noteworthy that Calvin, in expounding the doctrine of comprehensive divine providence, defended his position against the charge of contradiction (i.e., positing 'two contrary wills' in God) by arguing that the divine will merely *appears* manifold to us due to 'our mental incapacity' and 'the sluggishness of our understanding'. Calvin, *Institutes*, I.18.3. One thus finds in Calvin an appeal to mystery along the lines of the RAPT model.

writers, to the effect that 'sound doctrine' should be guarded and 'false teaching' condemned,[21] was honoured by the early church fathers. Accordingly, the trinitarian controversies of the fourth century culminated in the condemnation of heresies such as Sabellianism and Arianism, while the christological debates of the fifth led to the denunciation of Apollinarianism and Nestorianism.

One of the tasks of systematic theology is thus to articulate orthodox Christian doctrine and to set it apart from heterodox alternatives. Faithful expositions of the doctrine of the Trinity, for instance, ought to distinguish it from the deviations of modalism, subordinationism, and tritheism. Any epistemic model of Christian doctrinal beliefs that would serve to undermine this task will be anathema to the Christian community.

It might be thought that the RAPT model, which allows for appeals to mystery in defence of paradoxical sets of claims, faces this very difficulty. Dale Tuggy, for example, suggests as much in his critique of appeals to mystery in the context of trinitarian theology. According to Tuggy, many trinitarians are muddled in their thinking and fail to take a clear stance on the issue that divides social trinitarians (who claim in effect that God is numerically three divinities, not one) from modalistic trinitarians (who claim in effect that God is numerically one divinity, not three). Instead, they settle for some conciliatory claim such as the following:

(14) The Father, Son, and Holy Spirit are in some sense one and in some sense three.

Now while (14) is not clearly inconsistent, and thus avoids the spectre of logical contradiction, Tuggy considers it a 'shadowy and vaporous claim' which fails to do any useful work. It is far from clear that (14), even when conjoined with the following claims, rules out either modalism or polytheism:

(15) The Father is divine.

(16) The Son is divine.

(17) The Holy Spirit is divine.

(18) Whatever is divine is identical to at least one of these: Father, Son, Holy Spirit.

While this stance may avoid paradox, it does so at the expense of obscuring the distinction between orthodoxy and heterodoxy. Clearly this will not do. But does not my defence of a paradoxical interpretation of the Trinity, according to which God is one divine

---

21   Acts 20:28-31; 1 Tim. 1:3; 2 Tim. 1:13-14; Titus 1:9; 2:1; 2 Pet. 2:1; Jude 3.

being *in one sense* and three divine beings *in another sense*, face precisely this problem?

There are two issues to address in response to this objection. The first concerns the problem of *meaning*: specifically, whether or not claims such as (14) actually tell us anything of significance about God. Since I treat this question later on, I will refrain from doing so here and simply ask that the reader grant for now that a paradoxical set of claims can still convey meaningful information. The second issue concerns the problem of *distinction*: that is, how one should go about distinguishing orthodoxy from heterodoxy when faced with a paradoxical doctrine. As it turns out, there is no great difficulty in doing so; and illustrating this point, moreover, can shed considerable light on the epistemic roots of heterodoxy.

As I noted in Chapter 6, any doctrinal MACRUE can be rendered formally consistent by articulating distinctions on one or more terms. For example, the trinitarian claims that *God is one divine being* and *God is three divine beings* can be reformulated as follows:[22]

(T1A) God is$_1$ one divine being.

(T2A) God is$_2$ three divine beings.

Now the question at hand is this: according to this formulation, how would one censure the errors of modalism and tritheism? At first it might seem that one should simply repudiate the following two claims, taking them to represent the modalist position and the tritheist position respectively:

(H1A) God is$_2$ one divine being.

(H2A) God is$_1$ three divine beings.

But suppose that some alleged modalist were to reply thus: 'The fact is that I do not affirm (H1A) at all; I have merely been claiming (T1A) all along!' How could one refute such a reply, given that (according to the RAPT model) from our cognitive perspective the relations signified by 'is$_1$' and 'is$_2$' are conceptually indistinguishable?

The solution here is to admit that this alleged modalist is no heretic at all (at least, not on *this* count). For what the *bona fide* modalist claims is the following:

(H1) God is$_1$ one divine being and God is$_2$ one divine being.

More precisely, the modalist denies altogether that there *is* any unarticulated equivocation to be acknowledged. As he sees it, God is

---

22 The subsequent discussion applies *mutatis mutandis* any alternative formulations in which distinctions are posited (or terminology expanded) so as to avoid formal contradiction.

one divine being and that is the end of the matter; in no comparable sense should we also say, 'God is three divine beings.' Similarly for the *bona fide* tritheist, who insists that God is three divine beings, period; in no comparable sense is it correct to claim, 'God is one divine being.'[23]

We are now in a position to see what genuinely distinguishes trinitarian orthodoxy from heterodoxy: it is that the latter will have no truck with paradox, insisting instead on throwing in its lot with one side of the tension at the expense of the other. Rejecting outright an appeal to mystery in the face of apparent contradiction, the anti-trinitarian must opt for either oneness over threeness (modalism) or threeness over oneness (tritheism).[24] Likewise for christological heterodoxy: either the unity of Christ's personhood must be sacrificed in order to preserve his full divinity and full humanity (Nestorianism) or vice versa (Apollinarianism and kenoticism). Any solution will be deemed preferable to the scandal of paradox. And what this analysis suggests, perhaps, is an affinity between doctrinal heterodoxy and *theological rationalism*: a reluctance to subordinate human intuitions to the control of revelation and to acknowledge that our minds may not be conceptually equipped to resolve every logical puzzle thrown up by our systematization of the biblical data.[25]

7.3.3 Alternative Cognitive Design Plans

The RAPT model specifies that the paradoxical aspects of certain Christian doctrines are attributable to divine incomprehensibility (a function of both God's ontological profundity and human noetic finitude). Specifically, our cognitive apparatus is insufficiently equipped to grasp the metaphysical distinctions that would enable us to see just how the logical tensions in these doctrines could be eliminated and to refine our theological formulations accordingly. One might well ask, however, why things should have to be this

---

23 It thus follows that the characterisation of heterodox positions is independent of *which* terms in the doctrinal formulations bear equivocal senses.

24 Subordinationism also opts for oneness over threeness, in effect, but departs from modalism on the question of whether the Son and the Spirit are divine in the same sense as the Father.

25 One other lesson to take is that Christians ought to be more circumspect about charging this or that thinker with unorthodox views on the Trinity or the Incarnation, in light of the complexities thrown up by MACRUEs. The charge of modalism levelled at Barth springs immediately to mind.

way. After all, Christian theists typically take the view that human beings (our mental faculties included) are the product of divine design. Could not God, in his infinite wisdom, have given us cognitive faculties sufficiently advanced for us to *avoid* encountering paradoxes in our theological theorizing? Indeed, is that not precisely what we would *expect* to find? For if God wished to reveal his triune nature to us, presumably he would also want to arrange things so that we would not find it so logically perplexing.

It certainly seems true that God could have opted for alternative cognitive design plans. The question is whether we have good overall grounds for supposing (on Christian assumptions) that he would opt for a design that did not give rise to the occasional paradox when systematizing his self-revelation. All things considered, I doubt that we are in a position to answer affirmatively here. Although *we* might prefer such a design, we can hardly presume on that basis alone that God would share our preference. Besides, as Plantinga observes in his discussion of cognitive design plans, no matter how well designed our noetic faculties may be, the design plan will inevitably involve trade-offs and compromises, as any engineer can appreciate.[26] While the designer's primary aim is presumably that of producing predominantly true beliefs, there will also be other desiderata that will impose constraints on the design: accuracy, efficiency, flexibility, simplicity, material realizability, and so forth. Now for all we know (and that is the crucial qualifier) the optimal design for our cognitive apparatus, given God's purposes for us, does not involve the capacity to rationally penetrate some of the finer aspects of trinitarian and christological metaphysics. It may well be that if this capacity were added, it could only be at the expense of some other, more important feature of our cognitive apparatus. And given that we are not privy to such details of the divine design plan, we are hardly warranted in assuming that God ought to have done things one way rather than another.

In any case, the notion that the phenomenon of paradox in our theological theorizing is an intrinsic evil may well be misplaced, for it is plausible to think that God would have *positive* reasons for placing us in the epistemic situation posited by the RAPT model. In the first place, theological paradox reminds us of our creaturely limitations and of the transcendence of God. It confronts us with divine incomprehensibility and fosters reverent awe and epistemic humility.[27]

---

26 Plantinga, *Warrant and Proper Function*, 38-40.
27 Cf. Job 11:7-9; Isa. 55:8-9; Rom. 11:33-34.

Furthermore, in keeping with a central thread in the Christian narrative, paradox (with its attendant notion of divine mystery) invites *faith*, requiring us to trust God's self-revelation despite the fact that it disaccords at points with our rational intuitions (about identity, unity, personhood, etc.). We are thus faced with a stark choice: on the one hand, to conform the phenomena of divine revelation to our human intuitions about what must be the case, or on the other, to conform those human intuitions to the phenomena of divine revelation. Just as Abraham trusted God's self-revelation in the face of seeming absurdity—the pregnancy of a pensioner and the sacrifice of a son—and was commended for his faith, so it is possible that God means us trust the self-revelation of his triunity and his incarnation in the face of seeming illogicality, as opposed to leaning on our own understanding.[28]

Such suggestions might be dismissed (perhaps too hastily) as mere speculation, yet surely they are no more speculative than the claim that God *would not* place us in the epistemic situation posited by the RAPT model—and that is enough to conclude that this objection presents no serious threat.

7.3.4 *The Apologetic Mirror Problem*

One of the virtues of the approach to paradox defended here is that it offers resources for defeating a range of objections to Christian theism based on its alleged incoherence. It is commonly alleged that Christianity is false or irrational because it involves claims that are logically incompatible—and not surprisingly, the doctrines of the Trinity and the Incarnation often find themselves first up against the wall in this regard. My argument has been that at least some of these alleged contradictions are *merely apparent*, and, moreover, that Christians can be quite rational in believing this to be the case.

However, this strategy is arguably a double-edged sword. For if Christianity can avail itself of this form of defence, why not other religious or philosophical systems? Historically, apologists for Christianity have often taken the line that the best defence is a good offence, arguing that competing religious perspectives are untenable due to internal contradictions. But if the RAPT model is cogent, it would appear to pull the rug out from under such attacks. What is sauce for the goose is sauce for the gander: if Christianity can be insulated against critiques of this type, so can any other religious faith.

---

28 Rom. 4:18-21; Heb. 11:11-12, 17-19; Prov. 3:5.

Dale Tuggy has drawn attention to this problem for defenders of 'mystery':

> Even after one appreciates these problems [faced by the doctrine of the Trinity] and tries to address them, there is an almost irresistible temptation to spin a vice as a virtue. Many protest that the doctrine is 'supposed to be a mystery'. ... In any case, most Christian philosophers would not accept this sort of cop-out from members of other religions defending their distinct theses about God, Brahman, the Absolute, Nirvana, the Real, etc. They wouldn't applaud such moves, but would consider them an opportunity, a chance to point out insoluble problems with the world-view in question and the superior coherence of Christian theism. What is an intellectual vice for non-Christians can't be an intellectual virtue for Christians.[29]

It must be admitted that this objection has some bite—though it should be noted that even if the Christian's appeal to mystery *can* be mirrored by adherents of other religions, it does not follow that such appeals are illegitimate or irrational for the Christian. The most one need concede is that a non-Christian could *also* be rational in believing that the paradoxical doctrines of *his* religion are true. Furthermore, the rationality of those beliefs would still be contingent on the *truth* of the religion in question; for according to the RAPT model, the rationality of Christian doctrinal beliefs depends on whether or not biblical theism is, in fact, the case. Thus the issue is purely an apologetic one: it is the dialectical problem of debating *which* set of religious claims (if any) are true and rationally tenable, given that paradoxicality is not *necessarily* an indication of falsity.

Even so, Christianity is not fated to a stalemate with every competing religion with paradoxical doctrines. As I noted earlier, there are certain conditions that must be fulfilled in order for an appeal to mystery to be warranted, yet not every religious perspective has the metaphysical and epistemic resources to mirror the Christian's defence of paradox. In the first place, the RAPT model presupposes a robust Creator-creature distinction, giving rise to a doctrine of divine incomprehensibility which can account for the phenomenon of paradox. It also depends on the availability of a divinely authored propositional revelation, which alone can warrant the qualification of strong metaphysical intuitions when faced with a

---

29 Tuggy, 'Trinitarian Theorizing', 175. Cf. Scott R. Burson and Jerry L. Walls, *C.S. Lewis & Francis Schaeffer: Lessons for a New Century from the Most Influential Apologists of Our Time* (Downers Grove, IL: InterVarsity Press, 1998), 97.

set of claims that strike us as incompatible. Moreover, for any *particular* paradox to be defended via an appeal to mystery, the set of claims in question must be warranted by divine revelation and the appearance of contradiction plausibly attributable to divine incomprehensibility.

Given these constraints, it would seem that in principle only theistic religions whose teachings are grounded in special revelation from a personal deity can avail themselves of the RAPT model (or a similar model). In practice, that leaves us with species of Christianity, Judaism, and Islam. If it turns out that adherents of the latter two religions can mirror the Christian's appeal to mystery in defence of their own paradoxical teachings, then this is the price to be exacted for reconciling orthodox Christian doctrines with the rationality of Christian faith. In my estimation, it is a price worth paying.

7.4 Philosophical Concerns

7.4.1 Contradictions: Real and Apparent

The cogency of the RAPT model depends crucially on the distinction between *real* contradiction and *apparent* contradiction among theological claims. Not only must this distinction be formally coherent, it must also be plausibly instantiated; which is to say, it must be reasonable to suppose that there are, or could be, instances of *merely apparent* contradiction.

As I noted in Chapter 6, the fact that this issue can be raised and debated at all indicates that the distinction itself is intelligible, and the examples of MACRUEs provided there show that the phenomenon of apparent contradiction resulting from unarticulated equivocation is entirely credible. Nevertheless, some writers on the topic of theological paradox have maintained that the distinction between real contradiction and apparent contradiction is vacuous or misguided. Consider, for example, David Basinger's analysis of the 'theologians of paradox':

> [P]erhaps their real argument is the following. The Bible does present us with sets of truths that initially strike us as humans as incompatible and that some people believe are actually contradictory. However, it has not been demonstrated conclusively that such truths are really contradictory. Moreover since God would not have given us truths that are truly contradictory from a human perspective, we may be assured that no logical

incompatibility in fact exists. Such logical tensions are only apparent contradictions.[30]

Basinger grants that this position is coherent, but questions whether it is sensible to construe this as a *logical* difficulty (as the label 'apparent contradiction' would connote) since proponents of this view maintain that no *real* contradiction between biblical claims has been conclusively demonstrated.

> If the truths in question have not clearly been shown to be contradictory, then no 'logical solution' or 'defiance of logic' is required. Nor need the authority of revelation be evoked. If the truths are not clearly contradictory there is no logical problem as of yet to worry about.

> [A]s long as Biblical concepts are defined and applied in such a way that no logical incompatibility can be conclusively demonstrated, no logical apologies of the kind given by [the theologians of paradox] are necessary, for no logical etiquette has been disturbed.[31]

Basinger's thesis seems to be that either we are faced with a real contradiction, such that the contradiction has been 'conclusively demonstrated', or we are not, and only the former presents us with a logical problem. But this is an oversimplification of the range the epistemic situations that can obtain. It does not follow from the fact that no contradiction has been proven that there is no *appearance* of contradiction; indeed, it is usually the latter that motivates a deeper assessment of whether or not there is genuine logical inconsistency. Arguably it is precisely such a situation—a set of claims that initially strike one as inconsistent, though this *prima facie* assessment may be subject to revision—that has prompted such scrutiny of the doctrines of the Trinity and the Incarnation in recent decades. In short, if there *appears* to be contradiction between some set of claims, then there *appears* to be logical problem; and an apparent logical problem is a problem nonetheless.[32] The way to address such a problem is to

---

30 Basinger, 'Biblical Paradox', 211.
31 Basinger, 'Biblical Paradox', 211.
32 Consider the following parallel. I am presented with evidence according to which it appears that my father has committed a serious crime. You try to comfort me by way of the following argument: 'The fact that it *appears* your father has committed the crime is strictly irrelevant. Ultimately, either he has or he hasn't. But it hasn't been *conclusively demonstrated* that he's a criminal—and until that has been proven, there's no "legal problem" as of yet to be worried about!' Clearly appearances count for something, regardless of whether matters ultimately turn out to be as they appear.

consider whether what appears to be the case is *actually* the case. Basinger's dismissal of the appearance-reality distinction is far too hasty.

Another writer who finds fault with the notion of apparent contradiction is David Ciocchi. Analysing what he dubs 'the appeal to paradox' as a response to the tension between divine sovereignty and human freedom, he comments:

> To call a paradox an 'apparent contradiction' is very common, but not logically correct because it implies a distinction between types of contradiction. I follow David Basinger in maintaining that there is nothing ambiguous about the concept of contradiction or, more generally, the concept of logical inconsistency. A statement or set of statements either is or is not logically consistent, and hence there can be no genuine distinction between 'real' and 'apparent' contradictions.[33]

According to Ciocchi, the qualifier 'apparent' indicates that there are different *kinds* of contradiction. But in general, this is false: to say that 'X is an apparent F' is simply to say that there is something, X, which appears to be an F—and this entails nothing about whether or not there are different kinds of F.

In the context of the RAPT model, the notion of apparent contradiction implies only that some sets of claims *appear* to involve contradiction, while others do not; and the notion of *merely* apparent contradiction implies only that some sets of claims appearing to involve contradiction do not *actually* involve contradiction (on account of unarticulated equivocation). Both implications are entirely compatible with the notion that there is only one type of contradiction and furthermore that this concept of contradiction is quite clear to us. I have not claimed that we lack understanding of what 'type' of contradiction is involved in paradoxes or of what it means for two claims to contradict. On the contrary, I take it for granted that we do. Rather, my claim is that we lack understanding of *how* certain revelational data that strike us as inconsistent can nonetheless be logically harmonised by drawing relevant distinctions, on account of certain conceptual imprecisions in our noetic apparatus.[34]

---

33 Ciocchi, 'Reconciling Divine Sovereignty and Human Freedom', 397.

34 Somewhat perplexingly, Ciocchi goes on to explain that there is a sense in which we can speak of an 'apparent contradiction' after all, by distinguishing 'logical paradoxes' (real contradictions) from 'epistemic paradoxes'. As he explains: 'I will stipulate that a theological claim is a statement or set of statements employing vague, ambiguous, nontechnical

7.4.2 Consistency as Intellectual Virtue

'A foolish consistency is the hobgoblin of little minds,' averred Ralph Waldo Emerson, adding for good measure that 'with consistency a great soul has simply nothing to do.'[35] On this point Emerson arguably stands in a minority, for it is commonly held that logical consistency is the *epitome* of rationality and commendable epistemic practice. Above all else, goes the sentiment, one should strive to eliminate contradictions from one's set of beliefs; indeed, even the toleration of *apparent* contradiction is to be discouraged by the same principle.[36]

Life is never quite so straightforward, however, and there are rare instances where believing a set of incompatible propositions can strike us as more rational than withholding belief in one or more of those propositions. Consider the 'Paradox of the Preface', for

---

language to express a Biblical teaching [and] a theological formulation is a statement or set of statements employing clear, precise, even technical language to spell out the supposed meaning of a claim. ... With these stipulations I can define an epistemic paradox, or "apparent contradiction," as a theological claim for which it is (humanly) impossible to create any logically consistent formulations. Due to its imprecise language the theological claim itself is not logically inconsistent, but all of its formulations are logically inconsistent.' Ciocchi, 'Reconciling Divine Sovereignty and Human Freedom', 397-98. By distinguishing epistemic paradoxes from logical paradoxes, Ciocchi effectively concedes that there *is* a genuine distinction between real contradiction and apparent contradiction. As it turns out, Ciocchi's notion of epistemic paradox is similar to the analysis of paradox specified by the RAPT model. Nevertheless, he proceeds to criticise appeals to epistemic paradox by arguing that we have no reason to think that all *future* attempts at logical reconciliation will fail, i.e., that consistent formulations are *impossible* (for us). Yet the RAPT model does not involve this strong claim. Rather, it claims that: (i) we are *presently* unable to produce any consistent formulations of certain key doctrines (and for this very reason the doctrines *appear* to involve contradiction); (ii) while we may have no reason to think that all future attempts at logically reconciliation will fail, neither are we in a position to predict eventual success; and (iii) in the meantime Christians can still be rational in believing such doctrines, despite their apparent logical tensions.

35   Ralph Waldo Emerson, 'Self-Reliance', in *Essays* (London: J. Fraser, 1841).
36   Rescher's characterization of the epistemic burden presented by paradoxes is typical in this respect. 'The prime directive of rationality is to restore consistency... [I]nconsistency tolerance should be viewed as a position of last resort, to be adopted only after all else has failed us.' Rescher, *Paradoxes*, 10.

example. Sean writes a book on a certain subject in the confidence that each statement in the book is correct; thus, for each statement *S* in the book, on reflection Sean believes that *S* is true. Nevertheless, in humble acknowledgment of his own fallibility Sean also thinks it reasonable to suppose that there are one or two errors in the book (and he therefore writes a pre-emptive apology in the preface of the book). Accordingly, Sean believes that the *conjunction* of all the statements in the book is likely to be false, which appears to conflict with his other beliefs about the book. Strict consistency seems to demand that Sean believe this conjunction to be *true*, but given what he knows about his own abilities, that belief is quite unjustified.

Such anomalies notwithstanding, it remains an intuitively appealing axiom that inconsistency in one's beliefs should be avoided at all reasonable costs. To strive for systematic consistency in one's theorizing—theological or otherwise—is considered an intellectual virtue. If such is the case, then it suggests that there is something distasteful or shabby about defending paradoxical doctrines by appealing to divine mystery and thus it follows that the RAPT model is misguided *in principle*. Dale Tuggy, for one, expresses a view along just these lines: while we may derive a certain kind of intellectual pleasure by meditating on nonsensical or contradictory claims (such as Carroll's 'Jabberwocky' or the koans of Zen Buddhism), he maintains that 'an important intellectual virtue involves habitually refraining from this … pleasure'.[37]

Is the advocate of the RAPT model obliged to reject this principle—perhaps even taking the contrary view that *inconsistency* is an intellectual virtue? Not at all. Provided that certain important qualifications are made, the spirit of this counsel can be embraced wholeheartedly. I concur that one should never approve theories that one takes to be genuinely contradictory; this is consistent with the claim of the RAPT model that paradoxical doctrines merely *appear* contradictory, since real contradictions cannot be true. There is nothing virtuous about pure, unashamed irrationalism. Moreover, I would add that theories which avoid apparent contradiction should be preferred over theories that do not, *all else being equal*. It follows that Christians ought, as a rule, to strive to formulate their doctrines in a non-paradoxical manner. And for most such doctrines this is an attainable goal.

So in these significant respects, the sentiment expressed above can be endorsed. Still, if the argument of the preceding chapter is sound then it is plausible to think that in *some* instances the most rational

---

37 Tuggy, 'Trinitarian Theorizing', 178.

course for a Christian is to favour a paradoxical interpretation of a revealed doctrine over a non-paradoxical interpretation, treating the former as a MACRUE, provided (i) that the component claims of this formulation are adequately warranted by appeal to revelational data and (ii) that one can plausibly account for the presence of a MACRUE on the basis of divine incomprehensibility.

I venture that in such epistemic circumstances the intellectually virtuous course is to grant divine revelation 'right of way' over presumptions about our cognitive capacities, rather than the reverse. For on a thoroughgoing Christian theistic epistemology, what constitutes epistemic good practice will presumably be determined in part by what sort of things God means for us to know about himself and *in what fashion*. Consequently, if the state of affairs posited by the RAPT model is plausible then arguing that intellectual virtue demands a blanket rejection of all apparent contradiction amounts to begging the question against the model; for if the model is correct, intellectual virtue (by divine mandate) will demand otherwise.

7.4.3 Alternative Notions of Rationality

In Chapter 5, I endorsed Plantinga's proper function analysis of epistemic warrant (defined as that property which, in sufficient measure, distinguishes knowledge from mere true belief). According to this account, a belief is warranted if it is formed by way of properly functioning cognitive faculties successfully aimed at the production of true beliefs. A warranted belief must be rational in two important senses. First, it must be *externally* rational, that is, any sensuous or doxastic experience associated with the belief must not be attributable to cognitive malfunction.[38] Secondly, it must be *internally* rational, that is, the faculties responsible for producing the belief must be operating appropriately with respect to the believer's experience and other beliefs: thus, if it appears to S that the sky is blue, then S's belief that the sky is blue will be internally rational (absent any relevant defeaters). In particular, internal rationality requires that the relevant portions of one's defeater system, which

---

38 Simplistically put, everything must be proceeding normally with regard to how things 'seem' to the believer. In Plantinga's terminology, *sensuous* experience refers to that imagery in response to which perceptual beliefs are formed, while *doxastic* experience refers to the distinctive phenomenology which accompanies those basic beliefs that simply strike us as 'right' and 'obvious' (e.g., memory beliefs and *a priori* beliefs). Plantinga, *Warranted Christian Belief*, 110-11.

governs belief acceptance and revision in light of experience and other beliefs, be functioning properly. As Plantinga puts it, there must be proper function 'downstream from experience'.[39] I proceeded to defend Plantinga's extended Aquinas/Calvin model for warranted Christian belief and subsequently argued, in Chapter 6, that a model can be developed according to which even belief in paradoxical Christian doctrines can be warranted. If such beliefs can be warranted, then it follows that they can be proper function rational, i.e., both externally and internally rational.

Now it could be objected that even if such beliefs can be rational in the above respects, there are still *other* important types of rationality, and beliefs in paradoxical doctrines will invariably fail to be rational in these further respects. Even if this is so, I submit that the warrant question is by far the most important, given that warrant involves precisely that kind of rationality necessary for *knowledge*. Since other kinds of rationality are demonstrably not necessary for knowledge, one might ask how concerning it is for a belief to lack rationality in these respects. Nevertheless, it is worth briefly considering two other influential conceptions of rationality if only to show that neither raises a problem for the RAPT model.

First of all, one could argue that assent to a paradoxical doctrine cannot be *epistemically justified*, construed in a broadly deontological sense.[40] On this view, S is justified in believing p just in case S fulfils every relevant epistemic duty or obligation in so believing: S flouts no epistemic norms or responsibilities, so to speak. Hence the pertinent question would be to ask just *what* epistemic regulation might be transgressed by a Christian who holds to a paradoxical interpretation of the doctrine of the Trinity, say, in the manner specified by the RAPT model. Intuitively, one ought not to believe what one takes to be a contradiction, no matter what other epistemic grounds one might have. But the Christian considered here does no such thing, since she takes the logical conflict involved in the doctrinal claims to be *merely apparent* (and with good reason).

Perhaps then the relevant norm is something more subtle, such as the following: one ought not to believe a set of claims that one is unable to reconcile logically, even if one has reason to think that they could *in principle* be reconciled. Yet it is far from obvious that our

---

39 Plantinga, *Warranted Christian Belief*, 110-13.
40 For a discussion of deontological justification in Descartes, Locke, and various contemporary epistemologists, see Plantinga, *Warrant*, 3-29. See also William P. Alston, 'The Deontological Conception of Epistemic Justification', in *Epistemic Justification* (Ithaca, NY: Cornell University Press, 1989), 125-52.

reasoning is duty bound to this much stronger principle. So unless a good argument can be marshalled to defend the principle, there is no reason for an advocate of the RAPT model to feel intimidated by it. Indeed, it is difficult to see what alleged epistemic norm *could* be enlisted here that is both defensible and problematic for the construal of paradoxical doctrines that I have advocated. I conclude that the notion of epistemic justification, construed deontologically, offers no cogent basis for objection to the RAPT model.

Consider secondly the notion of *evidential justification*. According to this perspective, S is justified or rational in believing p just in case the truth of p is probable with respect to S's total evidence, where this evidence consists of the set of S's basic beliefs (those beliefs, such as perceptual beliefs or *a priori* beliefs, which are not held on the basis of inference from other beliefs).[41] This kind of rationality has been championed most notably by Richard Swinburne, who has objected to Plantinga's defence of the intellectual propriety of Christian belief on the basis that while such belief may be *proper function* rational, as Plantinga contends, a far more pressing question (apologetically speaking, at any rate) is whether it is *evidentially* rational in the sense outlined above.[42] It is precisely *this* flavour of rationality with which non-believers (and doubt-stricken believers) are most concerned, suggests Swinburne. In my view, Plantinga is correct to respond by arguing that this strongly evidentialist conception of rationality is rather less interesting and important than Swinburne thinks; for example, the deluded beliefs of a madman can be 'rational' in this sense, while other perfectly respectable beliefs (such as the memory that I was dealt a particular hand in a poker game last night) must be judged 'irrational'.[43] Such counterintuitive results indicate that the aetiology of belief is far more relevant to our commonsense notions of rationality than Swinburne acknowledges, while evidential probability calculations, though undoubtedly of great importance in certain epistemic contexts (such as the evaluation of scientific theories), stand in no simple relation to the

---

41 For a detailed explication of this understanding of justification, see Richard Swinburne, *Epistemic Justification* (Oxford: Clarendon Press, 2001).

42 Richard Swinburne, 'Plantinga on Warrant', *Religious Studies* 37.2 (2001), 207-8.

43 Alvin Plantinga, 'Rationality and Public Evidence: A Reply to Richard Swinburne', *Religious Studies* 37.2 (2001), 218-19; Alvin Plantinga, 'Swinburne and Plantinga on Internal Rationality', *Religious Studies* 37.3 (2001), 238.

propriety of beliefs *per se.*[44] Consequently, I am little concerned if it turns out that belief in paradoxical doctrines must be judged 'irrational' in a Swinburnian sense. Moreover, I suspect that few Christian beliefs—let alone full-blown doctrines (paradoxical or otherwise)—can be evidentially justified in the manner envisaged by Swinburne (including those held by Swinburne himself).[45] But surely they are none the worse for that.

There are, of course, various other conceptions of rationality that might be considered, though I believe the two treated above are those most likely to be employed in objection to the RAPT model. While there is no space for an exhaustive treatment here, my conclusion is that any notion of rationality wielded to this end will either be too weak to exclude the beliefs in question (as with appeals to uncontroversial epistemic norms) or too strong to be taken seriously as a general constraint on the propriety of beliefs (as with Swinburne-style notions of evidential justification).

7.4.4 Intuitional Inertia

Intuition—roughly, the power to immediately apprehend certain truths or concepts or relationships—is arguably one of the most valuable human cognitive faculties. Many of our most foundational beliefs are such that we are unable to prove them by philosophical argument, yet they simply *seem* to us to be true—even *obviously* true. The belief that $1 + 1 = 2$, the belief that the inferential principle *modus ponens* is valid, and the belief that there exist other minds than our own, would be just three examples. Similarly, while many of the concepts we possess are less than wholly distinct, others strike us as paradigmatically clear and precise: for instance, the concepts of individuality and plurality. Given the prominence and centrality of these *a priori* elements of human thought, our evaluation of proposed theses or theories is subject to what one might call 'intuitional inertia': a natural resistance to counterintuitive claims, to proposals that bring into question what naturally strikes us as true, possible, or necessary.

---

44 A number of difficulties with Swinburne's account of epistemic justification are identified by Michael Bergmann, including the observation that few believers have cognitive access to the sort of information needed to make the relevant probability judgements. Michael Bergmann, 'Epistemic Justification', *The Philosophical Quarterly* 53.211 (2003), 295-98.

45 Recall Alston's remarks on the prospects for internalist justification of religious beliefs. Alston, 'On Knowing That We Know', 22.

One of the more problematic aspects of the model I defend here is that it seems to run up against some of our most strongly held metaphysical intuitions. According to my proposal, the phenomenon of theological paradox arises because of present limitations and imprecisions in our cognitive apparatus: we simply do not grasp those metaphysical distinctions that would allow us to see *how* the apparent contradictions can be fully resolved. In the case of the doctrine of the Trinity, the difficulty seems to be located in our understanding of *identity* or *numerical unity*, at least in the application of these concepts to divine beings. The doctrine of the Incarnation, on the other hand, apparently runs into problems when we bring our intuitive notion of *personal unity* to bear on it, along with the various implications for mentality and consciousness that accompany that notion.[46] If the RAPT model is correct, however, it follows that these concepts are susceptible to refinement and qualification (at least in principle) in such a way that the relationship between the divine *ousia* and the divine *hypostases*, and the relationship between God the Son and Jesus of Nazareth, can be cognized without any logical difficulties. Yet many will find such claims dubious, to say the least. What could be clearer to us than the concepts of identity, singularity, and personal unity? How could notions so central and indispensable to our conceptual schemes, and thus to our understanding of the world, ever be thought 'coarse' in the manner posited by the RAPT model?

As a matter of historical fact, however, even elementary concepts such as these have been subject to considerable philosophical debate—and that in the absence of any discernible *theological* motivation. Take first the concept of identity. Some have argued that there is no such thing as *absolute* identity, as identity *per se*.[47] On this view, identity relations only hold relative to a sortal; it makes no sense to assert simply that X is the same as Y, only that X is the same F as Y. Others have contended (against the mainstream) that identity can be a *contingent* relation: hence in some cases, although X and Y are actually one and the same object, things could have been otherwise.[48] With regard to the properties of identical objects, both

---

46 Indeed, our notion of personal unity also raises difficulties for the doctrine of the Trinity, insofar as the biblical texts frequently speak of God in singular personal terms.

47 Peter Geach, 'Identity', *Review of Metaphysics* 21 (1967), 3-12; Peter Geach, 'Identity—A Reply', *Review of Metaphysics* 22 (1968), 556-59.

48 Allan Gibbard, 'Contingent Identity', *Journal of Philosophical Logic* 4 (1975), 187-221; Stephen Yablo, 'Identity, Essence, and Indiscernibility', *Journal of Philosophy* 84 (1987), 293-314.

the principle of the identity of indiscernibles and the principle of the indiscernibility of identicals have been called into question.[49] Likewise, the notion that individuals are identical across possible worlds has come under fire.[50] Even the idea that there is a theory-independent fact of the matter about what objects exist and in what quantity (with ramifications for the metaphysics of identity) has been soberly challenged.[51] Turning to the notion of numerical unity, the knotty question of material constitution—is the statue the same thing as the clay of which it is made, and if not, how many things are there on the podium?—has prompted some somewhat counterintuitive conclusions.[52] The concept of personal identity, meanwhile, has enjoyed its fair share of philosophical controversy. Is it analysable in terms of somatic continuity, or psychological continuity, or neither?[53] Is personal continuity a matter of degree?[54] Is it possible for a person to 'split' (via brain division or a process of instantaneous cloning) such that each of two distinct persons in the present is the same person as one in the past?[55]

---

49 Max Black, 'The Identity of Indiscernibles', in *Problems of Analysis* (Ithaca, NY: Cornell University Press, 1954), 204-16; Robert M. Adams, 'Primitive Thisness and Primitive Identity', *The Journal of Philosophy* 76.1 (1979), 5-26; Steven French and Michael Redhead, 'Quantum Physics and the Identity of Indiscernibles', *British Journal for the Philosophy of Science* 39 (1988), 233-46; Steven French, 'Why the Principle of the Identity of Indiscernibles is Not Contingently True Either', *Synthese* 78 (1989), 141-66. A. P. Martinich notes that the indiscernibility of identicals has been doubted by such luminaries as Aristotle and Leibniz. Martinich, 'Identity and Trinity', 179-80.
50 Roderick M. Chisholm, 'Identity through Possible Worlds: Some Questions', *Noûs* 1 (1967), 1-8; David K. Lewis, *On the Plurality of Worlds* (Oxford: Blackwell, 1986).
51 W. V. Quine, 'Ontological Relativity', in *Ontological Relativity and Other Essays* (New York: Columbia University Press, 1969), 26-68; Robert Kraut, 'Indiscernibility and Ontology', *Synthese* 44 (1980), 113-35.
52 For a succinct statement of the problem, and a taxonomy of proposed solutions, see Michael C. Rea, 'The Problem of Material Constitution', *The Philosophical Review* 104.4 (1995), 525-52.
53 For an overview of the different camps, see Eric T. Olson, 'Personal Identity', in Stephen P. Stich and Ted A. Warfield (eds), *The Blackwell Guide to Philosophy of Mind* (Oxford: Blackwell, 2003), 352-68.
54 Derek Parfit, 'Personal Identity', *The Philosophical Review* 80 (1971), 3-27.
55 David Wiggins, *Identity and Spatio-Temporal Continuity* (Oxford: Blackwell, 1967); Parfit, 'Personal Identity'; John Perry, 'Can the Self Divide?', *Journal of Philosophy* 69 (1972), 463-88; David K. Lewis, 'Survival and Identity', in Amélie Oksenberg Rorty (ed.), *The Identities of Persons* (Berkeley, CA:

My purpose in mentioning these ongoing debates is not to endorse any particular side, still less to advocate a sceptical stance, but rather to suggest that since so many aspects of these elementary concepts have been credibly contested we ought to be somewhat more circumspect about our understanding and application of them—and especially so when we apply the concepts to subject areas beyond our immediate experience and expertise. While our intuitions about such things serve us perfectly well in matters of everyday life, there are also 'grey areas': regions of theoretical inquiry where it is not wholly clear and beyond all controversy just what conclusions should be drawn. This being so, it is hardly unreasonable to take the view that our intuitions about what is metaphysically possible ought not to be treated, generally speaking, as the last word in doctrinal theorizing. Instead, Christians should be prepared to allow revelational data, if it carries sufficient force, to inform and qualify their understanding and application of *a priori* metaphysical convictions. Hence if (for example) the biblical claims about Yahweh, the Father, the Son, and the Holy Spirit prove extremely difficult to harmonize in terms of our 'natural' repertoire of concepts, we may well be justified in concluding that our concepts and vocabulary are in need of refinement (even if we are not in a position, cognitively speaking, to specify *how* that refinement should cash out).

Ultimately, one's approach to this issue will depend on how one relates and weights the contributions of natural intuition and special revelation to human knowledge: one's conclusions will thus depend on one's overall epistemology and, furthermore, on one's underlying metaphysic. Hence a variation on Plantinga's conditionality thesis, that the *rationality* of Christian belief crucially depends on the *truth* of Christian belief, will once again come into play. For if the orthodox Christian theistic view of the world is broadly correct, with its exalted conception of God, its positive yet modest view of human cognition, and its conviction that Scripture can furnish us with reliable information about the nature and activity of God (albeit accommodated to human thought and language), it follows that conclusions drawn on the basis of metaphysical intuitions will *normally* be warranted but nonetheless could *in principle* be subject to revision or qualification on the basis of revelational data which indicate we have run up against certain limitations in our cognitive apparatus. Faced with the triple constraints of (i) logically necessity

University of California Press, 1976), 17-40; Derek Parfit, *Reasons and Persons* (Oxford: Clarendon Press, 1984).

(the law of non-contradiction), (ii) revelational perspicuity (the most natural interpretation of biblical texts), and (iii) metaphysical intuitions (in effect, the assumption that certain notions adequate for consistent theorizing about immanent realities are likewise adequate for consistent theorizing about transcendent realities), proper function rationality will demand that one of these 'give way' in cases of conflict. If, as a matter of epistemic fact, we *do* lack the capacity to grasp various fine metaphysical distinctions needed to express some Christian doctrines in a transparently consistent way, it follows that (iii) is the point of weakness. I conclude therefore that resistance to the RAPT model due to 'intuitional inertia' not only underestimates the degree to which the sort of concepts in question are subject to debate in *non*-theological contexts, but also begs the question by assuming an epistemology of intuition at odds with the model itself.

7.4.5 Comprehension and Conception

I turn finally to what I suspect many readers will consider to be the most serious issue facing the RAPT model. This is the question of how Christian believers understand and assent to the theological claims involved in paradoxical doctrines and, indeed, whether there *can* be any such understanding and assent. I have argued that the paradoxical sets of claims typically involved in formulations of the doctrine of the Trinity and the doctrine of the Incarnation should be interpreted as MACRUEs, that is, as merely apparent contradictions resulting from unarticulated equivocation. On this view, some of the terms employed in those claims should be construed as being related *analogically* rather than univocally. If the relevant semantic distinctions could be identified, the logical consistency of the claims could be demonstrated; but in the absence of information *specifying* these distinctions, formally consistent expressions of these doctrines (and their implications) can still be constructed by indicating their presence explicitly with a suitable notation. To take an example, certain paradoxical implications of Chalcedonian christology could be expressed thus:

(K1) Christ did not know$_1$ every fact (by virtue of his humanity).

(K2) Christ did know$_2$ every fact (by virtue of his divinity).

There is, however, an obvious problem with this. Supposing we can be warranted in concluding that *there are* distinctions which could be made, perhaps even gaining some idea of *where* the distinctions are to be located (and hence which of the underlying concepts is subject to qualification), it remains that we are not in a position to specify the *content* of the distinctions. Thus, to continue with the example above, while we may have grounds for claiming that 'knowing₁' is relevantly different from 'knowing₂', we are nonetheless unable to say just *how* they differ. But if this is the case, how is one supposed to interpret claims like (K1) and (K2)? How can a Christian properly assent to claims he is unable to comprehend? And what is the Christian who affirms both claims supposed in practice to *believe*, given that he does not—indeed *cannot*—cognize the relevant distinctions?[56]

A number of points may be made in response, which taken together indicate that the difficulties here are not nearly so serious as they initially appear. In the first place, there is nothing incoherent about the idea of assenting to statements of which one has only limited understanding. Imagine that Bruce, an Australian unfamiliar with Scottish customs and cuisine, inquires of his friend Jock as to what Scots typically do on Burns Night. 'We eat haggis, neaps, and tatties,' Jock replies. Now even if Bruce is woefully ignorant of such delicacies, after accepting Jock's reply he could nonetheless meaningfully assent to this statement:

(BN) Scots typically eat haggis, neaps, and tatties on Burns Night.

If asked whether he believed this statement to be *true*, he could sincerely reply in the affirmative, despite lacking full comprehension of the terms used. In this connection we may speak of the *implicit meaning* of a statement, namely, whatever it is that is asserted by the statement when all of its terms are adequately understood (taking the original context of the statement into account).

In the example above, the implicit meaning can be identified with what *Jock* understands it to mean; and by affirming (BN) Bruce is effectively expressing his belief that everything this statement *says* to be the case, when ascribed this implicit meaning, is *in fact* the case. Furthermore, he is in a position to commend (BN) to *others* for acceptance, even though his comprehension is lacking in important respects; and those who accept it are consequently able to affirm

---

56 As Richard Cartwright remarks regarding the doctrine of the Trinity: '[A] mystery [is not] supposed to be unintelligible, in the sense that the words in which it is expressed simply cannot be understood. After all, we are asked to believe the propositions expressed by the words, not simply that the words express some true propositions or other, we know not which.' Cartwright, 'On the Logical Problem of the Trinity', 193.

(BN) on the same basis as Bruce, viz., by indirect reference to its implicit meaning.

On similar grounds, we can think of formulations such as (K1) and (K2) as also having implicit meanings; specifically, those meanings that would be understood by one who *does* grasp the relevant distinctions (and therefore comprehends enough of the underlying metaphysics to see clearly how there is no genuine contradiction involved). Christians who affirm such doctrinal statements are thus in effect committing themselves to the idea that whatever these claims state to be the case, when interpreted according to the relevant implicit meanings, is *in fact* the case. The idea that there *are* implicit meanings follows directly from the conviction that the doctrines in question are MACRUEs—for if the appearance of contradiction is due to unarticulated equivocation, then there are *in principle* distinctions available and hence there must be implicit meanings based on these distinctions.[57]

It is worth pointing out that the concept of implicit meaning arguably factors into many theological claims other than those involved in paradoxical doctrines, at least if something like the linguistic doctrine of analogy is accepted. The wisdom attributed to God is not the same as that attributed to Socrates, though it is similar in many important respects; thus when I echo the biblical affirmation that 'God is wise', my comprehension of that statement is *partial* and *approximate*. In making that affirmation, so it seems, I am committing myself to the notion that God exhibits a certain quality analogous to human wisdom—a quality that I understand and appreciate only imperfectly. The statement 'God is wise' can be thought of as having an implicit meaning grounded in a deeper comprehension of the divine attribute in question; and my belief that the statement is *true* when ascribed that implicit meaning is warranted by the biblical witness to God's character and by confirmation in my own experience (even if that full meaning is not something that I directly entertain).[58] If this general observation about analogical terms in theological statements is correct, it applies

---

57 Ultimately, of course, the presence of these implicit meanings is grounded in the divine testimony from which the doctrinal statements derive their warrant. The divine authorship of Scripture is thus the gold bullion which funds the claim that there *are* genuine metaphysical distinctions which resolve the paradox, even though we do not presently have cognitive access to them.

58 What I *do* entertain directly in my own mind is an *approximation* of that meaning—on which, more below.

in no less measure to analogical terms employed in paradoxical sets of doctrinal claims.

The doctrine of analogy can shed still further light on the meaningfulness of claims such as (K1) and (K2). In the illustration above, Bruce had a negligible understanding of the terms 'haggis', 'neaps', and 'tatties'. Other than what he might have been able to infer from the immediate context of his brief exchange with Jock (e.g., that these terms identify items of food indigenous to Scotland) the statement (BN) will have been largely uninformative to him. Now if the same cognitive vacuity were to afflict statements such as (K1) and (K2), that fact would invite serious objection to the thesis that doctrinal paradoxes can be usefully construed as MACRUEs. Yet this is not how things stand at all, precisely because each of the terms involved in the statements is related either univocally or analogically to the 'ordinary' sense of that term. None of the terms is wholly (or even mostly) unrelated in meaning to the sense it carries in ordinary discourse. Every word used is semantically anchored in everyday language.[59]

In statements (K1) and (K2) the terms $know_1$ and $know_2$ are such that both relate analogically (or one relates univocally and the other analogically) to the term $know$ in a statement such as 'John knows where Anne lives'. Consequently, we can say that (K1) and (K2) should be treated as *semantically approximate* to what would be deemed the 'ordinary' reading of those claims, that is, those interpretations in which each term is ascribed a univocal sense—just as the claim 'God is wise' should be treated as semantically approximate to a reading in which the term *wise* is univocal with the same term in 'Socrates is wise'. With this baseline of continuity in place, it then becomes a matter of judging how the analogical terms should be *differentiated* from their counterparts, in light of what we know about the subject matter and the broader context of the claims in view. This differentiation can be brought out in a number of ways—which leads me to my second point.

As I argued earlier, the phenomenon of linguistic analogy delivers paradoxical doctrines from the charge of logical inconsistency. Words adapt in meaning to resist contradiction, unless the context demands otherwise, and when the context in question is divine revelation (or a systematic summary of some part of that revelation) it is reasonable to assume that the linguistic tokens employed *do* so adapt. Nevertheless, a concern remains that analogical meaning

---

59   Cf. Ross's defence of the meaningfulness of religious discourse in general. Ross, *Portraying Analogy*, 165-70, 175-76.

relationships can be stretched *too far*—so far, perhaps, that the relevant terms are evacuated of any positive content. It will be useful therefore to identify some semantic test that can be applied to sets of claims so as to ascertain how meaningful they are in practice. Generally speaking, the meaningfulness of a particular claim can be assessed by considering the extent to which we can draw from it both *implications* (that is, what other claims follow from the claim in question) and *applications* (that is, what practical difference should be made by a commitment to the claim in question). The second criterion is particularly relevant to the question of meaning in Christian theology insofar as its practitioners have emphasised the inseparability of doctrine and praxis. The articles of the Christian religion are as much concerned with *behaviour* as with *belief*: faith without works is dead. James Ross rightly observes in his discussion of religious discourse that Judeo-Christian literature such as Bible stories, catechisms, creeds, stories of saints, and so forth, are not concerned merely with inducing certain mental states, but also with directing and regulating our *actions*:

> [They] are designed to modulate one's conception of oneself and of one's relationship to other people, to modulate one's judgments about the physical world, about the goals and values of life and one's judgments about God (who is to be encountered through faith, in obedience to moral law and in the pursuit of holiness). The discourse is inherently action-oriented, response, self-construal and judgment oriented. ... Living in God, in the spiritual Word, is the object of the craft of Christian doing; and Christian talking functions to prompt and modulate it.[60]

In judging the meaningfulness of such statements as (K1) and (K2) we should therefore consider what implications and applications one could properly draw from them. The answer, as it turns out, is reasonably straightforward in principle (and has been indicated earlier in this chapter): one is warranted in drawing any implications or applications that would also follow from an 'ordinary' reading of the statements, *except for those implications or applications ruled out by the body of revelational data on which those statements are based* (or by robust inferences from those data). Accordingly, one may take as valid implications of (K2) that Christ is divine and that Christ is worthy of our trust and our worship (indeed, these conclusions would comport with how the attributions of omniscience to Jesus often function in the theology of the New Testament writers). As a legitimate application of (K2) one might take encouragement from

---

60 Ross, *Portraying Analogy*, 167.

the notion that Christ is fully aware of our personal circumstances and knows what is best for us; moreover, one could offer encouragement to others on the same basis. Another application would be that Christ's teaching on both heavenly matters and earthly matters is trustworthy (cf. John 3:11-13) and thus ought to be followed. However, (K2) should *not* be taken to imply that Christ was less than fully human and is therefore unable to sympathise with us in our human weaknesses and limitations (cf. Heb. 4:15). On the contrary, the idea that Christ *has* genuinely experienced our human condition is a valid implication of the balancing statement (K1), and drawing comfort from that fact is a proper application of it. Furthermore, when the two statements are taken together they imply that Christ is a *personal* being (as opposed to, say, some kind of impersonal supernatural force) since *both* indicate that knowledge is the sort of thing that can be attributed to Christ; more significantly still, they should not be taken as implying that Christ is a *plurality* of persons, because this flies in the face of other revelational data.

Similar considerations can be applied to statements of trinitarian theology and to other doctrinal MACRUEs. In short, meaning can be invested in those theological statements that together express paradoxical doctrines (whether or not the equivocation has been formally articulated) in accordance with the constraints imposed by (i) standard linguistic and hermeneutic conventions, (ii) basic philosophical intuitions, and (iii) the total body of revelational data from which the statements are derived. No doubt particular care must be taken when interpreting such doctrinal statements, but the suggestion that the doctrines are altogether nonsensical or semantically vacuous is without foundation.

Finally, let us turn from *semantics* to *doxastics*. What does a Christian who holds to paradoxical interpretations of the doctrines of the Trinity and the Incarnation, for example, actually *believe* about the Godhead and Jesus Christ? I have already indicated that there can be a kind of *indirect* belief involved: a belief that certain propositions, identified indirectly rather than entertained directly in the mind of the believer, are true. It is in just this sense that Bruce believed that Scots typically eat haggis, neaps, and tatties on Burns Night. Similarly, Carol could ascribe truth to whatever propositions would be expressed by 'The Father is God and the Son is God and the Spirit is God', 'The Father is not the Son and the Father is not the Spirit and the Son is not the Spirit', and 'There is only one God' if each term were taken in the sense understood by one who actually apprehends the logical consistency of trinitarian metaphysics—even if Carol herself lacks this deeper understanding of the terms and the associated concepts.

Yet this alone is less than satisfactory. For presumably we also want there to be some kind of *direct* belief involved, some conception in the mind of the believer as to what state of affairs is said to obtain by the doctrinal claims in question. Put crudely, the pertinent question is this: just how should the Christian *think* of God and of Jesus Christ when reflecting on the doctrines of the Trinity and the Incarnation?

The answer, I suggest, comes by way of distinguishing two ways in which we can conceive of things. First, there is a sense in which we can conceive of something *concretely*: for example, I can conceive how my bathroom will look once it has been decorated. Concrete conception need not be perceptual in character; I can also concretely conceive of a novel algorithm for solving a certain computational problem, even though the algorithm itself is not a physical object. The rough idea here is that of *imagination*, of being able to 'see' the state of affairs under consideration.

In contrast to this, however, there is also a distinct sense in which we can conceive of something in a purely *formal* manner. This is our capacity to reflect on some proposed item or scenario, and to introduce it into discourse so as to invite others to reflect on it, regardless of whether subsequent thought and discussion lead to the conclusion that the item or scenario in question is coherent or metaphysically possible. To take some examples: one can *formally* conceive of such things as square circles, purple desires, and chocolate propositions, even though we recognise that each of these is impossible and nonsensical (although not nonsensical in quite the way that a 'fragmoss brimquack' is nonsensical). None of these is *concretely* conceivable, but nevertheless our ability to conceive of them in this purely formal sense is a *precondition* of our being able to deduce that there can be no such things and to state that conclusion to others. Less trivially, some philosophers maintain that libertarian free will is impossible because incoherent; but they are nonetheless able to specify and entertain that view with which they disagree. In a similar way, modal logicians can theorize in a meaningful way about 'non-normal worlds': possible worlds where 'logic is not guaranteed to hold' and thus contradictions may be true and impossibilities possible.[61] No one, I dare say, can really imagine what it would be

---

61 Graham Priest, *An Introduction to Non-Classical Logic* (Cambridge: Cambridge University Press, 2001), 58-73; G. E. Hughes and M. J. Cresswell, *A New Introduction to Modal Logic* (London: Routledge, 1996), 201.

like to inhabit such a world, but even *that* conclusion presupposes a
capacity to conceive of non-normal modality in *some* sense.

We can thus identify two distinct ways in which something can be
'conceived': concrete conception and purely formal conception. The
former entails the latter, but not vice versa.

With this distinction in hand, let us now consider the question of
belief in a paradoxical set of claims. Recall the earlier illustration of
the Flatlander who receives a propositional revelation from a
Spacelander about a three-dimensional object (a cone) and suppose
that the revelation includes the following two claims:

(S1)   The object O is shaped triangularly.

(S2)   The object O is shaped circularly.

As noted previously, even though these statements will appear
contradictory to the Flatlander, since his cognitive apparatus is such
that he can only conceive of objects two-dimensionally, he may
nonetheless rationally conclude that they constitute a MACRUE if
each of the statements is independently warranted to a sufficient
degree. In so concluding, he will have realised that there must be
some sense in which an object can be both triangular and circular,
even if he cannot grasp *how* that might be so. We might therefore say
that the Flatlander can *formally* conceive of the object O, even though
he cannot *concretely* conceive of it. The Spacelander may further
explain that this is rendered possible if the object exists in three
spatial dimensions, inviting the Flatlander to entertain the notion of
three-dimensional space by extension from his conception of two-
dimensional space (just as we can postulate a four-dimensional
space by extension from our conception of three-dimensional
space).[62] Nevertheless, the Flatlander will still lack the capacity to
conceive *concretely* of three-dimensional objects such as cones: to
picture in his mind's eye how such a state of affairs would obtain
(just as our cognitive apparatus prevents us from picturing an object
extended in four spatial dimensions).[63]

---

62   Abbott, *Flatland*, 81-89.
63   In Abbott's tale the protagonist, Square, is 'miraculously' granted the ability
     to perceive his own two-dimensional world from Sphere's point of view.
     After these revelations come to an end, however, he admits to great
     difficulty in recalling these visions and communicating their content to his
     compatriots; on his darker days, he is drawn back to his initial doubts about
     the very possibility of cubes and spheres, even questioning his own mental
     well-being. Abbott, *Flatland*, 115-18. Square's predicament helps to
     underline the relationship between conceivability (both formal and

Despite the element of paradox from the Flatlander's perspective, the notion of a cone will not be semantically vacuous by any means. What his conceptual limitations will entail in practice is an inability to think *simultaneously* and *unitedly* of object *O*, the subject of the revelational claims, as being both triangular and circular (in the senses familiar to him). At any point in time, he will either think of it as one or the other. He cannot concretely conceive of 'conicality', but he can concretely conceive of triangularity and circularity, each of which (in different ways) *approximates* the state of affairs under description.

Moreover, which of these two ways of thinking is appropriate in any particular context is not an arbitrary matter, but rather depends on what features of the underlying reality need to be emphasized (and perhaps acted upon). Suppose the Spacelander wants the Flatlander to appreciate that due to a cone's pointed end, it can hurt to fall upon it; in such a context, the Flatlander ought to think of *O* in triangular terms. However, if it is also important for the Flatlander to appreciate, in other contexts, that a cone can be rolled smoothly back and forth on a flat surface, it will clearly be most appropriate for him to focus on circularity instead. Hence the Flatlander is able to attain *after a fashion* a concrete conception of object *O* that is both meaningful and informative, albeit imprecise and unintegrated. Furthermore—and here we must reintroduce the theistic dimension to our fictional analogy—this combination of formal and concrete conceptions may be wholly adequate for the Flatlander to relate to transcendental realities as his Creator intends.

The principles illustrated in this analogy apply equally to the situation faced by a person *S* who affirms paradoxical formulations of the doctrines of the Trinity and the Incarnation. Although *S* cannot *concretely* conceive of a deity who is one indivisible being existing in three distinct persons, or a unified person who is omniscient yet capable of learning and susceptible to surprise, *S* can *formally* conceive of such things (and as I have pointed out, the latter claim is established by the very intelligibility of the former). Nonetheless, in both cases *S* can concretely conceive of *either side* of the paradoxical coin, on the understanding that such conceptions are only approximations and thus care should be taken about what implications are drawn. And depending on which aspects and implications of the doctrine are under consideration in a particular theological context, one or other conception may be more

---

concrete) and cognitive capacities. Despite his later concerns, of course, cognitive *limitation* need not imply cognitive *dysfunction*.

appropriate (even unavoidable). When reflecting on the Trinity in the light of God's uniqueness and aseity, conceiving of the Godhead as a numerical unity rather than a plurality of beings will be apropos. On the other hand, one naturally ought to think of the Godhead as something like a threefold personality when theorizing about the Trinity as the paradigmatic community of loving social relationships. The same principle applies to conceptualizations of Christ held in conformity to Chalcedonian orthodoxy: a 'two minds' perspective should take the fore when reflecting on (say) the pastoral implications of Jesus' genuine humanity, while a 'one person' perspective ought to assume prominence when expounding Christ's mediatory role as the agent of reconciliation between God and humanity.

The points raised in this section invite further explication and defence, but enough has been said to cast considerable doubt on the complaint that paradoxical doctrines must be semantically and cognitively vacuous. The various notions and distinctions to which I have appealed (implicit meaning, analogy rooted in ordinary discourse, implication and application as indicators of meaningfulness, formal conception versus concrete conception) can help us to see how one's understanding of doctrines such as the Trinity and the Incarnation can be informative and religiously significant, both in theory and in practice, even if the claims involved strike one as logically irreconcilable when subjected to analytical scrutiny.

7.5 Conclusion

In this chapter I have tried to address what I take to be the most serious biblical, theological, and philosophical concerns that might be raised against the RAPT model. No doubt each response could be expanded and strengthened, but nonetheless I believe the discussion above is sufficient to show that the RAPT model is viable and deserves serious consideration as a solution to the problem of doctrinal paradox that successfully navigates between the Scylla of rationalism (e.g., advocating theological models which avoid the appearance of implicit contradiction but distort the revelational data) and the Charybdis of irrationalism (e.g., renouncing logic or embracing anti-realism).

CHAPTER 8

Conclusion: The Prospects of Paradox

At the outset, I identified two key questions concerning paradox in Christian theology:

(1) Are any essential Christian doctrines genuinely paradoxical?

(2) Can a person be rational in believing a paradoxical doctrine?

These two questions have now received answers. As to the first, it appears that certain central doctrines of the Christian faith are indeed genuinely paradoxical when interpreted according to the constraints of credal orthodoxy. The doctrine of the Trinity, with its proscription of modalism, subordinationism, and polytheism, seemingly rules out all logically consistent positions; likewise for the doctrine of the Incarnation, with its claim that one undivided person, Jesus Christ, took on a fully human nature, in all its physical, mental, and spiritual aspects, yet without diminishing his divine nature. Attempts to excuse or evade these paradoxes by abandoning theological realism, denying classical laws of logic, substantially revising the doctrines, advocating 'semantic minimalism', or appealing to the notion of complementarity, either fail to relieve the problem or else exchange it for problems equally undesirable (or worse).

As to the second question, despite the paradoxicality of these doctrines, a Christian who confesses them need not be irrational in doing so. There are plausible models of Christian doctrinal belief available in terms of which the component claims of the doctrines can be held rationally and, moreover, will not suffer epistemic defeat on account of their apparent inconsistency provided certain plausible conditions are met. The RAPT model is one such model. According to this scheme, doctrinal paradoxes are best construed as merely apparent contradictions resulting from unarticulated equivocation, which arise on account of divine mystery—that is, a metaphysical state of affairs the revelation of which strikes us as contradictory due to present cognitive limitations and conceptual imprecisions. The model draws on the traditional Christian doctrines of analogy and divine incomprehensibility; furthermore, if the basic tenets of Christian theism are true (and if some central Christian doctrines *are* paradoxical) then I suggest that this model, or something similar, is *also* true. Various theological and philosophical objections might be levelled at the RAPT model, but none of those considered herein prove anywhere near fatal.

It remains for me to conclude by highlighting some of the implications of what has been said in the course of answering these two questions and indicating areas for further study and discussion.

8.1 Implications

The primary implication of the conclusions reached here is that Christians who hold paradoxical views of the Trinity and the Incarnation (whether knowingly or unknowingly) can be epistemically warranted in their doctrinal beliefs. This will be true for both intellectually sophisticated and unsophisticated believers. Whether these beliefs are *in fact* warranted will depend, of course, on whether the central Christian narrative is *true* (including its trinitarian conception of God and its incarnational claims about Jesus of Nazareth). But this conditionality applies equally to all distinctive Christian doctrines. It follows, significantly, that the positive epistemic status of Christian beliefs cannot be impugned by appealing to seeming contradictions implicit within central doctrines without also arguing that the fundamental tenets of the faith are outright *false*. For if they are true, and if the doctrines in question *are* paradoxical, then the RAPT model (or something close) is also likely to be true. Consequently, believers troubled by the phenomenon of theological paradox can breathe easy, while those taunted by sceptics with cries of 'incoherence' and 'irrationality' need not be intimidated.

There are also implications, as I have noted, for the disciplines of biblical interpretation and systematic theology (and the interaction between the two).[1] Once it is granted that the interpretation and systematization of revelational data *could* present us with paradoxical conclusions, given what Christians believe about God and human cognition, it follows that the use of logical inference and metaphysical intuitions needs to be qualified accordingly, lest the (worthy) goal of systematic consistency be pursued at the expense of fidelity to divine testimony. Furthermore, the conclusions reached

---

1   See §7.2.2 and §7.3.1.

herein regarding the circumstances in which adherence to paradox is epistemically acceptable can serve as a prophylactic against doctrinal heterodoxy—for if apparent logical tensions within a theological position are not *necessarily* the hallmark of falsity and irrationalism, then the typical objections raised against Nicene trinitarianism and Chalcedonian christology lose much of their force.[2] Theologians should recognise that one can shun *rationalism* without sacrificing *rationality*.

The practice of apologetics—that is, the reasoned defence and commendation of the Christian faith—also needs to be reassessed if the conclusions presented here are accepted. As noted already, the RAPT model offers resources for vindicating the rationality of belief in the Trinity and the Incarnation (and potentially other problem areas in Christian theism). Moreover, the model can be employed in a dialectical context to dissolve intellectual obstacles to *accepting* the Christian faith. For example, the following line of resistance can no longer be sustained:

> If I were to embrace Christianity, I would have to affirm the doctrine of the Trinity. But since this doctrine strikes me (and many others) as internally contradictory, it would be irrational for me to believe it; thus I cannot accept that Christianity is true without abandoning my intellectual integrity.

If the RAPT model is cogent, then the fallacy in this reasoning is evident, because it amounts to arguing that Christianity cannot be reasonably believed because it is *false*.

The reverse side of the apologetic coin is that Christians must treat advocates of other faiths as they themselves would wish to be treated. There can be no double standard. If Christians can be warranted in appealing to mystery in defence of paradoxical doctrines, so *in principle* can other religious believers. Nevertheless, as I pointed out, not every belief-system is on an equal footing here; the RAPT model involves specific theological and anthropological claims that do not comport with many non-Christian religions (let alone secular ideologies).

8.2 Further Research

Such are some of the implications of this study of paradox in Christian theology. But what does it suggest in the way of further research? In the first place, it invites continued creative reflection on

---

2   Fortunately for the Christian church, the Fathers were generally more tolerant of paradox than many modern philosophical theologians.

the doctrines of the Trinity and the Incarnation in the hope that deeper metaphysical insights will be uncovered, insights that allow us to comprehend and explicate these doctrines in a perspicuously consistent manner. This goal has not yet been reached, but it is still worthy of pursuit—*fides quaerens intellectum*. My defence of paradox is not meant to derail this project, but merely to show that the epistemic credentials of Christian beliefs do not stand or fall on its success.[3]

Secondly, there is the question of paradox with respect to *other* Christian doctrines. What about the relationship between divine transcendence and divine immanence? God's self-sufficiency and his decision to create? The necessity and freedom of the divine will? The relationship between divine sovereignty and significant human freedom? The need to locate God both inside and outside time?[4] If one accepts the general principle that divine revelation *may* present us with paradoxes, then these remain open questions.

Thirdly, I have suggested that while divine revelation may not provide us with sufficient information to penetrate the paradoxes in certain Christian doctrines, it might give some indication as to where the relevant distinctions are to be articulated in our formulations of those doctrines.[5] In our theorizing about the metaphysics of the Trinity, for example, is the paradox-generating imprecision to be attributed to our notion of *identity*, or *numerical unity*, or *being*, or *personhood*, or something else? If such revelational hints are to be discerned, it will require careful exegetical spadework.

Finally, there is room for a more detailed treatment of how the possibility of theological paradox bears on the practice of biblical

---

3 Compare, in this regard, the implications of 'Reformed epistemology' for natural theology. The proper basicality of theistic beliefs does not render arguments for the existence of God superfluous or impious; it merely follows that knowledge of God need not depend on the availability and cogency of such arguments. See Michael C. Sudduth, 'Reformed Epistemology and Christian Apologetics', *Religious Studies* 39.3 (2003), 299-321.

4 Consider the following recent comments by Richard Gale on the debate over divine eternality: 'What we really want is a God who can have the advantages of both views, which would enable Him to escape between the horns of the above dilemma argument. He would have the sort of self-sufficiency and completeness that mystics admire but also be a suitable object of communion for the theistic moral agent. *We really want something like a doctrine of the Trinity in which God has both a timeless and a temporal guise.*' Richard Gale, 'God and Time', *Religious Studies* 40.2 (2004), 234, emphasis added.

5 See §6.2.2.

interpretation and systematic theology. For those who continue in the tradition of formulating and justifying doctrines on the basis of special revelation mediated by inspired texts, various hermeneutical principles must be applied in the interpretation of those texts: logical norms, grammatical norms, lexical norms, cultural presuppositions, historical background, *a priori* philosophical intuitions, and so forth. These various factors need to be appropriately weighted if the correct theological conclusions are to be drawn, and in cases of purported paradox these factors will pull the theologian in different directions. In some instances, the sheer force of certain factors will be determinative; in others, it may be less clear whether a paradox doctrine is revelationally warranted.[6] I doubt that there are any cut-and-dried answers available here, but nevertheless more attention might be directed to where the lines are to be drawn.

8.3 Paradox: A Blessing in Disguise?

I began this book with a quotation from Kierkegaard extolling the virtues of paradox. The scope of the book has been restricted to defending the claim that although two central Christian doctrines are paradoxical, and all attempts to eliminate their paradoxicality have been unsuccessful, the epistemic credentials of Christian beliefs are none the worse for it. Could it be, however, that these paradoxes confer some *positive* epistemic benefit on the Christian faith and its adherents?[7] If nothing else, I suspect that had the church's claims about the nature of God and his plan for redeeming human beings been bereft of any logical perplexities, they would have garnered rather less intellectual attention and critical reflection over the last two millennia. (There is no such thing as bad publicity, so they say, and paradoxes seem to exhibit a remarkable power to draw human curiosity.) Beyond such psychological enticements, perhaps a case can be made that the presence of paradox adds some *evidential* value to a religion. Suppose one were faced with two historically established religions, R_1 and R_2. R_1 involves several striking claims which, while not explicitly contradictory, defy all attempts to express them in a manner that satisfies human intuitions about what is possible, while R_2 involves no such claims. All other evidential

---

6   As I have indicated, I believe that the doctrines of the Trinity and the Incarnation fall into the former category. Non-paradoxical interpretations of these doctrines (e.g., social trinitarianism and kenoticism) are notoriously difficult to square with plausible readings of the relevant biblical texts.

7   I have already remarked on some potential benefits of theological paradox in §7.3.3.

considerations being equal, which would be thought to bear the mark of transcendent origin and which the mark of mere human invention?[8]

---

8   'I believe that Kierkegaard was right to insist that the incarnation was paradoxical, contrary to our human expectations about what God could do and would do. However, I think he was also right to insist that this paradoxicality is actually a mark of its truth: "Comedies and novels and lies must be probable", but one mark of the transcendence of God's revelation in Jesus Christ is precisely that it is something that "could not have arisen in any human heart".' Evans, 'The Self-Emptying of Love: Some Thoughts on Kenotic Christology', 272.

Bibliography

Abbott, Edwin, *Flatland* (Penguin Classics: London: Penguin Books, rev. edn, 1998).

Adams, Robert M., 'Primitive Thisness and Primitive Identity', *The Journal of Philosophy* 76.1 (1979), 5-26.

Allgeier, J. L., 'Teaching Authority of the Church (Magisterium)', in *New Catholic Encyclopedia*, Vol. 13 (New York: McGraw-Hill, 1967), 959-65.

Alston, William P., 'The Deontological Conception of Epistemic Justification', in *Epistemic Justification* (Ithaca, NY: Cornell University Press, 1989), 125-52.

—, 'The Inductive Argument from Evil and the Human Cognitive Condition', in James E. Tomberlin (ed.), *Philosophical Perspectives 5: Philosophy of Religion* (Atascadero, CA: Ridgeview Publishing, 1991), 26-67.

—, 'Epistemic Desiderata', *Philosophy and Phenomenological Research* 53.3 (1993), 527-51.

—, 'On Knowing That We Know: The Application to Religious Knowledge', in C. Stephen Evans and Merold Westphal (eds), *Christian Perspectives on Religious Knowledge* (Grand Rapids, MI: Eerdmans, 1993), 15-39.

—, 'Epistemic Warrant as Proper Function', *Philosophy and Phenomenological Research* 55.2 (1995), 397-402.

—, *A Realist Conception of Truth* (Ithaca, NY: Cornell University Press, 1996).

Anderson, James N., 'In Defence of Mystery: A Reply to Dale Tuggy', *Religious Studies* 41.2 (2005), 145-63.

Aquinas, Thomas, *The Summa Theologica of St. Thomas Aquinas* (trans. Fathers of the Dominican Province; 22 vols; London: R. & T. Washbourne, 2nd edn, 1911-1920).

Astley, Jeffrey, 'Paradox and Christology', *King's Theological Review* 7.1 (1984), 9-13.

Austin, William H., 'Complementarity and Theological Paradox', *Zygon* 2.4 (1967), 365-81.

—, *Waves, Particles, and Paradoxes* (Rice University Studies: Houston, TX: William Marsh Rice University, 1967).

Baillie, Donald M., *God Was In Christ: An Essay on Incarnation and Atonement* (London: Faber and Faber, 2nd edn, 1961).

Barnes, Michel René, 'Rereading Augustine's Theology of the Trinity', in Stephen T. Davis, Daniel Kendall, and Gerald O'Collins (eds), *The Trinity: An Interdisciplinary Symposium on the Trinity* (Oxford: Oxford University Press, 1999), 145-76.

Bartel, Timothy W., 'Could There Be More Than One Almighty?', *Religious Studies* 29 (1993), 465-95.

—, 'Could There Be More Than One Lord?', *Faith and Philosophy* 11 (1994), 357-78.

—, 'Why the Philosophical Problems of Chalcedonian Christology Have Not Gone Away', *Heythrop Journal* 36.2 (1995), 153-72.

Barth, Karl, *Church Dogmatics* (14 vols; eds Thomas F. Torrance and G. W. Bromiley; Edinburgh: T. & T. Clark, 1936-1977).

Basinger, David, 'Biblical Paradox: Does Revelation Challenge Logic?', *Journal of the Evangelical Theological Society* 30.2 (1987), 205-13.

Bavinck, Herman, *The Doctrine of God* (trans. William Hendriksen; Edinburgh: Banner of Truth Trust, 1977).

Bayne, Tim, 'The Inclusion Model of the Incarnation: Problems and Prospects', *Religious Studies* 37.2 (2001), 125-41.

—, 'Inclusion and Incarnation: A Reply to Sturch', *Religious Studies* 39.1 (2003), 107-9.

Bergmann, Michael, 'Internalism, Externalism and the No-Defeater Condition', *Synthese* 110.3 (1997), 399-417.

—, 'Externalism and Skepticism', *The Philosophical Review* 109.2 (2000), 159-94.

—, 'Epistemic Justification', *The Philosophical Quarterly* 53.211 (2003), 295-98.

—, *Justification without Awareness: A Defense of Epistemic Externalism* (Oxford: Oxford University Press, 2006).

Black, Max, 'The Identity of Indiscernibles', in *Problems of Analysis* (Ithaca, NY: Cornell University Press, 1954), 204-16.

Bloesch, Donald G., *Essentials of Evangelical Theology*, Vol. 1 (San Francisco, CA: Harper & Row, 1978).

BonJour, Laurence, 'Externalism/Internalism', in Jonathan Dancy and Ernest Sosa (eds), *A Companion to Epistemology* (Oxford: Blackwell, 1992), 132-36.

—, 'Plantinga on Knowledge and Proper Function', in Jonathan L. Kvanvig (ed.), *Warrant in Contemporary Epistemology: Essays in Honor of Plantinga's Theory of Knowledge* (Lanham, MD: Rowman & Littlefield, 1996), 47-71.

—, *In Defense of Pure Reason: A Rationalist Account of A Priori Justification* (Cambridge: Cambridge University Press, 1998).

Bromiley, Geoffrey W., *An Introduction to the Theology of Karl Barth* (Grand Rapids, MI: Eerdmans, 1979).

Brower, Jeffrey E. and Michael C. Rea, 'Material Constitution and the Trinity', *Faith and Philosophy* 22.1 (2005), 57-76.

Brown, Colin, *Karl Barth and the Christian Message* (Eugene, OR: Wipf and Stock Publishers, 1998).

Brown, David W., *The Divine Trinity* (London: Gerald Duckworth & Co. Ltd., 1985).

—, 'The Logic of God Incarnate', *Modern Theology* 6 (1989), 112-13.

—, 'Trinitarian Personhood and Individuality', in Ronald J. Feenstra and Cornelius Plantinga, Jr. (eds), *Trinity, Incarnation, and Atonement: Philosophical and Theological Essays* (Notre Dame, IN: University of Notre Dame Press, 1989), 48-78.

Brown, Harold O. J., *Heresies: Heresy and Orthodoxy in the History of the Church* (Peabody, MA: Hendrickson Publishers, 1988).

Burson, Scott R. and Jerry L. Walls, *C.S. Lewis & Francis Schaeffer: Lessons for a New Century from the Most Influential Apologists of Our Time* (Downers Grove, IL: InterVarsity Press, 1998).

Buzzard, Anthony F. and Charles F. Hunting, *The Doctrine of the Trinity: Christianity's Self-Inflicted Wound* (Lanham, MD: International Scholars Publications, 1998).

Calvin, John, *Institutes of the Christian Religion* (trans. Ford Lewis Battles; London: Collins, rev. edn, 1960).

Cartwright, Richard, 'On the Logical Problem of the Trinity', in *Philosophical Essays* (Cambridge, MA: MIT Press, 1987), 187-200.

Chisholm, Roderick M., 'Identity through Possible Worlds: Some Questions', *Noûs* 1 (1967), 1-8.

Ciocchi, David M., 'Reconciling Divine Sovereignty and Human Freedom', *Journal of the Evangelical Theological Society* 37.3 (1994), 395-412.

Clark, Gordon H., *The Trinity* (Maryland: The Trinity Foundation, 1985).

—, *The Incarnation* (Maryland: The Trinity Foundation, 1988).

Clifford, William K., 'The Ethics of Belief', in Louis J. Pojman (ed.), *Classics of Philosophy, Volume 2: Modern and Contemporary* (Oxford: Oxford University Press, 1998), 1047-51.

Coakley, Sarah, '"Persons" in the "Social" Doctrine of the Trinity: A Critique of Current Analytic Discussion', in Stephen T. Davis, Daniel Kendall, and Gerald O'Collins (eds), *The Trinity: An Interdisciplinary Symposium on the Trinity* (Oxford: Oxford University Press, 1999), 123-44.

—, 'What Does Chalcedon Solve and What Does it Not? Some Reflections on the Status and Meaning of the Chalcedonian "Definition"', in Stephen T. Davis, Daniel Kendall, and Gerald O'Collins (eds), *The Incarnation: An Interdisciplinary Symposium on the Incarnation of the Son of God* (Oxford: Oxford University Press, 2002), 143-63.

Coffey, David M., *Deus Trinitas: The Doctrine of the Triune God* (New York: Oxford University Press, 1999).

Conee, Earl and Richard Feldman, 'Internalism Defended', in Hilary Kornblith (ed.), *Epistemology: Internalism and Externalism* (Oxford: Blackwell, 2001), 231-60.

Copi, Irving M. and Carl Cohen, *Introduction to Logic* (Upper Saddle River, NJ: Prentice Hall, 10th edn, 1998).

Craig, William Lane, 'Does the Problem of Material Constitution Illuminate the Doctrine of the Trinity?', *Faith and Philosophy* 22.1 (2005), 77-86.

Cunningham, David S., *These Three are One: The Practice of Trinitarian Theology* (Oxford: Blackwell, 1998).

Cupitt, Don, *The Sea of Faith* (London: BBC, 1984).

Dahms, John V., 'How Reliable is Logic?', *Journal of the Evangelical Theological Society* 21.4 (1978), 369-80.

—, 'A Trinitarian Epistemology Defended: A Rejoinder to Normal Geisler', *Journal of the Evangelical Theological Society* 22.2 (1979), 133-48.

Davis, Stephen T., *The Debate about the Bible: Inerrancy versus Infallibility* (Philadelphia, PA: Westminster Press, 1977).

—, *Logic and the Nature of God* (London: Macmillan, 1983).

—, *God, Reason and Theistic Proofs* (Edinburgh: Edinburgh University Press, 1997).

—, 'John Hick on Incarnation and Trinity', in Stephen T. Davis, Daniel Kendall, and Gerald O'Collins (eds), *The Trinity: An Interdisciplinary Symposium on the Trinity* (Oxford: Oxford University Press, 1999), 251-72.

Doepke, Frederick C., *The Kinds of Things: A Theory of Personal Identity Based on Transcendental Argument* (Chicago: Open Court, Carus Publishing Company, 1996).

Dole, Andrew, 'Cognitive Faculties, Cognitive Processes, and the Holy Spirit in Plantinga's *Warrant* Series', *Faith and Philosophy* 19.1 (2002), 32-46.

Dulles, Avery, 'Revelation, Fonts of', in *New Catholic Encyclopedia*, Vol. 12 (Detroit, MI: Thomson/Gale Group, 2nd edn, 2003), 190-93.

Emerson, Ralph Waldo, 'Self-Reliance', in *Essays* (London: J. Fraser, 1841).

Evans, C. Stephen, 'Is Kierkegaard an Irrationalist? Reason, Paradox, and Faith', *Religious Studies* 25.3 (1989), 347-62.

—, *Faith Beyond Reason* (Edinburgh: Edinburgh University Press, 1998).

—, 'The Self-Emptying of Love: Some Thoughts on Kenotic Christology', in Stephen T. Davis, Daniel Kendall, and Gerald O'Collins (eds), *The Incarnation: An Interdisciplinary Symposium on the Incarnation of the Son of God* (Oxford: Oxford University Press, 2002), 246-72.

Farrer, Austin, *Saving Belief* (London: Hodder & Stoughton, 1964).

Feenstra, Ronald J., 'Reconsidering Kenotic Christology', in Ronald J. Feenstra and Cornelius Plantinga, Jr. (eds), *Trinity, Incarnation, and Atonement: Philosophical and Theological Essays* (Notre Dame, IN: University of Notre Dame Press, 1989), 128-52.

Fine, Kit, 'Vagueness, Truth and Logic', *Synthese* 30 (1975), 265-300.

Foster, B. E., 'Kenoticism', in Sinclair B. Ferguson and David F. Wright (eds), *New Dictionary of Theology* (Leicester: InterVarsity Press, 1988), 364.

Frame, John M., 'The Problem of Theological Paradox', in Gary North (ed.), *Foundations of Christian Scholarship: Essays in the Van Til Perspective* (Vallecito, CA: Ross House Books, 1979), 295-330.

French, Steven, 'Why the Principle of the Identity of Indiscernibles is Not Contingently True Either', *Synthese* 78 (1989), 141-66.

French, Steven and Michael Redhead, 'Quantum Physics and the Identity of Indiscernibles', *British Journal for the Philosophy of Science* 39 (1988), 233-46.

Gale, Richard, *On the Nature and Existence of God* (Cambridge: Cambridge University Press, 1991).

—, 'Alvin Plantinga's *Warranted Christian Belief*' (2001). Available online at http://www.pitt.edu/~rmgale/ap.htm. Last accessed 15th May 2006.

—, 'God and Time', *Religious Studies* 40.2 (2004), 229-35.

Gavrilyuk, Paul, '*Theopatheia*: Nestorius's Main Charge Against Cyril of Alexandria', *Scottish Journal of Theology* 56.2 (2003), 190-207.

Geach, Peter, 'Identity', *Review of Metaphysics* 21 (1967), 3-12.

—, 'Identity—A Reply', *Review of Metaphysics* 22 (1968), 556-59.

Geisler, Norman L., '"Avoid. Contradictions" (1 Timothy 6:20): A Reply to John Dahms', *Journal of the Evangelical Theological Society* 22.1 (1979), 55-65.

—, 'Avoid *All* Contradictions: A Surrejoinder to John Dahms', *Journal of the Evangelical Theological Society* 22.2 (1979), 149-59.

Gettier, Edmund, 'Is Justified True Belief Knowledge?', *Analysis* 23 (1963), 121-23.

Gibbard, Allan, 'Contingent Identity', *Journal of Philosophical Logic* 4 (1975), 187-221.

Good, Kenneth L., *Are Baptists Rational?* (Lorain, OH: Regular Baptist Heritage Fellowship, 1986).

Goulder, Michael, *Incarnation and Myth: The Debate Continued* (London: SCM Press Ltd., 1979).

—, 'Paradox and Mystification', in Michael Goulder (ed.), *Incarnation and Myth: The Debate Continued* (London: SCM Press Ltd., 1979), 51-59.

Gribbin, John, *In Search of Schrödinger's Cat* (London: Black Swan, 1997).

Grillmeier, Aloys, *Christ in Christian Tradition: From the Apostolic Age to Chalcedon (451)* (trans. J. S. Bowden; London: A. R. Mowbray, 1965).

Grounds, Vernon C., 'The Postulate of Paradox', *Bulletin of the Evangelical Theological Society* 7 (1964), 13-14.

Hanson, A. T., 'Two Consciousnesses: The Modern Version of Chalcedon', *Scottish Journal of Theology* 37.4 (1984), 471-83.

Harnack, Adolf von, *History of Dogma*, Vol. 4 (trans. E. B. Speirs and James Millar; 7 vols; London: Williams & Norgate, 1898).

Harris, James F., *Against Relativism* (Chicago & La Salle, IL: Open Court, 1992).

Hart, Trevor, 'Revelation', in John Webster (ed.), *The Cambridge Companion to Karl Barth* (Cambridge: Cambridge University Press, 2000), 37-56.

Hasker, William, 'Tri-Unity', *Journal of Religion* 50 (1970), 1-32.

Hazelton, Roger, 'The Nature of Christian Paradox', *Theology Today* 6 (1949), 324-35.

Hebblethwaite, Brian, *The Incarnation: Collected Essays in Christology* (Cambridge: Cambridge University Press, 1987).

Helm, Paul, *The Providence of God* (Contours of Christian Theology: Leicester: InterVarsity Press, 1993).

Hepburn, Ronald W., *Christianity and Paradox: Critical Studies in Twentieth-Century Theology* (London: Watts, 1966).

Hick, John H., 'The Logic of God Incarnate', *Religious Studies* 25 (1989), 409-23.

—, *The Metaphor of God Incarnate* (London: SCM Press, 1993).

— (ed.), *The Myth of God Incarnate* (London: SCM Press, 1977).

Hill, William J., *The Three-Personed God: The Trinity as a Mystery of Salvation* (Washington, DC: Catholic University of America Press, 1982).

Hoekema, Anthony A., *Saved by Grace* (Grand Rapids, MI: Eerdmans, 1989).

Holmes, Augustine, 'The Paradox of God: Thoughts on Christian Theism', *Faith Magazine* (May-June 2002).

Howard-Snyder, Daniel, 'Trinity Monotheism', *Philosophia Christi* 5.2 (2003), 375-403.

Hughes, G. E. and M. J. Cresswell, *A New Introduction to Modal Logic* (London: Routledge, 1996).

Hurtado, Larry W., *Lord Jesus Christ: Devotion to Jesus in Earliest Christianity* (Grand Rapids, MI: Eerdmans, 2003).

Janz, Denis R., 'Syllogism or Paradox: Aquinas and Luther on Theological Method', *Theological Studies* 59.1 (1998), 3-21.

Jowers, Dennis W., 'The Reproach of Modalism: A Difficulty for Karl Barth's Doctrine of the Trinity', *Scottish Journal of Theology* 56.2 (2003), 231-46.

Kaiser, Christopher B., 'Waves, Particles, and Paradoxes', *Scottish Journal of Theology* 25 (1972), 94-95.

—, 'Christology and Complementarity', *Religious Studies* 12 (1976), 37-48.

Kelly, J. N. D., *The Athanasian Creed* (London: A. & C. Black, 1964).

—, *Early Christian Doctrines* (London: A. & C. Black, 5th edn, 1977).

Kierkegaard, Søren, *Philosophical Fragments* (Princeton: Princeton University Press, 2nd edn, 1962).

Klein, Peter, 'Warrant, Proper Function, Reliabilism, and Defeasibility', in Jonathan L. Kvanvig (ed.), *Warrant in Contemporary Epistemology: Essays in Honor of Plantinga's Theory of Knowledge* (Lanham, MD: Rowman & Littlefield, 1996), 97-130.

Knox, John, *The Humanity and Divinity of Christ: A Study of Pattern in Christology* (Cambridge: Cambridge University Press, 1967).

Kraut, Robert, 'Indiscernibility and Ontology', *Synthese* 44 (1980), 113-35.

Kvanvig, Jonathan L. (ed.), *Warrant in Contemporary Epistemology: Essays in Honor of Plantinga's Theory of Knowledge* (Lanham, MD: Rowman & Littlefield, 1996).

Layman, C. Stephen, 'Tritheism and the Trinity', *Faith and Philosophy* 5.3 (1988), 291-98.

Le Morvan, Pierre and Dana Radcliffe, 'Plantinga on Warranted Christian Belief', *The Heythrop Journal* 44.3 (2003), 345-51.

Leftow, Brian, 'Anti Social Trinitarianism', in Stephen T. Davis, Daniel Kendall, and Gerald O'Collins (eds), *The Trinity: An Interdisciplinary Symposium on the Trinity* (Oxford: Oxford University Press, 1999), 203-49.

Lewis, David K., 'Survival and Identity', in Amélie Oksenberg Rorty (ed.), *The Identities of Persons* (Berkeley, CA: University of California Press, 1976), 17-40.

—, *On the Plurality of Worlds* (Oxford: Blackwell, 1986).

Lonergan, Bernard, *The Way to Nicea: The Dialectical Development of Trinitarian Theology* (trans. Conn O'Donovan; London: Darton, Longman & Todd, 1976).

Loughlin, Gerard, 'The Basis and Authority of Doctrine', in Colin Gunton (ed.), *The Cambridge Companion to Christian Doctrine* (Cambridge: Cambridge University Press, 1997), 41-64.

MacKay, Donald M., '"Complementarity" in Scientific and Theological Thinking', *Zygon* 9 (1974), 225-44.

—, *The Clockwork Image: A Christian Perspective on Science* (Christian Classics Series: Leicester: InterVarsity Press, 1997).

MacLeod, Donald, *The Person of Christ* (Downers Grove, IL: InterVarsity Press, 1998).

Macquarrie, John, *Christology Revisited* (Harrisburg: Trinity Press International, 1998).

Mahoney, Timothy A., 'Christian Metaphysics: Trinity, Incarnation, and Creation', *Sophia* 8.1 (2002), 79-102.

Markham, Ian, *Truth and the Reality of God: An Essay in Natural Theology* (Edinburgh: T. & T. Clark, 1998).

Martin, Michael, *Atheism: A Philosophical Justification* (Philadelphia, PA: Temple University Press, 1990).

—, *The Case Against Christianity* (Philadelphia, PA: Temple University Press, 1991).

Martin, Michael and Ricki Monnier (eds), *The Impossibility of God* (Amherst, NY: Prometheus Books, 2003).

Martinich, A. P., 'Identity and Trinity', *The Journal of Religion* 58.2 (1978), 169-81.

McGrath, Alister E., *The Genesis of Doctrine: A Study in the Foundations of Doctrinal Criticism* (Oxford: Basil Blackwell, 1990).

Mizobuchi, Yutaka and Yoshiyuki Ohtaké, 'An "Experiment to Throw More Light on Light"', *Physics Letters A* 168.1 (1992), 1-5.

Moltmann, Jürgen, *The Trinity and the Kingdom of God* (trans. Margaret Köhl; London: SCM Press, 1981).

Moo, Douglas J., *The Letter of James: An Introduction and Commentary* (ed. Leon Morris; Tyndale New Testament Commentaries: Leicester: InterVarsity Press, 1985).

Moreland, J. P. and William Lane Craig, *Philosophical Foundations for a Christian Worldview* (Downers Grove, IL: InterVarsity Press, 2003).

Moroney, Stephen K., *The Noetic Effects of Sin: A Historical and Contemporary Exploration of How Sin Affects Our Thinking* (Lanham, MD: Lexington Books, 2000).

Morris, Thomas V., *The Logic of God Incarnate* (Ithaca, NY: Cornell University Press, 1986).

—, 'The Metaphysics of God Incarnate', in Ronald J. Feenstra and Cornelius Plantinga, Jr. (eds), *Trinity, Incarnation, and Atonement: Philosophical and Theological Essays* (Notre Dame, IN: University of Notre Dame Press, 1989), 110-27.

Moser, Paul K., 'Gettier Problem', in Jonathan Dancy and Ernest Sosa (eds), *A Companion to Epistemology* (Oxford: Blackwell, 1992), 157-59.

Moule, Charles, 'Three Points of Conflict in the Christological Debate', in Michael Goulder (ed.), *Incarnation and Myth: The Debate Continued* (London: SCM Press, 1979).

Nash, Ronald (ed.), *The Philosophy of Gordon H. Clark* (Phillipsburg, NJ: Presbyterian & Reformed, 1968).

Noble, T. A., 'Paradox in Gregory Nazianzen's Doctrine of the Trinity', *Studia Patristica* 27 (1993), 94-99.

O'Collins, Gerald, *The Tripersonal God: Understanding and Interpreting the Trinity* (London: Geoffrey Chapman, 1999).

O'Keefe, John J., 'Impassible Suffering? Divine Passion and Fifth-Century Christology', *Theological Studies* 58.1 (1997), 39-60.

Oderberg, David S., 'Coincidence Under a Sortal', *The Philosophical Review* 105.2 (1996), 145-71.

Oliphint, K. Scott, 'Epistemology and Christian Belief', *Westminster Theological Journal* 63.1 (2001), 151-82.

Olson, Eric T., 'Personal Identity', in Stephen P. Stich and Ted A. Warfield (eds), *The Blackwell Guide to Philosophy of Mind* (Oxford: Blackwell, 2003), 352-68.

Packer, J. I., *Evangelism and the Sovereignty of God* (Downers Grove, IL: InterVarsity Press, 1961).

Parfit, Derek, 'Personal Identity', *The Philosophical Review* 80 (1971), 3-27.

—, *Reasons and Persons* (Oxford: Clarendon Press, 1984).

Park, James L., 'Complementarity without Paradox: A Physicist's Reply to Professor Austin', *Zygon* 2 (1967), 382-88.

Pelikan, Jaroslav, *The Christian Tradition, Vol. 1: The Emergence of the Catholic Tradition (100-600)* (Chicago, IL: University of Chicago Press, 1971).

Perry, John, 'Can the Self Divide?', *Journal of Philosophy* 69 (1972), 463-88.

Phillips, D. Z., *Religion without Explanation* (Oxford: Blackwell, 1976).

Piper, John, 'Are There Two Wills in God? Divine Election and God's Desire for All to be Saved', in Thomas R. Schreiner and Bruce A. Ware (eds), *The Grace of God, the Bondage of the Will*, Vol. 1 (Grand Rapids, MI: Baker Books, 1995), 107-31.

Plantinga, Alvin, *God and Other Minds* (Ithaca, NY: Cornell University Press, 1967).

—, *The Nature of Necessity* (Oxford: Clarendon Press, 1974).

—, *God, Freedom and Evil* (London: Allen and Unwin, 1975).

—, 'Reason and Belief in God', in Alvin Plantinga and Nicholas Wolterstorff (eds), *Faith and Rationality* (Notre Dame, IN: University of Notre Dame Press, 1983), 16-93.

—, 'The Foundations of Theism: A Reply', *Faith and Philosophy* 3.3 (1986), 298-313.

—, *Warrant and Proper Function* (Oxford: Oxford University Press, 1993).

—, *Warrant: The Current Debate* (Oxford: Oxford University Press, 1993).

—, 'Reliabilism, Analyses and Defeaters', *Philosophy and Phenomenological Research* 55.2 (1995), 427-64.

—, 'Respondeo', in Jonathan L. Kvanvig (ed.), *Warrant in Contemporary Epistemology: Essays in Honor of Plantinga's Theory of Knowledge* (Lanham, MD: Rowman & Littlefield, 1996), 307-78.

—, *Warranted Christian Belief* (Oxford: Oxford University Press, 2000).

—, 'Rationality and Public Evidence: A Reply to Richard Swinburne', *Religious Studies* 37.2 (2001), 215-22.

—, 'Swinburne and Plantinga on Internal Rationality', *Religious Studies* 37.3 (2001), 357-58.

Plantinga, Alvin and Nicholas Wolterstorff (eds), *Faith and Rationality* (Notre Dame, IN: University of Notre Dame Press, 1983).

Plantinga, Cornelius, Jr., 'The Threeness/Oneness Problem of the Trinity', *Calvin Theological Journal* 23.1 (1988), 37-53.

—, 'Social Trinity & Tritheism', in Ronald J. Feenstra and Cornelius Plantinga, Jr. (eds), *Trinity, Incarnation, and Atonement: Philosophical and Theological Essays* (Notre Dame, IN: University of Notre Dame Press, 1989), 21-47.

Pollock, John L., *Contemporary Theories of Knowledge* (Totowa, NJ: Rowman & Littlefield, 1986).

Prestige, G. L., *God in Patristic Thought* (London: S.P.C.K., 2nd edn, 1952).

Priest, Graham, *An Introduction to Non-Classical Logic* (Cambridge: Cambridge University Press, 2001).

Priest, Graham, Richard Routley, and Jean Norman (eds), *Paraconsistent Logic: Essays on the Inconsistent* (Munich: Philosophia Verlag, 1989).

Quine, W. V., 'Ontological Relativity', in *Ontological Relativity and Other Essays* (New York: Columbia University Press, 1969), 26-68.

Quinn, Philip L., 'On Finding the Foundations of Theism', *Faith and Philosophy* 2.4 (1985), 469-86.

—, 'The Foundations of Theism Again: A Rejoinder to Plantinga', in Linda Zagzebski (ed.), *Rational Faith: Catholic Responses to Reformed Epistemology* (Notre Dame, IN: University of Notre Dame Press, 1993), 14-47.

Rahner, Karl, 'The Concept of Mystery in Catholic Theology', in *Theological Investigations*, Vol. 4 (London: Darton, Longman & Todd, 1966), 36-72.

—, *The Trinity* (trans. Joseph Donceel; London: Burns & Oates, 1970).

—, 'An Investigation of the Incomprehensibility of God in St. Thomas Aquinas', in *Theological Investigations*, Vol. 16 (London: Darton, Longman & Todd, 1979), 244-54.

Rea, Michael C., 'The Problem of Material Constitution', *The Philosophical Review* 104.4 (1995), 525-52.

—, 'Relative Identity and the Doctrine of the Trinity', *Philosophia Christi* 5.2 (2003), 431-45.

Rescher, Nicholas, *Paradoxes: Their Roots, Range, and Resolution* (Chicago and La Salle, IL: Open Court, 2001).

Richards, Jay Wesley, 'Is the Doctrine of the Incarnation Coherent?', in William A. Dembski and Jay Wesley Richards (eds), *Unapologetic Apologetics: Meeting the Challenges of Theological Studies* (Downers Grove, IL: InterVarsity Press, 2001), 131-43.

Roberts, Alexander and James Donaldson (eds), *The Ante-Nicene Fathers* (Edinburgh, 1867).

Robinson, J. A. T., *The Human Face of God* (London: SCM Press, 1973).

Rogers, Jack B. and Donald K. McKim, *The Authority and Interpretation of the Bible: An Historical Approach* (San Francisco, CA: Harper & Row, 1979).

Ross, James F., *Portraying Analogy* (Cambridge: Cambridge University Press, 1981).

—, 'Religious Language', in Brian Davies (ed.), *Philosophy of Religion: A Guide to the Subject* (London: Cassell, 1998).

Runia, Klaas, *Karl Barth's Doctrine of Holy Scripture* (Grand Rapids, MI: Eerdmans, 1962).

—, 'Knowledge of God', in Sinclair B. Ferguson and David F. Wright (eds), *New Dictionary of Theology* (Leicester: InterVarsity Press, 1988), 369-71.

Sadler, T. W., *Langman's Medical Embryology* (Baltimore, MD: Williams & Wilkins, 5th edn, 1985).

Sainsbury, R. M., *Paradoxes* (Cambridge: Cambridge University Press, 2nd edn, 1995).

Schaff, Philip, *History of the Christian Church* (New York: Charles Scribner, 1910).

— (ed.), *The Nicene and Post-Nicene Fathers: Series I* (New York, 1886).

Schaff, Philip and Henry Wace (eds), *The Nicene and Post-Nicene Fathers: Series II* (New York, 1890).

Schleiermacher, Friedrich, *The Christian Faith* (trans. H. R. Mackintosh and J. S. Stewart; Edinburgh: T. & T. Clark, 1928).

Sellers, R. V., *The Council of Chalcedon: A Historical and Doctrinal Study* (London: SPCK, 1953).

Senor, Thomas D., 'The Incarnation and the Trinity', in Michael J. Murray (ed.), *Reason for the Hope Within* (Grand Rapids, MI: Eerdmans, 1999), 238-60.

Snedeker, Donald R., *Our Heavenly Father Has No Equals* (Lanham, MD: Rowman & Littlefield, 1998).

Stead, Christopher, *Divine Substance* (Oxford: Clarendon Press, 1977).

Stiver, Dan R., *The Philosophy of Religious Language: Sign, Symbol, and Story* (Oxford: Blackwell, 1996).

Strawson, P. F., *Individuals: An Essay in Descriptive Metaphysics* (London: Routledge, 1959).

Studer, Basil, *Trinity and Incarnation: The Faith of the Early Church* (Edinburgh: T. & T. Clark, 1993).

Sturch, Richard, *The Word and the Christ: An Essay in Analytic Christology* (Oxford: Clarendon Press, 1991).

—, 'Inclusion and Incarnation: A Response to Bayne', *Religious Studies* 39.1 (2003), 103-6.

Sudduth, Michael C., 'The Internalist Character and Evidentialist Implications of Plantingian Defeaters', *International Journal for Philosophy of Religion* 45.3 (1999), 167-87.

—, 'Proper Basicality and the Evidential Significance of Internalist Defeat: A Proposal for Revising Classical Evidentialism', in Godehard Brüntrup and Ronald K. Tacelli (eds), *The Rationality of Theism* (Dordrecht: Kluwer Academic Publishers, 1999), 215-36.

—, 'Plantinga's Revision of the Reformed Tradition: Rethinking Our Natural Knowledge of God', *Philosophical Books* 43.2 (2002), 81-91.

—, 'Reformed Epistemology and Christian Apologetics', *Religious Studies* 39.3 (2003), 299-321.

Swain, Marshall, 'Warrant Versus Indefeasible Justification', in Jonathan L. Kvanvig (ed.), *Warrant in Contemporary Epistemology: Essays in Honor of Plantinga's Theory of Knowledge* (Lanham, MD: Rowman & Littlefield, 1996), 131-46.

Swinburne, Richard, *The Coherence of Theism* (Oxford: Clarendon Press, 1977).

—, *Revelation: From Metaphor to Analogy* (Oxford: Clarendon Press, 1992).

—, *The Christian God* (Oxford: Clarendon Press, 1994).

—, *Epistemic Justification* (Oxford: Clarendon Press, 2001).

—, 'Plantinga on Warrant', *Religious Studies* 37.2 (2001), 203-14.

Torrance, Alan, 'The Trinity', in John Webster (ed.), *The Cambridge Companion to Karl Barth* (Cambridge: Cambridge University Press, 2000), 72-91.

Torrance, Thomas F., *Trinitarian Perspectives: Toward Doctrinal Agreement* (Edinburgh: T. & T. Clark, 1994).

—, *The Christian Doctrine of God, One Being Three Persons* (Edinburgh: T. & T. Clark, 1996).

Tuggy, Dale, 'Tradition and Believability: Edward Wierenga's Social Trinitarianism', *Philosophia Christi* 5.2 (2003), 447-56.

—, 'The Unfinished Business of Trinitarian Theorizing', *Religious Studies* 39.2 (2003), 165-83.

—, 'Divine Deception, Identity, and Social Trinitarianism', *Religious Studies* 40.3 (2004), 269-87.

Turretin, Francis, *Institutes of Elenctic Theology*, Vol. 1 (trans. George Musgrave Giger; ed. James T. Dennison, Jr.; Phillipsburg, PA: Presbyterian & Reformed, 1992).

Van Inwagen, Peter, 'And Yet They Are Not Three Gods But One God', in Thomas V. Morris (ed.), *Philosophy and the Christian Faith* (Notre Dame, IN: University of Notre Dame Press, 1988), 241-78.

—, 'The Problem of Evil, the Problem of Air, and the Problem of Silence', in James E. Tomberlin (ed.), *Philosophical Perspectives 5: Philosophy of Religion* (Atascadero, CA: Ridgeview Publishing, 1991), 135-65.

—, 'Not by Confusion of Substance, but by Unity of Person', in Alan G. Padgett (ed.), *Reason and the Christian Religion* (Oxford: Clarendon, 1994), 201-26.

—, 'It Is Wrong Everywhere, Always, and for Anyone to Believe Anything upon Insufficient Evidence', in Ruth J. Sample, Charles W. Mills, and James P. Sterba (eds), *Philosophy: The Big Questions* (Oxford: Blackwell, 2003), 87-98.

Van Til, Cornelius, *The Defense of the Faith* (Phillipsburg, NJ: Presbyterian & Reformed, 3rd edn, 1967).

—, *Common Grace and the Gospel* (Phillipsburg, NJ: Presbyterian & Reformed, 1972).

—, *An Introduction to Systematic Theology* (Phillipsburg, NJ: Presbyterian & Reformed, 1974).

Vanhoozer, Kevin J., *Is There a Meaning in This Text?* (Leicester: Apollos, 1998).

Ware, Timothy, *The Orthodox Church* (London: Penguin Books, rev. edn, 1997).

Watson, Francis, 'The Bible', in John Webster (ed.), *The Cambridge Companion to Karl Barth* (Cambridge: Cambridge University Press, 2000), 57-71.

Wierenga, Edward, 'Trinity and Polytheism', *Faith and Philosophy* 21.3 (2004), 281-94.

Wiggins, David, *Identity and Spatio-Temporal Continuity* (Oxford: Blackwell, 1967).

—, 'On Being in the Same Place at the Same Time', *The Philosophical Review* 77.1 (1968), 90-95.

—, *Sameness and Substance Renewed* (Cambridge: Cambridge University Press, 2001).

Wolterstorff, Nicholas, *Divine Discourse: Philosophical Reflections on the Claim that God Speaks* (Cambridge: Cambridge University Press, 1995).

Wykstra, Stephen J., 'The Humean Obstacle to Evidential Arguments from Suffering: On Avoiding the Evils of "Appearance"', *International Journal for Philosophy of Religion* 16 (1984), 73-94.

Yablo, Stephen, 'Identity, Essence, and Indiscernibility', *Journal of Philosophy* 84 (1987), 293-314.

Yandell, Keith E., 'Some Problems for Tomistic Incarnationists', *International Journal for Philosophy of Religion* 30 (1991), 169-82.

Index